CASTLES
A History and Guide

First published in the UK 1980

Copyright © 1980 Blandford Press Ltd.
Link House, West Street, Poole, Dorset BH15 1LL

British Library Cataloguing in Publication Data
Brown, Reginald Allen
    Castles.
    1. Castles-Europe
    1. Title
    940   D910.5

ISBN 0 7137 1100 0

Typesetting & monochrome by
Tradespools Limited, Frome
Separations by Iberico, Madrid
Printed & bound by
Tien Wah Press (Pte.) Limited, Singapore

Half-title The entrance
to Krak des Chevaliers
(Syria).

Title page Gutenfels
Castle (Rheinland-
Pfalz).

Contributors spread
Sintra Castle near
Lisbon.

Foreword
Bamburgh Castle
(Northumberland).

CASTLES
A History and Guide

Foreword by Sir John Hackett

Special Consultant Professor R. Allen Brown
Dr Michael Prestwich □ Dr Charles Coulson

BLANDFORD PRESS
Poole   Dorset

SPECIAL CONSULTANT

Professor R Allen Brown Professor of Medieval History at King's College, London. He is an internationally acknowledged expert on Castellologie and is the author of several books on castles including *English Castles, The Normans and the Norman Conquest* and *The Origins of Modern Europe*. He is also co-author of the definitive *History of the King's Works* and has written a number of official handbooks and guides to castles published by Her Majesty's Stationery Office.

METALWORK CONSULTANT

Claude Blair MA, FSA Keeper of Metalwork at the Victoria & Albert Museum, London.

EASTERN EUROPEAN CONSULTANT

J.H. Sinicki formerly a member of the Institute of Historical Research, University of Warsaw, and of the School of Slavonic and East European Studies, University of London.

MAIN CONTRIBUTORS

Castle-building
28–43, 44–61
Dr Michael Prestwich Reader in Medieval History at the University of Durham and contributor to a number of historical journals including *Economic History Review* and *English Historical Review*. He has also written *War, Politics and Finance Under Edward I* and more recently, *The Three Edwards*.

Residence
100–113
Dr Charles Coulson History teacher at Dover College, Kent. He has had several articles on castles published in *Z.A.M.* and *Château-Gaillard*.

Residence
114–125
Alastair Hawkyard Co-Editor at the History of Parliament Trust in London and contributor to journals on history and archeology. He is co-author of *Great Dynasties*, a history of the Royal Families of Europe.

Fortress
80–97
James Petre Director of Studies at a private London College and contributor to various historical journals.

Fortress
64–79

144–145
Nicholas Hooper Researcher in Medieval History at King's College, University of London, specializing in Anglo-Saxon warfare.

CONTRIBUTORS TO THE GAZETTEER

146–151
Jim Bradbury Teacher of Medieval and Tudor History at the West London Institute of Higher Education. He is the author of *Shakespeare and his Theatre* and has published articles in *History Today* and *Teaching History*.

170–175
Martin Meade Inspector of Historic Buildings at the Department of the Environment and contributor to *Journal of Architectural Historians of Great Britain* and *Arts et Techniques*.

152–157
176–181
David Andrews Archeologist specializing in medieval Italy and contributor to various journals including *Archeologia Medievale*.

128–133
158–163
164–169
David Cook History teacher at Westminster School. He has contributed to various journals and is currently writing a doctoral thesis on the garrison and town of Berwick-on-Tweed in the fifteenth and sixteenth centuries.

134–139
Mark Taylor Archeologist working for the Department of the Environment in Wales.

141–143
Teresa Bonnick Researcher in Medieval History at King's College, University of London specializing in castles.

182–187
Matthew Bennett Researcher in Medieval History at King's College, University of London specializing in warfare of the feudal period.

CONTENTS

(centre) Inside of machicolations. *(top right)* Trecastle (South Wales). *(bottom right)* Eileen Donan Castle (Ross and Cromarty).

7

FOREWORD

by Sir John Hackett, GCB, DSO, MA, BLITT, LLD

'The splendour falls on castle walls ...'

Lord Tennyson's romantic vision is only one way of looking at a dominant element in our history – the strong place, the fortified dwelling. There are many others.

The functional importance of the castle lies in the ability to deny to outsiders, at will, access to a living space. When the earthworks and palisades of more primitive motte-and-bailey fortresses were replaced by structures of stone – more durable, less inconvenient and more readily defensible – the essential element was the big covered space, the so-called 'hall', in which everything was done which went on within the fortified dwelling. The archetypal building was a simple one. The great secure covered space we see at Oakham Castle (Leicestershire) could almost as well have served, with little change, as a tithe barn or a church. Roof and walls kept out rough weather. Small openings let in light and air. The space, thus enclosed, provided a place for work, for worship, for storage, or in general for the daily purposes of those who lived within it. It was to undergo modification to meet special needs.

The operational purpose of the castle was to keep out not only rough weather but also unwelcome intruders and to provide a safe refuge for those who dwelt within it. The strong place, the fortified dwelling, could thus also function as a secure base for the operations of armed men. The defense of the castle, and the resultant need for close watch upon the approaches to it, dictated its location in a commanding position, from which its influence upon the neighbourhood, and all that went on around it, became inevitably dominant. From many an upland spur in Western Europe a castle, often today more or less in ruin, continues to dominate the landscape, with strength and authority, exactly as it has for centuries.

In the weapons system which was to influence the whole course of history in feudal Europe for many hundreds of years the other principal element was the mounted, armoured man-at-arms. The soldier on a horse possessed not only more mobility than the foot soldier, but also a greater operational range. He could carry in addition more protective armour. The introduction of the stirrup, coming into Europe about the ninth century, furnished a stable,

mobile weapons platform from which effective use of the heaviest handheld weapon was now possible. The combination of the armoured mounted man-at-arms, operating from a fortified dwelling as a base, and the fortified dwelling itself – the dual weapons system, that is to say both offensive and defensive, of the castle and the knight – was to dominate the development of western civilization for nearly a millennium.

Castles, thrusting out from the landscape in an essentially assertive way, are bold and splendid things. They are as significant in the political, social, and economic aspects of our history as they are beautiful to look at. A first sight of Krak des Chevaliers in Syria is almost as exciting as a first sight of Venice. To see Saône for the first time, where local timber had been too short to bridge the minimal gap security demanded, is exciting in another way. The Frankish Seigneurs who built this uniquely imaginative stronghold carved out the rocky hillside around a slender needle of

stone, 40 feet high, upon which the middle of a bridge across a moat now wide enough, could be supported. To look at this is like being transported into a world where the impossible is commonplace. Little Saône has been my favourite castle since I first saw it more than forty years ago.

There is unlikely to be an early limit to the current steady growth of interest in the castle. It is a visible manifestation of one of the main components of that period of our history – the feudal – in which so much of the civilization of today was fashioned. This scholarly book, so carefully put together under the guidance of Professor Allen Brown of Kings College, London, one of the best of medievalists and a man who has few peers where castles are concerned, is a notable contribution to the better understanding of who and what we are, which is best reached through reflection upon the way we have come. There is much to reflect upon, with pleasure and with profit, here.

INTRODUCTION
Origins of the Castle

by Professor R. Allen Brown

Of all buildings castles belong uniquely to the so-called Middle Ages. Of course all architecture and all architectural forms reflect the type, the needs and the aspirations of the society which produces them, and so (to set aside mere houses and their appurtenances) there are not one but two fundamental architectural products of the Middle Ages, churches as well as castles. Further, the churches are the more fundamental of the two, for medieval society was Christian before it was anything, and the medieval polity, which has become Europe and Western Europe especially, was Latin Christendom to the end. The churches, however, for the most part are with us still, not just as ruins and ancient monuments or centres of tourist attraction, but generally in full working order, in many countries untouched even by the sixteenth-century Reformation and other modern deviations from the main road of history. Not so the castles, which belong uniquely to the Middle Ages in that they end with them. Some, of course, are still lived in by the fortunate few, significantly as the most lordly of all lordly residences and stately homes (in England, classic examples include Windsor, Arundel and Alnwick), but all have long since lost their military role which, throughout the long centuries of their proper functioning, was at least half their *raison d'être*.

Old Sarum (Wiltshire). The larger enclosure was the city and former Iron Age encampment whilst the central enclosure is where the castle stood.

Above The Norman castle at Portchester (Hampshire) occupied only one corner of the former Roman fortress which had become an Anglo-Saxon burgh.
Right Seal of Richard I (1189–99), King of England, Duke of Normandy and Aquitaine, and Count of Anjou.
Below Thirteenth-century seal of the Warenne earls of Surrey. (From the Barons' Letter in the Public Record Office, London.)

Definition of the castle

The castle was the fortified residence of a lord – any lord of sufficient status, not just the king or prince, though the king or prince is likely to have more castles (even if not necessarily grander ones) by reason of his primacy. It is this integrated combination of residence and fortress that is peculiar to the castle (giving us also the clue and key to its social significance, as we shall see) and differentiates it from all other known forms of fortification, earlier, later or, indeed, contemporary. All modern types of fortification, for example, are exclusively military and, furthermore, they pertain to the state or sovereign public authority, real or pretended. Roman fortification also pertained exclusively to the state, and Rome is our common ancestor in Europe and places further west. Other early fortifications are best differentiated from castles by emphasizing that they were communal, the fortifications and defences of communities as opposed to the fortified residences of individual lords. This was the case with Iron Age encampments (in England eg Dover or Old Sarum), with the burghs built in England by Alfred and his successors against the Danes, or the similar fortresses raised in Germany by Henry the Fowler. This was the case also with Viking camps and with the enigmatic *brochs* in Scotland and *raths* in Ireland (and in Wales). It was also the case, needless to say, with Roman camps, and with all fortified towns or cities of whatever date. The fortified town or city, of course, flourished throughout the so-called Middle Ages together with the castle, but the latter was different, more numerous, and more characteristic. Where, indeed, the two survive together, the difference is

of historical fact, the castle was the characteristic product of the ruling class of medieval Latin Christendom. But here we must be more precise. Sociologically and historically the castle is not so much medieval as feudal, and belongs precisely not to the Middle Ages but to the feudal period. And thereby hangs a tale. The terms 'the Middle Ages' and its derivative 'medieval' (*medium aevum*) are in any case both silly and misleading (*c.* 500 to *c.* 1500 is the middle of what, for goodness' sake?); 'Feudalism' and 'feudal' are something else again, not synonymous but much more meaningful. And the more one thinks about the castle, the more feudal it becomes.

Feudalism

Even before feudalism is defined, it may be said that the castle belongs exclusively to the feudal period, beginning with it and ending with it, and therefore appears at once as a manifestation of feudal society. That type of society found its origins in northern France in the ninth and tenth centuries. Its end, being more gradual and diffuse than its beginning, is more difficult accurately to place and varies somewhat from one country to another, but we must place it, generally speaking, in the sixteenth and/or seventeenth centuries. It was a society based upon and working through lordship of a particular kind (for mere lordship is older than feudalism), at first personal, soon and subsequently territorial also, and always military. This feudal lordship was the principal secular bond of society, the king himself, though he never lost his divinity, nor all his more ancient authority, being also the greatest lord, the lord of lords, the feudal suzerain. This bond was closely inter-twined with the bond of ecclesiastical discipline and hierarchy which was feudalized also, bishops and even abbots being not only princes of the Church but also vassals of the king or prince, owing knight-service for some of their lands, and some of them having castles. When in the ninth century the kingdom of the West Franks (later to be France), a successor state (though the term is anachronistic) of Charlemagne's empire of the Franks, collapsed under the manifold strains of internal strife and external attack by Moslems, by Magyars and, above all, by Vikings, and the old Carolingian order disintegrated, society painfully rebuilt itself on the basis of local and military lordship in the increasing absence of central or public authority.

> *It was agreed that it was God's will that His people should unite, but when the Vikings, the Moslems and the Hungarians were abroad, the urgent necessity was a safe stronghold and a lord whose protection would be at hand.*
>
> (R.H.C. Davis, *History of Medieval Europe*, London, 1957, p.173.)

Feudal society, it has been said, was society organized for war. Certainly feudal lordship is military in its origins, in its long continuing practice and its still longer-lasting ethos and mores. We are witnessing the evolution of a military aristocracy, and while the world has, of course, seen others in other times and places, we have yet to emphasize a fundamental peculiarity of this one. It was, so to speak, a mounted military aristocracy.

It is as impossible to dissociate warfare and military tactics from social history as it is architecture, and the advent of the mounted warrior in the West was itself one of the root causes of the origins of feudal society. Sometime about the mid eighth century the Franks, who like all the Germanic races had

entirely obvious even to the naked and unlearned eye. Carcassonne, perhaps the finest surviving example of a medieval fortified city in Europe, has a castle of residential lordship within the formidable amplitude of its double circumference. The Tower of London, ie the royal castle of London, raised by William the Conqueror himself in and after 1066, occupied one small corner of the pre-existing Old English and originally Roman walled city. Portchester is a dramatic surviving example of a similar arrangement, the Norman castle in one corner of a Roman camp which had become an Anglo-Saxon burgh. Five of Edward I's great castles in north Wales built at the end of the thirteenth century were combined with contemporary fortified towns; at Conway (p. 53) the two survive, almost complete and entirely distinct. The *hoi-polloi* of Conway, one may be quite sure, would have needed something more than a pass to enter the king's castle.

The castle is feudal

The castle, then, was a residential fortress, the fortified residence of a lord, and in that sense was private as opposed to communal or public, though it can and will be argued later in this book that a delegated public authority was also present in it. As such, though unfortified great houses and palaces were also known, it pertains peculiarly to the Middle Ages and was the fitting setting for that warrior aristocracy which dominated the period. There is no divine rule which says that a fully fortified lordly residence cannot be produced by some other society in some other time or place, but no equivalent in fact is known, and there is no doubt whatever that, as a matter

hitherto fought on foot, began to develop a cavalry arm, a heavy cavalry of mounted warriors increasingly capable not just of reconnaissance, pursuit and harassment, but also of fighting in the saddle. The knight, later to dominate both feudal society and contemporary battlefields and campaigns, was born. The classic medieval tactic of the cavalry charge, made possible by the stirrup and unknown in ancient times, evolved. And so did chivalry, the code at one and the same time, be it noted, both of the mounted warrior and polite society. (And be it noted also that, if words have any meaning, one cannot even begin to be chivalrous without a horse.) Sociologically what happened was that the new military élite of mounted warriors, who increasingly carried all before them on the battlefield (if properly used and judiciously combined with infantry), became, early and inevitably, a social élite also. Not only was military worth automatically reflected in social status (and, as far as possible, *vice versa*), but also and above all the horse made the new mounted warrior exclusive. Horses were expensive, then as now, and became more so as they were developed into the specially trained and specially bred warhorses, the *destriers* of the knights. One horse, moreover, would seldom suffice. If it now requires a string of ponies to play polo on a Sunday afternoon, how many warhorses would have been required to see a man through the Battle of Hastings, with life itself at stake, from nine o'clock in the morning until dusk on an October day? The knight's gear also was expensive, and became increasingly so as standards rose: the hauberk or long coat of mail, sword and helmet, shield and lance, saddle and other tackle – and all this long before the refinements of plate armour and armoured horses. Nor is this all by any means. The degree of horsemanship required to fight effectively in the saddle and survive was such as to require the total application and dedication of a lifetime. The knight, the specialist mounted warrior (of course he could fight on foot as well), was and had to be as professional as the age could make him, born and bred to war and horses, and for that it was necessary to be elevated above the sordid necessity of earning a living by any other means – and also to have servants. The social superiority of the man on the horse may be said to begin at this point.

Thus there was formed, rising phoenix-like from the ashes of the ninth century, a new secular upper class and ruling class of knights. In the strictest sense, the knight *is* feudal society, and certainly he is even more fundamental to it than those other fundamentals of the textbooks – the fief (Latin *feudum*, from which our words 'feudal' and 'feudalism' are derived), ie that land which he holds of his lord for his own support and to provide the expensive knight-service which he owes in return for it; and commendation, whereby the vassal is bound to his lord by the near-sacred ties of homage, fealty and investiture. In this society everyone who is a gentleman, but not a cleric or a monk, is or should be a knight. Of course in practice not all knights were social equals and most were vassals of some greater lord, but if not all knights were great men, all great men, from the king or prince downwards, were knights. Small wonder that the ethos of society was military, and mounted.

The castle as symbol and substance of feudal lordship

What then of the castle? We have already seen that as a matter of historical fact it belongs in time exclusively to the feudal period, and have suggested that as the fortified residence of a lord it was the perfect architectural setting for a military and feudal aristocracy. But we must go further. Castles pertain for the most part not to mere knights but to the greater lords of other knights and of greater lordships than a mere manor or two. They are the perfect architectural expression of feudal lordship of which they were the conscious symbol as well as much of the substance. First, as a matter again of historical fact, castles controlled the land. The warfare of the feudal period was dominated by heavy cavalry and castles, and the two go together. The castle itself was a military answer to cavalry, for you cannot take a castle by a cavalry charge. More than this, the evidence of surviving records and chronicles shows that the complement of any castle in time of war consisted of a very high proportion of mounted men, both knights and mounted sergeants (the latter being the military and social inferiors of the former). Clearly, save for the occasional sortie, walls and towers were not defended on horseback. The knights and sergeants were the strike force of the castle. Secure within from all but a full-scale investment, which was difficult to bring to bear and still more difficult to maintain (as we shall see later in this book, defence was probably in the ascendant over attack throughout the castle's active history), they could and did control the surrounding countryside, and the range of the castle was the range of the mounted men within it – about ten miles if you wanted to be back before nightfall.

Castles were thus the effective centres of military power and hence of territorial lordship, and that lordship was exercised by the direct lord of the land, whether or not the king or prince and most often not. Here, once again, we see that fragmentation of military power and public authority, no longer the exclusive attributes of the sovereign state, which is held to be a characteristic of feudalism – though such constitutionally negative aspects are too much emphasized in books. In reality feudalism was a positive not a negative political force, centripetal not centrifugal, cohesive not divisive. The greatest feudal lords were strictly bound by the feudal ties of homage, fealty and investiture to their own lord who was the prince, and the prince, like other feudal lords but more so, exercised a close control over the castles of his vassals as he did also over their military service. When on a famous occasion in 864, in the Capitulary of Pistes, Charles the Bald, king of the West Franks, prohibited on pain of demolition the making of fortresses without his licence, he sought control of non-royal fortifications rather than abolition.

Left The feudal prince, William, Duke of Normandy, beside the castle of Bayeux. (From the Bayeux Tapestry.)
Far left Norman knights at Hastings (Sussex) – a social and a military élite. (From the Bayeux Tapestry.)

Above La Tour Blanche at Issoudun (Indre), built *en bec* by Philip Augustus and once shining white.

Above A late thirteenth-century depiction of homage from the *Établissements de Saint Louis*.
Left The castle at Lavardin (Loire-et-Cher), and its donjon especially, standing as both the symbol and substance of lordship.

We will and expressly command that whoever at this time has made castles [castella] *and fortifications* [firmitates] *and enclosures* [haias] *without our permission shall have them demolished by the 1st. of August.*

(*MGH, Capitularies,* ii, p 328.)

Compare with this the 'Custom' of Normandy in the time of William the Conqueror, 'No one shall raise castles in Normandy', ie without the duke's licence (C.H. Haskins, *Norman Institutions*, New York, 1918, p. 282, c. 4).

However, the castle was no mere barracks. To think of it thus is anachronistic and to understand its role aright is to understand feudal society. The castle was a residential fortress. It was the residence of a lord who was himself a warrior and a captain, whose force and garrison (another anachronistic term) was his own household (*mesnil*), expanded in time of war and comprising his own vassals, knights and men-at-arms. The first two categories, at least, were gentlemen, for in this military society the higher you were the harder and the better you were expected to fight, as also in this society the ruling class really ruled. Here then, most often and appropriately assembled in the castle, were the captains and the kings, the eagles and the trumpets. When his lordship was in residence, shields were displayed on the walls, and banners flew from towers and turrets – like the Royal Standard now from Buckingham Palace or (a better and direct example) from the keep of Windsor Castle when the Queen resides. The castle was at the same time the centre, the seat and the visible expression of lordship.

Lordship is authority and authority was exercised from and by the castle, while its strength (and purchasing power) attracted adjacent settlement and trade. It was the headquarters of local government, whether royal or seigneurial. Royal castles were usually in the custody of the king's chief local officials, and baronial castles were usually the centres of the lord's honor and his lordship (and because honors and lordships were often multiple and territorially scattered, a great lord needed more than one castle). To the castle one went to render service, pay rent or plead one's law suit, or was summoned to attend court, hunt, joust or dine. The castle dominated the countryside in every way, military, socially, politically, administratively and economically, and all these potencies were integrated and combined in it, and given deliberate architectural expression by it. Castles are functional buildings, but so are churches, and both also consciously evoke concepts and aspirations. Side by side, indeed, as they often are, and notably in such grand juxtaposition as Durham or Rochester or a hundred other instances, they jointly symbolize the authority and divine order of the medieval world, secular and spiritual power, the Two Swords, *regnum* and *sacerdotium*. Certainly the castle stood for lordship in men's eyes and minds, whether representing the sheriff's authority on his official seal, or whitewashed and shining in the sun (Whitecastle, Monmouthshire, the White Tower at London, La Tour Blanche at Issoudun), or soaring to the sky in the background of those splendid illuminations of the medieval *dolce vita* in the *Très Riches Heures*. The contemporary word for the architecturally dominant feature of a castle, what the French call the *pièce maîtresse* of the building, was *donjon* – commonly but not always a great tower, and at one and the same time the ultimate military strong-point and containing the apartments of the lord himself. The word 'donjon', which in

French still retains much of its original meaning but in English has been debased ('dungeon'), was derived from the Latin *dominium* meaning lordship. In Spain the great tower is called 'the tower of homage'. Clearly feudal terminology is being applied to feudal buildings; the buildings no less than the words embody feudal concepts; language, architecture and social values are one. Similarly, intellectuals and clerical writers in that age loved to refer to monks, fighting their spiritual battles on behalf of society, as the knights of Christ, and their monasteries as the castles of God.

The geographical distribution of castles

Castles, then, are feudal, the architectural manifestation of feudal society and, more specifically, its ruling class. We may therefore expect to find them, and do, in all those countries where feudalism was established, eventually all over Europe and, in the case of the Middle East, beyond. In the beginning, however, this did not happen all at once, though the castle followed feudalism like trade used to follow the flag. Feudal society had its origins, as we have seen, in West Frankia and in northern France especially, in the area bounded on the east by the Rhine and to the south by the Loire. Appropriately, the

Above The fifteenth-century castle at Raglan (Gwent) with its great tower and no lowering of the guard.

Below Fourteenth-century seal of the city of Rochester showing the castle as the symbol of authority.

earliest castles so far known are there, at the recently excavated Doué-la-Fontaine (*c.* 950) and at Langeais (*c.* 994), (p. 45) both near the Loire. At the former site we seem to have a dramatic exposition of the very origins of the castle, wherein about the mid tenth century an unfortified, late Carolingian, lordly residence was fortified and turned into a castle, chiefly by strengthening and heightening its stone hall to make of it a great tower or donjon. The principal surviving strength of Langeais also is a great tower of stone containing residential accommodation. Both these earliest known castles, moreover, pertain absolutely to feudal lordship and can be seen like other early castles as integral parts of the very formation of the new feudal principalities then emergent in northern France, ie Anjou and Blois, Normandy, Maine and the rest. For castles 'made loyalty easy' (R.W. Southern, *The Making of the Middle Ages*, London, 1953, p 84) and riveted one's rule upon the land. Doué-la-Fontaine was fortified, it is thought, by Theobald, Count of Blois, and Langeais by Fulk Nerra ('Fulk the Black'), Count of Anjou. Fulk Nerra has been described as 'a pioneer in the art of feudal government' and also as 'the founder of the greatness of the county of Anjou' (Southern, op. cit. pp 86, 87), whose counts were to become kings of England and kings of

Jerusalem also, and of him his grandson and biographer could remember thirteen castles which he had founded as well as others by then forgotten. Meanwhile in Normandy, to cite another classic instance of a new and feudal principality, castles were becoming, in the tenth and early eleventh centuries, the bases of the power of the duke and his vassals – Rouen, Fécamp, Falaise, Bayeux, Ivry and Arques-la-Bataille. In this way we can see the castle as one of the foundations of the modern state.

From northern France and the Rhineland feudalism and thereby castles spread more slowly into the south, the Midi; more slowly yet into Germany, where the intact fabric of Carolingian kingship and society left little room or need of it before the twelfth century; later still into the eastern German provinces with the eastward expansion of Germany itself; and so late into Scandinavia, as Viking society declined, that it is arguable if it was ever established there at all. In northern Italy, also, things tended to be different, with a still Romanized and largely urban population including an urban aristocracy building high towers to fret the skyline of their cities instead of proper castles in the country like the landed nobility beyond the Alps. And then there are the countries of what Marc Bloch called 'imported feudalism' (*Feudal Society*, London, 1961, pp 187, 188). England in and after 1066 (and subsequently southern Scotland, Wales and Ireland) is a classic instance, for sociologically the Norman Conquest was the imposition of a new Norman and French ruling class upon the indigenous population, and was rendered permanent as much as anything by castles. It involved what was probably the largest single and most concentrated castle-building programme in history. There were more castles in England during the first century after the Norman Conquest than at any subsequent date, and the typical history of the typical English castle is of an early foundation soon after 1066, followed by continuous development thereafter, or, in not a few cases, abandonment. There were at the last count 1,223 castle sites in England and Monmouthshire alone, 367 in Wales (D.J.C. King and L. Alcock, *Château-Gaillard*, iii, London, 1969, pp 124–5), and most of them are, in Stenton's striking phrase, 'the most authentic memorials remaining of the age of militant feudalism' (F.M. Stenton, *The First Century of English Feudalism*, Oxford, 1932, p 197). The extraordinary race of Normans also took castles and feudalism with them in their concurrent conquest of southern Italy and Sicily, and were in the van of the First Crusade, launched in 1097, whereby the Frankish knights and chivalry from France wrested Jerusalem and the Holy Places from the Infidel. The Crusading States of Outremer, having been established – Antioch and Edessa, Tripoli and the kingdom of Jerusalem itself – were, needless to say, feudal in their organization, and their castles are amongst the most dramatically famous in the world, with Krak des Chevaliers (p. 75) justly the most famous of them all. After the near loss of all this to the Moslems under Saladin in the late twelfth century, the crusaders of 1204 took Constantinople and conquered the Eastern Empire of Byzantium, which accounts for castles in modern Greece and Turkey. Meanwhile another, and perhaps the greatest, territorial expansion of Latin Christendom in the Middle Ages was well under way, as the knights of a militant Latin Christianity slowly reconquered the Iberian Peninsula from the Moors (ie Arabs and Moslems again) to make a veritable land of castles. Here, however, as indeed in Outremer, there can be a difference, as

so many castles were held by the Military Orders of the Church (Templars and Hospitallers especially) to be thus fortified monasteries rather than the seats of individual lordship.

The military role of the castle

In this book the military and residential roles of the castle will necessarily be discussed separately, yet neither will be understood unless it is realized that each was complementary to the other in a military society in which the lord of the castle was a warlord and his househld his potential army. On the military side, subsequent chapters will discuss the warfare of the feudal period and the castle's role therein ('Strongholds and Strategy') together with the particular matter of siege-craft and defence ('Defence and Attack'). Here it is only necessary to forecast fundamentals by way of introduction, and by insisting that the castle was by no means only a defensive stronghold as it is so often exclusively represented in books and popular fancy. Of course it had to be as impregnable as the natural site strengthened by contemporary art, science and technology could make it, and defensive considerations no doubt chiefly controlled its design, development and architectural appearance. Beyond that, however, its purpose and function was at least as much offensive and aggressive, and indeed it could and should be argued that this was its primary military role. The castle was an armed base for active operations: it provided what we would call a 'military presence'. All those multitudinous castles studding the Welsh Marches, the frontier areas between Wales and England, are not there because the first Norman marcher lords and their successors were afraid of the wild Welsh tribes, nor even solely as the centres of new lordships won by the sword. They controlled the potentially hostile countryside and were used as bases for further advance. Some in consequence became redundant as that advance was duly achieved. Chester, for example, was never so important again as the gateway to north Wales after Edward I's great castles of Conway, Caernarvon, Harlech and Beaumaris nailed down Snowdonia, and those at Flint and Rhuddlan controlled the approaches to it.

The residential role of the castle

A subsequent chapter will describe the residential role of the castle ('Life in the Castle'), so that here again it is not necessary to do more than point to fundamentals and, as it

Left Rhuddlan (Clwyd) was one of the earliest of Edward I's castles in North Wales and was built (1277–82) on the concentric plan.
Far left Doué-la-Fontaine (Maine-et-Loire) is the earliest known castle site in Europe (*c.* 950) and has been recently excavated.

Above A detail from 'The Bear and Boar Hunt', one of the Devonshire Hunting Tapestries, depicting the castle as the seat of courtly life.
Left The month of April from the *Très Riches Heures* with the castle of Dourdan in the background. (From a facsimile in the Victoria & Albert Museum, London.)

Right Manorbier Castle (Dyfed) was the home of the de Barri family of Gerald of Wales, who lovingly described it for posterity in his *Opera*.
Below Acton Burnell (Salop) dates from the late thirteenth century and was the fortified manor-house of Bishop Robert Burnell.
Bottom Oxburgh Hall (Norfolk) is a moated manor rather than a castle. Even the great gatehouse was built largely for display.

were, set the tone. The most fundamental fact of all, of course, is that the castle was no less a residence than a fortress, however contrary that may be again to popular fancy. The castle was simply not exclusively a military building and cannot be understood as such. Music, troubadors and dancing, the rustle of ladies' dresses in a summer garden, even children's voices, these are no less authentic echoes for our ears to strain after than the clash of arms, the tramp of mailed feet or the shouts of battle. Sometimes the two sorts of sounds might mingle. There was a splendid wedding feast within while Saladin besieged the castle of Kerak in Moab (Petra Deserti) in far off Outremer in 1183. The lady of the castle sent out dishes to the sultan, and he ordered his great engines not to bombard the tower wherein the young couple lay. Residence may explain the siting of a castle: that a great man wanted or needed to live there was a prime consideration. Residence, and lordly residence, also of course explains all that sumptuous accommodation – great halls, splendid chapels (it may well be more than one of each) and integrated residential suites, in the donjon, chamber blocks and towers, for the various households of the lord, the lady and their guests. For the lords and ladies of the land lived not in family units in our suburban fashion but in the unit of the household, and their closer servants and retainers would also be of gentle birth. The nobles and the gentlemen, *de rigueur*, did much of their own fighting, and hence there were no barrack-blocks or other provision for soldiers as men somehow different and set apart from others. Humble and common servants and fighting men were certainly needed, but they slept where they could and wherever they could lay down a palliasse. The household also was itinerant as the magnates of the realm or principality, from the king or prince downwards, moved ceaselessly from manor to manor and castle to castle, for by this means alone could the personal kingship and personal lordship of the age be made to work. This, too, explains why so many castles were more than half

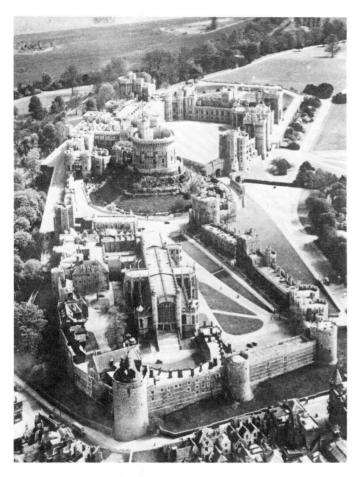

empty more than half the time.

Some of the greatest castles of the greatest lords, indeed, were nothing less than fortified palaces, as witness royal Windsor under Edward III in England (the Versailles of the age) or such great complexes of Continental princes of Loches, Chinon or Caen. But whatever its precise rank and status in the hierarchy of feudal society, the castle was the proper setting for the Beautiful People of the period. Gerald of Wales, in the twelfth century, describing his family castle of Manorbier in Pembrokeshire, makes it sound like a gentleman's country seat, which, of course, is precisely what it was. He duly stresses its defences, but then lists its favourable position with access to the sea, its fishpond, its vineyard, its orchards and its views (*Geraldi Cambrensis Opera*, ed. J.F. Dimock, London, Rolls Series, 1868, vi, p. 92). Some three centuries later, and towards the end, a fifteenth-century Welsh poet described the castle of Raglan in Monmouthshire in lyrical but enlightening terms, its

> *hundred rooms full of festive fare, its hundred towers, parlours and doors, its hundred heaped up fires of long dried fuel, its hundred chimneys for men of high degree.*

(Quoted by A.J. Taylor in the
HMSO Official Handbook, p.11.)

And when the end did come it simply stressed the fundamentality of the castle's residential role throughout, for what happened was that the military function faded away to leave those castles which survive as merely stately homes of an antique and traditional kind. Half the history of the castle is implicit in the fact that to this day in France the word *château* has come to mean no more than a grand country house. More still of its history ought to come to mind when one reflects that if one wants to find the real thing when travelling in France, one must ask the way to '*le château fort*', or even '*le vieux château féodal*'.

Ancillary roles

From the castle's twin basic roles of lordly residence and fortress other functions and uses directly followed. That it was the administrative as well as the social centre of the countryside, the seat of lordship and therefore of authority, has already been noted in this Introduction, and in the section of the book entitled 'Castles and the Community' these and other aspects of the castle's dominance in and over medieval society will be fully discussed. Meanwhile, however, one subsidiary role, namely the castle's use as a prison, is commonly so grossly distorted and absurdly exaggerated in popular guidebooks and, indeed, by guides, that it merits the advance publicity of a protest and a warning here. The scandal (for what else is the misrepresentation of the past?), based upon an arrogant ignorance of all things 'medieval', is not confined to Britain; though, were it not for Continental instances such as Loches or Ghent, one might suppose the Tower of London to be the most notorious example of a splendid castle, steeped in the true history of the land, presented to the public almost exclusively in terms of imprisonment, torture, murder and execution. Even so, it is only in the English language that the noble word 'donjon' has been debased in popular usage to 'dungeon', meaning a subterranean prison cell, preferably running with water and rats. Here, in short, is a vivid manifestation of that especially offensive heresy which sees something called 'the Middle ages' as the Dark Ages. What, then, is the truth of the matter, the grain of truth that has brought forth all this nonsense?

The castle as a strong place, surrounded by that almost mystical security still represented by the nightly Ceremony of the Keys at the Tower of London, and as difficult to get out of as it was to get into, was an obviously suitable place for the incarceration of prisoners. But in the medieval period such prisoners were usually political prisoners and prisoners of state, men and women of high degree, to be treated (in spite of some lurid stories in some contemporary chronicles) honourably. Part of the suitability of the castle for their incarceration, therefore, was that it could provide secure accommodation commensurate with their rank – which is about as far as one can get from the dank and rat-ridden 'dungeon'. In the medieval period, also, such socially elevated imprisonment was ocasional and subsidiary to the castle's basic functions as residence and fortress. Only when these waned or vanished did some of the subsidiary uses which had once followed from them in some cases take over to fill the vacuum – and so, to cite that famous instance once again, the Tower of London in the sixteenth and seventeenth centuries became increasingly a state prison and a manufactory of arms and armaments (there having been, amongst many other things including a menagerie and a mint, an armoury there since at least the time of Edward I). Even then the Tower remained a state prison for prisoners generally of rank and suitably accommodated. Norwich, to cite another and a different instance, did not become a common gaol, of horrid squalor, until the eighteenth century, in which philistine period the city fathers could think of no better use for it – and thus grievously mutilated one of the finest and oldest keeps in England. Dismal dank dungeons, it seems, like boiling oil poured from machicolations, are myths to be dismissed from any serious book on castles. As for the block and all those executions at the Tower, comprising ninetenths of every guide book and of every guide's discourse, indeed they happened; but they happened in the 'modern' period of the Tudors and Stuarts, for political executions were not a medieval habit. It was the bestial lusts and pathological policies of Henry VIII especially (the first 'modern' king?) who turned the Tower of London into a place of suffering and blood.

The architectural development of the castle

In the pages which follow, the architectural development and decline of the castle will, of course, be dealt with fully, as will the method of building and the impressive organization which lies behind it. Here therefore, and as usual, it is only necessary to forecast certain fundamentals. Thus while it may be true that most of the earliest castles were structures of earthwork and timber only (though even this is by no means so certain as was formerly supposed), it is not true that all were so. Stone building, stone fortification, was there from the beginning, ie in northern France in the ninth and tenth centuries, as witness Doué-la-Fontaine and Langeais, and as we might in any case expect. Timber defences, on the other hand, survived until very late (as witness Edward I's peel at Linlithgow, Scotland, in 1302), while earthwork in some form was almost always present (the ditch, fosse or moat). It therefore follows that the earlier structural history of the castle was not one of progress and development from earthwork and timber to masonry. It is moreover very clear that not all early castles which were of earthwork and timber were also of that best known type, the so-called motte-and-bailey castle, though without doubt the motte-and-bailey was particularly favoured by the Norman *conquistadores* of England in the first fine careless rapture of the Norman Conquest. Much recent work, therefore, especially by archaeologists, has been devoted to the uncertain origins of the motte as the dominant feature of many but by no means all early castles. Meanwhile it may be suggested that too much tends to be made of an assumed distinction between earthwork-and-timber castles and those of masonry. The two alleged types overlap in time, all three materials could be mixed and used at once, and the principles of medieval fortification were constant from start to finish in whatever medium, although, of course, they were applied with increasing sophistication. These, reduced to fundamentals, were the combination of wall (or its timber equivalent, the palisade) and flanking tower, the latter making possible the adequate defence of the former; and that other combination of the walled and towered enclosure and the donjon. The castle had to be big to house its possible complement of several large and self-sufficient households, their horses and their needs, but within it there seems always to have been an inner sanctum of lordly accommodation and ultimate military strength, namely the donjon. This could take the form of the motte with its integral tower (timber or otherwise), of the so-called 'shell-keep' or fortified enclosure on the motte-top (eg Windsor or Arundel), or of an inner bailey, but in an age of conscious symbolism it will be architecturally marked out and emphasized as the *pièce maîtresse* of the whole. The most formidable donjon of all, however, in all periods of the castle's history, was the 'great tower', *la grosse tour*, *magna turris* – what we call the 'tower keep', the most potent and evocative symbol of feudal lordship.

Castle building

The section entitled 'Castle Construction' also illustrates what ought to be obvious even to those who still believe in 'progress'

and the manifold advantages of modernity, namely, that our medieval forefathers could build a great deal better than we can. Further, a moment's thought may suggest that the great churches of Latin Christendom in the high Middle Ages were deeply impressive exercises not only of art but also of science and applied science too. Perhaps the greatest technological achievement of medieval masons was daringly to throw a high stone vault across the great and elevated spaces of their churches, yet this was done at least by the late eleventh century and, of course, without benefit of our vaunted modern technology. The great castles of the twelfth and thirteenth centuries and beyond – Château-Gaillard, Krak des Chevaliers, Caernarvon – are scarcely less architectural triumphs than the great churches, though customarily ignored by architectural historians in favour of the latter. The organization that lay behind these achievements and made them possible was scarcely less impressive than the buildings themselves and the expertise that raised them. England at least, unique in Western Europe, has preserved the evidence of its medieval building industry (for we can scarcely call it less) in the form of miles [*sic*] and miles of parchment rolls, building accounts especially, relating to the king's works if not to those of his magnates, clerical and lay. Masons and carpenters, plumbers and glaziers, smiths and plasterers, painters and common labourers were assembled in their thousands to construct Edward I's castles in north Wales, and paid at the standard rates, while, even more expensively, materials of every kind were brought as necessary over long distances, wherever possible by water. When Edward III was rebuilding Windsor castle in the mid fourteenth century, the complaint was that nobody else in England could obtain a mason for love or money, for medieval English kings had the right of conscription of labour and its direction also. Trade-union leaders now would be aghast, but though the first recorded strike in English history may have been at Dunfermline in

Left The nightly Ceremony of the Keys at the Tower of London echoing a past when the security of the realm depended on the security of its castles.
Far left The dramatically sited castle of Ortenberg (Bas-Rhin) with its tower *en bec* commands the surrounding countryside.
Below Chinon (Indre-et-Loire), known as 'the cradle of the Angevin race' – who were, amongst other things, kings of England. A great comital castle in Anjou, one third of which (the Fort St Georges) is off the picture to the right.

Above The splendid nineteenth-century castle at Peckforton (Cheshire) built for the Tollemache family by Anthony Salvin, who also restored the Tower of London.

Below The original White Tower of the Conqueror has become the centre of the great concentric castle known as the Tower of London.

1303 (for non-payment of wages by the king at Linlithgow), we know of very little opposition. The medieval building trade and all its various members were itinerant, moving from one site to the next, and were seemingly glad of employment. What they achieved was prodigious, and so, upon occasion, as necessity required, was the speed with which they accomplished it – five years for Conway and two for Château-Gaillard (p. 42). And there was generally no shortage of work for building and the patronage of the arts were attributes of lordship and, if medieval English kings are representative, more was spent upon them than any other lordly occupation save only war.

The decline of the castle

Although the latter will, of course, be dealt with in the pages which follow, it is in fact easier to discuss the origin of the castle than its decline, on which far less work has been directed. We can at least maintain that the advent of guns and gunpowder is superficial and erroneous as an explanation of its coming, as also are changes in the nature and conduct of warfare. Guns in particular seem for long to have been more effective in the defence of castles than in attack upon them, and, if so, another myth must be dismissed. Since the castle is the manifestation of a particular form of society, what we must seek and find to explain its decline in any given country is that change in social organization which can only be described as a change from feudalism to the nation state, as public authority becomes concentrated again in a sovereign central government, and military power, defence and fortification are gathered up into the hands of the king or prince. The decline of the castle when it comes is in practice the loss of its military value, yet we must be careful not to see the so-called 'fortified manor' – a great house thinly defended like, for example, Oxburgh Hall or Herstmonceux – as a measure of that decline to be associated exclusively with the later Middle Ages of, say, the

Left Haut-Koenigsbourg (Alsace) was the medieval castle of the Hohenstaufen German kings and emperors and was lavishly restored and largely rebuilt for Kaiser Wilhelm II in the first years of the twentieth century.

fifteenth century. The castle always was both residence and fortress. There always were unfortified lordly residences such as palaces and hunting lodges – in England, for example, the royal residences of Woodstock, Clarendon and Westminster itself. In between there always were what we may call 'halfway houses', fortified yet not full-bloodedly so, and as difficult for contemporaries to categorize as they are for us. Not everyone wanted, or could afford, a full-blown castle capable of holding out at length against the assault of armies. In England, thus, the fortified manor goes back to the beginning, with strong houses (*domus defensabiles*) mentioned in Domesday Book, via such examples as Stokesay, Acton Burnell (both in Shropshire) and Little Wenham (Suffolk) – all three built in the second half of the thirteenth century at the very time of the castle's apogee. The spirit and attitude behind the construction of such houses, at any time, is surely that of Patrick Forbes at Corse Castle (Aberdeenshire) in *c.*1500: 'Please God, I will build me such a house as thieves will knock at ere they enter.'

Survival, in reality and in tradition

The castle, which for half a millennium at least dominated society and history in Latin Christendom and the West, has naturally left its imprint not only on the land but also on the minds of men and women. The thing itself was a long time dying, what may be accepted as castles being built in Scotland as late as the seventeenth century and in Ireland as late as the eighteenth. Entrenched dues and customs lingered even longer, castle-guard rents being rendered to Eye in Suffolk in 1793 (and doubtless later), though that castle then as now had been ruined for centuries. In a sense, the castle has never died, retaining in many cases the half-life of its residential role. Some families continued to live nobly in their castles, and some still do. Certain royal castles, moreover, where monarchy survives, have themselves survived almost in full working

order to the present day, though their military parade is chiefly ceremonial. Dover, however, was refortified against Napoleon's French in *c.*1800 (with disastrous results upon the medieval fabric), though there, paradoxically, the true residential role had long been lost and no king had stayed in it for generations. At the Tower of London also, a shadow of the military function remains in its continuing garrison, though Charles II was the last king to reside there (but only traditionally on the night before his coronation), and the palace buildings for the king and court, south of the White Tower, were demolished under his predecessor, James II. Certain mere aspects of medieval military architecture also survived, though only as architectural traditions or fashions without practical role, notably the gatehouse and battlements or crenellation. The Radcliffe Quadrangle of University College, Oxford, for example, has both, though built in the eighteenth century. Soon after, the Romantic movement brought a new interest, however ill-informed, in all things medieval, including castles as places to write about ('Child Roland to the Dark Tower came') and if possible to live in. At the highest level, decent and even 'romantic' decay was stopped by more damaging restoration and improvement, as for example at Windsor, Arundel and Alnwick, or at Haut-Koenigsbourg – the last by Kaiser Wilhelm II in *c.*1900. In England in the nineteenth century, Anthony Salvin, while busily restoring the Tower of London, built a splendid brand-new castle for the Tollemache family at Peckforton in Cheshire. Elsewhere and less grandiosely, Victorian *nouveaux riches* and their equivalents in other countries at least grasped the fact, for whatever half-understood reasons, that castles were the noblest of residences, and did their best to ape their betters. Even today such phrases as 'the Englishman's home is his castle', and (Victorian sentimentalism notwithstanding) 'the rich man in his castle, the poor man at his gate', still faintly echo something of the castle's historic role.

The scope of the this book

Though from the reader's point of view there are many books on castles in all relevant languages, one has only to think of churches and the mountainous literature on every aspect of their history to realize the comparative neglect of our subject. It is significant, for example, that there is no such thing as even a bare list of castles even for the small and well-worked area of England and Wales, nor, one supposes, for any other country. This comparative neglect the present book will do its best to remedy a little, by dealing with all aspects of the subject, and by trying to be as comprehensive as possible geographically at least by reference to all countries and areas of Europe and the former Latin Christendom where castles can be found. In the Gazetteer section, itself divided into areas which take some note of historical reality, there can be no question of definitive lists of castles, but in each case some 20–30 castles have been selected on the basis of their particular interest or importance. In consequence one would like to think, and urge, that in a world of ever more far-flung tourism, so long as petrol lasts, no far-flung motor car with educated occupants will be complete without this companion on the back shelf. Time spent on reading it before one starts, or even in lieu of going, is also recommended.

Thelnetham, Suffolk.
October 1980.

R.A.B.

1

Castle-building

In the long centuries of its active history the castle of course developed architecturally like any type of building. Nevertheless its development is a more complicated process than a straight progression from the simplest to the most sophisticated. In the beginning Roman techniques of fortification had not been lost (eg the mural tower), and the preceding Carolingian epoch had already made its own contribution to the residences of the great (eg the hall). It is certain also that not all early castles were constructed of earthwork and timber only and that therefore a transition from timber to stone building is not the basic theme of early castle evolution. At the other end of the time scale another development cuts across any concept of a straight line of progress. As a generalization it seems true that later castles lost their military importance, the former balance of residence and fortress was upset, and residential splendours therefore triumphed. In consequence some later castles are less well fortified than some earlier ones.

Details aside, it is probable that the basic principles of castle design were constant from start to finish: a fortified enclosure with that inner sanctum of strength and lordship which contemporaries called the 'donjon'. In the context of the latter, the feudal period made its characteristic architectural contribution of the great tower, the 'keep' in English parlance.

The great castles of the High Middle Ages are, no less than churches, major architectural achievements by any standards, while even their simpler forebears, including those of earthwork and timber, are scarcely the results of a mindless application of unskilled and/or forced labour. It so happens that the extraordinary survival in England of the records at least of royal administration, from the twelfth century onwards, enables us to see in detail the medieval building industry (for such it was) at work, and to appreciate that necessary organization of finance, labour, materials and transport which is no less impressive than the buildings – castles as well as palaces and churches – which it produced.

Richard I's Château-Gaillard (Eure). A superb castle built in two years with a huge concentration of wealth and labour.

Castle Construction

Many aspects of medieval life which seem astonishing to modern eyes were treated as quite matter-of-fact by contemporaries. Even today, with all the advances of modern technology, the construction of a great castle would pose major problems. In the Middle Ages the task required not merely considerable technical skill in the art of building, from the cutting of the stone with simple hand tools to the design of complex vaulting, but also great powers of organization. Large numbers of workmen with their different skills had to be recruited, great quantities of materials had to be collected and the whole operation had to be carefully co-ordinated and financed. Yet few men thought it worthwhile recording how all this was done; there is an account of the rebuilding of the Syrian castle of Safad by the Crusaders in the thirteenth century, but such a text is unique. No chronicler thought it worth recording in any detail the way in which Edward I built his great chain of castles in north Wales in the late thirteenth century. Fortunately in that instance the survival of large numbers of building accounts enables the historian to piece together the story of how they were constructed in great detail, but outside the British Isles such documentary evidence is regrettably rare. In some instances it is possible to reconstruct the career of a medieval architect, or master mason to use the contemporary term. In others no more than the man's name is known, while the great majority of the men who were responsible for building castles remain anonymous. Examination of the material evidence of the buildings themselves often provides much evidence of the way in which they were built, making up for the silence of written records.

The requirements of a site

The first task in building a castle was to select a suitable site. Many considerations came into play here. There were the obvious military factors: if possible, the site should offer natural obstacles, such as a steep hillside or an expanse of water, to any attacker. It should not be too remote, and should command as much of the surrounding countryside as possible. It was important that water should be available as well as local supplies of foodstuffs. Ideally, building materials should be readily accessible. The bishop of Marseilles described what he considered to be the perfect site for a castle, namely the one he chose for the fortress of Safad. Offensively it provided a base for attacks on Damascus, while it defended one of the routes towards Acre used by Moslem raiders. The climate there was excellent. There was ample forest; vines, figs, almonds, pomegranates and olives grew in abundance, and there was good pasture for animals – this was a land of milk and honey. The local stone was ideally suited for building purposes and there was sufficient water in wells and cisterns. Selection of a site required the expertise of builders as well as of soldiers. In 1243 the civic authorities of Avignon selected a body of twenty men to choose a place for a new castle, among whom there were both knights and masons.

Once a site was chosen, a formal ceremony normally took place. An early eleventh-century charter refers to the foundation of a castle in Brittany by planting a stake in the ground one Sunday morning. At Safad the bishop of Marseilles laid the first stone. Edward I of England wheeled a token barrow of earth to the new ramparts he ordered to be built at Berwick-upon-Tweed.

Materials for the construction

The nature of the site did much to determine the materials from which a castle was built. Earth, stone, brick and timber were all used. Except for the rockiest of mountain sites, earthworks had a part to play in almost every scheme of defence. A ditch and bank could be dug quickly, and if the bank was then surmounted by a palisade, a surprisingly formidable obstacle could be created. If earth was piled up with care to form a tall mound, the equivalent of a tower could be constructed. This was known as a 'motte', and would be strengthened with a wooden superstructure in most instances.

Stone was the strongest building material. In ideal circumstances a castle would be built from the stone hewn from the ditch which was an integral part of the defences. There is a good example of this at Beeston in Cheshire, where the stone walls rise as a direct continuation of the rock face of the moat cut by the masons. More often, however, local stone was suitable for little more than the rubble infilling of the walls, as it was incapable of being properly cut and dressed. If that was so, stone would have to be brought to the site, often from a considerable distance and at great cost. One of the best known medieval building stones was the fine limestone of Caen in

Far left In the later Middle Ages brick was often used for castle-building, especially in low-lying lands where stone was scarce. Tattershall (Lincolnshire) is one of the finest English examples, built by Ralph Lord Cromwell in the fifteenth century.

Below A fifteenth-century illustration of a brickworks. The man in the shed can be seen moulding the bricks, which are then stacked up to dry out before firing.

Normandy, which was conveniently soft when first quarried and hardened on exposure to the air. It was widely used in England as well as in northern France and may be seen at the Tower of London where it was used for the dressings at the angles, while the walls themselves were of Kentish rag – a stone too hard to be cut into fine ashlar blocks. Similarly, the bulk of the stone used in Edward I's castles in Wales came from nearby quarries, up to ten miles away from the building sites, but window mouldings and similar parts were often of finer-quality stone brought all the way from quarries near Chester. Accounts for the building of Tattershall Castle in Lincolnshire in the fifteenth century show that fine ashlar and pre-formed tracery were brought from Ashby-de-la-Zouch in Leicestershire and from Northamptonshire, where the famous Barnack quarries were situated.

In the later Middle Ages brick was often used as an alternative to stone, particularly in low-lying regions where clay was plentiful and quarries far away. The Baltic lands, the Netherlands and eastern England all provide examples of castles built of that mellow material, whose richness of colour and variety of texture produced by irregular firing make a striking contrast with modern brickwork. The medieval mason

Right A reconstruction of Harlech Castle under construction. This view shows part of the gatehouse, and the curtain wall leading to the south-eastern tower. Note the use of helicoidal, or spiral, scaffolding: this technique was introduced to Britain by the Savoyard masons employed by Edward I.

took full advantage of the decorative potential of his medium.

Huge quantities of sand, lime and water were needed to make mortar to bond both stone and brick. Sometimes the lime was prepared by burning stone on the site itself; accounts show that on other occasions it was brought in ready-made. Iron and steel were needed both for nails and for the workmen's tools. Window glass and plaster were not required to add to the strength of the castle, but reflect its role as an aristocratic residence. Timber was extensively used in castles of all types. The Bayeaux Tapestry provides illustrations of wooden keeps and palisades, and even as late as the fourteenth century wooden castles were still being built. In a stone castle timber was needed for scaffolding during the construction stages, and for wooden floors, roofbeams, window-shutters, panelling and the like.

The provision and transport of materials

The lord was usually responsible for providing the workmen he employed with building materials. In 1224 the count of Dreux agreed with his master mason that he would supply all the stone, sand, lime, water and wood that was needed for the building works at his new castle. This was not an invariable rule: in 1378 an English mason, John Lewyn, made a contract with Lord Scrope for the building of Bolton Castle in Wensleydale, Yorkshire, under the terms of which Scrope agreed to provide all the timber, and Lewyn the stone. All the costs of transporting the materials to the site were, however, to be borne by the lord. This was often an expensive and difficult process. The twelfth-century builders of the castle of Ibelin in the Holy Land were highly fortunate in that they were able to use the remains of ancient buildings on the same site. A considerable saving was effected if stone could be quarried on the spot, for the evidence shows that the cost of transporting stone usually far exceeded that of the material itself. At the end of the thirteenth century it cost 120 *livres* to carry Tonerre stone worth 22 *livres* to the city of Troyes. Where possible, inland waterways or even maritime routes were used. It was not mere traditionalism that made the Normans in England use Caen stone so widely; it was probably cheaper to bring it by sea from Normandy than to have English stone carted overland.

The design process

Once the site for a castle was determined, the form that the building was to take had to be decided. Although the craft of building was an extremely professional one in the Middle Ages, it is clear that some lords took a very active part in the design of their castles. The tough and unscrupulous Anglo-Norman magnate Robert de Bellême was renowned for his expertise. He built extensively on his own account in Normandy and was employed by William Rufus to supervise the building of a new castle at Gisors. He gained military experience on the First Crusade, where his skill in building siege-engines assisted in the capture of Jerusalem itself. Robert had a predilection for hilltop sites; in England he abandoned his father's castle at Quatford, hard by the River Severn, and founded a far stronger fortification at Bridgnorth on high ground. It is hardly to be wondered at that a warrior like Robert should have been an expert in castle design. For the Normans the castle was as vital a military weapon as the mounted knight and an experienced soldier would naturally have strong views on the best form that defences should take.

It is rather more surprising, however, to find that Hugh de Noyers, Bishop of Auxerre in the late twelfth century, was considered to be an expert on military architecture. Great ecclesiastics were major lords in secular society as well as in the church and had responsibilities to defend their lands. Hugh's expertise was theoretical as well as practical, for he studied the classical texts on the art of war, notably the writings of Vegetius, and attempted to put ancient precepts into practice in his episcopal castles at Varzy and Noyers. The existing moats were greatly enlarged and new walls and towers were put up on his instructions. At Noyers careful arrangements were made to ensure that the garrison would be adequately supplied with victuals in case of siege. Water was provided though an elaborate plumbing system, and underground passages were dug to provide supply routes of which the enemy would be ignorant.

Even emperors and kings might take a close interest in castle-building. Extravagant claims have been made for Frederick II of Hohenstaufen, who died in 1250: he has been seen as an all-round genius, equally skilled in politics, science, literature and architecture. There is little doubt that he was also pathologically cruel, while his credulity in astrology does

not quite fit the picture of a Renaissance man born before his time. An inscription over an archway at Foggia in southern Italy suggests that the emperor was responsible for the design, if not the execution of the building: 'Caesar ordered this work to be constructed in this way; this is how Bartholomew built it'. Frederick probably also designed a great tower or gatehouse commanding the bridge at Capua, as well as the remarkable Castel del Monte in Apulia. His influence is particularly to be detected in the classical detailing of many of his castles, as in the portico of Castel del Monte, rather than in the fortifications themselves.

Edward I of England could not have been a passive onlooker as the chain of castles ringing North Wales was created; he undoubtedly took a great personal interest in the works undertaken at his command. His son, Edward II, took an even more practical interest in building and was rebuked by contemporaries because he enjoyed working as a craftsman. There is good evidence that he was responsible for the design of a new tower 'which we have devised to be done' at Knaresborough Castle in Yorkshire; on four occasions the master mason had to leave the works and seek out the king to ask for specific instructions.

CASTLE-BUILDING

Below Emperor Frederick II, who died in 1250, ruled Germany, Italy and Sicily. He built many notable castles, especially in southern Italy, and took a close personal interest in their construction.

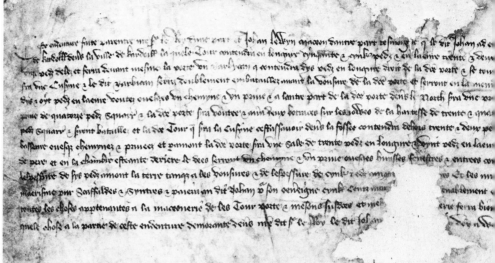

Below This late medieval illumination shows a mason's lodge. These were often no more than simple sheds, in which the masons worked carving the stones ready to be put in place.

Right A thirteenth-century drawing of a king instructing his master mason. Note the use of a windlass to hoist the stone to the layers, one of whom is checking the work with a level. Below, masons are using axes to carve stone.

1.

Left A contract between the Crown and John Lewyn for the building of the outer gatehouse at Carlisle Castle. The document was drawn up in 1378, and was written in Anglo-Norman. Lewyn built at many castle sites in the north of England; for his work on this occasion he was paid £333 6s. 8d.

The agreements that were made between patrons and the masons they employed reveal something of the design process. The count of Dreux asked his mason in 1224 to build a keep like that at nearby Nogent-le-Rotrou, though the surviving remains suggest that his orders were not strictly adhered to. In 1348 Lord Stafford provided a 'device and ordinance' for the castle he wanted built; these were perhaps a plan with instructions. A building plan for the castle at Courtrai in Flanders survives. The castle was built for Philip the Bold of Burgundy between 1394 and 1396. Accounts show that Philip was sent the plans while he was at Boulogne; they were vetted by some master masons from St Omer and then sent back, duly approved, to Henry Heubens, the mason in charge of the new works. In other instances it is probable that no plans ever existed. A contract might specify the precise measurements of the proposed building, which would be sufficient for a skilled mason. At Knaresborough the masons working on Edward II's tower had a tracing-house, where they could draw the shapes of vaulting and tracery full-size and transfer the patterns directly on to the stone – a technique much easier in many ways than working from scale drawings.

The master masons and their role

Even if the owner of a castle took an active interest in determining the plan of the fortifications, the actual work of supervising constructions was done by skilled professionals. Even the simplest motte-and-bailey castle of earth and timber had to be set out with care. The chronicler Lambert of Ardres described work on improving the castle at Ardres itself at the end of the twelfth century, with Master Simon laying out the lines for the moats and foundations with his measuring rod, the indispensable instrument for such work. Working in stone demanded very special skills, and the master masons in particular were men of great expertise who enjoyed considerable prestige. Master James of St George was paid half as much again by Edward I as he paid his household knights.

Much that has been written about the organization of the mason's craft in the Middle Ages belongs to the world of fantasy rather than of historical fact. Since many masons travelled widely in search of work, the craft was not universally organized into municipal guilds in the normal way, although there are some indications that in the later medieval period some general gatherings of masons were held, even on occasion on an international basis. Even in the fifteenth century, however, it was not necessary for a mason to work his way up through all the stages of being first an apprentice and then a journeyman. It is not clear whether the great master masons were trained from the first to be what are now termed 'architects'. They would have had to be literate and to have had a knowledge of practical geometry, while it is also likely that they would have had considerable experience in the various different types of mason's work.

There are references to the master craftsmen who built castles from as early as the late eleventh century, when Chaise-la-Vicomte was built by one Ingelbert, but no more is known of him than his name. At the same period Aubrée, wife of the count of Bayeux, had a castle built at Pithiviers by an architect (the chronicle uses that exact term) called Lanfred. So delighted was she with his work that she had him executed on the spot in case he should build so splendid a fortress for anyone else.

More is known about English masons than those of other countries, for the records of the English Crown are far fuller than those of any other European country in the Middle Ages. Henry II's exchequer accounts, the Pipe Rolls, reveal the names of several masons who worked for him. In the military sphere the most notable was Maurice the Mason, who worked both at Newcastle and at Dover, where the keeps show a strong resemblance. Initially Maurice received 8d. a day, the same wage as a knight, but later he was paid at the rate of a shilling a day. Although there is no equivalent series of French records, an early thirteenth-century memorandum of building work to be carried out for Philip Augustus gives the names of his leading masons. Some of the work was to be carried out 'as Master Aumary has devised'; he was clearly more important than the others, who were called Garnerius, Walter de Mullent, William de Flamenville, Odo, Adam, Ralph, Matthew and Alard.

More is known of the master masons of the thirteenth century than of the twelfth. Philip Chinard was an international figure who came from Champagne in France and settled in Cyprus, where he became acquainted with the techniques of fortification used in the Crusader world. He then entered the service of the emperor, Frederick II, and worked at Castel del Monte. The vaults there resemble those of the cathedral at Le Mans and the church at Châlons-sur-Marne – a clear consequence of Philip's French origin. Another French mason who worked in southern Italy was Pierre d'Agincourt, who went there to serve the ambitious Charles of Anjou and who built the walls defending the town of Lucera in Apulia, the place to which many Sicilian Arabs had been sent into exile by Frederick II.

The most notable example of the international mason is that of Master James of St George, whose genius was responsible for the magnificent chain of castles with which Edward I ringed north Wales. Edward probably first met James, a mason in the service of the count of Savoy, when he was returning from the Crusades in 1273. The count did homage to Edward at the new castle of St Georges d'Esperanche (Isère), on which James had worked. It was presumably because Edward was so impressed with the castle, rectangular in plan with octagonal corner towers, that he later took James into his employment. In 1278 James was sent to Wales 'to ordain the works of the castles there', and by 1285 he was termed 'master of the king's works in Wales'. His wife, Ambrosia, was promised a pension of 1s. 6d. a day should she survive him. In 1290 James was appointed constable of Harlech castle at a fee of 100 marks a year (£66 13s. 4d.), a rare example of a mason receiving command of a castle whose building he supervised.

The castles built by Master James in north Wales are among the finest surviving monuments of medieval secular architecture and, as the next chapter will show, it is possible by looking at them in order of construction to see the way in which one man worked out various solutions to the problems of castle design, elaborating his concepts with each successive project. Master James was not a man to remain content with his work; in each castle he tried to improve and develop his ideas. It is not, however, in the overall planning of the castles that his Savoyard origins are displayed. It is the detail of the masonry that reveals where he and some of his fellow masons had learnt their skills. At Harlech, in particular, the use of full-centred round arches reflect Savoyard practice. The design of the windows, with a low rounded arch, was unlike an English work of the period but echoes work at Chillon and Yverdon in Switzerland. The measurements of the Harlech windows match those at Chillon almost exactly. Similarly, one of the latrine chutes at Harlech is built to the same dimensions as one at the castle of St Georges d'Esperanche itself. It is clear that Master James was a craftsman as well as a designer. He could not, of course, exercise an equally detailed supervision of all the castles built by Edward I in north Wales. At Caernarvon much of the work was done by an English mason, Walter of Hereford, so that although the overall conception of the castle was James's, the castle lacks the Savoyard touches of detail so apparent at Harlech.

In his last years Edward I's attentions shifted from Wales to Scotland and Master James followed his lord. Unfortunately funds were no long sufficient to enable him to engage in a major castle-building programme and, as a unique surviving agreement between himself and the king for the fortification of Linlithgow reveals, he was reduced to building in wood rather than in stone. His engineering talents were probably also called upon to assist in the construction of siege-engines, for those skilled in building castles were often also adept exponents of the art of siege warfare.

Master James of St George was a genius of exceptional qualities. A more typical castle-builder, perhaps, was John Lewyn, who was active in the north of England in the late fourteenth century. Whereas Master James appears to have specialized throughout his career in military architecture, Lewyn began his career as a mason at Durham Cathedral. He built churches and castles with equal facility and was a good businessman, with interests in the wool trade as well as in building. His success was probably not due so much to the quality of his work as to the fact that he was an entrepreneur who could provide a corps of masons and other craftsmen to fulfil the contracts made with him. In the 1370s he seems to have had a near monopoly in the north of England. His work, at such sites as Carlisle Castle, Raby in Co. Durham, and Bolton in Wensleydale and Sheriff Hutton (both in Yorkshire), displays none of the virtuosity of Master James's castles. It is characterized by utilitarian square towers, plain exteriors and somewhat characterless masonry. Yet Lewyn's castles were practical and his costs reasonable. He deserves to be remembered as the chief English military architect of his age. His greater contemporary, Henry Yevele, built surprisingly few fortifications and the chief one with which he has been associated, the remarkable, circular castle at Queenborough on the Isle of Sheppey, now completely destroyed, was almost certainly not his responsibility at all but the work of Master John Box.

It is not always easy to identify the man primarily responsible for the building of a castle. At Cooling in Kent Lord Cobham employed Thomas Crump to build a new gatehouse in 1381. Henry Yevele was brought in to measure the work, as it was rightly suspected that Crump was overcharging, and it may be that the initial design was by Yevele but secure evidence is lacking. It has been argued from the building accounts for the fifteenth-century castle of Tattershall in Lincolnshire that the designer was a man called Baldwin Dutchman, who came either from the Netherlands or from Germany. He was a brickmaker, in charge of a brickworks set up a few miles from the castle site, and the documents in question do not suggest that he did anything more than supply the building material for the castle.

The identity of many of the masons who built the great French castles of the later Middle Ages is known. Raymond du Temple, Charles V's 'beloved sergeant-at-arms and master mason', worked at Vincennes with Guillaume d'Arondel. Jean Lenoir was responsible for Pierrefonds, while Guy de Dammartin served John, Duke of Berry, at such castles as Mehun-sur-Yèvre and Concresseault. They were master masons in a familiar mould. In fifteenth-century Italy, however, men of a rather different type began to take an interest in the problems

of castle design. Alberti, who died in 1472, was a Florentine nobleman, a man of all-round intellectual and even athletic ability: he is said to have been able to jump over a man, holding his feet close together. He wrote a treatise on architecture and devoted considerable attention to the problems of castle-building. Although he proposed a revolutionary transformation of civic and ecclesiastical architecture, by turning back to the classical tradition, he clearly respected the traditional solutions of castle design. He argued against those who considered high walls provided little defence against artillery, and advocated the retention of the keep.

Within the fortress ought to be one principal tower, built in the stoutest manner, and fortified as strongly as possible, higher than any other part of the castle, and not accessible by more than one way, to which there should be no other entrance but by a drawbridge.

(J. Rykwert (ed.), *Ten Books on Architecture by Leone Battista Alberti*, 1755, reprinted London, 1955)

Francesco di Giorgio Martini was another all-round Renaissance man keenly interested in the problems of fortification, as his treatise written in the 1490s shows. His drawings of star-

Above Leon Battista Alberti (1404–72), a Florentine of remarkable all-round abilities, was one of the most important of early Renaissance architects.
Left Henry Yevele was the most notable master mason in late fourteenth-century England and was extensively employed by Edward III and Richard II. He was not primarily a military architect, but his hand has been seen in the castles at Queenborough, Cooling and Portchester.

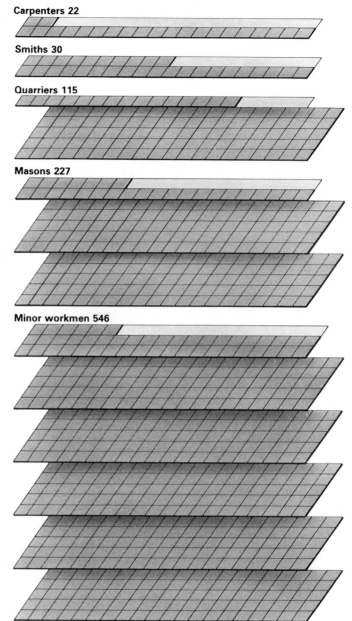

Right A diagram showing the enormous number of workmen employed under the master-mason Master James of St George during the building of Harlech Castle (Gwynedd). The large numbers of 'minor workmen' were chiefly employed as carriers, barrow-men and pick-men. (Figures from H. M. Colvin, ed. *History of the King's Works*, II, p 1030.

Carpenters 22

Smiths 30

Quarriers 115

Masons 227

Minor workmen 546

shaped forts and bastions reveal a quite different approach to the question of castle design than that of the medieval masons, although the actual fortifications he built were less revolutionary. Francesco, however, was an architect and an engineer in a quite different and more modern sense than a man such as Master James of St George. The role of the professional mason was far from over in the late fifteenth century but a new type of architect was emerging, at the very time that the role of the castle, as known in the Middle Ages, was dying.

The organization and supervision of construction work

The master mason could not organize the whole operation of building a major castle. It was necessary to employ a clerk who would pay the workmen, organize the supply of building material and keep the accounts. In the late eleventh century Gundulf, Bishop of Rochester, was described as 'very competent and skilful at building in stone'; not only was he responsible for the castle at Rochester itself but he also supervised work on the Tower of London. It is likely that his function was more that of a clerk of works than of a master mason. In the twelfth century supervision of building works was generally, as far as English royal castles were concerned, the work of the sheriff or the castle constable but in the succeeding centuries special clerks were appointed with increasing frequency. At Beaumaris in Anglesey Master James of St George was assisted by Walter of Winchester as his clerk of works. Under Edward III William of Wykeham rose to high office in both the church and the state after beginning his career as a royal clerk supervising the works at Windsor. Though he lacked the expertise of a master mason, Wykeham's own love of building is amply attested by the work he inspired at Winchester Cathedral, Winchester College and New College, Oxford. From 1378 the office of Clerk of the King's Works was firmly established; its holders had responsibilities extending over the whole of the royal building programme. Clerks of works were employed by private patrons as well as by the Crown. The fifteenth-century Tattershall accounts show that Lord Cromwell employed Thomas Croxby as his clerk to supervise the building work; he was succeeded by John Southall and then in turn by John Combe.

There was a similar pattern of development on the Continent, though it is far less well documented than for England. Thirteenth-century French royal accounts show that the *baillis*, like the English sheriffs, accounted for royal building works but in the fourteenth and fifteenth centuries special clerks were used. Pierre Magnier, who has been seen as the architect of the castles built by Count Peter I of Savoy, was more probably a clerk of works, performing the functions of an accountant and not of a designer. There was no specialist administration available at Courtrai in the late fourteenth century; there a local canon acted together with the *bailli* to organize the works.

The recruitment and organization of labour

It might be expected that since the castle was a feudal institution it would be built by making use of feudal services: in other words, that the lord would use his rights over his tenants to compel them to work on his new fortifications. In fact a public obligation to work on fortifications predated the appearance of the feudal castle and was probably not much used as a means of providing the labour for castle-building. In late tenth-century Catalonia, however, the peasants at Cardo-

na had to work one day a week on the castle. In England there had existed in Anglo-Saxon times, when there were no castles, the so-called *Trinoda Necessitas*, or triple obligation to work on bridges and fortifications, and to serve in the army. In a few cases this traditional duty to work on communal defences, or 'burghs', was transferred to the new castles built after the Norman Conquest. The men of several counties were compelled to work on a wall round the Tower of London, and as late as 1215 the men of Berkshire were summoned to repair the ditch of the town and castle of Wallingford, now in Oxfordshire. There were a few examples of feudal tenure associated with castle-building. At Corfe in Dorset a carpenter called Durand probably received his land as a reward for his work on the castle, and at Hereford some land was held in return for the interesting service of measuring the castle ditches and overseeing the workmen digging them. Sometimes the tenants who were obliged to perform military service in a castle, or 'castle-guard', were also held responsible for maintaining the houses within the castle where they lived during their spell of duty.

On the Continent there is little evidence to suggest that labour services were important in castle-building. In Germany *Burgwerk* probably developed so that communal defences

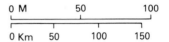

Left This diagram shows the way in which Edward I recruited workmen from almost every county in England in 1282–3 for his castle-building programme in North Wales. He had to use powers of impressment to bring together as large a force as this.

☐	Movement of Labour, May–June 1282
☐	Movement of Labour, 1283
●	Gathering points
♟	Carpenters
♦	Diggers
⚒	Masons
⚒	Counties providing some 1600 woodcutters (*coupiatores*), mainly for clearing tracks.
⌂	New castles under construction

```
0 M        50        100
0 Km   50   100   150
```

Below Part of a building account for Harlech Castle. The account ran from 30 December 1285 to 15 December 1286: this section covers three weeks from 20 January 1286. The different items cover expenditure on masons, quarriers, smiths, carpenters, minor works, horses for carriage, and the wages of a clerk. The total cost for the three weeks came to £10 19*s.* 8*d.*

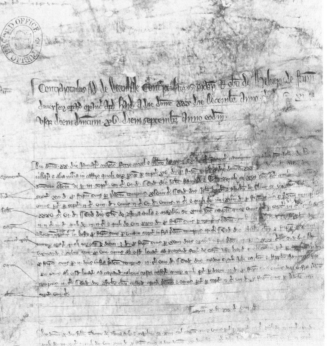

might be built in the tenth century to deal with the threat posed by the Slavs and Magyars; it was not related to the aristocratic castles built later. In France the *corvée* was the means of forcing men to work for their lord and for the king but the evidence suggests that castles were normally built by paid labour. Even the task of digging the earthworks for a simple fortification was a skilled task, better entrusted to experienced paid labourers than to peasants forced to work.

One very common means of recruiting the men to build a castle was for the lord to enter into a contract with a master mason. The latter would then be responsible for providing an adequate workforce. One contract survives from as early as the 1070s and it already displays features to be found in many later agreements. It was entered into by the abbot of Lérins and some unnamed masons and was for the building of a tower of refuge on the Ile St Honorat, off the south coast of France. The abbot agreed to pay the masons five hundred shillings for every five feet of tower. If the foundations were three feet deep the masons were to meet the cost of the work, but if they had to be four feet deep then the monks would be responsible for one foot of this. The stone was to be brought to the site by oxen supplied by the abbot, and the monastery was to provide all

Right A section of the Bayeux Tapestry showing William the Conqueror's men constructing a motte at Hastings, soon after their landing. The horizontal stripes may be intended as an indication of the way in which mottes were often formed, of layers of alternating material.

Right A section of the Bayeux Tapestry showing William the Conqueror's men constructing a motte at Hastings, soon after their landing. The horizontal stripes may be intended as an indication of the way in which mottes were often formed, of layers of alternating material.

the wood needed for the works. In 1224 the count of Dreux contracted with Master Nicholas of Beaumont-le-Roger for the construction of a castle at Dreux, where work had already begun. The count agreed to pay Nicholas 1,615 *livres* and to provide him with two robes, and undertook to provide all the building material. These are but two early examples of a type of agreement which was obviously very common.

For such great works as the building of Edward I's castles in north Wales, a contract system was not suitable, except when used for small sections of the operations. The Crown had the administrative capacity to supervise the masons closely, and employed them either on a daily basis or for task-work, when they were paid an agreed sum for a specific job. At Harlech the bulk of the initial work was done with wages paid on a daily and weekly basis. This took £1,157 out of the £1,602 spent in the first nine and a half months of 1286. By 1289, however, £1,700 out of £1,850 was spent on task-work. Master William of Drogheda, for example, was paid 45s. for each foot in height of the north-east tower, and 12s. per foot for the turret which surmounted it. Examination of the accounts for Caernarvon and Beaumaris suggests that the king's accountants exercised very tight control and that the costs of work done on a waged basis correlated remarkably closely with those of task-work.

It was not easy to recruit the large numbers of men required for a major undertaking. Edward I appointed special commissioners to hire the men he needed in north Wales. The Crown evolved powers to impress men into its service – powers which were badly needed both by Edward I and his grandson, Edward III. One chronicler even complained that it was almost impossible to find any good masons or carpenters while Edward III's works at Windsor were in progress. The compulsion involved was unpopular; the sheriff of Yorkshire on one occasion provided the masons he had collected together with red caps and cloaks to make it easier for the sergeant taking them to Windsor to prevent them from absconding on the way. The Crown also had powers of purveyance, enabling it to requisition building materials and transport. Private lords, in contrast, had no such extensive rights of compulsion and had to rely largely on the lure of good wages.

The division of labour

Society in the Middle Ages was highly ordered and evidence from as early as the twelfth century shows that the various tasks involved in castle-building were carefully differentiated. Lambert of Ardres described the labour-force involved in the initial stages of the refortification of Ardres. The role of the peasants was confined to bringing supplies in carts that they usually used to transport marl and dung. On the site there were ditchers, diggers, pickaxe men, hammerers, levellers, foundation workers, specialists in digging wells, stone-breakers, hodmen, men who carried barrels and turf cutters – not to mention officials and overseers who ensured that the labourers did their work properly. This remarkable degree of division of labour was not a literary contrivance by a chronicler anxious to impress his readers. The accounts for the building of Château-Gaillard on the Norman frontier which date from the same period paint a very similar picture. Carpenters, hodmen and other carriers, fencing workers, mortar-makers, barrow-men, water-carriers, porters of stone and wood, smiths, miners, quarriers, masons and lime-burners are all mentioned. There were distinctions between different types of mason throughout the Middle Ages. There were *hewers*, who

worked in the quarries, and *layers*, who did the actual work of building walls. *Roughmasons* were also usually involved in laying stone, while *freemasons* were skilled in the difficult art of cutting fine squared ashlar and carving complex mouldings and tracery.

The largest number of workmen were needed for the initial stages of building, for such tasks as levelling the site and digging the ditches. Again, the evidence is best for the castles built by Edward I in north Wales. For the first campaign in Wales, in 1277, the king recruited almost 3,000 workmen, some coming from as far away as Lincolnshire. Of the total, 320 were masons and no less than 1,845 were diggers. For the building of Harlech, the maximum labour force consisted of 227 masons, 115 quarriers, 30 smiths, 22 carpenters and 546 other workmen. The total of 940 compares interestingly with the 800 workmen said to have been employed on the Crusader castle of Safad in the 1240s. For the last of Edward I's castles in Wales, Beaumaris, those in charge of the works estimated that they would need some than 400 masons and 2,000 other workmen.

The characteristics of construction work

The medieval builder's methods probably did not change much over the centuries since few major technological advances took place during the period. For earthworks, all that was available was spades, shovels and barrows, and it is astonishing what could be achieved with these, given an adequate supply of manpower. Carpenters and masons had to rely on hand tools. Masons often provided their own specialist equipment, such as trowels, squares, plumblines and levels. For the cutting and dressing of stone they used pickaxes, crowbars, iron wedges, hammers, mason's axes and chisels. Some kinds of stone could be cut with a saw. Tools such as these wore out very easily and the employers were usually responsible for making proper arrangements for their repair and resharpening. A smithy was essential on any building site for this work. Machinery was sometimes used to hoist stone and other materials up to the level of the work as the castle rose in height. This might amount to no more than a simple block and tackle, but treadmill cranes were known: one such was in use at the Tower of London in 1282. Accounts for Caernarvon in 1319 provide details of a windlass which was probably used for this same purpose of hauling stone and timber up to the workmen.

A careful study of a castle can often reveal a great deal about the way in which it was built. Archaeological excavations have

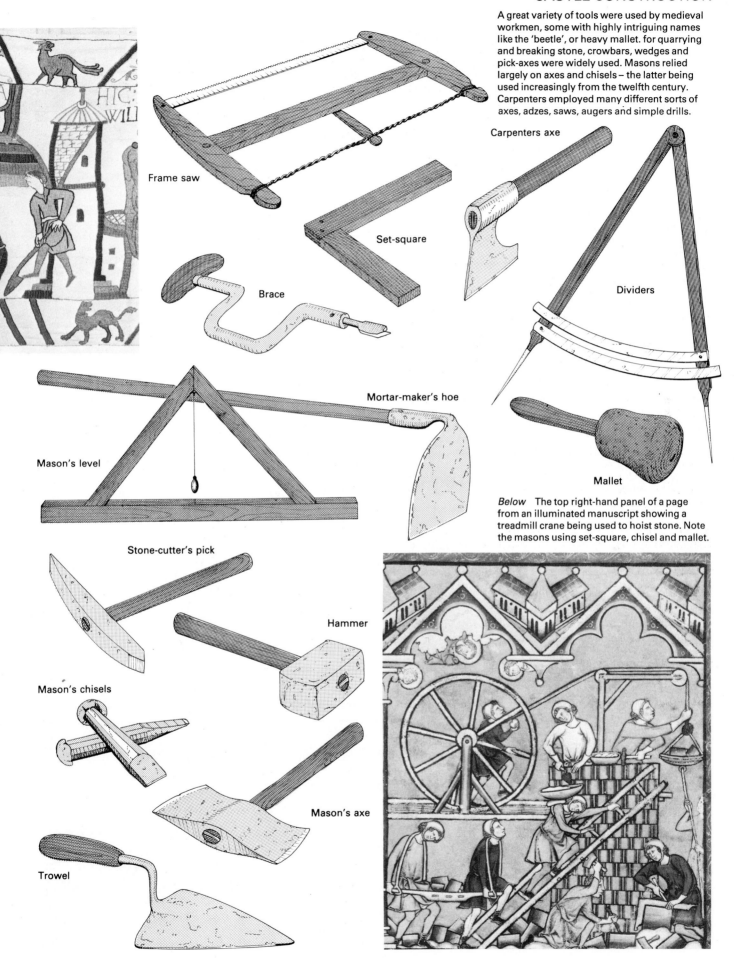

CASTLE CONSTRUCTION

A great variety of tools were used by medieval workmen, some with highly intriguing names like the 'beetle', or heavy mallet. for quarrying and breaking stone, crowbars, wedges and pick-axes were widely used. Masons relied largely on axes and chisels – the latter being used increasingly from the twelfth century. Carpenters employed many different sorts of axes, adzes, saws, augers and simple drills.

Frame saw

Set-square

Carpenters axe

Brace

Dividers

Mortar-maker's hoe

Mason's level

Mallet

Below The top right-hand panel of a page from an illuminated manuscript showing a treadmill crane being used to hoist stone. Note the masons using set-square, chisel and mallet.

Stone-cutter's pick

Hammer

Mason's chisels

Mason's axe

Trowel

CASTLE-BUILDING

Examples of the different varieties and styles of masonry used in constructing castle walls in the Middle Ages. The picture of Herstmonceux (Sussex) illustrates superbly the possibilities available in brickwork, whilst the 'mongrel' stonework shown below proves that even classical pillars could be incorporated in castle construction where materials were short.

Early small stonework (as at Langeais, Indre-et-Loire)

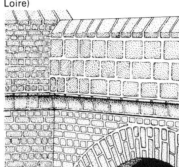

Ashlar facing with rubble filling behind

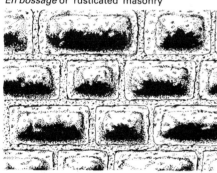

En bossage or 'rusticated' masonry

Mudéjar brickwork (as at Coca, Segovia)

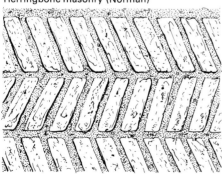

Herringbone masonry (Norman)

Isabelino work (as at El Real de Manzaranes, Madrid)

Banded masonry (as at Angers, Maine-et-Loire)

Left Medieval masons had their own individual marks, and in many castles these can still be seen. In some cases the marks were put on the stone at the quarry where it was cut, rather than at the building site itself.

shown that medieval earthworks were far more sophisticated than it appears at first sight. A motte was not just a heap of earth piled together. It might conceal wooden, or even stone, foundations for the tower which originally stood on its summit and great care was taken during its construction to ensure its stability. Construction was often in alternating layers of different materials, as is suggested by the Bayeux Tapestry illustration of the motte at Hastings under construction. At York the motte was composed of layers of clay and stones; at Oxford soil alternated with chalk, while clay was used as a coating for the completed mound.

Great care had to be taken with the foundations of massive stone buildings. Where possible, bedrock was used as a foundation but in many instances alternatives had to be sought. Wooden piles might be driven into the ground. This was done at Richmond Castle in Yorkshire in the eleventh century, and in 1324 piles were driven in with a machine called a 'ram' for part of the outer defences of the Tower of London. Sometimes a timber raft was constructed to provide stability if the ground was soft. Further stability was often given by piling up soil round the base of a keep or tower.

Castle walls were usually of composite construction, with the outer and inner faces carefully built, often of fine squared ashlar. The space between them would then be filled up with coarse rubble and mortar, forming a core of immense strength. Often the ashlar facings have been stripped from castles, so leaving this core exposed; the castles of Rhuddlan in north Wales and the Peak in Derbyshire provide good examples.

The style of masonry changed strikingly during the medieval period and often provides important clues as to the dating of castles. The earliest stonework, as at Langeais and parts of Chinon is characterized by the use of small square stones, which contrast strikingly with the larger rectangular blocks of later periods. It was quite common in the eleventh century to lay stone diagonally, with each row sloping in opposite directions, in a herringbone pattern. Some of the finest stonework dates from the twelfth century. The Norman keeps of the period feature well-cut ashlar, with the bare solidity of the walls often being broken by pilaster buttresses (slender rectangular projections) and simple mouldings. Notably in Germany and the Crusader lands there was a fashion for rusticated masonry, also known as masonry *en bosse*. In this technique the edges of the stone were cut square and smooth, but the centre was left rough, projecting slightly outwards.

This emphasized the joints in the stonework. At Krak des Chevaliers the contrast between this style of masonry and the smooth ashlar of the thirteenth century provides invaluable information for the dating of the various parts of the castle.

It would be fallacious to assume that the standard of masonry improved consistently as the Middle Ages proceeded. Quality had more to do with the type of stone available, the scale of the resources made available to the builders and the speed of construction. The fine ashlar of many twelfth-century keeps is far superior to most of the stonework of Edward I's Welsh castles. At Bothwell in Scotland there is a striking contrast between the excellent quality of the thirteenth-century work on the keep, with regular smooth-faced and close-fitting ashlar blocks, and the rough rubble walling erected by the picturesquely named Archibald the Grim in the late fourteenth century.

In many castles where ashlar survives in good condition mason's marks can be found incised on the stone. Every mason had his own mark but, although these provide an attractive reminder of the individual craftsmanship involved in castle-building, such marks must be used as evidence only with great caution. Their purpose was probably to identify the work of a single mason to the paymaster, and they were made by the man who shaped the stone, rather than the layer. In many instances, therefore, the marks were put on the stone at the quarry, not at the building site itself. It would be wrong to assume, as did the nineteenth-century expert on military architecture, Viollet-le-Duc, that as there were a hundred mason's marks to be found on the fabric of Pierrefonds, that was the total number of masons working on the site. It is nevertheless significant that at Broughton Castle in Oxfordshire, associated with William of Wykeham, two of the mason's marks there also appear on Wykeham's buildings in Oxford and Winchester.

To build high walls scaffolding was needed, and it is often possible to see from the holes left in the fabric how the structure was built up. Some evidence, particularly from the eleventh century, shows that on occasion stone walls were built up round a wooden framework of poles; the scaffold became an integral part of the wall itself. In Edward I's castles in Wales the putlog holes, as the holes where the scaffolding fitted are known, often run in a spiral pattern up the round towers. This type of helicoidal scaffolding was introduced by the Savoyard masons and it obviously provided an easy and efficient method for carrying stone and mortar up to the level where the masons were working. Many late medieval illustrations of the building of the Tower of Babel display a similar spiral ramp.

It is often possible to see from the fabric of a castle where one building season ended and another began. At Harlech Castle there are clear structural breaks half-way up the walls of the inner bailey. The west wall is particularly interesting because it is clear that initially the wall was built to only half its present thickness. This is confirmed by documentary evidence showing that in 1289 one group of masons was paid to double the width of this very wall.

Castles always relied on the sheer mass and solidity of their walls for much of their strength. There was little place for the ingenuity of pointed arches and flying buttresses which made it possible to build Gothic churches of such great height and delicacy. The architectural revolution which began in the twelfth century and radically transformed ecclesiastical build-

Right Bothwell Castle (Lanarkshire) showing the thirteenth-century keep on the left, half of which was cast down in 1337. As a result it is possible to see the way in which the walls were constructed, with a rubble infilling between ashlar facings. The tower on the right was built in the early fifteenth century.

ing did not, therefore, have so marked an impact on castle-building. The development of vaulting with pointed arches can be seen to have influenced the way in which towers were built; the circular donjons, or keeps, built by Philip Augustus of France with their stone vaulted ceilings would not have been possible a few generations earlier. Although castles rarely contain as much fine detailing as churches, the development of architectural styles can be seen from the way in which masons treated such features as loopholes. The earliest form is the absolutely plain slit. In twelfth-century work in the Crusader castles these were formed simply by leaving gaps between the stones; no shaping at all was involved. In Edward I's castles in Wales, the loopholes are mostly plain and angled out towards the interior to give the archer room but from the outside they feature no more than a slightly splayed foot. In the fourteenth century a small horizontal slit was often added, making a cross-shaped loop, frequently with elaborate detailing. In general, however, it was the internal domestic accommodation rather than the fortifications themselves which provided the masons with an opportunity to display the full range of their skills. Castel del Monte is a particularly fine example, with its magnificently vaulted rooms, elaborate capitals and splendid carving. At Kenilworth the buildings within the castle walls built by John of Gaunt in the late fourteenth century featured very fine traceried windows, worthy of any church, and elaborate vaulting, now largely decayed and ruined.

How long did it take to build a castle?

In the majority of examples the work of castle-building was in a sense never completed. Through the centuries additions, some minor and some major, would be made to the original fabric, and the castle would grow in an almost organic fashion. A great castle like Chinon in France would contain work dating from every century from the eleventh to the fifteenth. On occasion, however, astonishing speed was possible. In 1139 Henry, Constable of Beaubourg in northern France, sent surveyors and carpenters to measure up the site of an old castle at Ammerval. When they returned, he had a prefabricated tower and palisade constructed, and at dead of night the pieces were taken to the site and erected. To the astonishment of the local inhabitants, they were confronted the next morning by a castle standing on what had been empty ground the day before. That was an exceptional example, but it took the Conqueror's men only a few days to build a simple motte-and-bailey castle at Hastings, again probably using prefabricated wooden components.

A great stone castle could hardly be built in a couple of days. The normal rate of progress in building a great keep was for it to rise by a mere ten or twelve feet each year. In contrast, Richard the Lionheart's masons and their fellow workmen built the magnificent fortress of Château-Gaillard in little more than two years. The Crusader castle of Safad took two and a half years to build. More typical was Angers in France, where the main building programme occupied the period from 1228 to 1238. Harlech was built in seven and a half years; the Gascon castle of Villandraut which closely resembles it took nine years.

It was not possible, of course, for building work to continue at a steady pace throughout the year. Work on the fabric had to be halted in the winter, when frosts made it impossible for the mortar to set properly, and the longer hours of darkness reduced the length of the working day. At Kirby Muxloe,

Leicestershire, in 1481 the layers began work at the beginning of May and were dismissed at the end of October. An additional problem on that site was the danger of winter floods; one man was paid to watch the waters of the moat overnight when they threatened to overflow. The only work that could continue in the winter was the hewing and dressing of stone, which took place both in the quarries and the lodges that masons erected at building sites to serve as workshops and possibly also as accommodation.

The costs of construction

Many examples could be given of the costs of castle-building but in view of the changing value of money, particularly in late medieval France where repeated debasements caused frequent fluctuation, the figures often mean little. The cost of building operations at Angers in 1234 was 4,422 *livres*, at a time when the total royal revenue probably exceeded 400,000 *livres*. In north Wales, Harlech castle cost about £9,500 to build and the total of Edward I's works at all the castles there approached £100,000. To give these figures some meaning it is relevant to note that the most successful single tax of Edward I's reign, levied in 1290, was assessed at £116,000, and the least effective at £34,000. The total cost of the most expensive campaign in Wales, that of 1282–3, was approximately £150,000. The cost of castle-building to the Crown was therefore considerable. For a private landlord it must have been almost crippling on occasion and this helps to explain why many castles were built over a very long period of time. The Tattershall accounts suggest that the work was carefully budgeted at about £450 a year, at which level building would have to be a long-drawn-out process.

The references in contemporary chronicles and other documents, the many surviving building accounts and the actual fabric of castles which stand to this day all provide evidence as to how castles were actually built. The process is not surrounded in mystery like the construction of the Pyramids of Egypt; in the instance of a castle such as Harlech the historian can work out in very great detail the exact stages of construction, and can identify those involved, from Master James of St George down to John Colier who provided fuel for the smithy and carried lime, gravel and timber to the castle site. Yet even when the construction of a castle is completely documented it is impossible not to feel a sense of wonder and admiration that men could achieve so much with such limited equipment.

Below left Scaffolding was often no more than a simple framework as in (A). Sometimes a more elaborate structure was keyed into holes in the wall, known as 'putlog holes', as in (B). Spiral, or helicoidal scaffolding, as in (C) was often used for round towers; it was introduced into Britain from Savoy during the reign of Edward I and an elaborate version of this (D) was used at Coucy (Aisne).

Below This late medieval illumination of tiling operations shows the final stage of building work, with a mason in the foreground carving an elaborate capital, while tilers complete the roofs of the fortified town behind. A simple scaffold is used by those working on the castle.

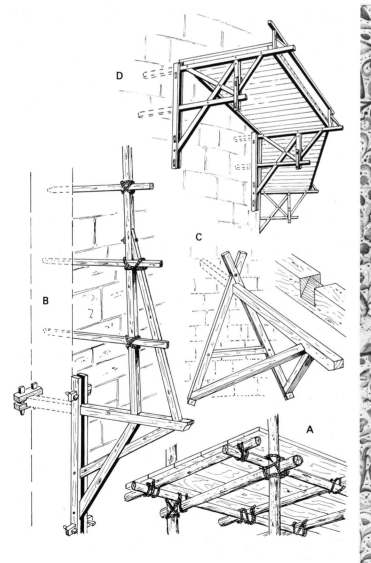

Development & Decline

The castle was the dominant type of secular architecture, both as a fortification and as a residence, from the eleventh to the fifteenth century. It took many different forms at different dates and in different countries, ranging from the simplest ditch-and-bank enclosure to highly complex stone buildings, redoubtable from without and palatial within. Development was not a straightforward progression from the simple to the sophisticated. The most magnificent medieval fortifications were those of the thirteenth century – the great Crusader castles such as Krak des Chevaliers, or the castles built by Edward I in north Wales. In the later Middle Ages the military elements declined, as more emphasis was placed on the castle as a comfortable residence. Castles still looked formidable but the show of strength was frequently illusory.

Castles in the ninth and tenth centuries
The art of military fortification was not new in the Middle Ages. The Romans were skilled engineers and designers and knew all the main elements later employed by castle-builders: ditch, bank, palisade, stone walls and flanking towers. Yet the Roman world did not know true castles, any more than did the Carolingian empire around the year 800. Fortifications were public works, serving a communal purpose. It was in the ninth and tenth centuries that the castle had its origins – in that dark period of European history when the Carolingian world reeled and collapsed under the onslaught of Vikings, Magyars and Moslems. It was only in exceptional instances, such as Saxony under the Ottonian dynasty or Wessex under King Alfred, that communal fortifications provided an effective form of defence. As new forms of lordship along feudal lines were established in western Europe so the castle emerged with its unique combination of functions, as lordly residence and powerful fortification. It was one of the corner-stones of the new feudal society and was not so much a refuge from barbarian attack as the product of the new aristocratic lordship which replaced the public authority of the Carolingian state.

The earliest evidence for the existence of castles is documentary rather than architectural. As early as 864 Charles the Bald, ruler of the western part of the old Carolingian empire, ordered the destruction of castles and other private fortifications built without his consent. The form of the earliest castles varied considerably. In some instances a simple enclosure wall or bank round a monastery was termed a castle, while in others old Roman defences were re-used. At Regensburg in Germany and Oudenburg in Flanders, to give but two examples, Roman walls were reinforced in the early tenth century. Many early castles probably consisted of little more than an oval enclosure formed by a ditch and bank, while particularly strong sites needed no more than a simple wall cutting off the one possible approach to a hilltop; the eleventh-century castle of the Peak in Derbyshire was of this type. At Plessis-Grimoult in Normandy a circular rampart was thrown up in the late tenth century and not long afterwards greatly strengthened by a stone wall and stone gatehouse. The castle of Hunnenburg bei Todenmann in Lower Saxony is of similar type, and probably of early date, while Eynsford in Kent is an example from late eleventh-century England.

It would be very wrong to assume that all the earliest castles were built of earth and wood. A very remarkable excavation at Doué-la-Fontaine in the Loire valley has shown how one early castle evolved. The original structure on the site was an

unfortified stone hall of late Carolingian origin. It was severely damaged by fire in the second quarter of the tenth century but the walls were left standing. In about 950 the original ground-floor entrance was blocked up and a new storey given to the building, so that it was now entered at first-floor level for reasons of security. A hall had become a castle. A few decades later the original structure was completely hidden from view when earth was piled up around it to create an artificial mound, or motte, to protect the foundations of the tower.

The motte-and-bailey and the shell-keep
In the first half of the eleventh century the motte came to dominate castle design. A tall conical mound would be surmounted by a palisade and timber tower, linked by a wooden bridge to a lower enclosure, the bailey. The Bayeux Tapestry provides invaluable contemporary illustrations of the type of structure which stood on the summit of an eleventh-century motte, while excavations at Abinger in Surrey have shown the way in which the earthwork itself was constructed around the massive wooden posts that served as foundations for the tower. In some other instances stone foundations ran down through

Above Founded in the late tenth century, Langeais (Indre-et-Loire) is a remarkably early stone castle, and the structure which still stands may have been begun in 994. From this type of building the great rectangular keeps of the twelfth century were to develop.
Left Chepstow Castle (Gwent) was begun in the late eleventh century; the lower part of the rectangular keep dates from that period. The final stage in the evolution of this complex castle came in the late thirteenth century, when the lower bailey with its twin-towered gatehouse and elaborate domestic accommodation was built.
Far left A well-preserved example of a motte-and-bailey castle, Pickering (North Yorkshire) was initially built of earth and timber, and then refortified in stone. The towered curtain wall was built in the 1320s on the orders of Edward II; it enclosed a new outer bailey. The original bailey is in the foreground.

the motte to the bedrock underneath. At South Mimms in Hertfordshire the twelfth-century motte was completely revetted in timber, so permitting it to be built at a steeper angle than was normal. Mottes were sometimes added to an existing castle: at Durham a fine Norman chapel is partly buried by a later motte and at Oxford the motte is probably later than the tower which stands just by it. In the majority of instances, however, the motte and bailey were both built at the same time, the motte providing a degree of security and strength which a simple enclosure could not offer.

One problem with a motte was that it was not easy to build a strong stone tower on top of an artificial mound, for it would not be sufficiently stable, at least not until it had had many years to settle. Doué-la-Fontaine must have been very exceptional among early castles in possessing a motte surmounted by a stone keep. An early example of a different tradition of castle-building is provided by Langeais (Indre-et-Loire), a site fortified by Fulk Nerra, Count of Anjou, one of the most remarkable early castle-builders, who was responsible for some 27 fortresses. The surviving fragment of Langeais consists of part of a rectangular stone building, its entrance at first-floor level. It was long thought that this was a donjon, or

keep, built in 994, but a recent controversial suggestion is that the castle at first consisted of the more conventional motte with a wooden tower, and that the stone building is a hall, or constable's lodging, added some 20 years later. Whatever the truth of this is, Langeais was an ancestor of the great square and rectangular keeps which were the most characteristic form of castle-building in the twelfth century. Langeais was not wholly unique when it was built. In about the year 1000 the naturally strong site of St Benoît du Sault in Berry was described as being fortified with 'an extremely strong stone house'.

Early castles were, therefore, very varied in type, but in the eleventh century the motte-and-bailey was the most successful. Such castles were quick and easy to construct but they had their disadvantages. The ditches needed to be recut fairly often, perhaps every 25 years, and the wooden buildings were vulnerable to fire and decay. At York the wooden tower on the motte was burned down in the ferocious anti-Jewish riots of 1190, and its successor, also of timber, was blown down by a gale in 1228. A characteristic development of this type of castle was for the wooden structures to be replaced in time by stone. It was not normally possible to build a massive stone

CASTLE-BUILDING

Above Restormel (Cornwall). A fine example of a twelfth-century shell-keep.
Right The castle at Gisors (Eure) was built by William Rufus on the advice of Robert de Bellême. It provides an example of a shell-keep, within which stands a polygonal keep, built either by Henry I or, more probably, Henry II.
Below Castle Rising in Norfolk was built in the second quarter of the twelfth century. In the centre of a large earthwork is the squat two-storeyed keep, notable for the highly decorated forebuilding. The design followed that of Norwich.

tower on top of an artificial motte, and so instead a stone wall would be built around its rim, thus forming what is termed a 'shell-keep'. The most famous example of this type is that at Windsor; the Cornish examples of Restormel and Launceston are also notable. At Farnham in Surrey and at Berkeley in Gloucestershire the entire motte was revetted in stone; a similar effect is provided by the walls built round some German hilltop castles. In general, however, the shell-keep was not common outside the Anglo-Norman dominions. Where the motte was sufficiently strong, a great tower or keep might be built within the shell-keep; Gisors in Normandy and Fréteval in the Loire valley provide two examples. It was more usual for the interior of the circular wall of the shell-keep to be occupied by relatively simple domestic buildings backing on to the wall. The fortifications of the bailey, the larger enclosure of the castle, could be replaced by stone with much less difficulty than those of the motte itself, and it would be tedious to list the many sites like Berkhamsted where stone walls simply follow the line of the original earthwork ditch-and-bank defences.

The rectangular keep in the twelfth century

The most typical feature of many twelfth-century castles owed nothing to the tradition of earthwork defences. The great rectangular stone keep was to be found in realms as distant as the Anglo-Norman lands, southern Italy and the Holy Land. The type probably had its origins in such buildings as the late Carolingian hall at Doué-la-Fontaine and the stone structure at Langeais. The concept of the keep was a simple one. Being a massive stone tower, it provided both a residence and a place of final refuge should the rest of the castle be overrun. From a defensive point of view, the occupants relied primarily on the massive thickness of its walls – up to twenty feet at Dover. Projectiles could be thrown at attackers from the wall-head, but few loopholes if any were made in the main fabric of the building.

Builders treated the keep in many different ways. Some were squat rectangular structures, two storeys high; others were square in plan, rising through four storeys. Contemporaries did not differentiate between the various types in their terminology, but modern architectural historians distinguish hall-keeps from tower-keeps. The size of keeps varied greatly, from simple towers some forty feet square to the massive one hundred and fifty feet by one hundred and twelve of Colchester. Development in England and France was

interrelated, and it is possible to trace family resemblances between keeps. That at Falaise in Normandy, built by Henry I in the 1120s, closely resembles Norwich, and in turn Castle Rising in Norfolk is in many respects based on Norwich. Newcastle upon Tyne was a prototype of Dover.

Rectangular keeps varied considerably in detail. The Tower of London and Colchester, both built under William the Conqueror, were exceptional examples with their apsidal projections for chapels and their first-floor entrances; they were probably based on the ducal castle at Rouen, now totally vanished. It was normal for entrances to be at first- or second-floor level and to be guarded by forebuildings which became increasingly elaborate as time went on. Most keeps of any size were divided internally by a cross-wall. Floors were of timber, although vaulted basements were an occasional feature. The fine keep at Loches in Touraine, of late eleventh- or early twelfth-century date, has a forebuilding but no cross-wall, and is enhanced externally by the addition of semicircular buttresses. In most examples flat pilaster buttresses were used to relieve the monotony of the massive walls, and in some examples, as at Norwich, the stonework was elaborately embellished with semicircular mouldings and rows of arches. By the late twelfth century the internal arrangements might be very complex, as at Dover, where galleries and chambers were constructed within the thickness of the walls and there was even an elaborate plumbing system.

The keep was taken by the Crusaders to the new lands they conquered in the Middle East but it developed there in a rather different way. Entrances were always at ground-floor level and were not protected by forebuildings. Internally the Crusader keeps, such as that at Safita, were not divided by cross-walls, and because of the shortage of good timber locally, they had stone vaulted ceilings. Externally there was none of the decorative detailing so common in the West. Militarily these keeps might appear less strong than those of the Anglo-Norman world but they were usually tightly enclosed by a curtain wall, as at Gibelet, and this more than made up for the absence of a forebuilding. Any attacker would find himself exposed to fire both from the curtain wall and from the top of the keep itself.

Sicily was part of the Norman world in the twelfth century, for all its exotic character derived from the Byzantine and Arab populace. At Adrano there is a fine Norman keep, probably dating from about 1100. It has a cross-wall, but no forebuilding, and like the Crusader examples lacks the corner turrets and pilaster buttresses familiar in France and England. Later in the twelfth century the tradition of the keep lingered in the palatial Sicilian castles of La Cuba and La Zisa, although with their decorative stonework and pointed arches a very strong Arab influence is evident.

One region where the rectangular keep was not the dominant feature of castle design was Germany. There the majority of castles were of simple earthwork construction, while the Crown and greatest magnates were still building in a style reminiscent of the Carolingian palaces, as in the margrave of Thuringia's work at the castle of the Wartburg (Eisenach, E. Germany) around 1200. Where towers were built, they were slender structures serving as look-out posts. They did not combine the functions of defence and accommodation as the great keeps did with such consummate success. One exception was Trifels, in the Rhineland, where the main tower did have more of the character of a true keep.

Round and polygonal keeps

There was one problem that could not be resolved with a rectangular plan: the corners of the keep were hard to protect. In the famous siege of Rochester in 1215 miners dug under one angle and succeeded in bringing down the whole corner turret of the keep. Excavation has revealed a similar mine under the corner of the keep which once stood at Bungay in Suffolk. The solution to this problem was to build round or polygonal keeps, and a number of interesting solutions took place in the twelfth century. The earliest round keep in France is probably that at Fréteval in the Loire valley, which may date from the late eleventh century. It consisted of a simple drum fifty feet in diameter and one hundred feet high. At Fougères in Brittany the foundations of a twelfth-century keep survive; it was round internally but octagonal outside. The polygonal keep at Gisors (Eure) may date from the early twelfth century. At Etampes (Essonne) a most remarkable plan was adopted in the second quarter of the twelfth century: that of a four-leafed clover. Another attempt to resolve the problem of the rectangular keep was made at Houdan in the same region, with a circular donjon reinforced by four massive semicircular buttresses.

Experimentation came later in England than in France. A great round keep, the only one with a cross-wall, was built at New Buckenham in Norfolk in the middle years of the twelfth century. In the mid 1160s Henry II built a polygonal keep at Orford in Suffolk. This ended up with few of the intended advantages, for three square turrets and a rectangular fore-building were added to the basic structure, which created the blind angles that the polygonal plan was intended to obviate. Chilham Castle in Kent was also given a polygonal keep with a square forebuilding. At Conisborough in Yorkshire, however, the forebuilding was abandoned and a plain cylindrical tower was strengthened by six massive tapering buttresses. The base, as in many twelfth-century keeps, was reinforced by being splayed outwards. This building so puzzled the late eighteenth-century antiquarian Edward King that he wrote: 'I cannot, therefore, but conclude this Tower to have been built by Hengist, or some Saxon king, before the conversion of that people to Christianity, if not much sooner.' There is, however, no doubt of its late twelfth-century date. Its buttresses suggest an affinity with Richard I's great keep at Château-Gaillard on the borders of Normandy. The plan there was essentially circular but was modified by a pointed, or 'beaked', projection facing the likely direction of attack; this was a common feature for a short period in the late twelfth and early thirteenth centuries. Great buttresses at Château-Gaillard were designed to bear a fighting gallery carried on arches – an early form of machicolation.

The round and polygonal keeps did not evolve into more complex forms as time proceeded but tended to become simpler. Philip Augustus of France built many plain round keeps in the course of his acquisition of new territory. A splendid example is that at Falaise, where he built a tower directly alongside Henry I's rectangular keep. The contrast is a striking one, and it is very clear that although the round keep may have been militarily superior, it offered less accommodation than the rectangular type despite its five vaulted floors. In south Wales the Earl Marshal built a round keep at Pembroke. Here the floors were wooden, with only the roof of the tower being of stone. All the twelfth-century complexities of buttresses and forebuildings were abandoned; the only sophistication in the thirteenth century was at the wall-head,

where stone corbels were frequently placed to carry the timber gallery from which defence was conducted, and which in time was replaced by stone machicolations. The keep at Coucy in France, destroyed in World War I, was the finest example of such a tower, with its walls twenty-three feet thick and each of its storeys vaulted in stone. A copy of Coucy was built at Bothwell in Scotland. Like its prototype, this keep was separated by a moat from the rest of the castle, but with its wooden floors Bothwell was far less strong. Half of the tower was cast down when the castle was razed in the fourteenth century.

The round keep never achieved quite the same popularity in England as it did in France. There is a group of such towers in the southern Welsh Marches, of which Skenfrith is one example. Here a semicircular projection carried a spiral stair to the upper storeys. In the north a fine round keep was built at Barnard Castle in Co. Durham. There may have been a French influence here, for the Balliol family who built the castle had important possessions in France. At York in the mid thirteenth century a four-leafed-clover plan was adopted in the remarkable keep built on the motte; the master mason was a man called Master Henry of Reyns, probably from Rheims.

Far left The keep at Orford (Suffolk), built between 1166 and 1172, is polygonal in plan, with the addition of three rectangular towers and a forebuilding to protect the entrance. The purpose of such a plan was to avoid the weakness at the corners inherent in a rectangular keep; this particular solution to the problem was not wholly successful.
Left The fine keep at Conisborough (Yorkshire) was built by Hamelin, half-brother of Henry II. Circular in plan, with massive buttresses which probably supported a fighting gallery, it represents another attempt to eliminate the weaknesses of the rectangular type of keep.
Below Built by Roger Bigod, Earl of Norfolk, on the site of a motte-and-bailey castle destroyed by Henry II, the late twelfth-century castle at Framlingham (Suffolk) is an early example of the trend to abandon the keep in favour of a curtain wall with flanking towers as the main defence against attack.

The possible influence of Crusader castles

For the most part castle-building in the thirteenth century was dominated by the concept of the keepless castle, where the defences consisted of a strong curtain wall with powerful flanking towers, and a well defended entrance. To see one possible origin of this type of castle it is necessary to turn back to look at the developments that took place in the Crusading lands in the twelfth century.

Many of the castles built by the Crusaders were of a simple quadrilateral plan, with a tower at each corner. Ibelin, built in the 1140s, was described by the great chronicler William of Tyre as 'a fortress with four towers'. Darum was 'a castle of moderate size, hardly a stone's throw across, square in form, with four angle towers, of which one was larger and stronger than the others'. A particularly complex development of the basic quadrilateral plan took place at Belvoir, where the addition of an outer wall with seven flanking towers, all square in plan, with a great barbican guarding the entrance, meant that attackers were confronted with a double line of defences arranged concentrically.

It is often assumed that the sophistication and complexity of the Crusader castles was the result of their designers' observa-tion of Byzantine fortifications. It may well be that the rectangular castles with their corner towers owed something to existing defences in the Middle East: forts of similar design were built by the Romans and provide a possible model, while the Omayyads constructed forts in Syria to a rectangular plan in the seventh and eighth centuries. It is equally possible that the Crusaders evolved castles of this sort quite independently. They would have been quicker and simpler to build than castles centring on a great keep. Nor was the type unique to the Middle East; it could have had Western antecedents. The castle of Druyes la Fontaine (Yonne), built in the late twelfth century is a French example. A detailed study of the Crusader castles suggests that Byzantine and Arab influence was largely confined to specific minor details of architectural practice, resulting from the use of some local craftsmen. The overall concept of the castles certainly fits in well with Western traditions of fortification. The way that the mural towers of Saône interrupt the wall-walk of the curtain-wall ramparts, rendering each section of wall completely independent, was typical of Byzantine practice, as was the use of a low relieving arch above a flat lintel to add strength. The Crusaders made use of the existing Byzantine defences at Saône

Right An imaginative reconstruction of a motte-and-bailey castle, based on Totnes (Devon).

but they transformed the whole defensive layout following their own principles. Interestingly, they incorporated three round towers into the curtain wall at a time when the general fashion was for square ones. These Crusader castles may have influenced trends in the West, but the case cannot be proved.

The castles of the thirteenth century

In Western Europe it was in the late twelfth and early thirteenth centuries that a shift in emphasis took place from the keep to the curtain wall defended with flanking towers. A striking example of the new style of castle is provided in England by the baronial stronghold of Framlingham in Suffolk, rebuilt in the 1190s. In place of a keep the castle featured an oval inner ward defended by 13 rectangular flanking towers, most of them open-backed. Henry II added a similar curtain wall to the defences of Dover. In Richard I's great castle of Château-Gaillard there was a keep, but attackers were faced successively by an outer and a middle bailey guarded by curtain walls with round towers before they reached the oval inner bailey with its curious curvilinear wall. It is tempting to see in this castle, on which Richard spent far more than he did on all the royal castles in England, the application of principles of fortification which he had learnt while on crusade in the Middle East. But there is no element of the castle which cannot be explained in terms of Western traditions and their skilful application to the specific site.

In the thirteenth century the keep was often wholly abandoned as an element in castle-planning. Angers, largely built in the 1230s, is one of the most magnificent examples of a castle relying on the strength of its curtain wall with round flanking towers; Boulogne is another. Both of these castles were polygonal in plan like that at Limerick in Ireland – a remote and early specimen of the type. In England the earl of Chester built in this style at Beeston in Cheshire and at Bolingbroke in Lincolnshire; only the former still stands today. The straightforward quadrilateral plan was followed as well as the polygonal one and examples of the former can be cited from Inverlochy in the Scottish Highlands to Catania in Sicily. In Germany, too, where development so often did not follow the general European trend, examples of this type of castle can be found.

In the thirteenth century increasing attention was paid to the problem of defending gateways. The entrance to a castle had always been regarded as a weak point. A common solution to the problem was to incorporate the gate into a tower; in the eleventh century at Richmond in Yorkshire and Ludlow in Shropshire the functions of keep and gatehouse were effectively combined by driving the entrance through a massive tower. In neither of these two instances was the concept satisfactory and the entrances were later blocked up. The most fruitful approach was to bring two mural towers close together to command the entrance. This was done at Dover in Henry II's time, with square towers, and in the 1220s at Beeston and Bolingbroke with round ones. In France the thirteenth-century castle at Carcassonne has its entrance defended in a similar way. At Dourdan (Essonne), built in the 1220s, the gatehouse is again composed of twin towers, but inside the curtain wall the building runs back into the courtyard, so that the whole forms a substantial block. This technique was followed up in Britain above all, notably in Edward I's castles in Wales. At Harlech and Beaumaris the gatehouse developed on the courtyard side into a magnificent building, flanked by

two slender staircase turrets.

The thirteenth century was the high-water mark of the medieval art of fortification, as may be seen by looking at the castles in France, at those built by the Crusaders in the Middle East, by Frederick II in Apulia and by Edward I in north Wales. In Palestine the most magnificent of the castles were those possessed by the knightly Orders, the Hospitallers and the Templars, who could draw on the resources of extensive landholdings in the West. Krak des Chevaliers is deservedly the most famous of the castles, although in power and strength Margat ran it close. The site at Krak was already fortified by the Arabs in the eleventh century; it underwent major rebuilding in the mid twelfth, and again in the early thirteenth century. The inner ring of defences dated from the twelfth century and consisted of a curtain wall with rectangular towers which barely projected beyond the line of the wall. This was strengthened by the thirteenth-century builders, who encased it in a new layer of masonry, with a powerful glacis (a sloping bank) and massive rounded towers. A new set of outer fortifications was added, lower than the inner ward, with round flanking towers and ample provision of loopholes from which fire could be directed at an enemy approaching from any direction. Entry to the castle was through a fairly simple gate-tower, from which a narrow ramp, carefully defended from every angle, led up to the inner ward. The castle was built on a huge scale, for it was in effect a military monastery, not the private residence of a great lord. It demonstrates very clearly how in the thirteenth century emphasis had shifted from the defence of a single massive keep, to which the outer works were a mere adjunct, to an integrated complex of great elaboration.

Frederick II's Apulian and Sicilian castles were thoroughly eclectic. Square, round and multangular towers were all employed. Notably at Catania and Augusta in Sicily the rectangular plan was adopted, with towers half-way along the

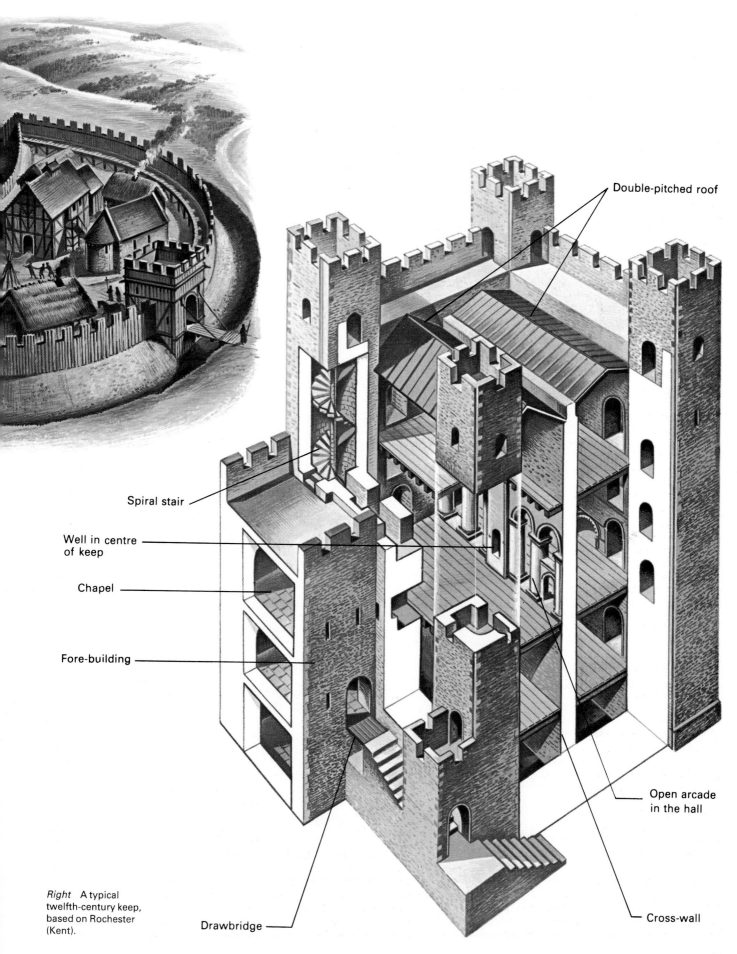

Double-pitched roof

Spiral stair

Well in centre
of keep

Chapel

Fore-building

Open arcade
in the hall

Cross-wall

Drawbridge

Right A typical
twelfth-century keep,
based on Rochester
(Kent).

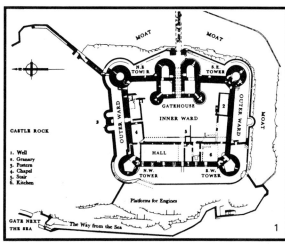

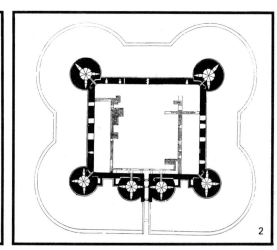

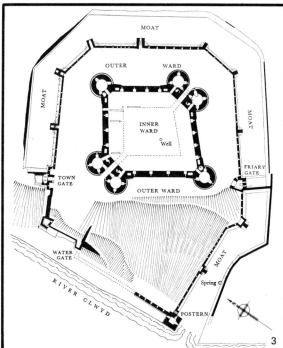

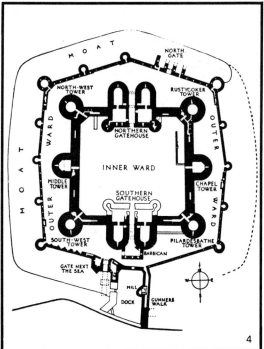

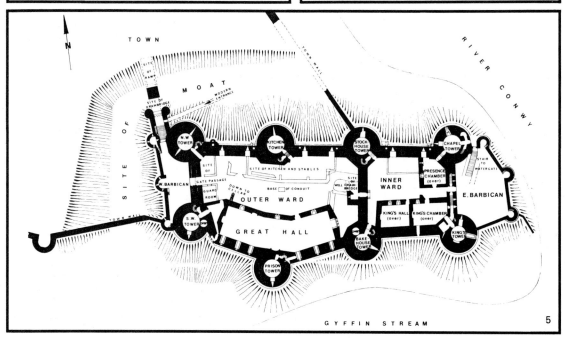

1 Harlech (Gwynedd) was begun in 1283. The rocky site did not allow much space for the outer ward, but the castle was built on a concentric plan.

2 Villandraut Castle in Gascony was built by Pope Clement V, who had served Edward I early in his career. The plan of the castle shows an obvious similarity to Harlech.

3 Rhuddlan (Clwyd) was built after Edward I's first Welsh war. Here Master James of St George adopted a fully concentric plan, with slender outer walls and a massive inner ward with twin gatehouses.

4 Beaumaris Castle in Anglesey was the most developed concentric design produced by Master James of St George, with its two large gatehouses and six towers dominating the inner ward, and outer defences far more formidable than those of the earlier castles. It was begun after the Welsh revolt of 1294–5, but funds were insufficient for it ever to be fully completed.

5 Conway (Gwynedd) saw Master James abandon the concentric plan; the site was unsuitable for it. He chose instead to give the castle two wards, separated by a massive cross-wall. The castle was built after the second Welsh war, of 1282–3.

Left The fine castle at Richmond (North Yorkshire) dates from the late eleventh century. At the top can be seen the great keep-gatehouse, while at the bottom right is Scolland's Hall, a fine early two-storeyed Norman hall.

curtain walls as well as at the angles. Many of the castles, such as Gioia del Colle in Apulia, were remarkable more for the opulence of their accommodation than the ingenuity of their defences. The greatest of all the castles were those at Lucera and Castel del Monte in Apulia. At the former site all that remains is the sloping outer wall, amply equipped with loopholes, which formed the base of one of the most remarkable towers of the medieval period. This appears to have been formed of two concentric rectangular walls. At the upper levels the interior was possibly open to the sky, making a kind of small courtyard, admitting ample light to the interior. The upper storeys were octagonal in form and the whole tower was elaborately decorated.

Castel del Monte is one of the most famous of medieval castles. It takes the form of a regular octagon built round a small courtyard, with polygonal towers protecting the outer angles of the castle. Again the interior is palatial, as befitted the grandeur of Frederick II's court. The closest affinities of the plan perhaps lie in Crusader architecture. The castle of Chlemoutsi in the Peloponnese, built by Geoffrey de Villehardouin in the 1220s, has an inner bailey of similar, though less symmetrical, design. A small open courtyard is surrounded by a six-sided building, with great barrel-vaulted rooms running right round the interior at ground-floor level. In the perfection of its detail and the regularity of its plan, however, Castel del Monte stands virtually unique. The one English castle to resemble it, the fourteenth-century one at Queenborough on the Isle of Sheppey, was totally destroyed in the seventeenth century.

The castles that Edward I built in order to cement his conquest of Wales provide a unique example of the way in which one man worked out his own solutions to the problems of castle design. The career of Master James of St George has already been outlined. He had his initial training in Savoy where Count Philip II and Count Peter built a number of castles on a simple rectangular plan with round or octagonal towers – the latter type can be seen at St Georges d'Esperanche. With the vast resources that Edward I made available to him Master James was able to employ far more sophisticated concepts in his Welsh castles, using all the familiar elements of keeps, curtain walls, flanking towers, gatehouses and concentric lines of defences, but articulating them in a way that was strikingly novel and imaginative.

For the first of the major castles, Flint, begun after the first

Welsh campaign in 1277, Master James adopted an orthodox rectangular design, using one of the angle towers as a keep. This was a far from orthodox structure, for it consists effectively of two stone cylinders, one inside the other. Attempts have been made to link this keep with the Tour de Constance at Aigues Mortes in the south of France, and with Castel del Monte, but these are not convincing. The partially ruined tower at Lucera might be a better candidate, even though it was not round; the arrangements of the upper floors may well have been similar. There is no reason, however, to suppose that Master James had a model in mind. Unusually, the keep at Flint was brought forward so that it could command the entrance to the inner ward, rather than form a last line of resistance. The concept of the keep was virtually abandoned in the later castles built by Master James, although at Caernarvon the triple-turreted Eagle Tower was larger than its fellows and possessed something of the attributes of a keep.

Like Flint, Rhuddlan was built after the first Welsh campaign. Here a concentric plan was employed, with a highly original treatment of the inner ward. It was quadrilateral in shape but at two of the opposing angles twin towers were placed to form gatehouses. Harlech, begun after the campaign of 1282–3, was a development of the same theme. Again this was a concentric fortification, with relatively slender outer walls pierced by ample loopholes, and a much taller and more massive inner ward. A great gatehouse dominated one wall of the inner ward; twin-towered, it projected back into the courtyard and provided spacious accommodation for the constable and a small garrison. Such buildings are often termed 'keep-gatehouses', but the briefest inspection of Harlech shows that this one was not intended to serve as a last refuge in time of attack. On the courtyard side it features large handsome windows, not mere arrow slits, with fine shallow arched heads in Savoyard fashion. Further accommodation at Harlech was provided within the inner ward, round which the hall and other buildings were ranged. Beaumaris in Anglesey, last of the castles, was a further development of this plan. There the inner ward was given two gatehouses, rather than one, as well as additional flanking towers. Regrettably the Crown lacked the resources to finish this most ambitious project, and today the towers stand at the level of the curtain walls, rather than rising proudly above them as had been planned.

Two of Master James's castles do not fit into the pattern of symmetrical concentricity observed so far. At Conway and Caernarvon, both built after the second Welsh war (1282–3), the castles consisted of two wards linked by a cross-wall. Each was connected to the defences of the town, which were built at the same time. The sites demanded a relatively long narrow plan, and at Conway in particular the rocky spur on which the castle was built was a sufficient natural defence for there to be little need for concentric lines of fortification. Caernarvon stands unique among the Edwardian castles with its polygonal towers contrasting with the round ones used elsewhere. These towers, together with the dark bands of masonry running along the walls, were intended to be a conscious echo of the defences of the imperial city of Constantinople. Edward I was deliberately expressing in stones and mortar an old Welsh legend which made Caernarvon the birthplace of the emperor Constantine himself. It may be doubted whether any of the king's newly conquered Welsh subjects appreciated such an elaborate architectural conceit. In the absence of concentric defences the offensive fire-power of the castle was limited. To

Right Arguably the finest of Edward I's Welsh castles, Caernarvon (Gwynedd) was built in deliberate imitation of the defences of Constantinople. This south curtain wall contained two mural galleries, with loopholes for archers, in addition to the loopholes contained within the battlements.

make up for this the massive south curtain wall at Caernarvon had mural galleries constructed within the thickness of the walls, providing a triple row of loopholes. This was a most formidable castle, arguably the finest single creation of any thirteenth-century military architect.

The achievement of Master James of St George and Edward I in Wales naturally had its imitators, though none could hope to match it. These castles were only made possible because England had developed new financial institutions, notably in the form of direct and indirect taxes, in place of the old feudal aids and dues, and because the king could draw on the credit facilities of Italian banking houses. The castles can hardly be categorized as feudal in any meaningful sense of the word. They were not built or financed by feudal means, and the duty of castle-guard was not introduced to provide them with garrisons. Nevertheless, at Caerphilly in south Wales the earls of Gloucester and their disreputable successors the Despensers built a castle which in many ways equals those in north Wales, and even exceeds them in the strength of its water-defences. At Dunstanburgh in Northumberland Edward I's enigmatic nephew Thomas of Lancaster built a great gatehouse in true Edwardian style but he lacked the time and the resources to complete the castle on the same scale. A more surprising imitation of the north Welsh castles is to be found at Villandraut in Gascony, where the overall conception of the castle is closely akin to that of Harlech. The castle was the work of Pope Clement V, who had, significantly, been one of Edward I's clerks for a time earlier in his career. It is also worth noting that at least one Savoyard workman was active in south-western France in the early fourteenth century.

Trends in the fourteenth and fifteenth centuries

Although such castles as Krak des Chevaliers, Harlech and Caernarvon can rightly be regarded as the crowning achievements of medieval military architecture, the solutions that they presented to the problems of defence and accommodation were not so perfect that no further development was possible. The normal view is that the later Middle Ages saw castles decline in military strength, while their domestic functions took an increasingly dominant role. As a result such features as gatehouses and machicolation were often reduced to little more than a formal symbolism, while stout curtain walls were weakened by being pierced by elegant windows. As will be shown, there is much to this view, but in some regions of Europe the needs of warfare and the confused state of politics meant that some remarkably fine warlike castles were still built. In France the Hundred Years War, accompanied as it was by widespread local violence, provided an undoubted impetus towards castle-building. In fourteenth- and fifteenth-century Spain an aggressive and confident nobility built on a massive scale, while at the other end of Europe the Order of the Teutonic Knights constructed a remarkable series of fortresses in the Baltic lands.

There were no major technical improvements in the methods of defensive fortification until the later fifteenth century. Builders remained content with the traditional vocabulary of castle design: keeps, gatehouses, towers both round and square, and curtain walls. There was ample room for experiment here. It is difficult to reduce the castles of any period to specific types and the problem is particularly acute for the later medieval period. Attempts at systematization fail in face of the great variety of plans that were then adopted. It is

Below Krak des Chevaliers (Syria), the finest of the Crusader castles. The complex concentric fortifications were not all planned at the same time; the original castle consisted of the inner defences. These were subsequently greatly strengthened, and the outer walls added.

Above Permission to build the splendid tower-house at Borthwick (Lothian) was granted in 1430. It consists of a rectangular tower with two massive wings, known as 'jambs', and is built of fine ashlar. The plain simplicity of the exterior contrasted with a luxuriously fitted interior.

possible only to discern and point to certain general trends that seem clearly evident.

The development of concentric lines of defence, so striking in Edward I's Welsh castles, was not continued. It may be that experience showed that the relatively slender outer defences were of little use. It was only in Spain, in castles such as La Mota at Medina del Campo, or Coca in the province of Segovia, that the concentric plan was much used. For the most part, defence was concentrated upon increasingly massive curtain walls, with elaborate wall-head defences. In place of the temporary wooden galleries, or hoardings, erected in time of danger, the late medieval builders constructed stone machicolations. French examples are particularly notable. At Pierrefonds (Oise) a machicolated gallery ran along the top of the curtain wall, while similar galleries some way below the summit of each flanking tower added greatly to the fire-power that could be directed from them. In southern France Tarascon, built in the first half of the fifteenth century, displays a similar emphasis on defence from the machicolated wall-head. Here the traditional emphasis on flanking towers was abandoned, though at Lassay (Mayenne) massive closely spaced D-shaped towers with heavily machicolated heads are highly characteristic of the period. In England the fourteenth-century Caesar's Tower at Warwick, with its six storeys and machicolated fighting gallery, echoes contemporary French practice, although there is no precise parallel to its curious tri-lobed plan. Fifteenth-century Raglan in south Wales likewise demonstrates the familiarity that its builders gained, while

fighting in France, with French techniques of fortification and ostentation.

In the majority of late medieval castles there was some form of keep, or donjon, or at least a clearly separate residence for the lord within the fortifications. In Spain in particular the keep, known as the *torre del homenaje* (meaning 'tower of homage'), was an essential element in any castle, though in England and France the keepless castle, as at Lassay, still had its advocates. Keeps could take many forms. At Vincennes the great donjon was built virtually as a castle within a castle. Rectangular in plan, it was totally self-contained within its own moat. As was common in this period, an encrustation of semicircular towers and turrets gave it the appearance of great complexity of design. Like many late medieval towers this one is very high, consisting of a ground floor and five storeys. One common plan for keeps was that of a rectangle with corner towers, as at Dudley (West Midlands) and Nunney (Somerset) in England, or Anjony (Cantal) in France. There was little standardization, however, in contrast to the great Anglo-Norman keeps of the twelfth century. There were some striking resemblances nonetheless: at Raglan, for example, the great fifteenth-century polygonal keep strongly echoes the late fourteenth-century Breton example of Largoët-en-Elven.

On a much smaller scale, the format of the keep was widely employed by lesser lords in what are often termed 'tower-houses'. Notably in the north of England and in Scotland, men found that the security they needed was best provided not by fortifying a large expanse of ground but by abandoning the tradition of curtain wall and flanking tower in favour of a simple, strong rectangular tower. Stark and uncompromising, these buildings were not designed to meet the threat of major sieges but they were ideally suited to the needs of border warfare. Equivalents of the tower-house are to be found elsewhere in Europe; they survive in some numbers in south-western France, and were common in Germany. They often

Left Pierrefonds (Oise) was one of the most splendid of late fourteenth-century French castles, and was extensively restored in the nineteenth century. The machicolated galleries are particularly noteworthy as being highly characteristic of this period.

was originally founded to fight in the Holy Land alongside the Hospitallers and Templars. With the failure of the Crusading movement in the thirteenth century, culminating in the fall of Acre in 1291, the attention of the Teutonic Knights was drawn to the eastern frontiers of Germany. Their castles had to serve, like Krak des Chevaliers, as both monastery and fortress. The garrisons were larger than was the case with a conventional royal or aristocratic castle; in the early fifteenth century Gotteswerde held 117 men, while Königsberg contained 252. The characteristic form of these castles was that of a square or rectangular building with slender corner towers and ample internal accommodation round the courtyard, but at Marienburg in Prussia, where the Grand Master of the Order resided, a whole complex of buildings was erected round a succession of courtyards.

The increasing emphasis placed on domestic comfort in the castles of the later Middle Ages is very striking. Many features of their design reflected aesthetic rather than military considerations: even such ostensibly warlike features as crenellations and machicolations often seem to have been included for reasons of prestige rather than of defence. Although round towers were preferable to square from a defensive point of view, the latter offered far greater convenience both to builder and occupier. In England it was notable that in the north of the country square towers were built in preference to round from the second quarter of the fourteenth century. In the south the late fourteenth-century castle at Bodiam in Sussex, like many English examples rectangular in plan with no keep, compromised with round corner towers and square turrets midway along the curtain walls. In France the towers at Vincennes were rectangular, as were the majority of those at Tarascon (Bouches-du-Rhône), although elsewhere, as at Pierrefonds, the circular or D-shaped plan still held sway.

The internal accommodation of halls and chambers was far more closely integrated with the design of the castle as a whole in the late medieval period than had been the case earlier. No longer were the domestic buildings little more than wooden lean-tos against the interior of the curtain wall. At Pierrefonds they were fully integrated with the curtain wall and ranged right round the interior of the castle, while one corner of the site was occupied by a massive seigneurial lodging. Bolton, in Wensleydale, provides another example of a fully integrated courtyard castle; no longer did the curtain wall merely enclose a large area of ground. At Herstmonceux in Sussex, another keepless example, the castle as originally built contained no less than four courtyards, each surrounded by a range of domestic buildings.

In order to make the chambers within the castle more comfortable, windows were frequently cut right through the curtain wall. At Tarascon an attempt was made to combine light with security by fitting massive iron grills over the windows, which pierced the ten-foot-thick walls, but in this as in very many other examples there is no disguising the fact that the castle was appreciably weaker as a result of the desire for comfort. In England the fine brick tower built by Lord Cromwell at Tattershall looks like a powerful keep but again its windows show that it would never have been sensible to take refuge there during a siege, even if it had possessed its own kitchen and water-supply. Spanish castles are in this respect something of a contrast to those of more northerly countries, with their walls left largely unpierced save by loopholes, but at the same time they provide ample examples

barely deserve to be described as castles. In Scotland, however, the type developed into surprisingly sophisticated forms as additional jambs, or wings, were added to the main building. At Borthwick, built in the fifteenth century, two such jambs flanked the entrance, but more often a Z-shaped plan resulted from such additions. The barmkin, or courtyard, attached to the tower acquired more elaborate defences, and at Crighton in east Lothian a series of additions to the original simple tower-house had by the sixteenth century created a courtyard castle containing an astonishing, and inappropriate, Italianate loggia and façade.

In Germany, military architecture had never been so dominated by the defensive panoply of curtain walls, flanking towers and gatehouses as was the case in France, Spain and England. In part this was because the Carolingian tradition of palace architecture survived longer in Germany than elsewhere, and in part it was the result of the way in which so many castles were perched high up on naturally strong craggy sites, which did not demand massive fortification. Many castles developed within a simple ring-wall, with a watchtower, or *Bergfried*, and a growing complexity of domestic buildings. Hilltop sites in particular offered little room for expansion, and so tightly-knit castles, often of great height, developed. As such examples as Kasselburg in the Eifel show, by the fourteenth century a French influence was beginning to be felt, with the *Bergfried* developing into a donjon as semicircular towers were added to it. The later Middle Ages in Germany witnessed a movement down from the high mountain sites, and in the low-lying lands castles of a more orthodox plan were built, as in the fourteenth-century Rhineland example of Gudenau. At nearby Kempen an interesting triangular plan was employed, with the castle depending on traditional curtain walls and round angle-towers for its defence.

A very distinctive German contribution to the history of castles was that made by the Teutonic Knights. This Order

Right The great round tower at Falaise (Calvados), known as the Talbot Tower, was built adjacent to the twelfth-century keep by Philip Augustus of France in the early thirteenth century. It is typical of the round keeps, externally very simple, built by this monarch.

of the late medieval emphasis on splendour and decoration rather than on true military strength.

The use of brick as a building material provided medieval craftsmen with splendid opportunities to create fine geometric patterns. This can be seen in the *mudéjar* work, built by Moslems who remained in the regions of Spain taken from their co-religionists during the Reconquest, which features at Coca and elsewhere. At El Real de Manzanares massive false machicolations serve a purely decorative function, while the turrets are finished in a highly ornate style known as *isabelino*, which could only have been produced in Spain. In the more sober climes of England, decorative brickwork featured at Tattershall and Herstmonceux, while in the Baltic lands the residence of the Grand Master of the Teutonic Knights at Marienburg displayed an astonishingly highly decorated brick façade.

In France the remarkable illustrations in the *Très Riches Heures* of the duke of Berry help to bring out the sumptuous, palatial quality of the castles. Here the material was stone, not brick. At Mehun-sur-Yèvre, in particular, the craftsmen brought to the castle the full skills of the medieval church-builder. Here the upper parts of an otherwise conventional castle were completed in an airy Gothic style with the most elegant tracery. Large windows in the outer walls increased comfort at the expense of security. The height of many castles built in this period of the fourteenth and fifteenth centuries again reflects the aesthetic rather than military considerations. Tall slender towers look grand and imposing but provided prestige rather than real security. In particular, height increased the vulnerability of any castle to gunfire.

Castles and artillery
It has often been supposed that the invention of artillery spelled the end of the medieval castle. Gunpowder was used as early as 1304 in the siege of Stirling Castle in Scotland, though probably as an explosive rather than as a propellant. Guns were certainly known in the 1320s, and by the early fifteenth century formidable siege-cannon were widely used. Castle-builders did not ignore the new weapons altogether, but their effect was not felt for some time and was hardly revolutionary at first. In England the earliest gunports appeared at Carisbrooke in the Isle of Wight in 1380, and they became a common feature in the fifteenth century. They were generally combined with loopholes, and were only suitable for firing light hand weapons intended to drive attackers away from the walls. Such gunloops, as they are termed, appeared rather later on the Continent than in England, and although they were known in the first half of the fifteenth century, it is significant that they rarely feature in contemporary illustrations. Such small gunloops made little difference to the strength of the castle.

In order to resist the heavy siege artillery of the fifteenth century, the obvious solution was simply to make the walls of the castle more massive. Towers became somewhat squatter, as at Rambures in Picardy, or in the late fifteenth-century D-shaped towers added to the curtain walls at Fougères in Brittany. This was hardly a sufficient response; more radical solutions were needed. It has been claimed that at Ravenscraig in Fife a true artillery fortress was built in the mid fifteenth century, for there two massive D-shaped towers flank a broad platform equipped with gunloops. This was open to the sky and apparently offered a far more intelligent solution to the use of

artillery than the piercing of loops in the lower storeys of towers, where the noise and fumes of gunfire would have made it impossible to fire more than a very few rounds. Examination of Ravenscraig suggests, however, that this broad platform is in fact an unfinished hall, subsequently adapted for the use of artillery. No attempt was made to ensure that the lines of fire raked across the routes that assailants were likely to take. It is not to Scotland but to Italy that the historian must turn to see the changes taking place in the late fifteenth century that were to see the end of the medieval castle. The development of the bastion, specifically designed with artillery in view, was an innovation of decisive importance.

Initially the Italian response to the problems of artillery was similar to that of the French. Walls were made thicker, and were heavily scarped in the hope that shot would ricochet off the oblique angle that they presented. Massive round or angular towers became the rule, with characteristic heavy machicolation. Theorists began to suggest new solutions. Drawings by Francesco di Giorgio Martini of star-shaped forts indicate a new approach to the question of providing sufficient angles of fire against besiegers, while among other suggestions he advocated the construction of casemates designed to command the bases of the walls. He described them as follows:

At the bottom of the ditch, where the bombards, crossbows and other weapons of the enemy cannot reach, there must be made a room of thick walls with the offensives (ie loopholes) set within all round, its diameter twelve to fourteen feet, its height eight feet, and so arranged that the crossbowmen and bombardiers can work shoulder to shoulder without getting in each other's way.

(S. Brinton, *Francesco di Giorgio Martini of Siena*, London, 1934, p. 98.)

An examination of the actual buildings for which Giorgio was responsible shows that for all his theorizing he was less of an

innovator in practice than men who achieved far less repute. Bacio Pontelli built the Rocca at Ostia Antica in the 1480s, with two round bastions and one pentagonal one. These were relatively low, massive platforms from which it was easy to operate guns and which presented a formidable obstacle to any would-be attacker. Giuliano da San Gallo's work at the end of the fifteenth century at Poggio Imperiale in Tuscany, with its huge low angular bastions, belongs quite clearly to a new tradition in fortification.

The new style spread rapidly. Some attempts were made to incorporate bastions or artillery platforms into existing castles. The remarkably complex defences at Bonaguil (Lot-et-Garonne), built by the Roquefeuil family in the fifteenth century saw outer works specifically designed for artillery added at the end of the period. In England such interesting forts as Deal and Walmer in Kent, built by Henry VIII, mark an early and not wholly successful attempt to assimilate the new science of artillery fortification. These were purely military buildings, lacking the residential element of the true castle. The twin functions of the castle, residence and fortification, were diverging rapidly in the sixteenth century with palaces on the one hand and fortresses on the other. The new techniques of bastions, hornworks and ravelins (both being types of low artillery outwork) were far more suited to urban defences than to aristocratic castles; typical of the developed style were the fortifications at Berwick-upon-Tweed.

Why did castles develop as they did?
The importance of imitation in castle-building is very obvious. The count of Dreux's instructions in 1224 that his new keep at Dreux should be like that at Nogent-le-Rotrou is a good example. Development was brought about as successful schemes of defence were copied and new improvements were incorporated. Yet it is not always easy for the historian to trace the links between one building and another, or even

Above Ravenscraig Castle (Fife) was built between 1460 and 1463 and is unique among Scottish castles with its two massive D-shaped towers. It was probably intended that they should flank a hall, but this was never completed, and was converted into a gun-platform.

Below Castel del Monte (Apulia) was largely built in the 1240s. Perhaps Emperor Frederick II's finest architectural achievement, the castle is a perfect octagon, with eight corner towers and eight rooms on each floor.

Below The castle of La Mota at Medina del Campo is a typical example of the elaborate fortifications of late medieval Spain; note the concentric defences and the complexity of the bartizans at the top of the keep.

Bottom A thirteenth-century round tower at Fougères (Ille-et-Vilaine); the pitched roof is a nineteenth-century reconstruction.

Below The castle of La Mota at Medina del Campo is a typical example of the elaborate

between different regions. The difficulty of determining the extent of Byzantine influence upon Crusader architecture, and of the latter upon castle-building in western Europe, brings this out. Many influential buildings have simply vanished, making it hard to trace the line of ancestry of specific types of castle.

The discussion of siege-craft later in this book (*see* p. 80) will show that improvements in methods of attack necessitate advances in defensive techniques. The introduction of the trebuchet with its high trajectory in the late twelfth century, for example, impelled men to build taller walls. The fall of the keeps of Rochester in 1215 and Bedford in 1224 does much to explain why so few keeps were built in England in the thirteenth century. Yet sieges were infrequent, and it is clear that Master James of St George did not improve the designs of his castles as a result of practical experience in defending them, for the Welsh did not even possess a full-scale siege-train. His castles represent the practical application of theoretical concepts, while their increasing sophistication owed much to the vast funds that the king was prepared to pour into the project.

Fashion and taste played an important part in the evolution of castle architecture. The design of Castel del Monte was clearly determined to a considerable extent by aesthetic considerations. There was no good military reason for building castles to a symmetrical plan, but appearance was important. The illustrations in the *Très Riches Heures* of the duke of Berry testify to the pleasure that men took in their castles as works of art. In the later Middle Ages height was often sought for show rather than for strength; the slender turrets of the late fourteenth-century gatehouse at Donnington in Berkshire lacked the solidity of thirteenth-century work but gave a fine impression. As has already been suggested, domestic comfort was a consideration of increasing importance in the fourteenth and fifteenth centuries.

The decline of the castle

The reasons for the decline of the castle are complex. It was perhaps impossible that the standard set by Edward I's works in north Wales could have been maintained. It can be argued that the later history of those particular castles shows that fortification on such a scale was over-ambitious. They were never garrisoned to their full capacity, their maintenance in a proper state of repair was rarely if ever achieved and they did not prove as invaluable in war as must have been hoped. Governments throughout Europe were beset in the later Middle Ages by financial problems which put major castle-building programmes in jeopardy. The shape of politics meant that in many instances it was no longer necessary for a government to establish and hold castles in all parts of its dominions, and when in England Edward III was in a position to build on a lavish scale he spent extensively on manors round London rather than on castles. He also poured funds into the rebuilding of Windsor, where the works were intended to create palatial apartments rather than to provide him with an impregnable fortress. Nor, of course, were the great castles of the twelfth and thirteenth centuries obsolete in the later Middle Ages. In 1418 Château-Gaillard withstood siege by English troops for sixteen months, and in the end the garrison only surrendered because they had no water left. When such powerful castles were in existence there was less incentive to build new ones.

In many instances governments adopted a deliberate policy of razing or destroying castles. As soon as Robert Bruce captured English-held castles in Scotland he ordered their destruction so that his enemies could not use them again. This policy was continued by his successors, as the shattered state of the keep at Bothwell so clearly demonstrates. In France during the Hundred Years War the French ordered the demolition of some of the castles in the Ile-de-France in 1358, and an ordinance issued by Charles V in 1367 set out that while all castles in good condition were to be made ready to resist attack, those which were not obviously defensible were to be destroyed. In the late fifteenth century the French monarchy took an aggressive attitude towards unlicensed private fortifications and during the same period the curbing of the power of the Spanish aristocracy by Ferdinand and Isabella meant an end to the lavish castle-building south of the Pyrenees.

In war, the development of the strategy of the swift mounted raid, the *chevauchée*, as practised by the English in France under Edward III with such effect, meant that castles were often of little value, for they could easily be bypassed. The English could only be challenged effectively by the French on the field of battle. It was only when the English were attempting to conquer territory by a steady advance, as Henry V did in Normandy, that castles could play their traditional role. There were great sieges in the Hundred Years War but the majority were of towns rather than of castles: Calais in 1346–7, Rouen in 1418–19 and Orleans in 1428–9. All too often in the fourteenth and fifteenth centuries, although castle walls were stout enough to resist attack, the will of the defenders was lacking. St Sauveur and Bécherel in France were surrendered by the English in the 1370s partly because the French offered substantial inducements in cash. During the Wars of the Roses the northern castles of Alnwick, Dunstanburgh and Bamburgh were won by the Yorkists in an arduous winter campaign in 1462–3 but they were soon back in Lancastrian hands, as a result of changes in political allegiance rather than of renewed siege warfare.

The decline of the castle was a symptom of fundamental social changes which took place over a long period. It can be argued that the process began as early as the twelfth century, for many simple motte-and-bailey castles were abandoned then and not rebuilt or replaced. The development of the great siege cannon, such as Edinburgh's Mons Meg, and of the artillery bastion, is only one small part of a complex process of change. It is very clear that no simple military and architectural solution to the question of the decline of the castle is adequate. The decay of the institutions of feudalism had their part to play. As the system of castle-guard fell into disuse, so it became harder to provide adequate garrisons. The growing sophistication of aristocratic life as the Middle Ages proceeded had, as an almost inevitable concomitance, the decay of the traditional castle, for at a certain point the requirements of privacy and luxury came into conflict with those of defence. Fifteenth- and sixteenth-century households were not, except in exceptional circumstances, as large as those of the thirteenth, and required a very different style of accommodation.

Castles may have declined by the end of the Middle Ages, but they have never lost their fascination. The architectural style of towers, curtain walls and crenellations did not die with the castle. Even Sir John Vanbrugh, steeped in the traditions of classicism, built a house for himself at Blackheath with round and square towers, and false machicolation. The nineteenth century found a wealth of inspiration in the castles of the past, and in Ludwig of Bavaria's Neuschwanstein the romantic view of the Middle Ages found perhaps its most astonishing expression, with fairy-tale towers perched on an Alpine crag. This was nearer to the fantasies of Disneyland than to the supremely practical realities of the medieval castle, which in its various forms represented a most successful solution to the problems of residence and defence.

Fortress

2

Although the castle's military function is its best known role, it is only one part of its total purpose and itself by no means generally understood. Understanding can only come from a knowledge of medieval warfare – more particularly warfare as waged in the feudal period – and that in turn is an aspect of medieval history most ignored by serious historians and travestied by others. A myth, represented in English-speaking countries by Sir Charles Oman's *A History of the Art of War in the Middle Ages*, has been allowed to establish itself, to the effect that the warfare of the feudal epoch was ineffective, disorganized, undisciplined and waged exclusively by exhibitionist knights, all of which is the exact opposite of the truth. One might rather suppose that the feudal upper classes of lords and knights, born and bred to war in a society whose ethos was above all military, would know what they were doing and do it very well – and so indeed they did. In the following section the warfare of the period will be properly analysed and described, and found to be effective, efficient, disciplined, and often as brutal as anyone could wish, though limited by a merciful absence of modern technology, and graced by a certain chivalry which, if finally rendered obsolete in our button-pushing age, is very much our loss.

The context and the explanation of the military role of castles is to us, of course, contemporary warfare, which came to turn especially upon them and upon heavy cavalry. Against them the shock tactic of the charge, near-irresistible elsewhere, was obviously useless, while successful attack and defence alike called for foot soldiers and support forces which, clean contrary to the myth, commanders of the period by no means despised. But the ultimate military value of castles, which made it so imperative either to capture or to hold them, was their offensive, not their defensive, role. They were the strong bases from which armed and mounted men controlled the surrounding countryside, and he who would control the land had first to control the castles.

Kerak in Moab (Jordan) was an aggressive base thrust out into the desert against Moslem communications. It took Saladin eight months to subdue.

Strongholds & Strategy

Feudal society was a society organized for war. Kings and princes, the men who acted as judges and officials, occasionally even bishops and abbots, were also warriors, and in the case of princes a successful reign depended on success in war, or at least on not being disastrously defeated. Rulers who were unsuccessful in war frequently faced unrest at home. Likewise the castle reflected this ambivalence, being a fortress and house as well as the centre of administration of its region. The very name of the tower, the donjon or keep, was derived from the latin term *dominium* meaning 'lordship' and from which in turn the modern English word 'dungeon' has developed. Rising above its surroundings, the donjon dominated the land and its inhabitants judicially, politically and fiscally, and it dominated the warfare of the Middle Ages. It is intended here to discuss first the armies and the practice of medieval warfare and then to set the castle into this context, and to attempt to illustrate both with examples.

The myth of medieval warfare

In the past the dominance of the castle and the proliferation of sieges in medieval warfare have been explained by describing medieval armies as inefficient and undisciplined, and their commanders as blundering idiots (with some worthy exceptions). Thus there were few pitched battles because armies could rarely find each other, and when they did by accident run into each other the result was a scuffle on a convenient hillside in which few men, apart from the wretched infantry, were killed and in which little or no tactical skill was shown. In addition, it has been assumed that castles and cities were less hard to find and it was far more simple to settle down to sieges that often proved futile. The origin of this myth is a fundamental misinterpretation of the sources and a misunderstanding of the role of the castle in medieval warfare. The myth is no longer tenable, yet it carries a surprising amount of weight.

The knight equipped for war

At the centre of medieval warfare was the knight. The word 'knight' is from Old English; Continental chroniclers used the Latin *miles*, meaning 'soldier', or the French *chevalier*, the Spanish *caballero* or the German *ritter*, all meaning 'horseman'. The importance of heavy cavalry in war has been dated to the Battle of Adrianople in AD 378 when an East Roman army was defeated by a Gothic force containing a substantial cavalry element. From then, the myth says, infantry forces were eclipsed and the supremacy of heavy cavalry established until the rise of the English longbowman and the Swiss pikeman in the fourteenth and fifteenth centuries. The importance of this battle has, however, been overemphasized. The value of infantry was realized by commanders throughout the Middle Ages, and heavy cavalry did not really come into force until the later eighth and ninth centuries.

In the middle of the eighth century a law-code gives us the cost of a full set of cavalry equipment:

the helmet	6 shillings
the *brunia* (mail-shirt)	12 *s.*
the sword	3 *s.*
the scabbard	4 *s.*
the leggings	6 *s.*
the shield and lance	2 *s.*
the warhorse	12 *s.*
total	45 shillings

Detail of mail showing riveted links

Alternative helmet known as a 'kettle hat'

Above (Late eleventh century, Norman) Hauberk over a gambeson; iron helmet with noseguard; wood and leather kite-shaped shield. *Right* (Early thirteenth century) Hauberk with hand extensions and mail hose under surcoat; great helm over mail hood; wooden shield in flat-iron ('heater') shape.

Other figures in the code show that a sound ox with horns cost two shillings at the same time, a sound cow with horns cost one–three shillings, and a sound mare cost three shillings. The military gear of a fully equipped heavy cavalryman was thus equal in cost to 15 mares or nearly 23 oxen and represented an enormous amount of money – an amount, indeed, that could only be drawn from a large estate. Kings and magnates could equip men in this way from their own resources and for centuries they did maintain armed men in their households, but another way of arming a soldier was to give him a grant of land sufficient to pay for his armament and his expenses on campaign on the condition that he performed military service when his lord demanded. This practice was central to the type of organized society that we call 'feudalism'.

The expense of the knights' equipment limited the numbers of such men that were available, and the expense of that equipment increased steadily. The hauberk of the tenth and eleventh centuries frequently consisted of plates or rings of metal sewn to a leather garment. This gave way to the more common employment of a mail-shirt which in turn gave rise towards the end of the twelfth century to the great hauberk, a long mail-shirt which had to be supplemented with mail

Left (Early fourteenth century) Habergeon over gambeson and under 'coat of plates' and short surcoat; habergeon sleeves and mail hose protected by metal or hardened leather plates; bullet-shaped helmet (basnet) with aventail attached, worn with visor or under great helm.

Detachable visor for basnet

Left (Early fifteenth century) Articulated steel plates over gambeson and habergeon, with arrest; steel-plated helmet (armet).

Alternative late fifteenth-century helmet (sallet) and face-defence (bevor)

Brigandine (fifteenth-century coat of plates)

Right (Late fourteenth century) Articulated metal leg- and arm-defences over habergeon with shortened surcoat (jupon) and plate gauntlets. Rowel spurs replace earlier 'prick' spurs.

Right (Late fifteenth century, Italian) Development of above with re-enforcing plates on the left arm and shoulder. Italian armour was widely exported in the fifteenth and sixteenth centuries. Note that the shield has now completely disappeared.

leggings and gauntlets. From the middle of the thirteenth century the mail-suit worn over a padded undergarment was additionally reinforced with metal plates and further development led to the appearance of the full suit of plates. As the expense of the latest in armour increased, the number of knights who could afford to equip themselves with it declined. The number of knights performing military service, probably at its greatest in the eleventh and early twelfth centuries, dwindled rapidly. It is estimated that William the Conqueror established over 6,000 knights in England after 1066, each required to serve for 40 days each year. Henry II in his Assize of Arms (1181) set out the arms to be maintained by free men, and, as well as knights themselves, those who had goods or revenues to the value of 16 marks annually (a mark was equal to 13s 4d sterling) were to possess the equipment of a knight – hauberk, helmet, lance, shield, sword and horse. This was an attempt to tap the growing wealth of the kingdom in the last part of the twelfth century, particularly of those who had grown rich from trade. John (1199–1216) enforced it, Henry III elaborated it in 1252 and Edward I repeated many of the most important ordinances in 1285. But it is clear that from the time of Henry III (1216–72) only one twelfth to one fifteenth of

Right 'July' from the *Très Riches Heures*, showing how the castle dominated practically every aspects of medieval life. (From a facsimile in the Victoria & Albert Museum, London.)
Below Especially bred and carefully trained, the war-horse or *destrier* was one of the most important part of the knight's equipment. (From the Bayeux Tapestry.)
Bottom A knighting ceremony showing the esquire pledging loyalty to his lord while spurs are strapped to his feet and he is blessed.

the assessed knight service was performed. The compensation was that the knights were better armed and served for more than the statutory 40 days.

The other great expense of the knight was his warhorse, the *destrier*. This horse was bred especially for its task of carrying heavy men into battle and had to be carefully trained. It is possible that a horse suited to carrying a heavily armoured man did not appear until the eighth century when the Arab breed was introduced. The Anglo-Saxons, who did not fight on horseback, did not have large horses for this anyway. The development of horse armour and the increasing weight of its load, meant that larger horses had to be bred – the closest living relative of the late-medieval warhorse is the carthorse. The use of armoured horses naturally strengthened cavalry units, at the expense of mobility, and in the thirteenth and fourteenth centuries the owners of such horses received higher wages. The destrier was the knight's most prized possession: it was ridden only in war and in the event of a surprise attack the first duty of the prudent knight was to save himself *and* his charger, and, only if there was time, to put on his armour. The *Story of William Marshal*, written about 1220, rarely fails to mention the value of a horse – £40, £50, even £100 appear at a time when a serf could be bought for £10. Many lords undertook to replace horses lost in their service, and figures from the end of the thirteenth century show that the warhorse was worth many times the value of an ordinary horse – 25 times as much in one case. (Compare the eighth-century Frankish law-code (see p. 64), where the warhorse was valued at four times the price of the sound mare.)

The origins and ethics of knighthood

In the armies of the barbarian successor kingdoms to the Roman Empire the nobles tended to fight on horseback and the free farmers on foot. But by the eighth century many free men could no longer afford to perform the military service required

amidst the meadows, tents and pavilions spread; it gives me great joy to see, drawn up on the field, knights and horses in battle array.

And it delights me when skirmishers scatter people and herds in their path; and I love to see them followed by a great body of men-at-arms; and my heart is filled with gladness when I see strong castles besieged, and the stockades broken and overrun, and the defenders on the mounds enclosed by ditches all round and protected by strong palisades.

And I like to see the lord who is foremost in the attack, mounted, armed and fearless, for thus he inspires his men to serve him boldly. And then when battle's joined every one will follow him with a good courage, for no man wins respect until he has given and taken many a blow.

Maces and swords and helms of different hues, shields that will be riven and shattered as soon as the fight begins; many vassals clashing together until the steeds of the dead and wounded run aimlessly above the field. And once he has entered the fray let each man of high birth think of nothing but the breaking of heads and arms; for it is better to die than to be vanquished and live.

I tell you I find no such pleasure in food, or wine or sleep as in hearing the shout of 'At them!' on both sides, and the neigh of horses that have lost their riders, and the cries of 'Help! Help!'; in seeing men great and small go down on the grass by the ditches; and in seeing the dead, with the pennoned stumps of lances in their ribs.

(J. Gillingham, *Richard the Lionheart*, London, 1978, p. 243.)
Barons, you should rather forfeit castles, towns and cities, than give up – any of you – going to war.
(J.F. Verbruggen, *The art of warfare in western Europe during the Middle Ages*, North Holland, 1977, p. 40.)

Bertrand was awarded a special place in Hell by Dante, with his head permanently severed from his body, for the discord that he had caused between lords by composing pieces such as the one given above.

Centuries after the Battle of Adrianople a revolution took place in the way in which heavy cavalry fought, and it greatly increased the military value of the cavalry. The introduction of the stirrup in the West around 800, and the development of the horseshoe, a better harness, and a saddle built up at the front and back and which supported the rider in his seat, all meant that it was possible to fight with the 'couched lance'. This meant that the knight, holding reins and shield in the left hand, and the lance rigid beneath his right arm, was able to use the forward momentum of the horse to give power to the blow delivered by the lance without being knocked off his mount as had happened previously. This manner of charging became widespread in the later eleventh century and the weight of the charge could break almost any body of troops. The warlike Turks of the East could not meet this charge and generally fled, hoping to exhaust the Frankish destriers or to kill them by archery. The princess-historian Anna Comnena recorded at the end of the eleventh century that her compatriot Byzantines thought that a Frank on horseback could pierce

of them. Charlemagne (768–814) ordered poor free men to club together to equip one of their number, but many found an easier way out. They surrendered their land and freedom to their chosen lord and agreed to work on his estates for a specified number of days. In return they received protection and were relieved of the burden of military service. The lord armed retainers with his increased wealth, either maintaining them from revenues or allocating them grants of land, and in this way he built up a contingent of warriors. Such men, who were later known as 'knights', came to predominate for a number of reasons.

The appearance of new ideas reflected the increased importance of heavy cavalrymen in war and society. Instead of a society in which all free men performed military service, a new model was advanced of a society comprising three orders. The *laboratores*, the class of unfree men, worked; the *bellatores*, the knights, fought to defend society, and the highest order, the *oratores*, prayed for everybody else. As might be guessed, the Church developed this idea in an attempt to curb the wars that disturbed public peace and, not least, led to the ravage and usurpation of the estates of the Church. The knightly class developed its own code of honour and shame – chivalry. How far these theories affected the knights is impossible to estimate. All had that peculiar medieval blend of piety and brutality which enabled them, for example, to massacre civilians and to amass lands and plunder while on such a holy mission as the Crusade. But it is likely that the greatest influences on them were the warlike and heroic ideals celebrated in the *chansons de geste* which were sung to them, works such as the famous *Song of Roland*. Bertrand de Born, a warrior-minstrel of the later twelfth century, expressed some of the ideals in this way:

I love the gay Eastertide, which brings forth leaves and flowers; and I love the joyous song of the birds, re-echoing through the copse. But I love also to see,

Right The stirrup, built-up saddle and method of couching the lance may be seen perfectly in this early thirteenth-century illustration.

Right below Devices such as the quintain made it possible to practise jousting before encountering the real thing in tournament or battle.

the walls of Babylon. Franks were highly prized as mercenaries, despite the myth of medieval warfare that they lacked military skills such as discipline and tactical sense.

Training and length of service

The knight was as professional a soldier as his time could make him. From an early age he was inured to the practice of arms, and a long apprenticeship in the arts of war and of *courtoisie* lay before him. Only when this had been served, frequently in the household of another lord, was he considered fit to be dubbed a knight (there is an excellent fictional description of the training of an esquire (an apprentice knight) in George Shipway's *The Paladin*, London, 1972). On some occasions large bands of esquires were dubbed (i.e. made knights) in a mass ceremony before a battle. The English historian Roger of Howden, a clerk in the household of Henry II (1154–89) who later went on crusade with Richard (1189–99), left this record of the training of the sons of Henry:

> They strove to outdo the others in handling weapons. They realised that without practice the art of war did not come naturally when it was needed. No athlete can fight tenaciously who has never received any blows: he must see his blood flow and hear his teeth crack under the fist of his adversary, and when he is thrown to the ground he must fight on with all his might and not lose courage. The oftener he falls the more determinedly he must spring to his feet again. Anyone who can do that can engage in battle confidently. Strength gained by practice is invaluable: a soul subject to terror has fleeting glory. He who is too weak to bear this burden, through no fault of his own, will be overcome by its weight, no matter how eagerly he may rush to the task. The price of sweat is well paid where the Temples of Victory stand.
>
> (J.F. Verbruggen, op. cit. p. 29.)

The *chansons de geste* make it clear that it was the sword with which noble deeds were performed but the esquire learned not only how to fight as an individual. There is evidence that knights fought in small units or *conrois*: their size depended on the number of knights that a lord had in his following, for this was the basis of the *conroi* (in England and Normandy there was some tendency to units of five and its multiples). These were grouped into larger units led by a *banneret* (ie. a commander distinguished by a pennon or banner), and these were in turn grouped into *battles*, which were the largest tactical formations in the medieval army. In mixed armies the national contingents frequently formed the basis of the larger tactical groupings. The array adopted in war might call for the host to be drawn up as two wings and a reserve, three battles drawn up one behind the other, or a number of brigades in line. These and other formations are found in the chronicles.

We do not know that knights were required to train regularly, and a lot doubtless depended on individual inclination. War and the feud provided a hard training ground but the most popular peacetime war game was the tournament. Not until the late Middle Ages was this the formalized jousting immortalized in the popular mind by Hollywood; for long it was a fullscale mock battle contested by 'teams' of knights, and here discipline and formation were instilled. Those who forgot were likely to find themselves considerably poorer, for the defeated party lost their horses and armour, or their monetary equivalents, to their captors. In this way a landless younger son could win fortune as well as fame. William Marshal, the fourth son of a Wiltshire baron, provides a good example of this. He rose to great fame, and a verse biography (see Bibliography), composed by a follower to celebrate his deeds, tells how landless William toured France with another knight when he was a young man. For two years they attended tournaments (in the time of Richard I it is estimated that there was one every fortnight) and in one ten-month period they captured 103 knights and did a very profitable business in ransoms as well as winning great renown for themselves. It was thought extremely clever tactics in these affairs for one team of knights to pretend not to be taking part and then to join in late in the day when the other teams were exhausted. The Church saw the tournament as a threat to public order and did not approve. Nor did Henry I, Henry II or Henry III like tournaments to be held in their English lands for the same reason and in 1215, for example, such a gathering was used as a means of keeping an army opposed to King John under arms. Mock battles could also turn into real ones, as might be imagined. Early in the thirteenth century Gilbert Marshal rode a new horse to a tournament near Hertford; the reins broke and he fell, but one foot caught in a stirrup and he was dragged along and received mortal wounds. The contest then degenerated into a brawl in which one of Gilbert's retainers was killed and many knights and esquires wounded.

As we have already seen, most knights were only required to serve 40 days each year and this, of course, limited their military value. One way to increase it was to pay those willing to stay on, and another was to levy a tax on the knights instead of obliging them to perform military service. This payment of 'scutage' was then used to hire mercenary knights, who were usually landless or disinherited knights who lived by the hire of their swords. In the second half of the twelfth century the kings of England tried other remedies: in 1157 and 1194 one

third of the knight-service of England was summoned to serve for three times the usual period; in 1196 Richard asked his English barons to join him in Normandy at Whitsun but to bring no more than seven knights each and to be prepared to serve for a long time, and in the following year he asked for only 100 knights but for these to be paid to serve for a whole year. A century later Edward I was still paying members of the feudal host to serve with his mercenary knights.

Above This carved ivory casket depicts a late form of the tournament. Ladies watch from stands while gentlewomen grant their favours to knights who pledge their faith (compare with the young knight receiving arms). Note that the lance points are shielded to prevent serious injury.
Below The tournament was not only a social gathering but also a mock battle where units of knights could be drilled. Defeat was costly and such war-games were taken seriously. (From the *Roman de Girard de Roussillon.*)

The composition and strength of armies

The knighthood was a social and military elite. It was rare for knights alone to form an army, although some chroniclers mention only the knights present. The value of infantry was well known, and not just as conscript labour for the digging of ditches. Large numbers of archers and spearmen appear to have been employed. The cheapest way of raising such forces was by means of the *arrière-ban*, which was the obligation of all free men to perform military service for various specified lengths of time. These forces were not always militarily useless, as has sometimes been claimed. Legislation such as Henry II's Assize of Arms, which Philip II (1180–1223) appears to have imitated in his lands in France, attempted to ensure that the levies (ie. the commoners performing the military service required of them) were equipped with a certain standard of weaponry – mail-shirts, iron caps and lances for the richer freemen and leather or quilted cloth tunics, metal caps and lances for the poorer. In the kingdom of Jerusalem the king was permitted to call on the services of all pilgrims in the land at a a time of crisis, and even on the crews of ships in his ports. More useful than the general levies were the militias of the towns. The citizens frequently organized useful spear-armed forces that had the necessary *esprit de corps* to face a cavalry attack. The communal militias of the towns of north Italy gave a good account of themselves against the hosts sent against them by their overlord, the German

Right This illustration to a fifteenth-century translation into French of archbishop William of Tyre's popular history of Outremer (the Frankish settlements in the Middle East) shows the foot-soldiers marching out before the knights at the Battle of Antioch.

emperor, in the twelfth century; the citizens of the Flemish towns defeated invading French hosts on more than one occasion at the beginning of the thirteenth century, and the schiltrons (hedgehog-like formations of spearmen) of the Scots defeated the English at Bannockburn in 1314. Archers could also be found among the commoners, although for long the English tended to recruit both their spearmen and archers from among the south Welsh.

Other troops were highly specialized and ranked just below the knights in the military hierarchy. In 1210 we know that John had a corps of *ingeniatores*, the builders of siege-engines, and individual names are known from the eleventh century. The idea of the crossbow was an ancient one. There were several different sorts, but among the most common was the two-foot crossbow where both feet were placed in the stirrup and the cord hauled over the trigger, while the one-foot version, worked by the same process, was the standard weapon. Nobody seems quite sure what happened to the weapon in the Dark Ages; it may have been in use at the Battle of Hastings (1066), but what is certain is that the Church condemned its use in wars between Christians in 1139. Nevertheless it was widely used in eastern and southern Europe, and the princes of the north and west tended to hire their crossbowmen from these areas. Richard the Lionheart was said to have enjoyed demonstrating his skill with the weapon during sieges. The English, for example, recruited most of their crossbowmen at the end of the twelfth century from Genoa and Gascony and later from Flanders. It is interesting to note, however, that at the same time those employed by the French king appear to have been of French origin. The profession was a demanding one and the rates of pay and conditions of service were correspondingly good. In the last decade of the twelfth century knights in Richard's service received six shillings a day in the coin of Anjou (about 1s. 6d. in sterling), crossbowmen four shillings, mounted sergeants (non-noble and less well equipped and mounted than knights) 2s 6d. and foot sergeants 1s. 8d. (at a time when a quarter, ie. 28lb, of wheat cost only 4s., a cock 1d. and a ram 1s.). The king undertook to pay for and to repair those crossbows used in his service and supplied the quarrels (ie. the projectiles) that they shot. Companies of crossbowmen were generally employed on garrison duty.

Beneath these in rank were the true mercenaries of the period – the loathed and hated *routiers*. They comprised elements drawn from many areas: the overpopulated towns of Flanders, neighbouring Brabant and north Italy, and also from the Rhineland, Gascony, the Basque lands and Aragon. They had rejected society and wandered in gypsy-like bands fighting on the side of the highest bidder, and in between were plundering for their livelihoods. So long as princes waged wars they required the services of such bands of full-time mercenary soldiers, who had no estates or homes to worry about. But they were feared and often summarily dealt with: in 1171 Louis VII of France and Frederick Barbarossa, the German emperor, agreed not to employ or permit the presence of such bands between the Rhine, Alps and Paris, and elsewhere mutually hostile lords allied to expel or slaughter them. The English historian Walter Map described them in about 1180.

A new and particularly noxious set of heretics arose, which formed bands of up to a thousand men. The fighters of these bands were protected from head to foot by a leather jerkin, and were armed with steel, staves and iron. They went about in bands of thousands, and reduced monasteries, villages and cities to ashes. With violence, yet thinking it no sin, they committed adultery, saying 'There is no God'. This movement arose in Brabant, hence the name Brabançones. From the start these marauders drew up for themselves a curious law. Fugitive rebels, false monks and renegade clerks, and all who had forsaken God for any reason, may have joined them. Their number has risen so sharply ... that they can with impunity stay where they are or wander about all over the land, greatly hated by God and man.

(Walter Map, *Courtiers' Trifles*, in Verbruggen, op. cit., p. 124.)

And yet their leaders rose high in the service of princes. Richard's closest companion was his mercenary captain Mercadier. He boasted that so highly did the king trust him that he was put in command of the army; at the same time one of Philip II's most trusted lieutenants was a Welsh mercenary, one Cadoc. John took this to extremes, trusting a number of such captains above all others, granting them rich lands and pensions and giving them the custody of important strongholds. Not all, however, repaid his trust, and some surrendered their charges to the French. The biographer of William Marshal asked:

Do you know why king John was unable to keep the love of his people? It was because Louvrecaire (a mercenary captain) maltreated them, and plundered them as though he were in an enemy's country.

(F.M. Powicke, *The loss of Normandy*, Manchester, 2nd ed, 1961, p. 230.)

Of course he was in an enemy's country, for the *routier* had no homeland outside the band. Wherever war raged such bands were to be found; the Hundred Years War caused another surge in their numbers and on this occasion many of them were English archers and men-at-arms.

Finally, something should be said about the strength of medieval armies. It is generally accepted that the medieval chronicler had no head for figures and in many cases this is true. But on occasions the figures given sound detailed and reasonable; sometimes it is clear that certain chroniclers had access to official figures, and from the later Middle Ages administrative records survive. It frequently happened that a

TACTICS IN MEDIEVAL WARFARE

The pitched battle was not vital to medieval warfare – more could be won, and less risked, in ravaging and siege operations. Tactics were not neglected, however, as these examples show.

1. Battle on the march (Battle of Arsuf, Palestine, 7 September 1191).
The formation chosen by Richard I for the march south from Acre enabled him to give battle and at the same time protect the vulnerable supply train and knights' horses. Half the infantry protected the army 'like a wall' while the rest of the host marched within in relative safety. On the seventeenth day of the march Saladin launched a full-scale attack. The knights counter-attacked before Richard gave the order, but their charges were well-ordered and Saladin's army was shattered.

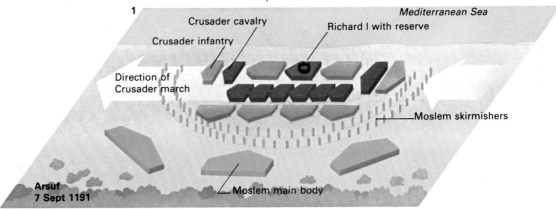

Arsuf map:
- *Mediterranean Sea*
- Crusader cavalry
- Crusader infantry
- Richard I with reserve
- Direction of Crusader march
- Moslem skirmishers
- Moslem main body
- **Arsuf 7 Sept 1191**

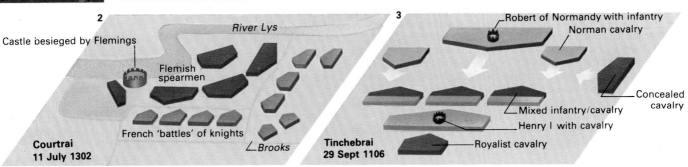

Courtrai map:
- Castle besieged by Flemings
- *River Lys*
- Flemish spearmen
- French 'battles' of knights
- *Brooks*
- **Courtrai 11 July 1302**

Tinchebrai map:
- Robert of Normandy with infantry
- Norman cavalry
- Concealed cavalry
- Mixed infantry/cavalry
- Henry I with cavalry
- Royalist cavalry
- **Tinchebrai 29 Sept 1106**

2. Phalanx of citizen spearmen (Battle of Courtrai, Flanders, 11 July 1302).
An army of 8–10,000 spearmen (levied from the Flemish towns) supported by archers and a few hundred dismounted knights took up a position defended by brooks. They were attacked by the flower of French chivalry (about 2,500 knights) under Robert of Artois with units of crossbowmen and javelin-men. French missiles did little harm to the Flemish formation and the charge of their knights was unable to break the hedge of spears. The Flemings attacked and drove back the French killing up to 1,000 knights in an almost unprecedented disaster for French arms.

3. Ambush and dismounted knights (Battle of Tinchebrai, Normandy, 29 September 1106).
Henry I drew up his army in three lines: Norman infantry and some 700 mounted knights in the front, then himself with English and Norman foot-soldiers stiffened with dismounted knights and in reserve about 700 mounted knights. About 1,000 mounted knights were placed in ambush to one side. His brother Duke Robert of Normandy's outnumbered army of about 700 knights and 5–6,000 infantry was drawn up with a centre of infantry and dismounted knights and two mounted wings. The main bodies met and the day was decided by the charge of the knights in ambush.

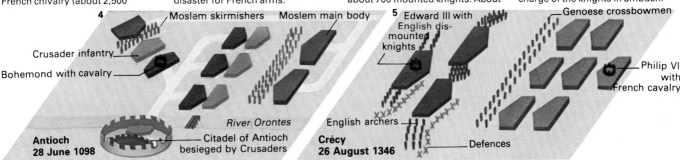

Antioch map:
- Moslem skirmishers
- Moslem main body
- Crusader infantry
- Bohemond with cavalry
- *River Orontes*
- Citadel of Antioch besieged by Crusaders
- **Antioch 28 June 1098**

Crécy map:
- Edward III with English dis-mounted knights
- Genoese crossbowmen
- Philip VI with French cavalry
- English archers
- Defences
- **Crécy 26 August 1346**

4. Infantry and mounted knights (Battle of Antioch, Syria, 28 June 1098).
The infantry of each 'battle' of the Crusaders' army under Bohemond preceded the knights and kept the Turkish horse-archers at bay until the moment for the charge arrived. The reserve beat off a Turkish force that had reached the Crusader rear; the main charge routed the enemy.

5. Archers and dismounted knights (Battle of Crécy, 26 August 1346).
Philip VI of France's army, estimated at 8,000 knights and esquires and some 4,000 infantry came up against Edward III's force of about 8,500 men including some 5,000 archers drawn up in battle array on a hill. The right flank of the front line and the reserve were defended by hastily-dug earthworks. The Genoese crossbowmen made little impact on the English line and the French cavalry were thrown back by concentrated archery and dismounted knights and squires. The combination of dismounted knights and archers, almost always protected by hedges, ditches, stakes or other defences, was the standard English tactic throughout most of the fourteenth and fifteenth centuries, and it was nearly always successful. There is no evidence, however, that the archers were deployed anywhere but on the flanks or that there was a revolution in the archery or tactics of the fourteenth century. The success enjoyed by the English may have been due to the number of trained archers employed.

Right Matthew Paris drew this illustration to accompany the description of a sea-fight between the Pisans and Genoese (1241). The fearful array of weaponry shown could be used on land or sea. Once opposing ships had been grappled together the combat proceeded rather as in a land battle.

chronicler knew the strength of his own side but not that of the enemy and this gave rise to some fantastic exaggerations, such as 400 against 80,000, or two against 10,000, and the one million Englishmen said to have been at the Battle of Hastings. The number of knights were limited because they were expensive to equip and were drawn from a land-holding elite, and while the infantry were more numerous their numbers in general were limited by those required for agriculture. All the evidence points to most medieval armies consisting of hundreds, not thousands. Thus a comparison of figures given for crusading armies up to 1125 shows that the largest consisted of 1,200 knights and 9,000 foot, but much more frequent were the armies of 700 knights and 2,000–3,000 foot or as little as 200 knights. The administrative records of fourteenth-century England show that royal armies rarely exceeded 10,000 horse and foot. At the Battle of Brémule in 1119 the kings of England and France had only some 400–500 knights respectively, and one chronicler says that at the second Battle of Lincoln in 1217 the regent of England brought a force of 400 knights and 347 crossbowmen against an army of rebel barons and French numbering 611 knights and 1,000 infantry. It is quite clear that the largest armies of the period, those raised by kings, were rarely over 10,000 men of all arms, but that this sort of figure represented a significant proportion of the small populations of the times and also of those free to fight cannot be doubted.

The losses suffered in battle also seem to have been small, at least among the knights, and there are two reasons for this. First, the armour of the knights protected them from serious injury, despite the recurring tales in the *chansons de geste* of helmets and heads cloven to the neck by sword blows, and of men cut from collar-bone to saddle. The Moslems were surprised that the knights that they captured after the Battle of Hattin (1187) had suffered only minor injuries, although every horse had been seriously wounded and could have fought no more. Ordericus Vitalis, the twelfth-century chronicler, tells us that of the 900 knights involved in the Battle of Bremule he had heard that only three were killed, although 140 of the French were taken captive. He said quite correctly that the reason that few were killed was 'they were all clad in mail'. Second, throughout the Middle Ages a fortune could be made from the ransoms of captured knights. Ordericus thus continued that they 'were more concerned to capture than to kill the fugitives' and that they did this 'out of fear of God and fellowship of arms' (Ordericus Vitalis, *The Ecclesiastical History*, ed. and trans. M. Chibnall, Oxford, vol 6, 1978, Book XII, cap 18). These motives may well have been in their minds, but each knight knew that a live captive was worth considerably more to him than a dead enemy. The less well-armed infantry did not get off so lightly and there are tales of the captured infantry being massacred at the end of a battle, although this was probably not common. Ordericus Vitalis tells us of the Battle of Tinchebrai (1106) (see Chibnall vol 6, Book XI, cap 20) that in the first charge of the royal knights 225 of the rebel infantry were cut down (an impossibly precise figure); Henry I in a letter to the Archbishop of Canterbury stated that he had captured 400 knights and 10,000 infantry, and that the number of slain was not known. The fact that the horses of the knights were the most vulnerable element of any medieval army was not lost on commanders, and they used their archers and spearmen to inflict casualties here and to defend their own horses (see diagram illustrating battle

tactics). Thus there is evidence that medieval commanders were capable of intelligent tactical and strategic plans, and that medieval armies possessed the discipline to carry them out (although of course some commanders and armies were lacking in such capacities).

Medieval warfare and the castle

It is still true, however, that medieval warfare was dominated by the sieges of castles until the fourteenth century, and that for a long period battles were relatively rare. A partial explanation for this may be found in the nature of medieval armies. Armies raised by purely feudal means were short-service forces: the warriors who served in them were also landowners or farmers and could not devote their whole time to war. Armies of paid troops, whether volunteers from the feudal host or mercenaries, were extremely costly to raise and to maintain. It may thus have been that commanders were loath to commit their forces to battle. In addition practically no medieval battles were decisive. The entire concept of 'decisive battle', so beloved of some military historians, is on the whole invalid. At Hastings William killed the king of England and destroyed the main field army but the English did not submit to him until he approached London at the end of the campaign.

None of the great English victories in the Hundred Years War – Agincourt, Crécy and Poitiers, to name only the most famous – had any marked effect on the war, and the greatest achievements of both the English and the French came in those periods which consisted of prolonged siege operations and skirmishes. In these phases of the war either side extended its control not through spectacular victory in battle but by a creeping advance based on the control of strongholds. In only one instance, the Battle of Hattin in 1187, may a medieval battle be spoken of as decisive: the field army of the kingdom of Jerusalem was destroyed by a Moslem force led by Saladin; the king was captured along with many of the barons and knights of the Kingdom, and the captured Hospitallers and Templars (see p. 80) were beheaded. This was because, according to the Moslem chronicler Ibn al-Athir (quoted in a most informative and enjoyable book by F. Gabrieli: *Arab Historians of the Crusades*, London, 1969, p. 124), they were well known as the fiercest troops in the Christian armies and the Moslems thought themselves well rid of them. These two Orders formed the equivalent of two standing armies in the Latin East with a large fund-raising and back-up network in

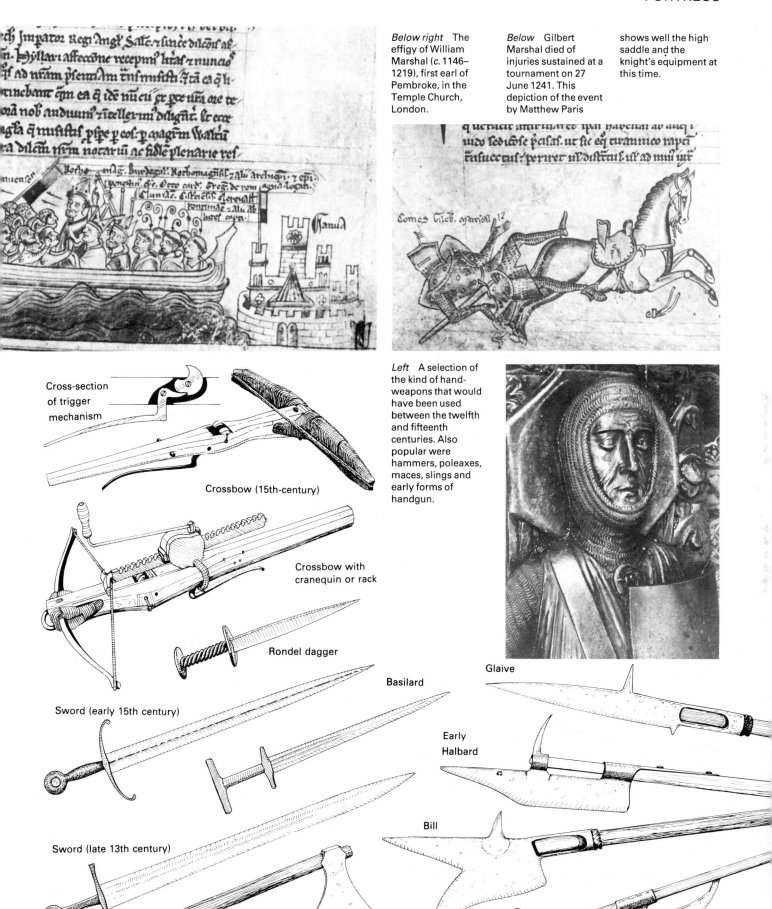

Below right The effigy of William Marshal (*c.* 1146–1219), first earl of Pembroke, in the Temple Church, London.

Below Gilbert Marshal died of injuries sustained at a tournament on 27 June 1241. This depiction of the event by Matthew Paris shows well the high saddle and the knight's equipment at this time.

Cross-section of trigger mechanism

Crossbow (15th-century)

Crossbow with cranequin or rack

Rondel dagger

Left A selection of the kind of hand-weapons that would have been used between the twelfth and fifteenth centuries. Also popular were hammers, poleaxes, maces, slings and early forms of handgun.

Sword (early 15th century)

Sword (late 13th century)

Basilard

Danish Axe

Glaive

Early Halbard

Bill

Gisarme

Top An Egyptian portrait of *c.* 1180 thought to represent Salah ed-Din Yusuf (Saladin) (d. 1193), Vizier of Egypt who united all the Moslem states bordering the Crusader kingdom. *Centre* The death of a commander often led to rout and defeat. This Matthew Paris drawing shows Philip Augustus, during the Battle of Bouvines (27 July 1214). *Bottom* Odiham Castle (Hampshire), was built for King John.

Western Europe. The Kingdom of Jerusalem was in a unique position among the western Christian states of the time in that it was ruled by an alien minority and had no reserves of military manpower. Nor did it have access to the reservoirs of mercenary soldiers who were employed in the West, and thus when an army was put into the field the 'garrisons' (see p. 69) were stripped and any losses, even in the event of a victory, were extremely difficult to replace. Nevertheless an army was frequently put into the field as the best way to discourage Moslem attacks, and when battle was given the Franks usually avoided defeat. Hattin was different. One of the leading barons of the time is reported to have counselled: 'Do not endanger the kingdom by endangering the field army' (Smail – see p. 76 – discusses this fully in his section concerning the Battle of Hattin). The king and assembled barons chose to march across an arid and waterless plain, exposed to harassment, and were demoralized and half beaten before the battle proper even started. Having destroyed the army, Saladin marched the length of the kingdom receiving the surrender of the now weakly defended towns and castles.

And yet this battle did not result in the extinction of the principalities set up less than a century earlier in the aftermath of the First Crusade. King Guy was released and gathered an army of survivors of Hattin and new Crusaders. Vastly outnumbered he besieged the important port of Acre, which was taken after the kings of England and France arrived on what is known as the Third Crusade. Following this a rump of the kingdom was re-established and Saladin's death soon after led to the breakup of Islam's temporary unity. A battle should never be viewed in isolation from its context.

A greater part of the truth is to be found in the role that the castle played in medieval warfare. It has been noted that the castle dominated the land surrounding it in many ways, and the sight of a castle perched high on a crag has led to such comments as 'the castle commanded the valley' or 'closed the

Left The massive fortress of Krak des Chevaliers (Syria) as seen from the southwest. The castle was acquired by the Knights Hospitallers in 1144 and from it parties of mounted men were able to harass enemy lands up to Homs in Syria.

route' or 'guarded the frontier'. The sight of castles on a map has led to the idea of lines of defence made up of a number of castles. There have been times when fortresses have been able to perform such functions by reason of their artillery, but the primitive artillery of the Middle Ages, even after the discovery of gunpowder, rendered this impossible. Nor were medieval armies tied to particular routes. Since they were small they lived largely off the countryside and did not rely on convoys traversing certain routes from supply depots. The idea of castle defence lines in the style of the Maginot line is also a false one.

The exceptions to these rules only prove them. Château-Gaillard, overlooking the Seine in Normandy, is one example of a castle that did block a route. It was probably late in the summer of 1196 that Richard I began work at Les Andelys, a site on which fortification had been forbidden by the Peace of Louviers (December 1195). The site was a valuable as well as strategic one, but so highly did Richard value it that he ignored the sanction of the Church and later paid generously for it. A palace on the site became his favourite residence during the last two years of his life and he planned and oversaw every aspect of the building of the fortress. Richard called it his 'fair castle of the Rock' (*bellum castrum de Rupe* in the Pipe Rolls) or his 'saucy castle' (Château-Gaillard) and the contemporary English historian William of Newburgh recorded that:

> he took such pleasure in the building that, if I am not mistaken, if an Angel had descended from heaven and told him to abandon it, that Angel would have been met with a volley of curses and the work would have gone on regardless
>
> (Gillingham, op. cit., p. 263.)

It is clear that a master of the art of siege-warfare was at work, and Richard boasted that so perfectly was its design that he could hold it even if its walls were made of butter. The accounts for the two years taken to build it (an incredibly short

time for a work of stone) show that over £11,000 sterling was paid to the men in charge of construction. The next largest item of expenditure at the same time was £1,300 spent on a town wall, and in England Richard spent only £7,000 on *all* English castles during his whole reign. The most spent on any English castle in the period was the £8,250 expended on Dover, but that was spread over the years 1164–1214.

Richard thus attached great import to the 'saucy castle'. The work consisted of the castle itself perched on a crag above the Seine, a fort on an island in the river connected to each bank by a wooden bridge, a new town with wall and water defences at one end, similar defences around the old town at Les Andelys, a stockade across the river and a number of outlying forts. It has been generally accepted that the purpose of this impressive work was the defence of Normandy, which had been considerably weakened by the loss to the French of the major fortress of Gisors. An invading army following the Seine, its baggage and siege-train carried on the river, could be at Rouen, the capital of Normandy, in two days and could be provisioned along the river. The castle was thus positioned to cut the navigation of the Seine, to separate the two divisions of an army advancing along the banks of the river, to make their communication with Paris impossible and to place them in danger of both divisions being defeated before Rouen was reached (William the Conqueror had achieved just this in 1053). The whole complex at Château-Gaillard, of which the castle was only the centre, was well suited to this purpose but, as John Gillingham has pointed out (op. cit., p. 265), Richard was thinking not of the defence of Normandy but of the reconquest of the Vexin – that region of the Seine valley where France met Normandy and which had been a battleground between the kings of France and dukes of Normandy for over a century. Château-Gaillard was designed as an offensive forward base to which men and munitions could be sent from the arsenal at Rouen in preparation for the hammer-blows to be launched against the French castles in the Vexin. It was only in the reign of the next king of England, John, when the defences of Normandy collapsed, that the 'saucy castle' was called on to defend the Seine valley and Rouen.

Where the borders of Normandy marched with those of France, castles were grouped together for the defence of the March. Throughout the twelfth century, groups of royal castles acquired in various ways (by purchase, confiscation, or, as with Château-Gaillard, custom-built) were united into military districts, but even these could not prevent the French from raiding into Normandy.

The castle as the key to the land

The true importance of the castle lay in its intimate relationship with the region around it. This relationship has best been summed up as follows:

> wherever they stood, fortified buildings provided a base from which power could be exercised, and within which it could be protected and preserved. As in Europe, so in Syria, castles had only occasionally to withstand a siege, but they continuously filled their function as the physical basis of overlordship [...] a medieval fortress could not halt an attack at the frontier, and many times during the (twelfth) century Muslim armies penetrated deep into the Latin states. The Franks temporarily lost control of any area occupied by the invader.

(R.C. Smail, *Crusading Warfare*, Cambridge, 1956, pp. 60–2.)

But while a castle stood unconquered, such loss of control was only temporary. The castle buildings were designed to resist capture for as long as possible and were therefore passive, but it was the men in the castle who enabled it to perform an active role in war. The defenders are frequently referred to as a 'garrison' but, although convenient, this word is not entirely correct. On the whole the men (and women, in some cases) who defended castles in war also lived there in peace, for the castle was residence as well as fortress (as we shall see in a later chapter). In war, however, the strength of a castle could be increased by the employment of hired troops, and in times of crisis we find, in the English administrative documents for example, records of money spent on repairs, munitions and bodies of troops.

The size of the defence force depended not least on the capacity of a castle. The rebel barons threw a force of some 100 knights and men-at-arms as well as crossbowmen into Rochester in 1215, and in 1216, Dover, described by the thirteenth-century historian Matthew Paris as the 'key to England', was held against the rebel barons and their French allies under Prince Louis by some 140 knights and men-at-arms, in addition to lesser men. But these were large 'garrisons'. We are told that the castle at Odiham held out against prince Louis in 1216 with a force of only three knights and ten men-at-arms. After the Battle of Hattin, Jerusalem was found to hold just two knights. In desperation 60 sons of rich merchants were admitted to the knighthood.

Small as they were, these garrisons, which contained a large number of mounted men, exercised an importance out of all proportion to their numbers. From their base, parties of mounted men could roam the land surrounding them. Their range was dictated by the journey that could be made from and back to the castle in one day, estimated at about ten miles, and by this means they controlled the land unless a major force was led against them. Le puiset was a castle in the region of Paris taken by King Louis VI 'the Fat' in 1111. His biographer, the abbot Suger, indicated that the castle simply had to be taken because when it was in hostile hands nobody dared approach within eight to ten miles of it. Montlhery in the same region was a thorn in the flesh of Louis's father, Philip I. It was said that the inhabitants of the towns of Paris and Orleans could not pass from one town to the other without either the permission of the lord of the castle or a strong escort to keep his knights at bay. The Muslim chronicler Ibn Jubair wrote of the town of Homs:

> what do you think of a town that is only a few miles from Hisn al-Akrad (the massive crusader fortress, Krak des Chevaliers), the stronghold of the enemy where you can see their fires whose sparks burn you when they fly, and whence each day, should they wish, the enemy may raid you on horseback?
>
> (*quoted in* The travels of Ibn Jubair, *trans. R.J.C. Broadhurst, London, 1952, p. 268.*)

Thus did a castle dominate the land and prohibit movement. Its defenders were powerless in the face of a major force, but unless the enemy was prepared to besiege the castle, which could take a long time and might anyway be frustrated by a relief force, it could not conquer the land.

This aggressive aspect of the castle made it a most useful instrument for the conquest of a country. In England and Syria the alien Normans and Franks built castles from which they exercised their domination. When expansion was contemplated a new castle was built and the defenders pacified the land from that base. Then another castle was built further into the land of the enemy and another parcel of land pacified and colonized. In this manner the Normans extended their domination into Wales, Spain was reconquered from the Moslems, Germany conquered from the Slavs and the Christian dominion advanced in Outremer.

This principle had other applications too. Castle could be used to fight castle. In the case of a siege it was not unusual to find a temporary siege-castle erected to cover a gate or postern and to prevent the enemy from getting out for any reason. A force of knights would be stationed in the siege-castle from which they could repel any sortie. In a wider context a castle could be used to deny the defenders of a nearby castle the revenues and produce of the land. This practice vastly increased the expense to the enemy of maintaining a 'garrison'. In 1199 Richard and Philip II agreed on a truce to last for five years. Philip was allowed to retain certain castles that he had taken but was to surrender all claim to their lands. At first Richard was furious because he thought that he had been tricked into the truce by the papal legates, but the biographer of William Marshal modestly tells us that his hero pointed out to the king

> when he can get nothing from the land and has to keep up the castles at his own cost, he will find that he is carrying a burden heavier than a war. That is what will happen: I wager they will come back tomorrow.
>
> (Powicke, op. cit., p. 199.)

A force was detailed under a mercenary captain to harass the French garrisons on the Epte so that they could collect nothing from the land. So successful was he that Richard was presented with the customary dues from the Vexin even though the castles were in the hands of the French. Elsewhere in Normandy the garrisons of his castles aggressively patrolled up to the gates of enemy fortresses, in one case with such effect that it seems that Richard was able to hold a council just outside a French-held castle without being disturbed.

Nor have we yet exhausted the potential of the castle. Some major castles contained arsenals from which arms and armour, siege-engines and projectiles, provisions and all the other

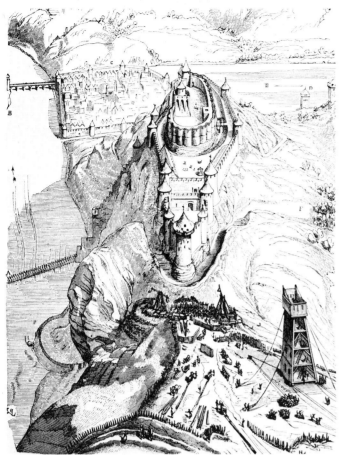

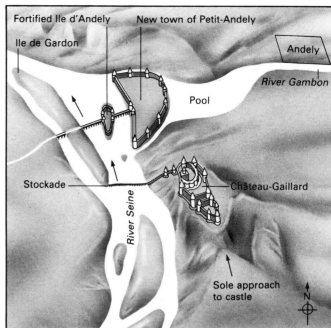

Left King John made one attempt to raise the siege of Château-Gaillard in August 1203, but failed, and the loyalty of Normandy to John melted away in the following weeks, until the castle was finally captured in March 1204.
Above A diagram to illustrate the system of defences at Château-Gaillard on the Seine.
Below Exemplary punishment used as psychological warfare was well known in the Middle Ages.
(From *Les Histoires d'Outremer.*

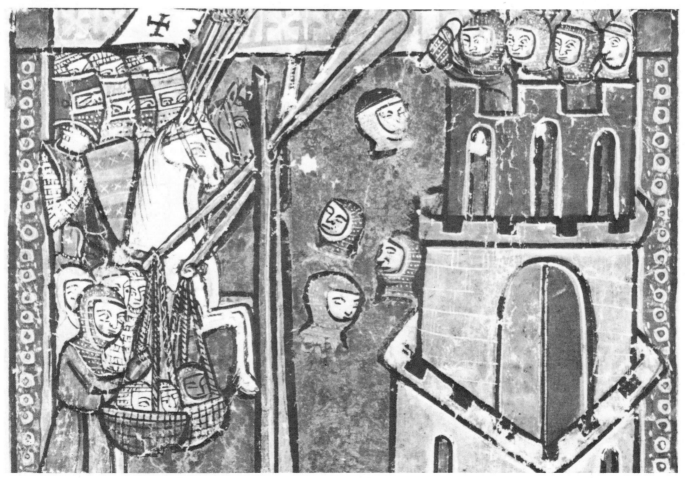

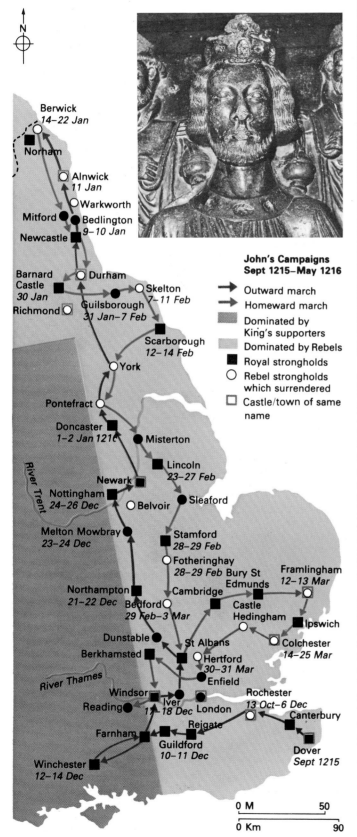

Below *Below* King John died at Newark (Nottingham) on 18 October 1216, reputedly of a fever aggravated by supping on peaches and new cider, the loss of his treasure in the Wash, and the news that Dover Castle was close to surrender. His body was taken to Worcester Cathedral where he wished it to rest.

N

John's Campaigns Sept 1215–May 1216

→ Outward march
→ Homeward march
▨ Dominated by King's supporters
▨ Dominated by Rebels
■ Royal strongholds
○ Rebel strongholds which surrendered
□ Castle/town of same name

Berwick *14–22 Jan*
Norham
Alnwick *11 Jan*
Warkworth
Mitford
Bedlington *9–10 Jan*
Newcastle
Barnard Castle *30 Jan*
Durham
Skelton *7–11 Feb*
Richmond
Guilsborough *31 Jan–7 Feb*
Scarborough *12–14 Feb*
York
Pontefract
Doncaster *1–2 Jan 1216*
Misterton
Lincoln *23–27 Feb*
Newark
Nottingham *24–26 Dec*
Belvoir
Sleaford
Melton Mowbray *23–24 Dec*
Stamford *28–29 Feb*
Fotheringhay *28–29 Feb*
Framlingham *12–13 Mar*
Bury St Edmunds
Northampton *21–22 Dec*
Cambridge
Bedford *29 Feb–3 Mar*
Castle Hedingham
Ipswich
Dunstable
St Albans
Colchester *14–25 Mar*
Berkhamsted
Hertford *30–31 Mar*
Enfield
Windsor
Iver *17–18 Dec*
London
Rochester *13 Oct–6 Dec*
Reading
Reigate
Canterbury
Farnham
Guildford *10–11 Dec*
Dover *Sept 1215*
Winchester *12–14 Dec*

River Trent
River Thames

0 M 50
0 Km 90

paraphernalia of war might be drawn. In the event of a lost battle, a friendly castle was a safe base to which to retreat and re-form. In 1177 Saladin led an army into the south of Palestine and was defeated at the Battle of Mont Gisard. The defeat in itself need not have been disastrous but his nearest friendly base was in Egypt across the desert and in the long retreat his army suffered badly from lack of water, supplies and shelter, and broke up as a fighting force. As with the countryside, so with towns: a castle built in a town enabled the town to be dominated. Thus William the Conqueror had three castles built in London and two in York, and any English rebels would have had to take not only the city walls but also the castles before either city could have been safely controlled. By these means the defence of a city could be prolonged, or a city whose inhabitants were untrustworthy or rebellious could be kept firmly under control.

The castle played a central role in medieval warfare because it represented the key to the land. Even assuming that an invading army could gain a clear victory in the field, it still had to take the castles of the enemy. This, however, was a risky business. While an invader was slowly besieging fortresses the enemy had ample time to re-group and raise the siege in progress or attempt to launch a counter-stroke. The troops of the invading army might even wish to return home for the harvest or to enjoy their revenues. The use of hired troops solved this problem to a great extent, but they were expensive to maintain and we have seen some of the problems connected with their employment. It was thus unusual for a land defended with manned castles to be conquered, and wars tended to follow a less ambitious pattern (the completion of the conquest of Normandy by the French King Philip II in 1204 was due above all to a collapse of resistance and the defection of half the Norman baronage, and to John's inability to relieve those who did hold out for him). What was to be attempted depended of course on the military resources available for a

Left In September 1198 Richard I's scouts
informed him that Philip Augustus was in the
vicinity of Gisors in Normandy. Although
outnumbered Richard charged the French as
they marched, putting them to flight. Richard
boasted that he had unseated three of the
enemy knights with one lance.

exerting economic and financial pressure on an opponent (J. Gillingham, op. cit., pp. 55–6). By ravaging the lands of an enemy he might be brought to terms, he would certainly lose revenues, and if he did not retaliate he would lose face as well and might find his vassals changing sides. It is in this context that raiding must be seen, for it was an essential part of medieval warfare. The raid, far from being the spiteful, futile act it has often been written off as, was a calculated insult to an opponent. In a twelfth-century work (*Jordan Fantosme's Metrical Chronicle of the War between the Scots and English*, ed. and trans. R. Howlett, Rolls Series, London, 1886, vol. 82) these words of advice to the Scots are put into the mouth of Count Philip of Flanders, a member of the coalition formed against Henry II in 1173–4.

> *Destroy your foes and ravage their country,*
> *By fire and burning let all be set alight;*
> *That nothing be left them outside, either in wood or meadow,*
> *Of which in the morning they could have a dinner.*
> *Then with his united force let him besiege their castles;*
> *They will have nor succour nor aid within thirteen leagues.*
> *Thus should war be begun: such is my advice.*
> *First destroy the land and then one's foe.*
> (lines 444–451.)

A description of an army on the march makes it clear what this entailed.

> *The march begins. Out in front are the scouts and incendiaries. After them come the foragers whose job it is to collect the spoils and carry them in the great baggage train. Soon all is in tumult. The peasants, having just come out to the fields, turn back, uttering loud cries. The shepherds gather their flocks and drive them towards the neighbouring woods in the hope of saving them. The incendiaries set the villages on fire and the foragers visit and sack them. The terrified inhabitants are either burned or are led away with their hands tied to be held for ransom. Everywhere bells ring the alarm; a surge of fear sweeps over the countryside. Wherever you look you can see helmets glinting in the sun, pennons waving in the breeze, the whole plain covered in horsemen. Money, cattle, mules and sheep are all seized. The smoke billows and spreads, flames crackle. Peasants and shepherds scatter in all directions.*
> (Chansons des Lorrains, Gillingham, op. cit., p. 118.)

The raid was obviously a brutal exercise, but it was a way of exerting pressure on the enemy and also of softening him up. It became, in fact, as important as the battle and the siege, and should never be dismissed.

In a short space such as this it has only been possible to give a brief outline of the organization and practice of medieval warfare, and the importance of the castle in that context. Many more examples may be found from a wider geographical area and a wider time-span than has been covered here, but all will reflect the same basic truth. Medieval warfare was dominated by the knight and the castle. But it was neither sterile nor anarchic, and the evidence shows that all aspects of the so-called 'art of war' were well-known and understood.

given campaign, but the capture of a small number of castles and therefore the land that they controlled – perhaps a strip of land along a border – could be counted a success.

Truces, sieges and raids
During such a campaign it was perfectly acceptable for the defenders of a castle to agree to a truce. During that time they were still under siege although the besiegers might have gone on to another siege. When the truce had expired it might be renewed or the defenders might have agreed to surrender if relief had not arrived by the time the truce ended. This was an extremely practical approach to war for only a few castles were so strong that they could hope to hold out until the besiegers had to go home. An example of this is to be found in the war of 1173–4 when a coalition of France, Flanders, Scotland and disaffected barons, led by Henry II's son the Young King Henry, invaded England and Normandy. The king of the Scots, as his part of the conspiracy, was to invade the north of England. In the autumn of 1173 he duly invaded but failed to make an impression on either the castle of Wark-on-Tweed or of Carlisle, after which he was driven back into Scotland and begged for a truce which he was granted. In the following year he returned and once more laid siege to Wark. Again he was unsuccessful and moved on to Carlisle which he blockaded, detaching part of his army to capture the castles of Liddel, Burgh, Appleby, Harbottle, Warkworth, Brough and Brougham – all in the far north of England. The defenders of Carlisle promised to surrender by Michaelmas (29 September) if they had not been relieved, so William of Scotland used the intervening time to besiege Prudhoe on the Tyne. His plans were brought to nothing, however, when he was taken by surprise by a royal force, and although he fought bravely he was captured and the rebellion collapsed.

It has been said that making war in the twelfth century was like going on strike in the twentieth, for it was a way of

Defence & Attack

The king had built this stronghold with a view to extending his boundaries; he also had in mind the fact that from this place he could more easily collect the full revenues due annually from those dwelling in the surrounding villages which our people call casalia. A fixed toll could also be levied on those travelling past on the road.

> (*William of Tyre – A history of deeds done beyond the sea*, trans. and annotated by E.A. Babcock and A.C. Krey, Columbia, vol 2, 1943, p. 373.)

Thus William of Tyre explained why King Amalric of Jerusalem founded the castle of Daron in the Gaza strip shortly after his accession in 1162. It is but one example of the indisputable fact that during the feudal period the castle dominated the land, and that largely as a result it also dominated warfare. Possession of castles was vital whether you were fighting a war of expansion in another land, or at home taking part in a rebellion or civil war. It is true that victory in the field, if sufficiently crushing as at the Battle of Hattin in 1187, could so incapacitate your enemy as to render further opposition extremely difficult, but if your foe kept control of all of his castles your success might well be transitory. The resilience of only a few castles and towns after Hattin prevented Saladin from completing his conquest of Outremer. In fact, victory in full-scale battle could be quite superfluous if it was not part of a campaign to occupy an enemy's territories through his strong-points. The Battle of Agincourt, for example, was an irrelevant sideshow in the war against France compared to the systematic conquest of Normandy by the victor – Henry V of England in 1417–19. And 1066 might not have been so memorable a year, if the Anglo-Saxons had possessed castles.

Alternatives to attack

Given the crucial role of the castle, it was inevitable that it became increasingly complex and sophisticated. Just as modern politicians and soldiers tend to employ horrendous weapons of destruction as deterrents, so too the feudal lord tended to improve the offensive and defensive capabilities of his castle so as to convince potential aggressors of the futility of besieging him. He would not necessarily make his castle 'impregnable' (a rather abused word in works on castles) but he would strengthen it to the point that its reduction would cost a foe a good deal of time and a good deal of money. This in itself might well be sufficient to avert an attack. The castle of Newcastle upon Tyne was far from 'impregnable' in 1173, but it was strong enough to make an ill-prepared Scottish King William think twice about a siege:

> *Well sees the king of Scotland that he will never complete*
> *The Conquest of Newcastle on Tyne without military engines.*
> (*The Metrical Chronicle of Jordan Fantosme* in *Chronicles of the reigns of Stephen, Henry II and Richard I*, vol III, ed. by R. Howlett, Rolls Series, London, 1886, lines 582–3.)

In 1191, the Anglo-Normans of the Third Crusade likewise had reservations about assaulting St Hilarion in Cyprus:

> *Dieudamour is of too great might*
> *To be taken by storm or fight*
> (*Estoire de la Guerre Sainte* by Ambroise,

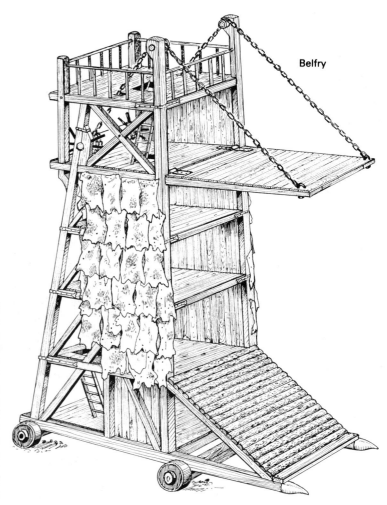

Belfry

trans. by M.J. Hubert and J. La Monte, New York, 1976, p. 104, lines 1987–8.)

Clearly the full scale siege of an adequately defended castle was not to be undertaken lightly, so it is hardly surprising to learn that a commander would choose some other means to his end if he could. Besieger and besieged might enter into some form of contract involving surrender of the castle if it was not relieved after a stipulated period during which there would be a truce. If diplomacy failed, the besieger might try intimidating his enemies into capitulating. At the siege of Nottingham in 1194 King Richard executed some of Prince John's men outside the castle as a timely reminder to those who still withstood him within. In 1285 Sultan Kalaoun invested Margat and mined under its remarkably strong donjon. Instead of firing the mine and bringing down the tower he invited the Hospitallers of the garrison to inspect this siege-work. Duly impressed they promptly capitulated. Alternatively, one might have recourse to subterfuge, as in 1271 when the Sultan Baibars forged a letter commanding the Hospitallers to yield up the great Krak des Chevaliers. In 1401, the Tudor brothers determined to capture Conway castle, largely so as to be better able to bargain with Henry IV for remission of sentences for their misdemeanours. Adam of Usk relates the trick by which they took the castle '[...] the two warders being slain by the craftiness of a certain carpenter who feigned to come to his accustomed work; and, entering therein with other forty men they held it for a stronghold.' (*Adam of Usk – Chronicon A.D. 1377–1421*, ed. and trans. by E.M. Thompson, London, 2nd ed, 1904, p. 226.)

In spite of its strength, a castle could only resist as long as its garrison, and in many cases this was a matter of pure logistics. Whenever possible, the men of a castle would build up their stock of provisions as much as they could if they believed they were about to be besieged. In this connection it is of interest to look at the Crusader castles, built be it noted

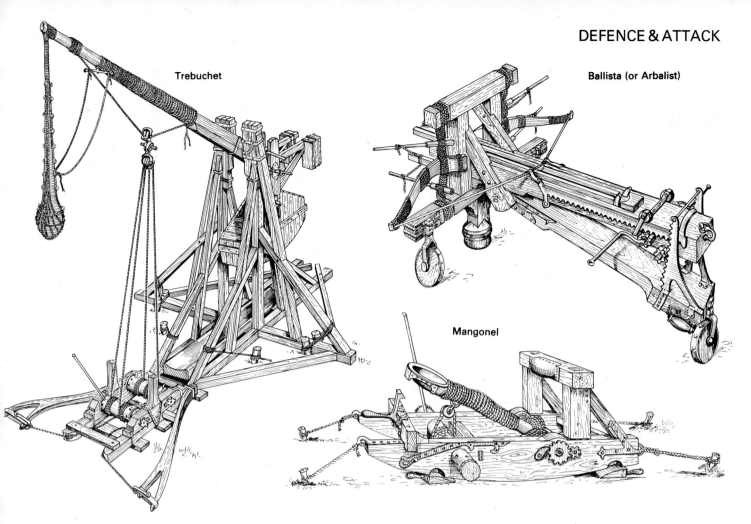

Trebuchet

Ballista (or Arbalist)

Mangonel

Ram

Bore

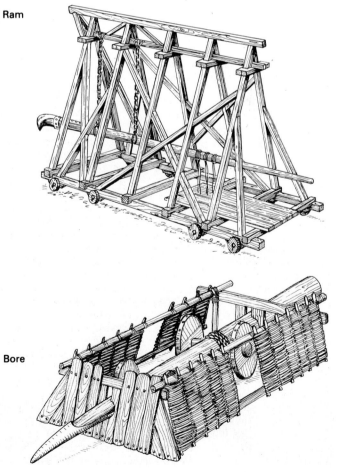

where warfare was endemic, and study the large edifices which it is believed may have served as storage spaces. Water was naturally of prime importance in the Crusader castles as it was elsewhere, and not surprisingly an attacker might well cut off a castle's water supply if he could, as in one of the sieges of Desenberg in West Germany for example. Where a castle was given little or no warning of an impending attack, its commander had to be most careful to eke out his ammunition and rations. At Wark-on-Tweed in 1174, the constable – Roger d'Estuteville – exhorted his men:

Shoot not your arrows, except in great need [...]
If we have food, let us save it willingly
Spare your weapons, I say it to you, archers.
        (*Fantosme*, op. cit., lines 1230 and 1236–7.)

King William of Scotland gave up the siege of Wark before its defenders exhausted their supplies, and Roger, like a wise commander who knows when to keep a low profile, did his best to ensure his men did not provoke the Scots to return:

Say nothing abusive: for God's sake let be!
Nor shout nor follow with cries these Scotchmen.
        (*Fantosme*, op. cit., lines 1299–1300.)

King William's enemy, Henry II of England was altogether more stubborn. In 1173 he besieged certain rebels in Dol which rapidly surrendered because

They had not the provisions sufficient to sustain life
        (*Fantosme*, op. cit., line 211.)

In the long run, a castle was bound to succumb if a close blockade could be sustained. An attacking force might cut trenches and take no further offensive action than preventing fresh supplies from reaching the beleaguered. This means of taking a castle could be an especially expensive one, however, so a wise general would seek some other means of eliminating a castle's sources of supply. One alternative was to devastate the areas surrounding a castle, as Count Philip of Flanders advised the Scots in the twelfth century (see p. 79).

Above The siege of Dinan in 1064. (From the Bayeux Tapestry.)

Below The great tower of the Hospitaller castle of Margat (Syria), the largest of all Crusader castles.

Frequently these castle environs, sometimes known as *châtellanies* or *castellarie*, contained the lands, rents and services of the fees of the knights who performed castle-guard. If the fees were plundered, then the economic position of the knights and therefore the castle itself would be severely undermined, for as Sir Maurice Powicke pointed out 'the possession of a stronghold without its source of revenue was inconvenient and unprofitable' (op. cit., p. 199). The best examples of this policy of reducing a foe's castles are most probably the offensives of Philip II of France into the Norman lands of the Angevin king-dukes, Henry, and his sons Richard and John, in the late twelfth and early thirteenth centuries. In fact the French were so successful at this that several Norman castles were dismantled on the orders of the English Crown when Philip was merely threatening to destroy their *châtellanies*. Naturally enough Richard I and his brother John tried to play Philip at his own game, and in Richard's time, at least, with some success. But because the continental wars of Richard and John were fought mainly on their own territories, this policy of destroying the *châtellanies* hit the Angevins far more than Philip. All this shows quite clearly the quintessential relationship of castle and land: the land was controlled by the castle and at the same time supported it; without the land there was neither point nor possibility in the castle's continued existence.

Attack by escalade

Yet however else one might try to capture or seriously weaken a castle, the ultimate sanction remained that of a direct attack on its towers and walls. Perhaps the most obvious way was to use scaling ladders, but this was a risky business in the extreme and certainly was not a tactic for a commander who had to husband his manpower. A more efficient if elaborate form of escalade was to use a great wooden tower known as a 'belfry'. This was undoubtedly the largest 'engine' used in

mondsworth, 1969, A rendering of the following extract will be found on p. 403.)

> *A wooden tower was built on a square base and carried to such a height that it overtopped the towers of the city by five or six cubits. The wooden tower had to be constructed in the way described in order that by letting down the hanging drawbridge, the soldiers could run easily down to the lower level of the city wall [...] Its base was raised on a number of wheels, and, it was levered along with crowbars by the soldiers inside [...] It was completely covered in from top to base and divided into several floors, and all around were openings in the shape of loopholes through which arrows were shot. On the top floor stood high spirited men, fully armed, with swords in their hands ready to stand on defence.*

Once it was in position the attacking Franks took off its wheels, but before long 'that whole terrific construction' was burnt to the ground by the defenders. At the siege of Damietta in 1169, we learn from William of Tyre that the Christians built a belfry of seven storeys, and then levelled the approaches to the wall.

> *The fighters in the movable tower kept up a continual pressure upon the besieged. Without intermission, they hurled forth showers of arrows and stone missiles together with such other weapons as their fury and the confined space furnished.*

(*William of Tyre*, op. cit., p. 364.)

Breaching the walls

A more effective and therefore favoured means of attacking a castle was to create a breach in its walls through which an assault could be made. At first castles were generally, though not always, built of wood, so a besieging force could use fire to rupture the palisade. The Bayeux Tapestry depicts William of Normandy's men doing just this at the siege of Dinan in 1064, and in Suger's account of the siege of Le Puiset in 1111 we again hear of the besieging force using fire against the wooden defences of the castle. The bailey stockade at Le Puiset was finally breached not by fire, but by a party who simply hacked their way through. Nonetheless this took time and obviously required extreme determination as the assailants would be exposed to showers of missiles from the outraged garrison. Where stone castles superseded wooden ones, this rough-and-ready form of attack became impossible, unless the assailants were equipped with proper picks and crowbars and given the protection of a movable shed or penthouse under cover of which they could deliberately chisel away. Yet even then success was far from certain: to create a breach by the use of hand tools only was a long and arduous process during which the garrison could devise a number of counters, such as dropping heavy stones or incendiaries on the shed, making a sortie, or reinforcing their wall from within. Small wonder, then, that it is rare indeed to find an occasion where soldiers attempted to rupture walls without the protection of a wooden shed. We see this at Acre in 1191, but evidently the recklessness of the individuals in question was induced by the cash rewards put on offer by King Richard I.

More commonly a besieging force would attempt a breach by using a battering-ram slung within the protective framework of the movable shed. The ram might well be a large tree-trunk

siege warfare since it was built to tower above the parapet of the besieged castle wall so that archers and crossbowmen could command the interior, and, more especially, clear the battlements of defenders before the drawbridge was dropped and the assault troops went in. At Tyre in 1111, for example, one was 65 feet tall and another 80 feet tall, while a little later at Lisbon in 1147 we find one belfry of 83 feet and a second of 95 feet. The belfry consisted of a number of storeys known as *coenacula* or *solaria* which enabled it to carry a great many men: the Arab historian Baha ed Din tells us that three belfries of the Crusaders at Acre in 1191 'could each, according to report, accommodate more than five hundred men.' ('Sultanly Anecdotes and Josephly Virtues' in *Recueil des Historiens des Croisades*, Historiens Orientaux, vol III, Paris, 1884. This has the full text. There are also useful extracts in Gabrieli, op. cit.). This also imparted greater strength and of course this was vital if the belfry was to survive the barrage of stone missiles the defenders would use against it. Equally it had to be capable of surviving an incendiary attack, and accordingly it was covered with hides, vines and mats which were repeatedly doused with water and vinegar. Once the belfry was constructed, the next task was to level the approaches to the objective: no mean feat if, as at Tyre, this involved filling in three ditches. It would then be wheeled up against the wall, the wheels taken off, and the assault attempted. Success was more likely than with the simple method of using ladders, but more often than not the belfry proved vulnerable to fire in spite of its damp coating. On occasion it was countered by a similar tower constructed by the defenders behind the threatened section of wall, as at Dyrrachium in 1108 and at Damietta in 1169.

Anna Comnena's account of the siege of Dyrrachium in 1108 is an outstanding record of the construction and employment of the belfry. (*The Alexiad of Anna Comnena* is available in Penguin classics, trans. by E.R.A. Sewter, Penguin, Har-

which would be tipped with a heavy iron head. As with the belfry, the approaches to the objective would have to be levelled before the ram and its shed could be moved up. Once in position it would be swung repeatedly by its crew which might number as many as 60 men. At Acre, the Archbishop of Besancon built a ram for the Crusaders with a head 'in form like the giant axle of a mill-stone' as Baha ed Din relates. Ambroise adds that

> [...] Twas underneath,
> As twere, a kind of house or sheath.
> Therein a great ship's mast it had,
> Knot-free, with each end ironclad,
> And underneath the ram were those
> Who were to deal the wall stout blows
> (op. cit., p. 169, lines 3849–54.)

Closely related to the ram was the bore, or the *musculus* as the Romans called it. Similar, if a little smaller than the ram, its purpose was to bore away into the masonry, and we find it especially directed against sharp angles. Like the ram, it too would receive the protection of a shed beneath which its operators might more securely go about their work. Yet even with this covering many rams and bores were destroyed by a barrage of heavy stones or were burnt down. Alternatively they might be caught up in devices lowered from the walls which caught them by the head and immobilized them. At Tyre in 1111, a Moslem seaman invented grappling irons that caught the Crusaders' ram and pulled it sideways so that it nearly overturned its protective housing. In the Albigensian Wars of the thirteenth century, Beaucaire in Provence was similarly attacked by a ram

> but the besieged, when they perceived this, are not discouraged. They make a noose of rope, which is attached to a machine of wood, and by means thereof the head of the bosson [the ram] is caught and held fast
> (from a passage of Provençal poetry)

The ram especially might also be countered by the careful lowering of material like baulks of timber or mattresses, as at Jerusalem in 1099, as a kind of buffer to absorb the shock of the battering.

Undermining

Although these devices remained in use throughout the period of the castle's military importance, by far the most effective means of creating a breach was to undermine. Sappers, often specialists in their craft, would tunnel their way beneath their objective, supporting their mine with strong beams of timber as they went. When the work was completed, combustible material – brushwood, faggots, even pig fat as at Rochester in 1215 – would be introduced and ignited; the mine would collapse and simultaneously bring down the masonry standing above it. This tactic worked well against even the strongest of castles, as in 1215 at Rochester, in 1216 at Dover, in 1224 at Bedford, and in 1271 at Krak des Chevaliers. Unless the castle was reasonably secure, having been built on the living rock or behind large water defences, there was in reality very little that could be done to defend it against this sort of attack. The defenders could attempt to countermine – to dig their own tunnel and hope to break into the enemy's mine – before it was too late, but this was far from a foolproof answer to the threat. To begin with, mining was frequently a complete surprise to a castle's defenders since the entrance to the mine might well be

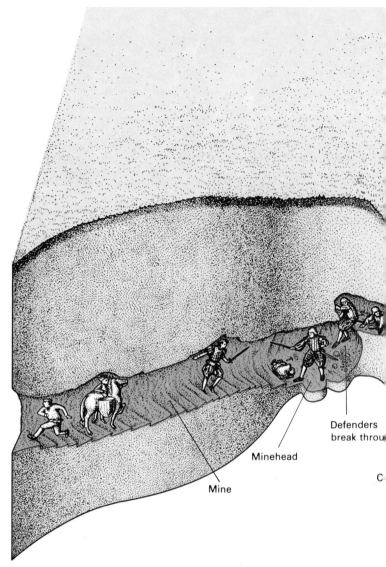

Defenders break throu

Minehead

Mine

C

protected by sheds or fences known as 'hurdles'. Even when it was plainly apparent that mining was in progress it was not easy to deduce the exact direction it was taking and needless to say the very countermining itself was a risk to the masonry the process was meant to safeguard. If a countermine did succeed in breaking into the mine of the besieger there might then be a hellish underground mêlée at Dyrrachium. There the Greeks used reed pipes to blow a form of Greek fire into the faces of the Franks in the mine, and by this means succeeded in foiling them.

Astonishing as it may be, it is still possible for us to see for ourselves exactly what these tunnels were like, for at St Andrew's in Fife, Scotland, there is an extremely rare example of an intact mine and countermine dating from the siege of 1546–7. The assailants sank a tunnel six feet wide and seven feet high in order to undermine the castle's Fore Tower. It is perhaps worth noting that the mine was high enough for ponies to be used and certainly their help would have been valuable, for the tunnel leads down into a wide minehead that evidently required not a little effort to excavate. It was apparently intended to run branches from this in order to cause the breaching of the tower in several places, but before

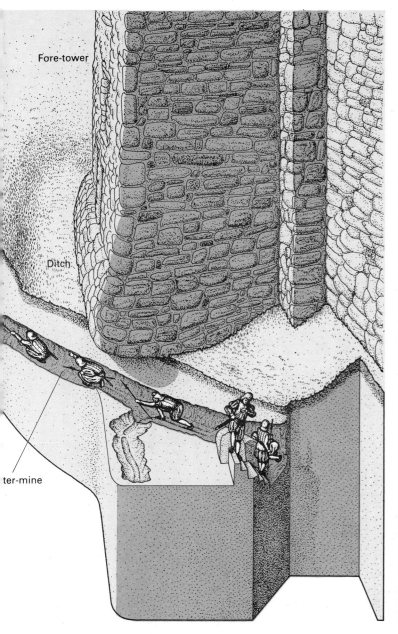

Fore-tower

Ditch

ter-mine

Left Cross-section of the mine and counter-mine at St Andrews (Fife) in Scotland.
Below A view of part of the tunnelling at St Andrews dating from the siege of 1546–7.

this could be realized, the defenders had skilfully run out their own countermine under their own walls and broken through into the minehead from a slightly higher level. But perhaps the most fascinating feature of the tunnelling at St Andrew's is that it is clear that the defenders were at first far from certain as to where to direct their digging: two trial pits were first dug and given up, and the eventual mine itself follows an uncertain course in its early stages: a timely reminder for us of the difficulties of countermining and of the poor success it more generally encountered.

If a breach at a particular point was expected, an alternative was to erect some barrier within the castle to deny entrance to the enemy's assault troops. At the siege of Carcassone in 1240, the garrison built a good strong palisade between themselves and the wall which was being undermined. Similarly they built a dividing wall within a threatened barbican so that when one part of this outwork collapsed, the enemy would find the garrison still in control of the remaining part (cf the keep at Rochester in the siege of 1215). At Lisbon in 1147, the Christians undermined a wall before the Moors could do anything about it, but their quick reaction staved off immediate disaster for they rapidly erected a barrier of beams in the

breach. In the long run, however, *ad hoc* wooden fencing proved to be as unsatisfactory a defence as countermining, and to the end of its time as the centrepiece of warfare, the castle's deadliest enemy remained the mine.

Bombardment

Having looked at the ways in which escalade and breach could be effected, we now come to the subject of bombardment – in essence those great stone-throwing engines, commonly known as *petrarie*, which were used to batter the objective in much the same manner as modern artillery pieces. This is arguably the most difficult matter with which we have to deal: our sources are far from consistent in identifying their types, and even less helpful in explaining their mechanism. This in itself is of interest for it is in marked contrast to the detailed accounts we have of belfries, rams and mines. One explanation may be that petrarie generally aroused less excitement in chroniclers for the simple reason that they were very much a standard feature of siege warfare.

Broadly speaking, we may divide petrarie into two main types, of which the mangon, or mangonel, was the earlier, and being slightly smaller probably remained the commoner.

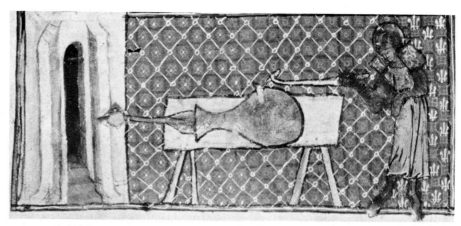

Right Cannon of 1326 in the Walter de Milemetes MS. at Christ Church, Oxford.

Above An attack on a castle, showing the use of incendiary arrows and cannon, from a German Firework Book *c.* 1450.
Above right Perhaps the most famous cannon of all: Mons Meg, which dates from about 1450. She blew up in 1680 but was subsequently restored in 1829.
Right Bamburgh Castle on the coast of Northumberland. In 1464 it was captured by the Yorkists after a bombardment by cannon fire.

Left Greek Fire dropped from the battlements, from *Les Commentaires de César* (1473). Originally developed by the Byzantines in the seventh century, the Crusaders made great use of Greek Fire at the sieges of Montreuil – Bellay (1151) and Nottingham (1194).

Basically this engine constituted a long arm with a spoon or sling for its projectile at the free end, inserted through a skein of ropes or strong hair stretched between uprights at its other end. The ropes would be twisted towards the target by windlasses, and the long arm pulled down hard against the pressure. Thereupon the stone would be secured in the spoon or sling. When triggered the device would release its projectile and catapult it towards the objective. The mangon could accommodate extremely heavy ammunition: stone balls weighing up to 600 lbs were used in the reduction of Saône in 1188. Occasionally a besieging force went to great trouble to fetch its stones from great distances: on the Third Crusade King Richard is supposed to have had rocks transported all the way from Messina with which to bombard Acre. In 1287 Rhys ap Maredudd, Lord of the Vale of the Towy, rebelled against the English administration in south-west Wales and seized the castle of Newcastle Emlyn. The English used a great petraria to recapture it, and teams of men were employed to scour the seashore below Cardigan to find 480 suitable stones to use. These were transported by boat up the Teifi to Llechryd and from there moved up by 120 packhorses and horse-drawn carts. It appears that mangonels were also capable of surprisingly rapid fire: the chronicle of the conquest of Lisbon in 1147 tells us that two such engines were in action over a period of ten hours, worked by relays of men, during which time they cast some 5,000 stones, a rate of one stone every 15 seconds per machine. Whether we believe this or not, the comment of the chronicler that 'the enemy were greatly harassed by this action' (*The Conquest of Lisbon: De Expugnatione Lyxbonensi*, New York, 1976, p. 143) remains something of a euphemism.

Whereas the mangonel worked by torsion, the trebuchet worked by counterweight or counterpoise. It was superior in that by adjusting the position of the weights on the pole relative to the pivotal point, it was possible to impart a greater degree of accuracy than was possible with the mangonel.

Unlike many other siege devices this was not it appears, a legacy of the Romans, but a completely new weapon. It seems to make its appearance towards the end of the twelfth century, and we see what is probably one, named Mal Voisin used by Philip Augustus at Acre. It is found in Italy *c.* 1199, and an especially large one, nicknamed Cabulus, was used by the French against Château-Gaillard in 1203–4. In the spring of 1217, Prince Louis procured a trebuchet 'about which there was much talk, for at that time few of them had been seen in France'. In spite of this interesting extract from the *Histoire des ducs de Normandie et des Rois d'Angleterre*, ed. F. Michel, Société de l'Histoire de France, Paris, 1840, p. 188, it is apparent that the weapon was being used with increasing frequency in the early thirteenth century. It played a prominent part in the sieges of the Albigensian Crusade, and it is perhaps significant that by 1228 we have the first known mention of the word *trubechetarius* or maker of trebuchets and siege-engines in general.

Although both mangonel and trebuchet were occasionally used to hurl incendiaries and perhaps even dead horses in the hope of spreading disease, they were essentially instruments of bombardment, and in this respect they differed from the third basic type of engine – *ballista* (sometimes called the *arbalist*) which was primarily an anti-personnel weapon. Like several other siege-devices, this had been used by the Romans in various forms, most notably the *carro-ballista* or spring gun (cf the *springald*, a name given to the ballista in the fourteenth century and after). In form it was rather like a gigantic crossbow, and though it could be adapted to project stones, like a crossbow its fundamental purpose was to shoot bolts. These bolts might well be made of iron and would be feathered with wood; when released they would achieve such momentum that they could skewer several individuals who were unlucky enough to be in alignment, as at Paris in the ninth century. The ballista was arguably of greater value in the defence of a castle than in the reduction of one: the bolts themselves were of little use against masonry and naturally a castle was designed so that its defenders were exposed as little as possible to its fire. Moreover, the ballista required comparatively little space in which to operate, and in this respect could the more readily be accommodated by the defences of a castle than the large petrarie.

The direct descendant of these engines was the cannon of the later Middle Ages, and indeed the word 'gun', from 'gonne', may be derived from mangonel, or the word 'gunners' from the professional 'gynours', such as those who worked Cabulus at Château-Gaillard. Contrary to general belief, the advent of gunpowder had little immediate effect on siege warfare. If we look at the illustration from the Walter de Milimetes manuscript, depicting the earliest known use of a cannon in England (in 1326), we may see how pathetic a challenge it offered a castle's defences. Indeed, if anything, cannon were as much of a danger to the users as to the enemy, as James II of Scotland discovered at the siege of Roxburgh in 1460 when he was killed by a gun which burst on firing. On occasion, guns could have seemingly devastating effects, as at Bamburgh in 1464 when King Edward's pieces so pounded the walls that chunks allegedly flew off into the sea. Yet even by this time there is not much to suggest that cannon were much more superior than petrarie. If by this point the castle was in decline, it was not because gunpowder had rendered it obsolete, but rather for more complex reasons altogether. The importance of castles in

Right The fourteenth-century drawbridge at the castle of Vitré on the frontier of Brittany in France.

the English Civil War of the seventeenth century and the trouble taken by Cromwell's men to slight so many argue that the castle still had some answers to even the more sophisticated cannon of post-medieval times.

Before passing on to other forms of attack, it is worth noting a common predilection for giving siege-engines nicknames. In a way this is a pity because we tend to find the same nicknames used for different devices; thus at Acre in 1191 'cat' seems to be the name given to both a movable shed and to a belfry, simply because both could be described as creeping up to the wall in the manner of a cat and sticking fast to it. 'Tortoise' or 'testudo' is more certainly a name applied to the movable shed, often, though not always, with a ram, while the 'mouse' seems to refer specifically to the bore. Stone-throwing engines are given a wider variety of pet names, such as Mal Voisin (Bad Neighbour) referred to above, as at Acre and at Dover in 1216, or Mal Cousin (Bad Kinsman) again as at Acre, or rather appealingly Warwolf as at Stirling in 1304. Cannon too received their individual names: at Bamburgh in 1464 we hear of the King's guns Newcastle, London, Dysion and others, and of course all visitors to Edinburgh castle know of Mons Meg which is of fifteenth-century origin.

In discussing the various machines of siege warfare there is an inevitable tendency to relegate the ordinary soldier with his personal arms to obscurity. This would most certainly be foolish as the records show incontrovertibly that he played a leading role. For a major siege such as Bedford or Kenilworth, tens of thousands of quarrels (crossbow bolts) along with arrows would be procured and expended in spite of the presence of a formidable array of engines. The archers would position themselves behind hurdles, otherwise called mâtlets, which were also acquired in abundance, and attempt to pick off those manning the battlements or less frequently would rain their fire from the top floors of a belfry. In the early Middle Ages, the crossbow was much preferred to the bow when attacking a castle in this way. Occasionally even a king would condescend to use one, as with Philip Augustus at Acre:

Neath the testudo oft would go
The king himself with his crossbow
(*Ambroise*, op. cit., p. 203, lines 4819–20.)

But like the ballista from which it developed, the crossbow was more effectively used in defence than in attack. Requiring less operating space than bow or longbow it was the favoured hand weapon for defence throughout medieval times.

Incendiaries

As with the large engines, crossbows could be adapted to fire incendiaries against castles as can be seen from the German Firework Books of the later Middle Ages. Mention has already been made of the most famous incendiary of all: Greek fire. This was very much the secret weapon of the period, shrouded in mystery as indeed it still is. Crude oil, refined oil, naphtha, pitch, resin, sulphur, quicklime, bitumen have all been suggested as ingredients, but what is certain is that it was highly inflammable and that water alone was insufficient to extinguish it. It is thought that it was developed in the seventh century by the Byzantines who used it primarily in naval warfare. Michael Psellus and Anna Comnena relate how Byzantine fleets were able to dispose of Russian and Pisan enemies in the tenth century, principally by use of Greek fire. It could also be used on land, however, as we saw at Dyrrachium. Before long the Crusaders became conversant

with it, and this most likely explains its appearance in the West, first at the siege of Montreuil-Bellay in 1151 and then at Nottingham in 1194. Generally speaking, the mixture would be placed in some appropriate receptacle, and then hurled at the objective, igniting on impact. It had a devastating effect on timber constructions, such as siege-engines, and thus was probably more profitably used in defence of stone castles than against them. Equally it might have a tremendous influence on morale for it certainly impressed those who saw it. Listen to the words of the lord of Joinville:

This Greek fire was such that seen from the front as it darted towards us it appeared as large as a vessel of verjuice, and the tail of the fire that streamed behind it was as long as the shaft of a great lance. The noise it made in coming was like that of a thunderbolt falling from the skies; it seemed like a dragon flying through the air. The light this huge, flaming mass shed all around it was so bright that you could see right through the camp as clearly as if it were day. Three times that night the enemy slung Greek fire at us from their petraries, and three times they shot it from their arbalestres à tour.
(*The Life of Saint Louis by Joinville*, trans. by M.R.B. Shaw, Penguin Books Ltd., 1963, p. 216.)

The siege-castle

We began this section by emphasizing that the role of the castle was fundamentally offensive in nature. The potential or actual threat posed by a rival's castle might prompt a lord to construct a new stronghold by way of a counter. In 1165 King Henry II of England began to build a new castle at Orford in Suffolk which, as R. Allen Brown (in *Orford Castle*, HMSO, London, 1964, pp. 6–8) points out, was part of the king's attempt to wrest the military control of East Anglia from the great magnates of the area. It is but a short step from this strategy to the building of a siege-castle, close to an invested fortress, from which the attacking forces could launch raids and dominate the roads and surrounding area so as to prevent victuals from reaching the castle. The history of the Crusader States contain good examples of these monumental siege-works, and we can identify instances in the sieges of English castles. Thus in 1139, King Stephen marched against William de Mohun in Dunster Castle.

Left The main gateway, with two portcullises, at Hever Castle near Edenbridge, in Kent.

Above Here at Saône in Outremer (now Syria), the gateway and the adjacent eastern curtain were defended by a ninety-foot-deep channel which had been hewn from the rock. Opposite the gate, the Crusaders left a slender needle of solid stone to support their bridge which spanned the sixty feet across.

Left Caerphilly (Mid Glamorgan) was begun in 1271 by Gilbert de Clare, Earl of Gloucester and Hertford. In 1266, he had been present at the siege of Kenilworth, and it seems very possible that this inspired certain features of Caerphilly, most obviously its broad water defences.

Three kinds of spurs
(*right*) Dover, Kent
(*below*) Goodrich,
Herefordshire
(*bottom*) Chepstow,
Gwent.

When he saw the unconquerable fortifications of the place, [...] he entirely despaired of a siege, and taking better advice he fortified a castle before the very eyes of the enemy, whence he might keep them more sternly in check, and at the same time possess more securely the surrounding district.

(*Gesta Stephani*, ed. and trans. by
K.R. Potter, Oxford, 1976, pp. 81–3.)

At Huntingdom it is still possible to detect the remains of the motte-and-bailey siege-castle of 1174. As we might expect, it was built opposite the principal gate of Huntingdon Castle just out of arrow range in order to be best placed to impede the egress of the besieged.

The castle's defences

Of course the gateway was always a potential weak spot in the defences of castles and as a result was frequently the particular objective of an assault. When King Louis' men arrived at Le Puiset in 1111, their first thought was to destroy the castle's gate, and we see the same happening at Dover in 1216 when Prince Louis' army focused its attention on King John's main gate and its barbican at the northern apex of the outer bailey wall. It is not surprising, then, to find that gates became increasingly elaborate in design and sophisticated in concept. Nowhere perhaps is this more apparent than in England, though obviously there are many European gates well worthy of our attention. We can trace their development from the relatively simply beginnings discernible in the Bayeux Tapestry (though note that even here the provision of such devices as the flying bridge (ie one linking motte and bailey) suggests that the approaches to gates were rarely ever without some special form of protection) to the gate encased in a single tower as at Exeter, or in the side of a tower to make two right-angled turns as is common in Outremer, to the splendours of the Edwardian castles of north Wales. In such places as Harlech

Left Founded in 1066, Dover is one of the earliest of English castles. Its present appearance is mainly the result of building between 1168 and 1256.

Carcassone or it might be highly irregular in shape in order to exploit fully the lie of the land as at Scarborough, Yorkshire. A slightly different arrangement exists at Caen in Normandy where access to the gateways is obstructed by small forts bound with their own round towers and connected to the gateway complexes by drawbridges. At Caen too we can see a large hornwork (an earthen spur), which, complete with its own ditches, provided substantial protection in time of siege. As we would expect, such works were often laid out immediately in front of gateways. In Wales for instance there is no better example than that opposite the west gate of Caerphilly, very possibly based on the inspiration of the similar hornwork, known as the Brays at Kenilworth, Warwickshire. These earthworks were, like other features of a castle, offensive as well as defensive in nature, and this is most readily appreciated at Dover, where the spur was linked to the rest of the castle by an underground passage which terminated in a three-pronged fork permitting the defenders of the castle to launch surprise sorties, possibly in the rear of a besieging force.

The royal castle of Dover, Matthew Paris's 'key of England', is in many respects a first-class example of a superbly strong castle. With walls up to 21 feet thick, its keep could have resisted bombardment for a very long time. Here, of course, as in so many castles, lay the principal point of the defence: the keep was the strongest single part of the castle and at the same time the final refuge when all else was lost. Like many other donjons and towers, the keep at Dover stands on its own plinth, which with similar constructions known as the 'batter', 'spur' and 'talus', was some guard against bore or ram and was perhaps used by defenders as a means of ricocheting missiles dropped from above into the ranks of adversaries. Possibly the most magnificent of such works is the great talus on the south side of Krak des Chevaliers, the castle once called the 'key of Christendom'. One can only feel sorry for the Sultan in 1271 when, having taken the *burgus* (the walled suburb), then the triangular outwork and finally the outer curtain, he was confronted by the three great towers with their talus behind the gulf, certainly one of the most formidable pieces of medieval military architecture anywhere. Little wonder that, as we saw, he resorted to subterfuge. Returning to Dover, however, we have 'the first known castle in Western Europe to employ concentric lines of fortification, one within the other.' (R. Allen Brown, *Dover Castle*, HMSO, London, 1974, p. 13.) Its curtain walls are studded with mural towers – a great asset in any defence, for by thrusting out beyond and above the wall, they provided platforms from which enfilading fire could sweep the areas before the walls, and furthermore divided the curtain into sections that could be isolated if any fell. At Dover we find that the rectangular towers of the inner bailey and eastern outer bailey are of twelfth-century origin while the semi-circular ones of the western outer curtain derive from the next century. This is a pattern of development which is fairly representative of an increasing preference for rounded towers. We are generally told that this was because such towers had no sharp angles and were hence less prone to bombardment, the bore and the ram, and that they possessed a better field of fire. All this may be true, but only to a rather limited extent, for if we think about these things it seems dangerous to conclude that the round tower, or for that matter the round keep, was so very superior to the rectangular one. It may be argued that fashion, as much as military expediency, dictated

and Beaumaris, and in the contemporary works of the nobility (Caerphilly, Tonbridge and Dunstanburgh), we see the total conversion of what may once have been the weakest point of a castle into what was certainly its strongest point. Gateways became complexes of doorways, portcullises and drawbridges or turning bridges (*pontem torneicium*). Sometimes they were designed to include right-angled turns and were covered along their length by loopholes, spy-holes and *meurtrières*, or murder-holes, which in spite of their sinister name were probably used more to douse burning doors than kill assailants. As if this was not enough, the gateway was then given its main strength in its close-fitting flanking towers which projected outward to the field. An outstanding example of the fully developed gateway may be seen in the King's Gate at Caernarvon, of which it has been said that 'Nowhere in Britain were the safeguards of a castle entrance so highly developed.' (*The History of the King's Works*, ed. H.M. Colvin, HMSO, London, 1963, pp. 390–1.) Lying behind the north moat of the castle, it was planned so as to include two drawbridges, five great doors and six portcullises, numerous loopholes, spy-holes and murder-holes, and a right-angled turn, all within the stout protection of adjacent polygonal towers with their own offensive capabilities. All that is missing from this royal entrance still used today, as at the Investiture of H.R.H. the Prince of Wales, is a barbican or a fortified outwork, though in a sense the King's Gate did possess such extra protection in the borough walls which surrounded it.

As often as not the barbican constituted two parallel walls projecting outward from the gate, with their own battlements or crenellations, ending in a further gateway as at Warwick for example. Quite apart from its obvious purpose of further strengthening the main gateway to its rear, it could also be used in much the same way as a flanking tower – as a projecting elevation from which to offer the adjacent wall enfilading fire. Its design might be quite complex as at

the proliferation from around 1200 of semi-circular towers as in the south curtain wall at Corfe or of horse-shoe towers as at Ilan and elsewhere in Turkish Armenia, of towers *en bec* as at Loches or the Norfolk Towers and FitzWilliam Gateway at Dover, and of drum towers and polygonal towers as in Edward I's works in Wales.

At the same time we find an ever increasing use being made of various refinements that enabled the defenders to do their job more efficiently while simultaneously remaining unexposed. On both tower and wall we see the straightforward crenellated wall-walk supplemented by well sited loopholes pierced through the merlons. Sometimes embrasures were sunk right through the thickness of the wall as at Til Hamdoun in Armenia or at Krak des Chevaliers; even more splendidly, passageways with their own embrasures and loops might be built within the wall beneath the wall-walk as at Caernarvon. Timber hoarding, sometimes called 'brattice work', and stone machicolation also served to give defenders almost total protection while going about their business of dropping projectiles through the openings between the supporting corbels. In addition to this, we may argue that emplacements were specially constructed to accommodate a castle's own engines. This is perhaps reflected in names such as Gunners' Walk at Beaumaris, and the Engine Tower at Criccieth which in 1343 is recorded as possessing its own springald. At Harlech, platforms were cut into the castle rock, probably for engines and it is held (by R. Fedden and J. Thomson, *Crusader Castles*, London, 1957, p. 66) that at Krak des Chevaliers there are embrasures especially for ballista. Generally, though, it was unnecessary to make such provision in a castle's plan, as engines could always be placed within the enceinte, and from the later twelfth century it may well be that keeps and towers were given flat roofs of lead which served as convenient platforms. An early instance of this is the siege of Daron in 1191 when King Richard's Crusaders were particularly troubled by a mangonel which the Moslems had set up on their great tower. Of course, there was always a chance that the vibrations of stone-throwing engines would damage the masonry, and this was a problem that became more acute with the introduction of cannon into a castle's defence system. Still, by the time cannon came to dominate warfare, the life of the castle had just about run its course, so it is hardly surprising to find that generally little more than the occasional gunport, as at Bonaguil in France, or as at Raglan, bears witness to this weapon's influence on the defences of castles.

Of all the architectural features of a castle, nothing symbolizes its potential for an active defence more than the postern gate or sally port. From these often discreetly located exits, the mounted contingent of a castle's garrison could issue forth and deliver a surprise, and hence possibly devastating, attack on a besieging force. From here it is but a little way back to our starting point of the castle's fundamental role of offence. As was pointed out in the Introduction, this may be seen on a lavish scale in the Welsh marches or in grand style in the Edwardian castles of north Wales. In England we might note Leicester Castle which in 1174 was used by the king's enemies as a base for raids on Nottingham and Northampton, or Bedford Castle from which Fawkes de Bréauté *exploited* the surrounding country for nine years. Fawkes, it appears, was so confident in the strength of his position that in 1224 he went so far as to order his men to capture the royal justices who had

met in Dunstable in order to fine him for his depredations. Forewarned, most of the justices escaped, but one of their number – Henry de Braibroc – was taken and incarcerated in the castle. This was the last straw for King Henry III who accordingly resolved to reduce Fawkes's power base by whatever means he could. A large portion of the kingdom's military resources was concentrated around Bedford and the siege pressed with the utmost vigour. Fawkes's confidence was not entirely misplaced, however, for it took two full months before his castle finally succumbed to this formidable opposition.

The siege of Kenilworth

Forty years after the fall of Bedford, King Henry was at war with a substantial part of his nobility under the leadership of Simon de Montfort, Earl of Leicester. Simon was killed and his army broken at Evesham in August 1265, but up and down the kingdom the rebellion persisted. Many who remained disaffected to the king rallied in the castle of Kenilworth, and from there totally dominated a very extensive area round about. The local sheriff, for example, was unable to hold county courts for over a year and a half because he was impeded by 'those who were in the castle of Kenilworth' (*Exchequer Plea Roll* I e.

Far left The keep at Dover Castle (Kent) was built by Henry II in the 1180s. It reaches a height of 95 feet and measures 98 feet by 96 feet above the plinth.
Left Krak des Chevaliers (Syria): the gulf, talus and towers on the south side of the inner curtain.
Below The great round drum towers of Edward I's castle at Harlech, in Gwynedd, Wales, viewed from the south. Begun in 1283, it was largely completed by 1290 and successfully withstood a siege during the Welsh revolt of 1294–5. On the west were the platforms cut in the rock for *petrarie*.

m. 23, Public Record Office), and in the Patent Rolls we hear how the men of the castle 'do not cease to make assaults, invasions, depredations, burnings, homicides, and other grievous offences, in throwing down, burning and devastating the castles and dwellings of the king's faithful subjects' (*Calendar of Patent Rolls* 1258–1266, HMSO, London, 1910, pp. 654–5). Obviously the king could not tolerate such open defiance indefinitely, and so in November 1265 began to organize the means with which to eliminate this thorn in his side. Writs were sent off ordering the sheriff of Warwick and all the tenants in chief of the Crown to muster at Northampton for St Lucy's Day (13 December) prior to marching on Kenilworth. The country, however, was still in a state of war; rebellion was still to be suppressed elsewhere and many of those loyal to the king had fulfilled their feudal obligations already. Consequently little came of this initial summons, and similarly a subsequent attempt to concentrate the strength of the shires at Northampton for St Hilary's Day (13 January) proved just as unproductive. Local forces under captains like Osbert Giffard did their best to contain the situation, but they proved utterly unequal to the task; the rebels continued to make mounted expeditions into the surrounding countryside, frequently at-

Right Timber hoarding and stone machicolation served much the same purpose. They involved a parapet which projected beyond the wall below so that stones and other missiles could be dropped through openings between the supporting corbels.

tacking any royalist contingent that ventured too close to the castle. Not surprisingly, King Henry tried other tactics: we are told that he brought earl Simon's son, young Simon, before the castle to request the garrison to relinquish the stronghold, though this ploy failed. A little later, in March, a royal messenger was sent into the castle to speak with the rebels who cut off his hand by way of a reply to the King. This was as tactless as Fawkes's treatment of Braibroc for it served nothing other than to intensify Henry's resolve. Further summonses were issued, and eventually a full siege was mounted in late June.

The siege of Kenilworth is a classic, yet unsung, case of the castle in defence and attack, so we can conclude this section in no better manner than by attempting some examination of it. In one respect it was rather peculiar in that the numerical strength of the garrison was abnormally large: one of our best informed sources claims that it was as many as 1,200 men, not to mention 53 ladies, girls and handmaidens. This, however, was only an asset as long as provisions were plentiful. What mattered more was the extraordinary strength of the place itself, for in 1266 Kenilworth was undoubtedly one of the two or three most heavily defended castles in the British Isles. To the south and west lay the Mere – a great artificial lake ponded back by the fortified causeway, now called the Tiltyard from the jousting that took place there in later times. The Tiltyard itself also served to connect the main gate with the complex earthworks of the Brays to the south, binding the two together, as it were, to give Kenilworth a main entry point fit to rival any other castle's. A large pond guarded the south-east perimeter while the north-east corner was skirted by its own ditch which very likely contained a moat. Within this ring of earth and water lay the outer curtain wall, complete with mural towers on the comparatively vulnerable north and north-east sides, and this in turn surrounded the inner curtain, giving us, as at Dover, an example of an early concentric castle based on the core of a stolid late twelfth-century keep. Well might the rebels feel confident in their ability to withstand even King Henry's forces, variously described as 'innumerable' (*de Antiquis Legibus Liber. Cronica – Maiorum et Vicecomitum Londoniarum*, ed. T. Stapleton, Camden Soc., London, 1846, p 87) and as 'a mighty host from all England'. (*Brut y Tywysogyon – Peniarth*, MS 20 version, ed. and trans. by T. Jones, Board of Celtic Studies, University of Wales, History and Law Series II, Cardiff, 1952, p 114).

The Dunstable Annalist ('Annales Prioratus de Dunstaplia', in *Annales Monastici* vol. III, ed. H.R. Luard, Rolls Series, London, 1886) tells us that the king's army set up its tents about the castle in four divisions: Henry personally commanded one and assigned the others to his sons Edward and Edmund, and the fourth to Roger Mortimer. Nine petriarie were set in position around the north-eastern quadrant, and working incessantly day and night, succeeded in causing some damage to the walls and towers, though more especially to domestic buildings which were not specifically constructed to resist bombardment. While this 'softening-up' process was in progress, the king procured two belfries with which to assault the walls. One of these was prepared by Edmund, and it is described as a lofty and broad wooden structure containing 200 crossbowmen and archers. A second one 'which was called the bear *(ursus)* because of its size' (*Chronicon (de bellis Lewes et Evesham) – William de Rishanger*, ed. J.O. Halliwell, Camden 1st series, vol 15, 1840, p 56) contained separate compartments

also housing crossbowmen and archers. It seems that neither of these two great edifices ever even reached the wall, for both were bombarded and ultimately destroyed by the castle's own petriarie. These were also used against the stone-throwing engines of the besieging forces some of which were certainly damaged in consequence. The king, however, was able to order spare parts and wholly new machines to supplement and replace those already in action, and so the artillery fire continued unabated, the hurtling stones frequently meeting and shattering in mid-air, until eventually all Kenilworth's engines had been knocked out. This, however, does not seem to have occurred until the siege was quite well advanced by which time another plan of attack had been devised. This, as the *Chronicon*... relates, involved obtaining barges from Chester to use to attack the castle across the Mere. In one respect this was quite intelligent, for the outer curtain by the lake had never been given much strength in that it was entirely without mural towers. Furthermore, such a plan was certainly feasible as was proved in 1097 when the Emperor Alexius of Byzantium made a waterborne attack on Nicaea with boats that had been dragged by oxen 'over the mountains and through the woods until they reached the lake' (*Gesta*

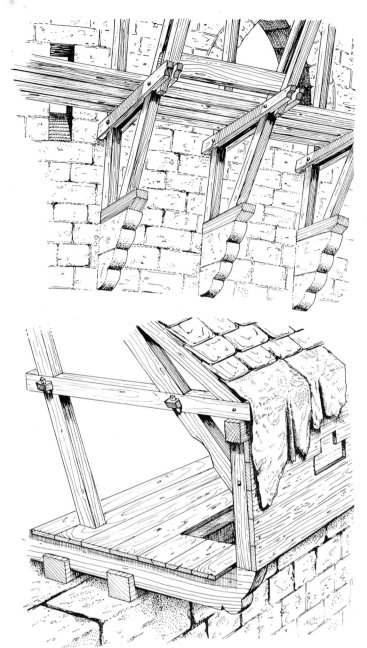

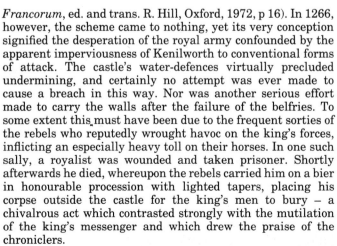

Below The remarkable keep at Raglan (Gwent) complete with gunports and in the background the machicolated, polygonal flanking towers of the main gate.

Francorum, ed. and trans. R. Hill, Oxford, 1972, p 16). In 1266, however, the scheme came to nothing, yet its very conception signified the desperation of the royal army confounded by the apparent imperviousness of Kenilworth to conventional forms of attack. The castle's water-defences virtually precluded undermining, and certainly no attempt was ever made to cause a breach in this way. Nor was another serious effort made to carry the walls after the failure of the belfries. To some extent this must have been due to the frequent sorties of the rebels who reputedly wrought havoc on the king's forces, inflicting an especially heavy toll on their horses. In one such sally, a royalist was wounded and taken prisoner. Shortly afterwards he died, whereupon the rebels carried him on a bier in honourable procession with lighted tapers, placing his corpse outside the castle for the king's men to bury – a chivalrous act which contrasted strongly with the mutilation of the king's messenger and which drew the praise of the chroniclers.

King Henry had vowed to maintain the siege until he had reduced the castle, but he found he was having to spend too much time and money in the process. Moreover he was beset with other problems, including bickering nobles, a very

depleted Treasury, trouble from the Welsh, and from August, a new and highly dangerous concentration of rebels under John d'Eyvill in the Isle of Ely. Consequently he attempted to negotiate, initially in July through the mediums of the Archbishop of Canterbury and the visiting papal legate. When the rebels refused the king's terms, the two senior churchmen solemnly excommunicated them, just as had happened at Bedford. Completely unperturbed, the rebels called for their surgeon, a Master Philip Porpeis who was by all accounts quite a character, and dressed him up to imitate the legate.

> *And he stood like the legate upon the castle wall*
> *And excommunicated the king and legate and their*
> *men all*

> (*Robert of Gloucester*, Part II, ed.
> W.A. Wright, Rolls Series, London,
> 1887, p 772, lines 11928–9.)

A further attempt to define the position of the rebels was made with the issue of the Dictum of Kenilworth on the 31 October. This laid down a procedure by which the rebels could redeem their confiscated estates and added that anyone not coming into the king's peace within 40 days would not afterwards be allowed the terms offered by the ordinance. Henry permitted the garrison and their comrades from Ely to confer over this, and about the same time there was an exchange of prisoners. In the end, however, both parties of rebels rejected the Dictum and prepared to continue the resistance. By this date, though, both sides seemed to be showing signs of weariness. Outside Kenilworth, the royalists appear to have contented themselves with a blockade, realizing of course that the rebels must be running short of victuals. Within the castle, the men were reduced to eating their horses, and with the worst of winter approaching were badly in need of firewood which was in very short supply. Early in November, a truce of 40 days was arranged, and three knights were given leave to go and see if they could obtain help, providing that, if they failed, the castle would surrender on terms at the expiry of the allotted time. Clearly, though, the rebels had no illusions of relief, for in the event they capitulated before the envoys returned and on or about 14 December, with only two days' supply of food remaining, they marched out, overcome as they were by hunger and disease.

The siege of Kenilworth leaves us in no doubt of the supremacy of defence over attack, for the castle was not taken but rather had been yielded up on certain conditions, and then only after it had successfully resisted a phenomenal concentration of military resources for some six months. A detailed study of the Chancery records shows just how great this concentration was: two of the king's engines were sent from Somerset and Devon by water to Worcester and thence to Kenilworth; more engines, including one of the belfries, were sent from Gloucester, and yet more again from London and Worcester. Local workmen and 24 carpenters from London were summoned to maintain these and more specifically assemble others from parts that also came from far afield: iron from Gloucester, horsehair from Oxfordshire and Berkshire, hemp, cords, and cables from Bridport, timber from Bedfordshire and the Forest of Dean. Further to the north, the Constable of Nottingham castle provided 'one *balistam de trullio* and four *balistas ad duas* pedes of the king's baliste' (*Cal. Pat. Rolls*, 1258–1266, p 632), while the bailiffs of Lincoln sent no less than 30,000 crossbow bolts, as did the sheriff of London. In the west, the constable of St Briavels

Castle dispatched his stock of 4,000 quarnels and shortly after was ordered to have his men work day and night to produce a further 6,000 specifically for the two foot crossbows, while from Surrey and Sussex came 300 sheaves (*glanetas*) of well prepared arrows. Of especial interest are the 2,500 hurdles ordered from the sheriffs of Oxford, Worcester and Northampton. These ranged in size from eight feet long by seven feet wide to ten feet by eight, and are described as 'thick and close-wattled' (*densas et spissas*) (*Calendar of Liberate Rolls*, vol V, 1260–1267, HMSO, London, p. 226). The need for so much protective fencing argues that the men within the castle were well equipped with their own crossbows and bows, and indeed at least one narrative source speaks of an incessant exchange of crossbow bolts. But of course these munitions were only a part of the king's logistics service which was also responsible for the procurement and supply of the foodstuffs required by his forces. Again this is reflected by the records which show vast amounts of wine and venison, oxen, porkers, wheat, corn, oats, and malt for beer, and salt and herrings transported to the siege from diverse parts of the realm. Here, of course, lay much of the expense of siege warfare, for generally speaking, all these supplies and their carriage had to be paid for, from allowing credits to the sheriffs against their dues to the Exchequer, to the simple payment of individuals like John de la Linde who received 13*s.* 4*d.* for carrying a whale to the King at Kenilworth.

The exact cost of the siege would be very hard to compute, but it is clear that it was largely instrumental in straining the Exchequer's resources to breaking point. In all his long reign, King Henry had known only one marginally worse financial year, and that was 1264 when the country was in the hands of his arch enemy, the Earl of Leicester. Why then had the King felt so constrained to persist at Kenilworth in spite of the knowledge that it was ruining him? It was simply because he knew that while the rebels retained their base they would continue to dominate much of Warwickshire and at the same time inspire disaffection elsewhere in the realm. Further, by openly disdaining the king's authority, the disinherited rebels rejected his lordship and cast aspersions on his Crown, a symbolism no king could ignore. Rather similar considerations lay behind many sieges in every country where society was feudalized, but in Britain at least, probably no other single castle ever stood for so much or was ever so much trouble to a monarch as Kenilworth.

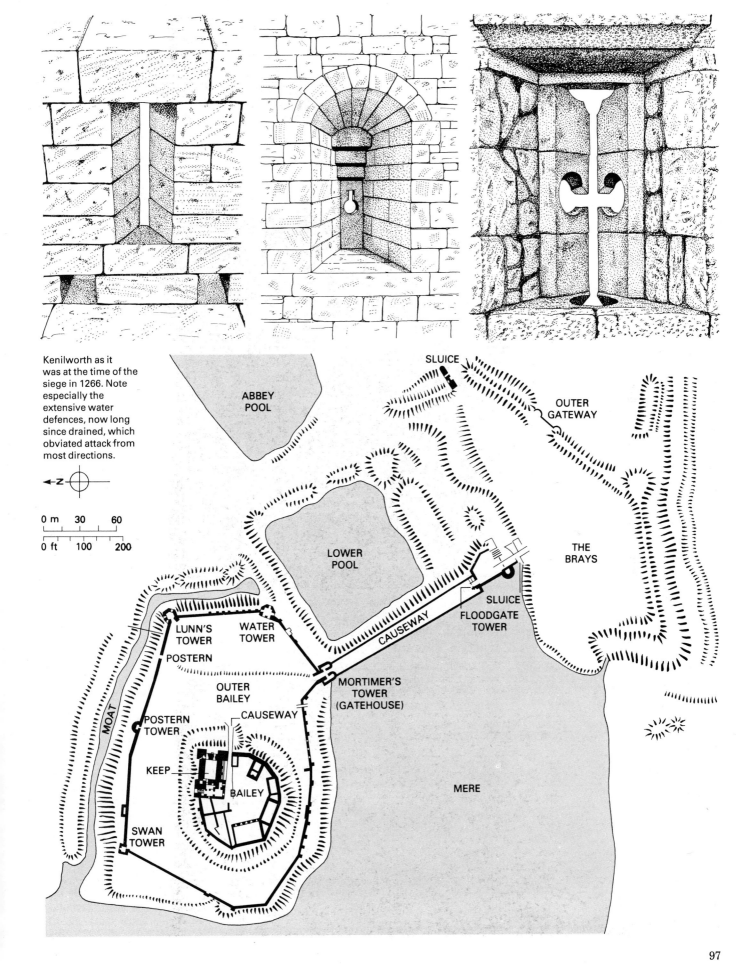

Kenilworth as it was at the time of the siege in 1266. Note especially the extensive water defences, now long since drained, which obviated attack from most directions.

ABBEY POOL

SLUICE

OUTER GATEWAY

THE BRAYS

LOWER POOL

LUNN'S TOWER

WATER TOWER

POSTERN

CAUSEWAY

SLUICE

FLOODGATE TOWER

MORTIMER'S TOWER (GATEHOUSE)

OUTER BAILEY

MOAT

POSTERN TOWER

CAUSEWAY

KEEP

BAILEY

SWAN TOWER

MERE

0 m   30   60

0 ft   100   200

3

Residence

Castles were not just fortresses but also residences, albeit the residences of the great. It is this unique combination of the military and the residential functions which makes a castle, and makes it differ from other types of fortification of other periods, earlier or later, and from the contemporary fortified towns and cities of the Middle Ages. The residential role of the castle was at least as important as the military, and may do much to explain, for example, its siting or its internal arrangements and the buildings within it. Nor shall we find within it any barracks or separate accommodation for a separate soldiery or garrison, for in this society the lords and their households who occupied the castles would also defend them or operate from them in time of war. What we should find – though now vanished or ruined or at least stripped of all rich furnishings and colours – is accommodation as sumptuous as the age and personal resources could make it: halls and chapels (it may be more than one of each) and a multiplicity of chambers, for the several households of the lord, his lady and their guests; together with all the necessary appurtenances of a self-sufficient medieval stately home – gardens, parks, vineyards, dovecotes, fishponds, mills and stables.

Because castles were also the residences of a ruling class which ruled, we should expect to find them integrated with the local community, whether of town or countryside, of which they were the centres. Not for nothing did their architecture deliberately express the concept of territorial lordship, for they were its focal point, not only socially or for the rendering of rents and services but also as the headquarters of local government, whether royal through royal officials or seigneurial through the constables and stewards of some other lord.

Herstmonceux in Sussex (built *c.* 1440) was never heavily fortified and thus reveals more than usual of the fundamental residential role of the castle.

Castle & Community

'Community' means the entire population of a distinct region and period considered as an interdependent whole. Industrialized societies in modern Europe are notably homogeneous and integrated; differences of wealth, occupation and life-style being insignificant compared with what is general and universal. We take this as obvious and natural often forgetting what a recent phenomenon it is in the whole space of human history. Castles were produced by a society very different from our own: a society closer to the eighteenth century in so many ways than to ours. Medieval society was divided into segregated classes (the 'estates of the realm') though more or less held together by common allegiance to a ruler and lord, and by deference to a common religious code. Who you were (nobleman, ecclesiastic, townsman, peasant) depended essentially on your family. Status and occupation were inherited not chosen, as a rule. A non-noble ('gentility' was the great social divide) might receive knighthood for military valour. The profession of arms was an ennobling vocation (M.H. Keen, *The Laws of War in the Late Middle Ages*, London, 1965, pp 254–7). A serf might be freed, leave the land and become a citizen of a borough as a craftsman or trader. He might even obtain education and enter the Church as a priest or a monk (with his lord's permission). But the vast majority of people were fixed for life in the social rank and function (and frequently also the place) in which they had been born. By birth nobles had rule and dominion as leaders of their men in peace and in war. They constituted a tiny minority of the population and formed an increasingly exclusive caste whose especial function, by the medieval concept of society, was to defend the community as a whole. Their seals depict them mounted on horseback, fully armed and riding sword upraised, or charging with couched lance in the forefront of the battle. Castles were their homes, grand or modest according to their wealth but always centres of lordship and seigneurial administration, places of pride and prestige and occasionally also of warlike cavalcade and sortie, or, in adversity, of secure refuge from a more powerful enemy. Crenellation and portcullis, towers and archery-slits denoted a noble residence and formed the environment of courtly and aristocratic life. Castles were essential to the noble minority in an abundance of ways, but the chivalric aspects of the lordly fortress appeared very differently and had little appeal to the 'common people' of the countryside and to the labouring poor of the towns. It is with them that we are mainly concerned.

Castles and the common people

The Church was much affected by the aristocratic cult of castellation. Conventual and secular buildings were often embellished with battlements and almost all higher ecclesiastics (bishops, archdeacons, abbots, priors) were themselves younger sons of the nobility. Cathedral and monastic precincts obviously needed walls to set them apart from the life of the laity. The segregation of the clergy from the commons or 'third estate' arose from their spiritual functions and was entrenched in canon law and in the Monastic Rule. Precinct walls both expressed this seclusion and made it effective in very much the same fashion as, for instance, did the enclosure of walls and towers around the earl of Huntingdon's castle of Maxstoke in Warwickshire, built early in the reign of Edward III. As a celibate order the 'first estate' recuited its manpower from both nobility and commonalty. But the ethos of the medieval Church was predominantly aristocratic. Bishops ranked as barons, counts (earls) and dukes (a rank held by some

archbishops, eg of Reims and Narbonne). Castles, castellated manor-houses and city episcopal palaces were part of their landed possessions or 'temporalities'. Naturally enough the abbots and priors of monasteries, together with the chapters of Cathedral communities, copied the ways of other prelates and nobles by crenellating their bell-towers and houses. Walls and gatehouses of precincts and ecclesiastical buildings of all kinds were castellated, whether for defence or for display as local conditions might require. Most often the cause was a combination of both motives. All such structures had some of the seigneurial attributes of the castle, and a few were defensible enough as well to be fully-fledged fortresses. Tynemouth Priory in Northumberland and Albi Cathedral in the south of France are examples. At all levels of defensibility, however, ecclesiastical fortifications compare closely with their lay counterparts (eg gatehouses: see M.E. Wood, *The English Medieval House*, London, 1965, pp 155–65). And in using castles to enforce lordship, defend fiefs and rights and to proclaim their noble status (by rank or by blood) the princes of the Church stood shoulder to shoulder with the lay aristocracy. It was not for nothing that in the English great councils of the Crown, the Parliaments, Lords spiritual and temporal sat

Left Maxstoke Castle (Warwickshire); aerial view from the north-east. Within the courtyard the medieval hall and other buildings of the house (now entirely gone) of William de Clinton, Earl of Huntingdon, had a peaceful and domestic character seemingly belied by the martial display of walls, towers and great gatehouse.

Below Equestrian seal of Henry de Percy, Lord of Leconfield, Topcliffe (Yorkshire) and Petworth (Sussex), who died in 1314. (From the original letter patent in the Public Record Office.)

Above Gatehouse, curtain wall and angle tower of Maxstoke Castle which was built following a royal licence to crenellate issued in 1345.

together in the upper house. Together they mustered only a small and select minority of the medieval community. Severe though the conditions were by which they enjoyed their privileges of wealth and power under the Crown, a yawning gulf still separated them from the labouring majority on whose work depended almost solely the economic viability of the entire community. The poor have left few records of their own in the nature of things.

Castles are such conspicuous and characteristic monuments of aristocratic activity, in war and in peace, that their impact on the rest of society can easily be neglected. Since they were both instrument and symbol of lordship to the ruling class who possessed them, castles were conversely reminders of inferior status to the commons. William the Conqueror and the Normans brought castles in large numbers to England (probably in excess of a thousand in all). The verdict on his life given by the Anglo-Saxon Chronicle was written from a different standpoint: 'He had castles built and poor men hard oppressed' (D.C. Douglas, *William the Conqueror*, London, 1964, p 373). It is a familiar theme repeated in more detail and with lurid elaboration in the Chronicle's well-known description of the Anarchy in the reign of Stephen (1135–54). In both

the castle is the associate in crime and the instrument of cruel oppression. Their lord's castle, as it might be, crowning the height overlooking the village (such sites are rare in England) and dominating the pasture and ploughland of the valley, constantly affirmed the villagers' subordination and their duties of labour, obedience or simple deference to the lord. Rents in cash or in the form of produce were paid at the castle. The lord's manorial court was normally held there and frequently near by stood the lord's gallows, stocks and pillory by which as a *seigneur haut justicier* he, or his representative, under the authority of the ruler, executed on offenders punishment for crimes. In case of rebellion the castle walls protected the lord and his household administrative staff of clerks and others until help could arrive. Noble tenants were closely bound by ties of personal fealty to aid their lord in arms on his summons. Peasants and commoners were in a collective relationship with the lord rather than a personal one. But the castle also existed for their benefit. If there was invasion and war the peasantry sought shelter with their cattle, movable possessions, harvested crops and fodder within the castle walls. As the peasant husbanded his fields so the lord husbanded him, for on peasant labour ultimately depended the

reciprocal and not unjustly balanced as a result.

Labouring on the castle

Let us take two examples from France, one concerning such a rural castellary as we have just described, and the second a small township attached to a castle. The first is from a document dated 1215 (*Recueil des Actes de Philippe Auguste*, III, Paris, 1966, no. 1359). Robert de Courtenay, Lord of Nonancourt (south-east of Normandy), drew up a statement of the position as it was between himself and his men of the lordship. It has some special features which are of interest to us in that the administrative centre was a castle, not an unfortified manor-house. On summons by the lord and 'when it shall be reasonably necessary' the men must carry wood to the castle of Nonancourt for repairing the lord's lodgings and also the timber defensive barriers outside the walls. This necessity would evidently be mutually agreed. In wartime, 'they shall bring their harvested crops into the castle so as to stock it and provide their food'. Danger of a kind to compel the community to take refuge within the castle would not be hard to define. Co-operation is of the essence. At the castle of Tournan, near Paris, agreement between lord and community is still basic but the position differed in that the dependants of Anseau de Gallande, a lordling of the Ile de France, were organized in a township (or *burgus*), as we have mentioned, which had its own walls to protect them. Evidently, though, some of the men lived in the open country, not within the town. In our second example, the following are their reciprocal obligations as laid down in a charter of 1193 (*Layettes du Trésor des Chartes*, I, Paris, 1863, no. 410). To the lord is due a hearth tax (a normal house had one fireplace only); recourse to his court for civil litigation and criminal trials, as the court of first instance; and certain fines are payable to the lord for various minor infractions. Labour services are also stipulated, in particular declares Anseau: 'Once a year, if I decide to strengthen my castle of Tournan, those who are of the lordship shall help me for one week with whatever cart each man may have'. Men too poor to possess a cart and team (at this period probably still of oxen, not horses) shall labour personally or provide a substitute. To keep the town gates and bridge in repair is the men's duty but Anseau undertakes to provide the timber which his men must carry to Tournan 'from as far away as Paris, or beyond, if necessary'. They must also guard and defend the town and escort their lord at his expense, in arms, when required. Such arrangements are far from one-sided. Each man exactly knowing his role, people of different classes consorted readily though without any equality. Anseau de Gallande even promised that whenever a new lord inherited the fief in future, the incoming heir must first swear to his men to observe his side of their contract before they make their oath of fidelity to him as his subjects.

Of course it was not always so evenly balanced. Power as well as ethical principles influenced political arrangements. When castles were established by force in newly conquered territory (as in England after 1066) the security of the conquerors in face of a hostile populace which greatly outnumbered them demanded harsher methods. Peasants might be forced to work on the unskilled but back-breaking tasks of digging ditches, carrying the spoil and constructing earthwork ramparts and mounds topped by palisades. Except for some of the carpentry, such a motte-and-bailey castle did not require a skilled labour force. The famous Bayeux Tapestry may well

revenues of the lordship and the survival of the castellary as an economic (and political) unit.

Such were the everyday impacts of the castle on the life of the labouring people. Despite the great variety of structural forms and political and geographical circumstances all over medieval Europe and beyond, the role of the castle in the community changed but little. Through castles lordship was exercised over the peasantry and the whole superstructure of the feudal state was maintained. The castle's military function (in the narrow modern sense) should not be exaggerated. Even in the warlike Crusader States in the Holy Land during the twelfth and much of the thirteenth century most of the tasks performed by castles were administrative (revenue, jurisdiction, police, residence) rather than strictly military. 'As in Europe, so in Syria, castles had only occasionally to withstand a siege but they continuously fulfilled their function as the physical basis of overlordship' (R.C. Smail, op. cit., p 61). In what follows we shall see what this meant for the peasantry of the castle fief. The mutuality and interdependence of the relationship between lord and community must first be illustrated. Too often the castle-owner, the lord-castellan, is regarded as a mere exploiter. In reality, rights and duties were

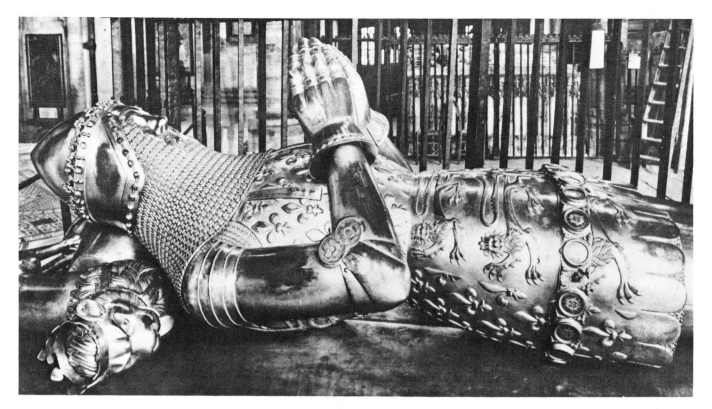

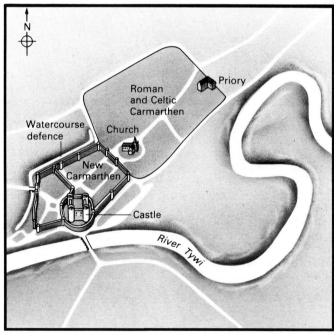

Top Effigy of Edward, the Black Prince (d. 1376) from his tomb in Canterbury Cathedral (Kent). His surcoat bears the combined arms of England and France adopted by his father. He was the *beau ideal* of chivalry in his day and universally respected.

Above Old and New Carmarthen (South Wales) show how townships were founded adjacent to castles. Although the site was a Roman and Celtic one, the medieval walled borough clusters around the quadrangular castle by the river crossing.

depict such a scene where labourers are shown working with picks, pointed wooden spades and shovels on the new castle of Hastings (*The Bayeux Tapestry*, ed. F.M. Stenton *et al.*, London, 2nd ed, 1965, p 51). In Ireland during the Anglo-Norman campaign a century later, forced labour was undoubtedly used to erect the invaders' earthwork castles. The same could occur as a result of localized anarchy as well as from organized conquest. Such a breakdown of authority occurred in Normandy following the death of the Conqueror (1087). His youngest son, count Henry, fortified the Cotentin peninsula against duke Robert, William's eldest son, and forced the people of the area to toil on castles for himself and his supporters. Among the sufferers were the populace of the town and district of Quetthou whose lords, the monks of Holy Trinity at Caen, bitterly complained. Regrettably, perhaps, their reason was not so much sympathy for the hardships inflicted as fear of loss of their own rights over their men's labour; the clergy were especially sensitive to such acts of usurpation as this (*Calendar of Documents Preserved in France*, London, 1899, nos. 424, 724). From the same source we learn that in 1124 woods belonging to Mont-Saint-Michel abbey were felled for timber to build a castle. The usurper made his peace with the monks but we are not told whether any attempt was made to compensate the peasantry for loss of advantages. Their rights tended to be damaged first and rectified last, if at all. It was much the same when the lord of Brancion, near Cluny in Burgundy, agreed with the great Benedictine monastery (*c.*1147) that he had no rights of lordship over the inhabitants of the abbey lands. For quietness of conscience before setting out on pilgrimage to Jerusalem (very likely with the Second Crusade of 1147–9) he confessed that his demands for lodging in their houses, for military service and work on constructing fortifications had been unjust and unwarranted (*Recueil des Chartes de ... Cluny*, V, Paris, 1894, no. 4131). Again, usurpations were resented not as social injustices to the peasantry but on account of the harm done to another lord's own legalized exactions. Similarly, the Church council at Reims in 1148, under Pope Eugenius III, concerned itself about the impact on clerical property of the various 'new evils' of that era of prolific lordly castle-building in many

regions of France. Excommunication and anathema were threatened and the council pronouncements forbade 'all undue exactions for works of castles'. The strong arm of the Church, in default of any sufficient royal power, did help to repress lawless compulsion which harmed the agrarian population most directly. From the later eleventh century also the Peace of God movement, backed by threat of spiritual sanctions and by secular force as well, helped to establish a code of non-aggression against the defenceless classes of society, the non-combatants of the medieval community, namely clergy, peasantry and women (*Thesaurus Novus Anecdotorum . . .*, IV, Paris, 1717, 121–4, 141–4; also R.W. Southern, *The Making of the Middle Ages*, London, 1959, pp. 74–117).

Lay lords and the Church worked together in France to assert the rule of law. In England and its appendages the strong government of the Anglo-Norman kings and the success of the Norman Conquest ultimately protected the peasantry with a strong if harsh hand. Castle-work by the peasantry was regulated and legalized in France. In England it quite rapidly passed into oblivion, except for emergencies, with frequent and wholesale charters of exemption. Peasants came to know where they stood in this respect; labour on the lord's castle was still arduous and irksome, but it was more exactly defined and less arbitrary. When King John asked for help (1202) from the knights and freemen of the lordship of Dunster in Somerset to fortify the castle there, he asked it as a favour, pointing out that the work was being done for their benefit and safety (*Rotuli Litterarum Patentium*, London, 1835, p 6b). Lords of unfree serfs are not likely to have made grave demands of them as a result of the king's request. In the warlike borderlands more was still expected of the peasantry although the help of the knightly classes with money and materials was now taking the place of massed labour gangs. William the Marshal's tenants were instructed (1220) to help him rebuild the castles of Narberth and Wiston, near Pembroke, destroyed by the Welsh. No doubt unfree tenants contributed, for warfare was a ruthless taskmaster. Edward I directed the men of Annandale (1299) to work on strengthening the palisading around his castle or 'peel' of Lochmaben for the campaign against the Scots. Apart from such emergencies, by the

thirteenth century it had also become normal in Scotland for peasants to be required to work on castles only if established by precedent. Thus King William the Lion called on his own men (1211–13) for his campaign of castle-building to consolidate his power in the county of Ross, but formally recognized that the men subject to Dunfermline Abbey had assisted of their own good will. Such gratuitous help was for the one occasion only; giving it was not to be turned to the volunteers' disadvantage subsequently (*Foedera*, I, I, London, 1816, p 163); *Cal. Documents Scotland*, II, Edinburgh, 1884, no. 1112; *Regesta Regum Scot.*, II, Edinburgh, 1971, no. 500). Pressure could still be applied, of course, and might be impossible to resist, but as fortifications were built increasingly of fire-proof masonry the part to which peasant labour could contribute correspondingly shrank. Impressment was widely used by kings and princes of the blood to secure carpenters, masons and other craftsmen for castle-building (and other) projects. Edward I's castle-construction in Wales required skilled and semi-skilled men to be forcibly recruited from all over the kingdom (A.J. Taylor, in *The History of the King's Works*, I, London, 1963, pp 293–408). But these men were highly paid and their profession was of necessity both seasonal and peripatetic, quite different from the peasant communal labour with which we are concerned. In Wales it survived under native rule and law remarkably late. It is recorded in 1315 that the men of Colwyn, north Wales, were still liable to castle-work and in addition were bound to make (or repair) the outer barricades, called *le hériçon* or 'thicket', and to repair the lord's lodging in the castle. Once every three years, however, was considered sufficient for the barricades (*Cal. Chancery Rolls Various*, 1277–1326, London, 1912, pp 171–3). Stone building was a tradition which continued much less interrupted in southern Europe so the peasant's contribution was less. Overseas, in the Frankish conquests of the Crusades, in the Holy Land from 1099 and in Greece from 1204, castles were built from the first in masonry. Timber was scarce and the advanced siege techniques of the Moslems required castles to be solid and fire-proof. In place of the timber superstructures (*hourds*), stone machicolation was soon developed. Although the labour of excavating such a rock-cut ditch as that at Saône was prodigious, the work was familiar to masons apprenticed as quarriers. As a result the Crusaders relied heavily on native craftsmen, frequently drawn from the friendly Christian principality of Lesser Armenia, north and east of Antioch, or from the subjects of the Byzantine emperor. These men were highly paid professionals whose skill was much sought after.

The peasant's labour on castles was very different. Wherever possible, personal service was replaced by cash payments – if the peasant was prosperous and the lord prepared to accept money in lieu. Payment of rent was much less demeaning, being closer to free-tenure, and did not disrupt work on the villager's own holding. The fact was two-edged, of course. In France, notably, the lord held on tenaciously to personal labour because it might be hard or expensive to replace, which motive operated in England also particularly when labour became scarce after the Black Death in 1348–50. But there was a further reason. Having unfree serfs living and working on the land was a particular *cachet* of lordship. Personal labour was the mark above all of unfree status. If the lord possessed a castle, this social distinction was rubbed in. The kind of fortification was immaterial, as can be seen from a verdict

Below Apocalypse Tapestry imagining the destruction at the end of the world of the French royal fortress of Angers (Maine-et-Loire) built under Louis IX.

delivered in 1210 by the duchy court of Normandy. The judges ruled 'that the men of Roger Caperon who dwell within his hauberk fief must repair his earthwork castle (*mota*) at Bonneville, or construct one anew if there is none there'. Roger was no more than a lowly knight, but he held by noble service. His hauberk (*lorica*) and fighting on horseback distinguished him as the social kinsman of the great lords and set him rigidly apart from his 'rustic' and 'villein' dependants. In central France the custom in the Nivernais was similar. As late as 1268 it was held by the royal court that a palisaded earthwork entitled its possessor to seigneurial prerogatives. Conversely, a noble was a castle-holder as of right. Castle-work was only one of the obligations which branded the serf but it epitomizes the whole social gulf between the noble 'estate' and the *ruptarius* (*roturier*), or tiller of the soil. Another Exchequer Court verdict (1223) is more specific.

> It is adjudged that the men of Roger d'Argences shall do him adequate aid and service for repairing his earthwork castle, situated within his hauberk fief, since they have admitted that it does lie within that fief and that they are resident within the fief.

Far left Dunstanburgh Castle
(Northumberland): an imaginative scene
showing refugees flocking into the newly-
completed fortress to escape a Scottish raid,
some time between 1316 and 1322.
Left Aerial view of the castle today.

survive on the one side accessible from the land. In 1337 the King's patent granted to Mathew de Sausmarez the proceeds of a sales and purchase tax for ten years to finance 'the repair of his castle or fortlet of Girburg in that island, to serve as a place of refuge for the king's subjects there in time of war or disturbance'. (*Cal. Pat. Rolls*, 1334–8, p 413). Evidently the islanders concurred in the project but they were notoriously independent-spirited and the king felt it necessary in 1342 to order his keeper of the Channel Islands to make compulsory what was for their own good, in view of the heightened danger of raids from the nearby French coast. places were to be allocated within the cliff-top castle to each family group and community. To make sure that the people obeyed the proclamation and duly went to the castle they were threatened with confiscation of any goods and chattels left unprotected outside. The castle was a joint responsibility and the king had, he considered, performed his part by forgoing his revenue to finance its construction. So the men of Guernsey were expected to reciprocate. In the proclamation they were told that 'it is just that what is built for the common advantage and defence [...] shall be defended at the common cost in time of war' (*Calendar of Close Rolls*, 1341–3, HMSO, London, p 375). Compulsory guard services by the peasantry occur in England at times of especial crisis (eg 1322) but they are still extempore in nature, whereas in France during the Hundred Years War peasant *guet et garde* (watch and ward) became highly organized. Service was done by all non-exempt dwellers within the castellary. In war it had to be done in person. At other times a money payment was customary, the proceeds funding repairs or substitutes' wages. In this way ancient duties of labour on castles became merged with guard services and rights of refuge in a systematic way largely absent in England except for exposed and warlike districts. The peasant had always had an ultimate duty to fight if a general summons to arms (*levée en masse*) should be proclaimed as a last resort. In England it was seldom necessary. The peasant's labour, however, was always fundamental to the society as it was to the system of castles which protected the land. When Lord John de Cobham built his castle of Cooling, on the vulnerable coast by Rochester, in the 1380s, he acknowledged in a strikingly original fashion the debt to the whole community which he was discharging. Within the two baileys there was space for numerous refugees and their possessions. Beside the archway of the outer gatehouse a plaque with archaic English lettering proclaims still:

> *Knoweth that beth and schal be*
> *That I am mad in help of the cuntre.*
> *In Knowyng of whyche thyng*
> *This is chartre and wytnessyng.*

Castles and the open country

Danger could stimulate common endeavour by the scattered rural population of a lordship but the spirit of co-operation was prone to evaporate once the immediate peril had passed. The defenceless 'open country', or *plat pays*, needed the castle just as the castle needed the revenues, food and manpower of the countryside around it. Castle-building was a lengthy and expensive undertaking. Emergency works alone were not enough. A planned distribution of fortresses capable of supporting armies in the field and of protecting refugees required central royal organization, or at least effective local initiative on a sufficiently large scale. Northern England felt the scourge

Roger's men are put at the King's mercy for having refused service and gone to court
(*Jugements de l'Echiquier de Normandie*, Paris, 1865, nos. 73, 341; *Les Olim*, ed. Beugnot, Paris, 1839, no. 20).

Heavy as it was, the burden of castle-work was mitigated by law and custom. Only the unfree layman bore it, as a rule, whose birthright was manual labour. Until the Anglo-French conflict of the Hundred Years War (*c.* 1339–1453) all men of the Church, all 'tonsured clerics', were exempt. After that, if they lived in walled towns they were increasingly taxed to pay for repairs to the fortifications. Eventually in France their fiscal immunity was almost entirely taken away but like the nobles they still enjoyed exemption from physical labour. The *corvée* afflicted the peasant alone but castle-work was still much better than not having the protection which castles provided. There are many examples of concerted action by the rural community to make fortified refuges for themselves, almost invariably in co-operation with the local lord. In the case of the castle of Jerbourg, on the Isle of Guernsey, this was King Edward III. The site is a spacious headland defended by sheer cliffs. Of its man-made defences only the earthworks

Right The outer gatehouse at Cooling Castle (Kent) licensed to be crenellated in 1381. Heavily machicolated parapets and simple circular gunloops are combined with crosslet slits for crossbows. The plaque overlooks the entry from the right-hand flanking tower. Originally there was a moat and drawbridge.

of Scottish incursions following Edward II's inept mismanagement of the campaign aginst King Robert Bruce, which ended disastrously at Bannockburn, near Stirling, in 1314. Thomas, Earl of Lancaster, cousin to the king and the greatest lord in the North and Midlands, resolved to tackle the problem. Just evacuating the country in advance of raids across the border was a defeatist solution. Failing success in battle, fortification was the answer. Before even seeking royal approval he began to fortify the headland of Dunstanburgh on the Northumberland coast. It is a site like that of Jerbourg. A great gatehouse of so-called Edwardian type, with two great round towers flanking the gate-passage, was placed facing inland on a line of massive curtain wall cutting across the neck of the peninsula from cliff to cliff. Earl Thomas no doubt used his own resources of cash and manpower for the task, masons' skills and peasant muscle. Much of the stone used was quarried on the spot, from the ditch. Work obligations which had fallen into disuse, or in the long years of peace had been 'commuted' to a money payment, again had to be done personally. It was the same in France. King Philip IV in 1300, with no inklng of the long war ahead of his country, agreed to accept cash in lieu of the cartage services due to the castle of Epernay, in Champagne, from the men of the castellary. He made two routine reservations. Should the king be present in person (ie to emphasize his lordly right as count of Champagne) or if there was war, the work must be done by the peasants themselves (*Registres du Trésor des Chartes*, I, Paris, 1958, no. 103). War, as Philip the Fair knew it, was an affair of short duration, most likely an adventure of a few months, or at most a full-scale but brief and decisive summer campaign. Philip's humbling of the count of Flanders, and even his ancestor's seizure of Normandy in 1204 from King John, typified contemporary experience. Long-term intermittent hostilities separated by troubled periods of truce, with elements of endemic civil war, were quite another matter. The Hundred Years War was certainly not a continuous century of fighting but it was an entirely new type of war (K. Fowler, *The Age of Plantagenet and Valois*, London, 1967, pp 13–15, etc). The traditional techniques of resistance, active and passive, were to undergo drastic change before it was over. In most of the regions of France the rural community suffered grievously. The direct effects of devastation of the land were compounded by the indirect impact of high taxation and labour demands.

France, from the Channel coast to the borders with the Empire of Germany and down to the foothills of the Pyrenees, was afflicted. Deep in the south are the castle and barony of Lapenne (Ariège). The district was alarmed into readiness to resist attack by rumours of the great raid, or *chevauchée*, or Edward, the Black Prince, which culminated in his decisive victory at Poitiers in 1356. Striking across Languedoc from the English duchy of Gascony, spreading terror and devastation as it went, his rapidly-moving mounted force did not, in fact, have with it any of the heavy equipment required to attack any place of strength. The prince's purpose was quite different (H.J. Hewitt, *The Black Prince's Expedition of 1355–7*, Manchester, 1958). In 1356 he turned northwards not back towards the regions of Langeudoc. But precautions had to be taken in good time. Strong-places could be destroyed indirectly, if the economy of their castellaries was ruined. All over the south-west within reach of the Gascon border it was the same story. At Lapenne Lord Thibaud asked the men of his barony to help strengthen the walls and ditches of the castle. His relations

with his dependants were apparently already rather embittered but they complied, no doubt by clearing out ditches, carting timber for palisades and erecting *hourds* to protect and defend the wall-tops. The work was in full swing when Prince Edward's army passed to the north on their march to Narbonne on the Mediterranean. His return to Gascony also went clear of Lapenne. Then, early in 1356, the prince's target was heard to be Poitou and the north (Hewitt, op. cit. maps pp 51, 103) for a second, great, demoralizing and destructive foray against the Valois dominions. This second raid led to victory and the capture of King John of France but for the peasantry of Lapenne it meant that they were out of immediate danger. Promptly they stopped work on the castle and refused to continue. Thibaud, their lord, took the longer view. The attack might be repeated and precautions were still advisable. Perhaps also he had an eye to getting improvements made to his castle with unpaid labour, and he may well have hoped to strengthen his hold over the men of the castellary by securing permanent and regular castle-work from them. At all events, he brought a case against them in the court of the royal seneschal of Carcassonne. Before him Lord Thibaud argued that his men had broken their agreement with him and that the court should enforce it as the work was primarily for their benefit since they could take refuge in Lapenne castle with their goods whenever danger was near. The public interest and central policy concurred. The seneschal upheld him but the community of the castellary was still not satisfied. Choosing representatives to go all the way to Paris they appealed to the highest court in the kingdom, the royal *Parlement*. Apparently the justices felt that the men of the castellary had more right on their side and they adopted a compromise. Although they rejected the men's appeal they made no award of costs against them and ruled so as to protect both parties' interests while reconciling them with general policy. The seneschal of Carcassonne should make an inspection of Lapenne castle and decide what works were essential to put it in a state of defence. Only that much was to be done by the community and neither they nor Thibaud were to acquire or lose any right or obligation towards the other. The relationship between lord and men was kept in its former delicate balance (P-C. Timbal, *La Guerre de Cent Ans...*, C.N.R.S., Paris, 1961, pp 108–9).

To ensure effective defence of the rural populace, every part of the open country had to be within convenient reach of a castle. At the time of Poitiers twelve miles was considered the

Left Ransoms were a rich source of gain from war. In this fifteenth-century illumination the Duke of Orléans is depicted in honourable captivity in the Tower of London. Traitors' Gate, the White Tower (white-washed as it normally was) and, in the background the City of London are shown both accurately and artistically.

Below Distant view of Krak des Chevaliers, near Homs, in the modern state of Syria. Ceded to the Knights Hospitaller in 1142, and held by them until lost to the Mamelukes in 1271, the Order continually poured wealth and skill into making it the most formidable castle in Outremer. An arab settlement has grown up in and around the castle just as there was a dependent *burgus* outside the walls in Crusader times.

maximum practicable distance to go in hasty emergencies. The fortress of refuge, be it a castle or a walled town, was not necessarily that of the lord to whom the refugee was subject, although this was most usually the case. Everything possible was done to ensure that men and movables were put behind walls in good time – from advance warning by proclamation of impending attack and free access without tolls on entry or leaving the strong-place, to threats of confiscation of portable property abandoned to sustain and attract the enemy raider. In return for protection the peasant contributed labour. In the eastern province of the Dauphiné, protection was paid for by a tax of one twentieth of produce, paid usually in cash, and for that reason called the *vintaine*. Throughout the kingdom no lord of a castle was allowed to demand castle-work, *guet* or *garde* unless protection was given in return and the castle kept in a defensible state. Lords were compelled on pain of demolition of their fortresses to maintain them properly, and weak ones which could never be used but for enemy 'lodgement' were ruthlessly razed, without compensation. All ranks of men were affected. Inevitably, for all that could be done, the hapless peasantry were hardest hit. Recurrent outbreaks of war and brigandage by the 'free companies' did great damage from which the Plantagenet dominions were mostly immune. But in the Marches of Gascony and in northern England, and in Ireland nearly continuously beyond the territories of the English Pale, castles also protected refugees and acted as arsenals and military bases for active defence of the country-side. The role of Jerbourg, on Guernsey, has been mentioned. Edward III in 1342 had to insist that no goods brought within the castle for protection by the community of the isle should be kept back by the constable 'while they do what they ought for the custody of the castle'. Bamburgh, on a coastal promontory closer to the Scottish border than Dunstanburgh, had long been a traditional place of refuge. In 1318 and again in 1323 its constable had to be admonished for trying to levy toll on refugees' goods leaving the castle when the Scots withdrew (*Cal. Close Rolls*, 1318–23, pp 40, 662, 597). The royal concern was always that peasants should not be deterred from seeking safety. Their labour and working animals were the mainspring of the medieval economy. To leave cattle or harvested crops in the open country only encouraged raiding parties to attack, and where there was food they could remain to devastate the land, before moving on to fresh fields. All interests coincided to get the rural populace with their wealth within walls at the earliest news or rumour of impending attack. It almost amounted to a true 'scorched earth' policy, and occasionally was supplemented by deliberate destruction in the invader's path. Such methods of defence were not very honourable to the ruler who resorted to them. Both Edward II of England (1307–27) and Philip VI of France (1328–50) suffered discredit and loss of prestige for doing so, but, when the enemy could not be met in the field, fortresses minimized the damage he could wreak. Castles were a vital part in this inglorious but essential function of passive defence.

Castles multiplied in early medieval Europe for precisely these reasons. Pressure from Viking and Norse attacks, and in the south from the Moors crossing the Pyrenees from Spain, or raiding the Mediterranean coastline, fell upon a region where central authority was collapsing. Local action was the only remedy. Lacking the manpower to defeat an attacker by force of numbers a fragmented system of castle lordships was the only viable formula of safety for localities left to defend themselves. What was happening is clearly illustrated by a document drawn up in the late tenth century (986) about the foundation of the castle of Cardona, in north-eastern Spain, at the turn of the century. The situation was quite unlike that of England after the Norman Conquest. The populace and their leaders were united in resisting the Moorish Infidel. Large castles, not small forts for the minority to resist and quell a hostile mass of peasants, arose naturally in response. The powerful Islamic state which had overrun Spain rapidly after 711 and virtually extinguished Christianity in the peninsula forced the population in the Christian enclaves surviving in the Pyrenees to work closely together. From the upland valleys of Navarre, Andorra and Catalonia was launched the counter-attack. Castles enabled the Christians to fight back, to regain control of territory bit by bit, to police, tax and protect the peasantry of each little lordship and, most vitally, castles enabled them to escape annihilation from Moslem incursions too sudden or too strong to be checked by an army in the open. Count Wilfrid of Barcelona, who founded Cardona in about 900, was carrying forward, as hundreds of other lords were independently doing, that long conflict of the Reconquest which ended only in 1492 with the fall of Granada. Such an epic struggle had incongruously humble methods, but they were intensely practical. Every person who came to inhabit the territory controlled by the castle, and who took refuge within it, was guaranteed security of property. In war this was afforded by the fortifications; in peace by the lord's court of justice. On their part, the community of the castellary promised to make no tribute to any other lord (apart from Church dues), and undertook to labour on the defences and to guard them whenever necessary. The work specified was on

> the tower of the castle, on the walls and superstructures, digging to deepen the ditches and to strengthen the ramparts, for one day in each week through the year. In grave peril as much must be done as the people's safety required.
>
> (*Amplissima Collectio* ...
> I, Paris, 1724, 336–40.)

Self-help and common endeavour were the original principles of communal labour on 'works of castles'. Although at some periods these elements were subverted, peasant duties becoming almost absolute lordly rights, war and common danger restored the first situation which had given birth to the castle in medieval Europe. Peasant obligations could harden

Right A peasant tills the light soil of the valley below the Hospitaller castle of Margat (Syria) using a simple plough and a single yoke of oxen. The scene is almost timeless. The great fortress stretches across the sky-line with its keep and heaviest defences massed to confront the adjacent high ground.

Below Marienburg on the River Vistula (Poland), headquarters of the Teutonic Knights and the continuously garrisoned fortress of the Grand Master of the Order. Founded as a crusading order in the Levant, they turned their attention from 1225 to Europe's other Crusade at home, which ultimately created the Kingdom of Prussia (1701).

Left A distant view of Beaufort Castle (Lebanon). Only constant vigilance against Moslem attacks and careful protection of the labouring peasantry could preserve the economic viability of a community in such a harsh and forbidding environment. This was the *raison d'être* of the castle.

In the Levant conditions were harsher. Manpower was so scarce that walls had to do the work of soldiers and the castles' dominance of the countryside was primarily a military one. In the words of R.C. Smail (op. cit., pp 60–1): above all they were centres of authority. The commander of a castle and its garrison was master of the surrounding district, and had means continuously at his disposal to meet any challenge to his authority (op. cit., pp 60–1). During the twelfth century the difficulties of holding territory in subjection by armed occupation grew inexorably. The military orders took over more of the key and inland castles. With revenues derived from their network of commanderies and preceptories all over Europe these military monks could afford the prodigious cost of effective fortification. Templars and Hospitallers had the dedicated and war-hardened knights and lower ranks to keep castles on a constant war footing. In Europe this was almost unknown. Only in Spain fighting the Moors (where military Orders were again prominent), or in north-eastern Germany and along the southern shores of the Baltic Sea, where the order of Teutonic knights fought the heathen Prussians and Slavs, were castles so maintained.

Levantine conditions brought castles closer in many ways to modern military practices. They had standing garrisons entirely distinct from the surrounding civilian population. There could be little question of admitting peasants of doubtful loyalty as refugees if they consumed precious stores and threatened treachery. They had to be kept to the outer ward or excluded entirely. Auxiliary troops recruited as mercenaries, sometimes men of partly European descent, tended to be unreliable when danger was acute. In face of such a united Moslem campaign as that of 1187 by Saladin, which reduced the kingdom of Jerusalem to a coastal fragment with a few inland strong-points only in Christian hands, it was all the Franks could do, after defeat in battle, to keep a few of their castles. Native subjects and auxiliary troops could not remain loyal and risk being treated as traitors. Krak des Chevaliers and Margat, both Hospitaller castles, held out inland. At Krak des Chevaliers a garrison of two thousand, early in the next century, was the castle complement with provisions for a year (R. Fedden and J. Thomson, op. cit.). Vast storerooms, stables, water-tanks and undercrofts catered for a large, permanent force of cavalry. In Europe only temporary lodges not permanent barracks were needed. They were erected and then dismantled when their temporary occupants departed. Magnificent though they are and compelling the admiration of the twentieth-century visitor even in ruin, it remains true that the castles of the Crusaders were not integrated into the economy of the countryside as the European castles normally were. We like to think of castles as military posts, bristling with armed men, frowning defiance over a barren land. But the castle was dead and its purpose vanished unless that country was well cultivated and securely protected. King Edward III of England wrote to his justiciary of Ireland in 1341 about the castle of Ballykine with just this fact in mind. The castle must, he said:

> be delivered to one who is able and willing to defend
> it against the attacks of enemies and to maintain it
> in a suitable state, as the king has learned that
> several lands pertaining to that castle, because they
> are up on the march and among the lands of the
> king's Irish rebels, lie fallow and uncultivated [. . .]
> owing to the negligence of the keepers of the castle.
> (*Cal. Close Rolls*, 1341–3, p 312.)

into unilateral seigneurial perquisites, with nothing given in return, but the true and most characteristic role of the medieval castle was a communal not a sectional or minority one. This was the nature of the castle throughout that prolonged era in which it remained an integral part of the life of the entire community both in peace and during war.

Such admirable castles were built in the Frankish states of Outremer that something must be said about the special conditions in which they operated. The way in which castles dominate their rural setting is seldom more conspicuous than in the Levant. Palestine and Syria of the Crusaders, east of the coastal strip, was a barren country compared with their well-watered European homelands. So every one of the castles sheltered and exploited a pocket of fertile soil, often surrounded by bare mountains (Saône, Krak des Chevaliers, Margat) or beleaguered by the desert (like Kerak in Moab). The Franks were an alien aristocracy (however orientalized in some instances). They had imposed their rule by force and it remained essentially a military occupation. Castles were all the more important, but not quite as in Europe. European settlers were too few to be true colonists. Indigenous village communities were left under their own laws and paid their dues largely in cash. Racially this peasantry had no kinship with the invaders. Christian Syrians, Armenians and others belonged to sects considered heretic by Byzantium and little closer to Rome than were the native Moslems and Jews. These factors severely limited the common interest which in Europe united the community of the castellary in the face of danger. Whether the overlord was Frank or Seldjuk made little difference to the peasantry in most parts of the Holy Land. So the castles were alien enclaves rather than true centres of community life. The cities of the Mediterranean seaboard were more European in population, but cosmopolitan and mercantile, divided into separate districts and quarters. Venetians and Pisans, Templars and Hospitallers all lived in jealous rivalry and virtual independence. Commercial individualism prevailed while the castles of the interior kept a lonely vigil over an increasingly hostile countryside. To the medieval artist landscape was hardly complete without castles perched on the distant hill-tops. Even the Last Judgement and the Resurrection were imagined with castles in the background. Towns grew up under the tutelage of the castle-lord and received protection. Edward I's castles in north Wales were an effort of town plantation as much as of aggressive penetration.

Life in the Castle

House and home

The significance of the castle was not limited to times of disturbance, war, rebellion or social unrest. Castles were homes, and apart from their military design and function they were barely distinguishable from other houses of the Middle Ages. Recent excavation at Castle Acre in Norfolk has shown how a house without military pretensions was transformed over several decades in the eleventh and early twelfth centuries into a building of military importance. But the evolution of Castle Acre from domestic dwelling to fortress was not unique: many castles replaced houses formerly on the same site or else nearby while keeping all the functions of the superseded buildings. A house that was also a castle bestowed prestige on its owner, and social advancement often explains the transformation of a modest family home with an estate or seignory, limited sometimes to no more than the land in its immediate vicinity. Local rivalry between two or more families, and the conflicting interests of Church and State or king and magnate, could result in a crop of castles; for instance there were two each at Stafford and Winchester, three at Poitiers, over 40 at Bologna and 72 (14 survive) at San Gimignano. Towers, turrets, battlements, machicolations, shooting points and armouries should not be allowed to deceive the modern visitor to such places, the castellar features incorporated in some structures being of little real use. With their decline as military bases castles did not cease to be occupied, but remained in use as residences. This was not a newly discovered purpose; it was simply that one of several functions performed by castles in their heyday was to emerge eventually as the sole one.

Components of the residence

The domestic focal point of a castle was the great hall. In some castles it was situated originally in the lord's quarters, but the tendency early on to have separate halls, as at Richmond in Yorkshire, became the standard later. The great hall was, as its name implies, the most spacious room in the complex of accommodation and facilities which made up a castle. A somewhat bleak place, it had a raised dais at one end for the use of the lord and family or their representatives or social superiors. The hall served a variety of purposes: originally it was the main living room of the castle and all the chief functions were held there. The occupants met there to eat, to do business, to enjoy themselves and, for some, to sleep. But increasing wealth and more sophisticated management as the Middle Ages advanced led to a lessening in its importance, with the lord's desire for greater privacy and the addition of rooms meant only for certain uses. Yet the hall remained the centre of the castle and of activity there until castles ceased to be built.

Near to, but not always adjoining, the great hall were the kitchens, the buttery (the storeroom for liquor) and the pantry (the storeroom for bread and other provisions). Until stone became readily available, and later, brick, kitchens were often made of wood and regularly burnt down. The danger from fire meant that kitchens were often detached from the halls which they served and it was only the general adoption of less combustible building materials that enabled them to be situated nearer the halls. This improvement did not result in food prepared in the kitchens arriving at the table any the warmer. The most important diners sat furthest from the kitchens and the ceremonial accompanying the serving of

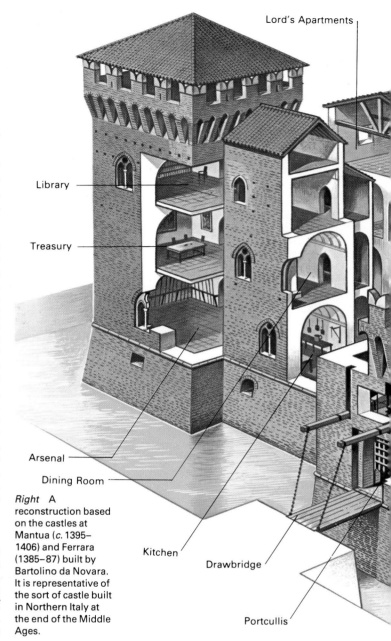

Right A reconstruction based on the castles at Mantua (*c.* 1395–1406) and Ferrara (1385–87) built by Bartolino da Novara. It is representative of the sort of castle built in Northern Italy at the end of the Middle Ages.

their food became more elaborate as the years passed. Eating in public became such a ritual that by the fourteenth century the great preferred to dine privately, in rooms further away from the kitchens. In some of the grander, earlier castles the kitchens were situated immediately adjoining, or else beneath, the great hall with stairs linking the two. But such close proximity meant that the smell of cooking always reached the users of the great hall and detracted from its desirability as the centre of the castle. Thus by the time the papacy moved to Avignon it had become the practice to have the kitchens on the same level as, but apart from, the great hall. Only in less prestigious buildings or when other needs enforced it did the kitchens remain close to the great hall, as for instance at Methoni in the Peloponnese, Trogir in Dalmatia and Kastel Kastelli in Crete.

The living quarters for the lord, his family and servants were situated as far away as possible from the kitchens. In some of the earlier and poorer establishments such accommodation was limited to a handful of rooms, or even to a single room, and it is not possible to be certain from the evidence of the surviving structures who in many cases the occupants were. The best fitted rooms were those of the lord. In the richer

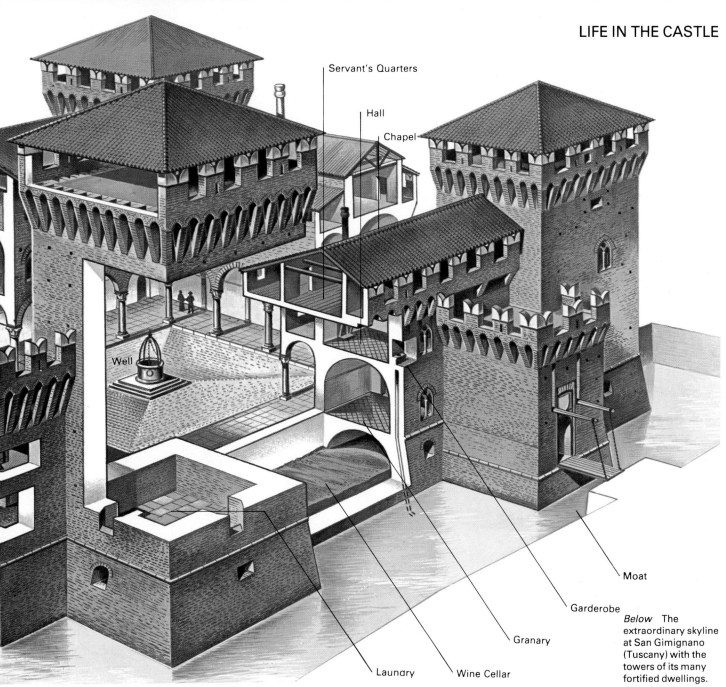

Servant's Quarters

Hall

Chapel

Well

Moat

Garderobe

Granary

Laundry

Wine Cellar

Below The extraordinary skyline at San Gimignano (Tuscany) with the towers of its many fortified dwellings.

and larger castles the lord had a suite of rooms for his own use which were closed on his departure and only vacated by him if a visitor more distinguished than himself arrived. The lord, if a king or a magnate, owned more than one house or castle and, for a number of reasons, one being the frequent difficulties in supplying food, he moved from place to place taking with him his chief servants. His wife did not always travel with him but often stayed behind with their children and other companions, living in one or two of the better equipped castles, and joining, or being joined by, her spouse only at given times. These women had accommodation separate from their husbands. There were also quarters for a small household which kept the castle in running order during the absence of the lord, his wife and their servants. This household seems to have varied in size between six and a dozen people, there being usually a porter, a watchman, a cook, a steward, a chaplain and a washerwoman. Thus in the greater castles there was separate accommodation for the lord and his wife as well as for the permanent household and the travelling one. In addition there was housing for men in the lord's fee, retained to advise him on financial and legal issues or employed in the management of his property, and for dependents of his, bound by homage,

Right Originally the main living room of the castle, the status of the hall gradually diminished with the increase in wealth and desire for privacy during the Middle Ages. But it continued as the centre of the castle's activity. This picture shows the lower end of the great hall at Stokesay Castle (Shropshire).

Above The main residential range at Wressle Castle (Yorkshire) with lodgings in towers at either end of the great hall, as seen from the site of the former gardens.

Right The centre-piece for the high table was often the pretext for display as can be seen from this elaborate early sixteenth-century German example, known as the Burghley Nef.

Far right A beaker with a cover for show on the buffet or dresser, designed to resemble a walled town with church and castle.

Right A lavishly carved stool made in France in the fifteenth century.

Left the late fourteenth-century great hall built
for John of Gaunt at Kenilworth Castle
(Warwickshire). Note the magnificent traceried
windows, the chimneypiece and the remains of
the second hall beneath.

service, tenancy or political and social connexion. There was
also accommodation for visitors because a great man was
expected to show hospitality to the traveller, but such mag-
nanimity did not extend to one and all since poor pilgrims were
often denied entry although provided with food at the gate.
One hall and one kitchen sometimes proved insufficient to seat
and feed all present at one time, and rather than suffer the
ignominy of failure as a host some castellans built a second
and third hall and kitchen.

The need to provide quarters for so many and such a variety
of people and for periods of differing lengths meant that castles
were made up largely of *camera*, that is chambers or sets of
rooms called lodgings, which could be opened or shut as
needed. The size of the individual rooms, their number and
furnishing depended on the rank and wealth of the user. The
clustering and arrangement of such lodgings was well suited
to the overall layout of castles. They were placed either in
blocks along the edges of the baileys and smaller courtyards
within the baileys, or else in towers. Their design in separate
units with their own access accorded well with the concept that
any part of a castle could be defended separately.

There was also provision for religious devotion and the
saying of mass. The responsibility laid upon landowners by
Church and State to set a Christian example to their social
inferiors was taken seriously. Where there was a parish
church nearby often with a living in the gift of the castellan,
there was sometimes no chapel within the castle walls. But if
there was no chapel, portable altars were available and
oratories were common. In some castles, such as the Tower of
London, there were sometimes two or more chapels, each with
its own priest and staff. In the earlier chapels the lord joined
the other members of the congregation in the body of the
chapel, although he, unlike they, had a seat. Later he had a
pew of his own overlooking the chapel, sometimes with a fire to
keep him warm. After the building of Sainte Chapelle within
one of the royal fortresses in Paris, castle chapels became
showpieces to demonstrate the piety of the lord as much as to
adorn the castle itself. They were often structures of great
beauty and of much embellishment, and some, such as St
George's Chapel at Windsor, were manned by a host of men in
holy orders, choirs, organists and other musicians. Sometimes,
in unabashed emulation of Sainte Chapelle, they had shrines
and reliquaries but none could rival the prime model in its
possession of the crown of thorns thought to have been worn by

Christ. To house the staff in such chapels it became common
for colleges with masters of their own and separate facilities to
be founded beside the chapels. Such colleges, although the
product of benefactions by the castellan, were usually semi-
autonomous bodies within the castle, and divine service
continued to be said however few were staying in the castle.
Where possible, collegiate churches were erected in the lower
bailey or outer courtyard of a castle, but as they became
fashionable only during the last phase of castle-building, space
was sometimes no longer available within the existing enceinte without its redevelopment. Although this was done
occasionally, it was a costly process and some, like Ralph Lord
Cromwell at Tattershall in Lincolnshire, preferred to build
outside the walls. Elaborate religious foundations linked with
castles, however, were not a phenomenon of this last phase. In
the eleventh and twelfth centuries monasteries were often
built in the neighbourhood, for instance as at Castle Acre in
Norfolk and Lewes in Sussex.

Each of the parts of a castle had a specific use, but unlike a
building today each part was not restricted to that use.
Adaptability was a basic concept of medieval design and
castles illustrate better than most buildings of the period how
this was realized. Each room, whatever its function, was used
for sleeping. Men slept at night in the rooms where they
worked during the day: the cooks slept in the kitchen, the
chaplain in the chapel and the stablemen in the stable.
Medieval stories, manuscript illustrations and inventories
show that beds and bedding were to be found in almost every
room. Where they were not provided, mattresses or simply
straw were brought in as needed. In some castles there were
orders regulating the distribution of pallets and straw. Some of
the rooms situated over gates or posterns housed the raised
portcullis and its machinery. A somewhat whimsical yet fairly
accurate idea of the inconvenience usually caused by this
arrangement can be seen in the Windlass Room at Castell
Coch in Glamorgan, designed by William Burgess for the
eccentric third marquess of Bute in the 1870s. At Caernarvon
the chapel accommodated the portcullis which when raised
served as a screen to divide the altar from the main body of the
chapel and thus to protect the sacrament. The floors of such
rooms over gates, and others similarly placed over passageways, were often fitted with meurtrières, openings about a foot
square with removable wooden covers through which fires
could be quenched with water and unwelcome visitors could be
attacked with pikes and bills stored in the rooms themselves
for such a contingency, while other rooms had similar lids
covering the openings to the machicolations through which to
drop items on assailants. Bows and sheaves of arrows were
kept near windows looking outwards, and after the introduction of guns in the fourteenth century handguns and even
cannon adorned bedchambers. Where possible these armaments were placed, sometimes quite decorously, so as not to
interfere with the domestic use of the rooms. The guardrooms
with arms and armour displayed on their walls to be found in
later buildings were undoubtedly copying medieval examples.
Such an example, albeit much depleted and now refurbished
with later items, is still to be found in the chapel of Farleigh
Hungerford Castle in Somerset.

Each part of a castle was designed to be put on a war-footing
at a moment's notice, to become a refuge against attack or the
headquarters for an offensive. Similar adaptability was expected of the occupants: everyone had to don armour in an

emergency. A castle prepared for war was little more than a household ready to fight. With this notion accepted by one and all there was little need for regular garrisons, an expensive outlay even for a king, let alone a lesser figure. Garrisons were features of castles only in areas where order was inadequately kept, usually on account of a conflict of jurisdiction or on the boundaries of Christendom. Garrisons were maintained by kings only as long as a particular crisis or problem lasted. The more serious matter of preserving Europe against the Infidel was entrusted to the Military Orders, Poland being defended by the Teutonic Knights and the Crusading States by the Hospitallers and the Templars. These Orders maintained the only permanent garrisons throughout the Middle Ages and thus their castles were first and foremost fortresses. Yet even the castles which they built were demonstrably no more than religious households basically organized for war, and thus they should not be rashly distinguished from other centres of lordship in the period.

Furniture and furnishings

It has already been noted that all parts of a castle were used for sleeping, and beds and bedding could be found in every room; the only exceptions to this were the castles of the Military Orders which were essentially fortified monasteries. Beds varied according to rank, the great occupying ones covered with furs and costly materials, the lowly having to content themselves with straw. The design of beds evolved during the Middle Ages. To keep snug in bed in large rooms beds with headboards, canopies and various other hangings were invented. Such beds first became popular in France but by the late thirteenth century other countries had adopted their use, Henry III of England ordering one for himself in the 1240s. Often the focal point of a room, hung beds became objects of display, cloth of gold and silver often being used and one ordered by the duke of Burgundy in the 1390s having over 100 square yards of material. Given as gifts and passed on as heirlooms such beds gradually became showpieces only to be used on certain occasions; they were appropriately called 'beds of state'. A less expensive type of bed resembling a bell-tent and called a *sperver* came into vogue in the fourteenth century and within a hundred years it was the standard design. Like beds of state *spervers* were employed to indicate rank.

The doubling of beds for seats during daytime and the increasing cost and elaboration of the main beds led to most rooms being furnished with a second. For the richest this was for the use of the occupant's personal servant or companion, but often he slept there himself with his manservant. Beds were invariably shared, single beds being a later innovation.

Beds often provided the only seating in a room. Once windows became larger in the twelfth century, stone window-seats were introduced into the design of the bays, often with a raised foot-rest. Chairs tended to be kept only for the great and occurred singly, usually being placed beside the bed. Foot-stools were supplied for the use of the most important in an effort to raise the sitter above draughts. The use of footstools thus served to distinguish the sitter further from his companions who, until other seating was provided, either stood or sat on the floor, as can be clearly seen in Rogier van der Weyden's 'Magdalen Reading'. Where other seating existed it was made up of benches, forms and stools. Towards the close of the Middle Ages these items were sometimes carved with an

opulence quite at variance with the purpose and simplicity of the item itself. To save space, forms were at times placed against the walls of a room. Tables completed the furniture to be found generally. As space was at a premium trestles were preferred to legged tables which seem to have been almost unknown, any occurrence being cause for comment.

Wall lockers fitted with shelves were the standard method of storage throughout the Middle Ages, the most famous perhaps being the sixteenth-century ones designed for Catherine de Medici at Blois, and were a feature of many rooms within castles. Their doors were often the excuse for elaborate ironwork and other decoration. Free-standing cupboards were known in the tenth century but seem not to have become common for another four hundred years. Drawers in cupboards are thought to have been another innovation popularized by the French. Chests and caskets do not figure much in castle inventories but while the lord and his retinue were in residence they would have been found in almost every room

Below Réné of Anjou in his bed of estate dreams of meeting the personification of Love. Note the bell-tent for Réné's man-servant, the window with its shutters, the rush-matting covering the floor and the unusually advanced fashion of carpets over the matting. (From the *Livre du Coeur d'Amour Espirit*.)

Left The great chamber at the fifteenth-century castle of Langeais (Indre-et-Loire) restored as it was about the time of the marriage there of Charles VIII of France to Anne of Brittany. Langeais was the work of Jean Bourré, the minister of Louis XI from 1465, though only two wings were completed.
Above 'The Magdalen Reading' by Rogier van der Weyden. Only the great were provided with chairs in medieval times. Their absence meant that many people had to sit on beds or window bays or even squat on the floor.
Below One of the Apocalypse Tapestries at Angers (Maine-et-Loire) showing the Heavenly Jerusalem.
Far left The mid fourteenth-century lodging range at Woodsford Castle (Dorset).

because they went with the lord on his journeying. Buffets and dressers completed the items of furniture to be found in castles by the end of the Middle Ages. Placed in the hall and the other main rooms they provided sideboards for the display of plate and for the serving of wine and other drinks to important persons. Popularized by the French, a buffet can be seen in the miniature for January in the *Très Riches Heures* of the duke of Berry.

To help reduce draughts wall hangings embellished the main rooms for living. Originally these seem to have been used only in the hall behind the lord's seat on the dais, but increasing prosperity and standards of luxury led to their use throughout. Embroidered cloths and woven cloths were common from the outset of the Middle Ages, while painted cloths were not introduced until the fourteenth century. None of these compared with the sumptuous tapestries produced at Arras in Artois as early as the twelfth century for the courts of France and Burgundy and later bought with such avidity by all who could afford them throughout Europe. To meet the demand, tapestry manufacturing sprang up elsewhere but none of these could match the products of Arras. The most common subjects chosen for depiction were plants, trees,

Right One of the richly carved fireplaces at Tattershall Castle (Lincolnshire) adorned with the arms of Ralph Lord Cromwell, his purse of office as Treasurer of England and a number of figures.
Below right An enamelled casket once owned by William de Valence, Earl of Pembroke (d. 1296). Chests and caskets of this sort would have been a common feature in most rooms of a castle when the lord was in residence.
Below The aqueduct at Krak des Chevaliers (Syria). Due to the difficulties of storing water in Southern Europe, Asia Minor and Palestine, huge cisterns were often built within the castle, with aqueducts of the type shown here to keep them full.
Right An early sixteenth-century glass roundel for a window depicting the knight Paulus von Seckendorff with arms and crest.

Left The Camera degli Sposi at Mantua (Apulia), decorated by Mantegna and glorifying the house of Gonzaga. This late fifteenth-century scheme reflects the Renaissance preference for ornate design, in direct contrast to the earlier medieval tradition of painting every available surface with bright colours.

way to a more restrained and deliberately contrived form of decoration but even that by standards of today frequently jarred with the contents of the rooms themselves. There is no reason to believe that the rooms painted at Mantua by Pisanello and Mantegna were admired solely for their design and that their furnishings took account of the frescoed walls. When not painted the floors were tiled, often laid in elaborate patterns sometimes bearing heraldic devices or showing scenes from everyday life or from popular tales. Late medieval fireplaces were similarly exercises in ostentation, being emblazoned with the owner's arms like those at Tattershall or flamboyantly carved like those at Poitiers.

Heating

In the earliest castles fires were to be found only in the hall and kitchens, the other rooms being heated by means of braziers fed with embers. As elsewhere, central hearths seem to have been the norm, but to judge from the Tower of London wall fireplaces were not unknown, even if a luxury, in the eleventh century. These central hearths may have had hoods with flues to draw the smoke up, but if they did the later preference for wall fireplaces suggests that the hoods were not successful. In some parts of the Continent, especially central and north Europe, a variant on the fireplace, a stove, was preferred. A notable series of encaustic tiled stoves dating from the fourteenth and fifteenth centuries is to be seen at Haut-Koenigsbourg in Alsace. The occupants of castles, like those of other dwellings, tried not to waste heat and by means of a number of devices more or less sealed up their rooms and sat huddled close to their fires. The result was that the rooms became stuffy. To counter this herbs and scented leaves were strewn on the floors. Later it became fashionable to have pots to hold this mixture but despite the frequency of their depiction in fifteenth-century Flemish paintings such pots do not figure often in inventories or household accounts from the period.

Floor coverings

The wooden floors of upper storeys were plastered and cemented over. This was doubtless a fire precaution but as it was also the practice in purely domestic dwellings it should be seen too as a further effort to reduce draughts. Over this base flagstones, bricks or tiles were laid in the castles of the rich. The predilection for floor-tiles seems to have been a peculiarly English enthusiasm but it was shared to a lesser degree on the Continent. Whether painted or paved, floors were rarely left uncovered, rushes being used to cover them. It is usually claimed that these rushes were simply strewn without any preparation, but if this was the habit in poor establishments it was not so in the homes of the well-off where the rushes were woven into matting, which was replaced each year during the spring. An example of this matting can be seen in the January miniature in the *Très Riches Heures*.

Lighting

As far as possible castellans relied on daylight to lighten the interiors of their buildings, but with so many openings in the walls designed primarily for defence this could rarely be achieved. Where it was, windows were provided with iron stanchions and internal shutters. Sometimes there were also grilles on the outside. By the fifteenth century there were often two sets of shutters, one of them holding glass. So that the

animals and monsters. Larger and more costly items depicted the Virtues and scenes from the Bible, histories, romances, classical legends and contemporary tales as well as the lives of the saints and other worthies and the more worldly pursuits of hunting, hawking, fishing and other pastimes. Heraldic items were also in demand. These usually displayed the owner's coat of arms or those of his affinity but sometimes bore his name, rebus (a punning device on the owner's name), crest and motto. Carpets introduced by Italian and French merchants in the fourteenth century as coverings for tables remained too dear for everyone except the wealthiest to buy.

Decoration

All the available wall surfaces, both inside and out, were painted as were the roofs on the inside, the ceilings and sometimes the floors. The exteriors were usually only whitewashed, hence the name the White Tower given to the keep in the Tower of London, but it was not unknown for various designs to be picked out in another colour on the white background. The interiors of the early and high Middle Ages were awash with colour, without any evident regard for overall harmony in their decoration. This riot of colour gave

occupants could make the most of the light, seats were set into the bays. Artificial light was provided by torches, tapers and candles which were allocated according to the rank of the occupant. Stands and holders were usually brought in for these as needed, but in the better-off establishments more permanent fixtures to take them were fitted to the walls or suspended from the ceilings.

Water supply

Water was sometimes available from streams, rivers or lakes, but for a variety of reasons, including the avoidance of polluted water drawn from those sources, most castles were dependent on a well for their supply of water. In southern Europe, Asia Minor and the Crusading States huge cisterns were built to hold water against the heat of summer and aqueducts were sometimes constructed to keep them full. Save in the kitchens there was generally no running water (a notable exception being the provision for piped water in the keep at Dover in the 1180s) and then only cold. Hot and cold water was taken to other parts of the building as needed for washing, and bowls and tubs were provided as required. The French popularized the use of bath-houses in the late fourteenth century. These rooms with their pools and costly fittings proved difficult to maintain and within 150 years they had largely ceased to be built or used.

Sanitation

Most of the rooms in a castle were supplied with chamber pots which were emptied daily. These were supplied even when superior latrine facilities were available. Garderobes, which were small closets invariably situated in external walls, featured in the earliest castles such as the Tower of London, but became more common as the standard of living enjoyed by the magnates rose, individual suites or rooms being built with ones used solely as latrines. For general use there were also communal garderobe blocks housing many cubicles. Herbs and scented leaves were put in the garderobes to help keep the air sweet and water from the washing bowls was thrown down the shutes. Letters no longer wanted and other pieces of paper and material found their final destination there. When these were not available straw seems to have been provided. The pits sometimes opened into the moat or flowing water but where this was not possible they had to be cleaned out regularly by 'gong-farmers' who travelled the country just to perform that task.

Wardrobes

A component which figures prominently in any household account or inventory of a castle is the wardrobe. As we have seen, it was originally just the room where cloth was stored until made up for wear or put to other use; it later became the storeroom for the lord's garments with a staff of its own. Each New Year new clothes were distributed among the household. As the material for these clothes was the same, only varying in quantity and quality, all the occupants of a castle, except the lord and his immediate family, wore a set of clothes which marked them out from other establishments and from visitors. Alliance, connexion and dependence on a castellan were readily discernible to a visitor. Unstable dyes and expense often limited the colour of the cloth handed out to green, brown or an indeterminate grey to black. Lengthy spells of mourning meant that the residents at a castle were often dressed in

black. In later medieval castles separate wardrobes were maintained for the lord and his wife.

Arsenals

One element often given undue emphasis in an examination of castles is the storage of arms, armour and munitions. At times these were used to terrorize the locality and by a show of strength to pervert the course of justice, but their function was to strengthen a lord's authority in his maintenance of law and order and to guarantee some preparedness in the event of rebellion or war. Royal regulations in England and elsewhere gave legal backing to this purpose. Large depositories of arms and armour only became a feature of castles in their final phase. Until then arms were normally scattered throughout the complex ready for use in an emergency. The evidence is scanty but armourers seem to have been employed in the larger establishments from the thirteenth century onwards. Their work was to maintain the arms on the premises in good order but the upkeep of pieces used only in the mock warfare of the tournament took up most of their time. Tiltyards for tournaments are mentioned in guidebooks but the evidence for these is untrustworthy.

Left A woman bathing in a tub, from a fifteenth-century glass roundel for the month of June in a series depicting labours of the months (from Brandiston Hall, Norfolk).
Far left The miniature for the month of January in the *Très Riches Heures* depicts feasting at Christmas in the great hall of one of the duke's castles. (From a facsimile in the Victoria & Albert Museum, London.)
Below The harbour enclosed by walls and towers of the early fourteenth-century castle at Sirmione on Lake Garda (Venetia).
Above The outside of Conway Castle (Gwynedd) is shown to have been entirely whitewashed in this early fifteenth-century French miniature of Richard II staying there before his capture by Henry of Bolingbroke.
Above left The miniature for the month of February in the *Playfair Hours* showing a servant bringing in fuel and the master sitting close to the fire.

Other features inside and outside the castle

In addition to parts already covered some castles had a number of other facilities within their walls, and these varied from place to place. The most obvious of these was the provision of stabling. For a society where the knight on horseback played a major role it seems odd at first sight to find that stables were rare in fortresses, but expense accounts for stables make it clear that they accommodated horses used for travelling and conveyance, not those for war which were bred and kept at special stud farms. The stables included an area for the storage of hay. There were separate storehouses for foodstuffs produced in the locality for consumption by the household, and the most common of these were the granaries. There were mills for grinding corn – at Krak des Chevaliers in Syria driven by the wind, at the Tower of London by the tide and at Carisbrooke in the Isle of Wight by a donkey – but the majority were worked by hand. Separate laundries and brewhouses existed in the larger and more sophisticated establishments. Sometimes there were forges where work ranging from the shoeing of horses to the maintenance of armour was undertaken. A few castles situated at the water's edge had quays for berthing ships within their walls, such as Beaumaris in

Right the elaborate window-bays of the lord's quarters overlooking the inner garden at Thornbury Castle (Gloucestershire) built in the early sixteenth century for Edward Stafford, Duke of Buckingham.
Below right A Flemish bronze candlestick of the thirteenth century resting on a base formed from a grotesque winged monster.
Below The fine ashlar exterior of the late fourteenth-century castle at Nunney near Frome in Somerset. Nunney was built in the grand manner by Sir John de la Mare during the reign of Edward III. An extensive enclosure to the north and west has now gone but the impressive moated and machicolated donjon remains.

Anglesey and Sirmione in the Veneto, Italy. Gardens existed mainly for the growing of herbs and other plants for use in the kitchen but vines and roses were also cultivated. Roof gardens had been introduced in France and England by the fifteenth century and to judge from the architectural evidence were popular earlier. Kennels for dogs, mews for hawks and dovecotes for doves and pigeons completed the ensemble.

Contrary to general belief walls with battlements did not define the extent of a castle and many elements making up a castle were to be found outside the walls. In addition to further gardens there were orchards and vineyards to give pleasure as well as fruits. There were also parks for deer, warrens for rabbits and pounds for other animals, besides fishponds, lodges and banqueting houses. Moats and lakes were supplied with small boats for rowing. Although initially rare these facilities multiplied in the wake of the pursuit of pleasure from the thirteenth century onwards. Some castles had hermitages but whether these housed anchorites or were follies is unclear.

Centres of administration

As the residence of a lord a castle was more than a home, indeed its functions were manifold. Rank brought with it land

Left More a fantasy than serious fortification, the early sixteenth-century castle at Azay-le-Rideau (Indre-et-Loire) is seen reflected in its moat. It was built for the financier Gilles Berthelot and served a largely residential role, but an impression of fortification can be seen in the turrets and machicolations.

rooms, each successive room being smaller than the one immediately before, and the last the most private. Even there a lord was waited on by his personal servants who rarely left him unattended. To get away from others in a castle was almost impossible and for someone not naturally gregarious life there cannot have been happy.

Provision for leisure

Evidence of amusements is scanty. For the most part the residents of a castle had to find their own. Pieces and boards for chess and backgammon are mentioned in a variety of sources but other games remain a matter of guesswork. Tennis became fashionable in France in the late fourteenth century and others elsewhere soon took it up. Music-making was presumably a regular pastime; towards the end of the Middle Ages some of the more expensive instruments, such as lutes and virginals, are mentioned in accounts and inventories. The larger households maintained musicians of their own from the earliest phase of castle-building and later had troupes of actors as well. Their skills were sought after by the great and the patronage offered to anyone with talent was thought to add lustre to a lord as well as to his household and residences. Books were rare, even after the advent of the printing press, but by the fifteenth century collections of works of devotion, manuals, histories and contemporary popular fiction seem to have been common in western Europe. Some Italian castles had galleries of classical sculpture as early as in the thirteenth century, such as that owned by Frederick II at Lucera in Apulia, and secular paintings were displayed at Ferrara a hundred years later, but novelties of this type remained rare until the Renaissance.

Aesthetic consideration and appreciation

Lords often sang the praises of the castles in their ownership as homes, not as fortifications. The phrases used for the most part are terse but Gerald of Wales, more articulate than most, described his birthplace at Manorbier in Dyfed with undoubted affection. That Gerald's outpouring was not the product of an acute sensibility is borne out by the descriptions of castles left by travellers, chroniclers and other writers. The description of a castle in *Sir Gawain and the Green Knight* epitomizes many of these.

> *There were fair turrets fashioned between, with many loopholes well devised to shut fast. Gawain had never seen a better barbican. Further in he saw the hall rising high, with towers all about, whose pinnacles rose aloft, with carven tops cunningly wrought. On the tower roofs his eye picked out many white chimneys that gleamed like chalk cliffs in the sunlight. And there were so many pinnacles, gaily painted, scattered about everywhere and climbing one above another among the embrasures of the castle, that it looked as though it were cut out of paper.*

Fit II, stanza 34 (modernized English)

Visual impact was desired and the interest aroused today by buildings such as Castel del Monte in Apulia, El Real de Manzanares in Madrid province, Nunney in Somerset, Thornbury in Gloucestershire and Wardour in Wiltshire was deliberately contrived. Castles were meant to be homes and objects of joy – and when necessary, but only when necessary, seats of war.

and authority, and thus castles were power houses. The area managed by some extended no further than the adjoining manor but many were the centres for liberties, honors, seignories, counties and palatinates. Some were the headquarters for a series of estates. Castles served not only a variety of domestic purposes but also of administrative ones. Their buildings were used as the meeting place of local courts, of assizes and of other assemblies. As centres of justice they had prisons for holding malefactors captive. As centres of management they had areas reserved for the safe-keeping of accounts and other records. Those administering major lordships also housed writing offices and treasuries called respectively chanceries and exchequers. A few had mints for coining money.

Public life without privacy

As the residence of a lord, a castle was a place for show and ceremony was vigorously observed. The elaboration of codes of etiquette by the Burgundians, French and Italians made the life of a lord in public highly ritualistic. A wish on his part for privacy led to a withdrawal into apartments of his own, to the resentment of others who saw in this a sign of moral decline. The quest for privacy resulted in the construction of series of

GAZETTEER
& Reference

While there can be no question of a complete and definitive list of the thousands of castles which survive or are known to have existed in Europe and the former Latin Christendom, the purpose of the following Gazetteer is to provide as generous a selection as space will allow of the best or most informative sites. These are arranged alphabetically within regions which are themselves, it is hoped, a reasonable compromise between areas of modern tourism and those historical units – kingdoms and principalities – which produced the castles and are thus the proper context for their understanding. As a further aid to this understanding, each region is given a short introduction of its own, noting its peculiarities whether historical or architectural. These regional introductions are not the least valuable part of the Gazetteer, for no building can be appreciated in isolation, and even in the so-called Middle Ages, when Latin Christendom had a cultural and social unity long since lost, not all countries were the same either in their historical experience or their architecture. The phrase 'the feudal system' is frowned upon by historians (and examiners) because it implies a degree of uniformity which did not exist, and of castles even less than other types of building, perhaps, can the philistine cry be uttered, 'when you have seen one, you have seen them all'. For each castle in each region a brief description and history is given noting points of particular interest, together with an indication of its location and accessibility as accurate as information at the time of publication can make it. It should be noted with regret that in England at present the well-known standard hours of opening for Ancient Monuments in the custody of the Department of the Environment are subject to arbitrary alteration without notice, in the name of economy.

A map of Europe in the Middle Ages by Mercator (1512–94).

TERRAE POLARIS PARS

PETZOREKE MORE

ASIAE

PONTVS EVXINVS
Italis Mare maior.

MARE HYRCANVM
siue
CASPIVM
nunc
MARE DE SALA
Ruthenis
Chualenske morie

PARS

MEDITER · RANEVM

EVROPA,
ad magnæ Europæ ge:
rardi Mercatoris P. imitati
onem, Rumoldi Mercatoris F.
cura edita, seruato tamen
initio longitudinis ex ratio
ne magnetis, quod Pater
in magna sua vniuer:
sali posuit.

Medius Meridianus eo reliqui ad hunc
inclinantur pro ratione 60. & 40.
parallelorum.

Duysburgi Chuorsum typis æneis.

England

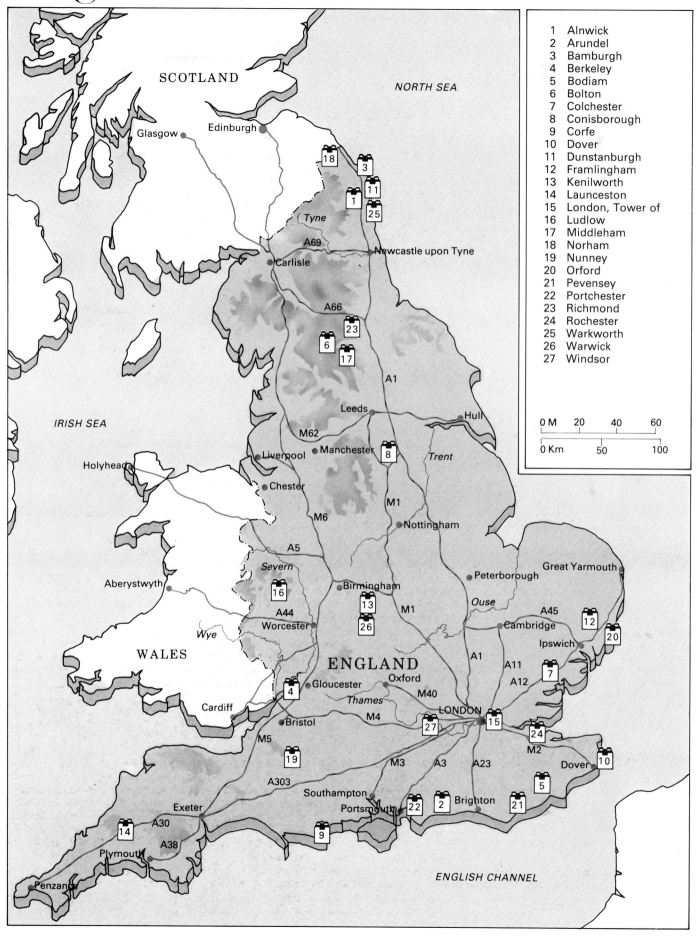

SCOTLAND

NORTH SEA

Glasgow   Edinburgh

Tyne

A69

Carlisle

A66

IRISH SEA

Holyhead

Liverpool   Manchester

Chester

Trent

Leeds

Hull

M62

M6

M1

Nottingham

A5

Severn

Aberystwyth

A44

Worcester

Wye

WALES

Cardiff

Bristol

Gloucester

Thames

Oxford

M40

M4

Birmingham

M1

Peterborough

Ouse

Cambridge

A45

Ipswich

A11

A12

Great Yarmouth

ENGLAND

LONDON

A1

M5

A303

A30

A38

Exeter

Plymouth

Penzance

Southampton

Portsmouth

M3

A3

A23

Brighton

Dover

M2

ENGLISH CHANNEL

1	Alnwick
2	Arundel
3	Bamburgh
4	Berkeley
5	Bodiam
6	Bolton
7	Colchester
8	Conisborough
9	Corfe
10	Dover
11	Dunstanburgh
12	Framlingham
13	Kenilworth
14	Launceston
15	London, Tower of
16	Ludlow
17	Middleham
18	Norham
19	Nunney
20	Orford
21	Pevensey
22	Portchester
23	Richmond
24	Rochester
25	Warkworth
26	Warwick
27	Windsor

0 M   20   40   60

0 Km   50   100

Castles are found across the length and breadth of England. Indeed those listed below can only be a mere selection from the countless examples of this peculiarly medieval type of building (or earthwork) which is so integral a feature of the English heritage. Introduced by the Normans as part of their new feudal regime, the castle reached its apogee here as elsewhere between the late 12th and earlier 14th centuries, as witness Dover, Corfe and the Tower of London, each fully developed within that period. In the north especially, distance from London and the need of constant vigilance against the Scots ensured maintenance of the castle's strength longer until it ceased to have military importance. A large number of English castles are administered by the Department of the Environment. Because of the sometimes complicated system operated by the Department and other bodies we have provided a standard reference for opening times as follows:

SH	Weekdays	Sundays
Mar–Apr	9.30am–5.30am	2pm–5.30pm
May–Sept	9.30am–7pm	2pm–7pm
Oct	9.30am–5.30pm	2pm–5.30pm
Nov–Feb	9.30am–4pm	2pm–4pm

SM: Sunday mornings from 9.30am, April to September.

1 Alnwick

Location: Alnwick (Northumberland), on the A1 34 miles (58 km) north of Newcastle.
Description: Splendid but much restored castle, seat of the dukes of Northumberland. Museum.
Opening hours: (8 May to 29 September) 1pm–5pm. (Closed Fridays.)
History: Though now associated with the Percy family, who obtained it in the 14th century, Alnwick was previously held by the Vesci family and probably founded by Ivo de Vesci c. 1100. Beginning as a motte-and-bailey, it was fortified in stone during the 12th century, rebuilt by the Percy family in the 14th century and again, unfortunately, in the 18th and 19th centuries. The principal features include the elaborate towered shell-keep or donjon – 'the seven towers of the Percies' – and the outer west gate and barbican with, here and elsewhere, intimidating figures (modern replacements of medieval originals) on the battlements.

2 Arundel

Location: Arundel (West Sussex).
Description: Magnificent but much restored castle, in continuous occupation from the 11th century, now the seat of England's premier duke.
Opening hours: Almost daily.
History: The castle was founded soon after 1066 by Roger of Montgomery, close friend of the Conqueror and also Earl of Shrewsbury, as the centre of the Sussex rape, or military lordship, of Arundel conferred upon him by the king. Since then it has almost always been held by some of the noblest in the land – the Albini (Aubigny) earls of Sussex, the Fitz Alans and, since the 16th century, the

Howard dukes of Norfolk. The residential buildings in the southern or lower bailey were substantially rebuilt in the 19th century but that ward is entered through Roger of Montgomery's gatehouse (with 13th-century barbican). To the left Earl Roger's motte remains, crowned by a 12th-century shell-keep, its original entrance blocked and replaced by the 13th-century Well Tower.

3 Bamburgh

Location: Bamburgh (Northumberland) on the B1341 off the A1.
Description: Vast but much restored castle built on a site of natural strength overlooking the North Sea.
Opening hours: (April to September) 2pm–dusk.
History: The castle was founded soon after the Norman Conquest within the site of an ancient citadel of the kings of Bernicia. It was taken by William Rufus from Robert de Mowbray, Earl of Northumbria, in 1095 and besieged with heavy guns by Warwick 'the Kingmaker' in 1464. The rectangular keep is attributed to Henry II and the inner bailey contained the King's Hall, the Captain's Hall and a large kitchen, all originally of 13th-century date. The castle was fully developed by c. 1250 but has undergone drastic restoration in the modern period.

4 Berkeley

Location: Berkeley (Gloucestershire) on the B4509 off the A38 or M5.
Description: A mainly 12th-century castle still in the possession of the Berkeley family.
Opening hours: (May to August: Tuesday to Saturday) 11am–6pm, (Sundays) 2pm–6pm. (April and September) 2pm–6pm. (except

Bodiam

Mondays). (October: Sundays) 2pm–4.30pm.
History: The castle, basically a motte with two baileys (cf Arundel, Windsor), was first founded here by William fitz Osbern, Earl of Hereford and close friend of William the Conqueror. In the 1150s it was granted to Robert Fitz Hardinge, direct ancestor of the present lord, by Henry II who built the remarkable shell-keep. This (cf Farnham) revets the motte rather than crowning its summit. The fine domestic range, including the great hall, in the eastern bailey is 14th-century. The castle is famed especially as the place of the confinement and savage murder of Edward II in 1327.

5 Bodiam

Location: Bodiam (East Sussex) 15 miles (24 km) north of Hastings.
Description: Very photogenic 14th-century castle now owned by the National Trust. Museum in the caretaker's cottage.
Opening hours: (April to September: Monday to Saturday) 10am–7pm, (Sundays) 2pm–6pm. (November to March) 10am–4.30pm or dusk (closed on Sundays).
History: Bodiam was built under licence granted by Richard II in 1385 to Sir Edward Dalyngrigge for the defence of the adjacent country against the urgent danger of French raids. It is a quadrangular castle of late medieval type (cf Bolton), the sumptuous residential ranges neatly articulated and integrated within its walls and towers and set about a central courtyard. There are four drum towers at the angles, a fine rectangular twin-towered and machicolated gatehouse, a rectangular and machicolated postern tower opposite and a projecting rectangular tower in the centre of each of the two remaining sides. The castle is particularly notable for its wide water defences, originally traversed by a right-angled approach via outworks and drawbridges.

Bolton

6 Bolton

Location: Castle Bolton (North Yorkshire). A684 west from the A1 for 23 miles (37 km) and then north-west at Wensley to Castle Bolton.
Description: Quadrangular castle contemporary with Bodiam. Museum.
Opening hours: Open during daylight hours. (Closed Mondays.)
History: This castle was built by Richard, Lord Scrope under licence granted in 1379. Very similar to Bodiam in general design, all its towers are, however, rectangular and there is no separate gatehouse, the well-defined entrance passage being through the eastern range. The ample and lordly accommodation here comprises eight distinct residential suites, twelve single-chamber apartments for lesser men, a communal great hall and chapel, kitchen, service rooms and stables. Towards the end of its history, Mary Queen of Scots was imprisoned here from July 1568 to January 1569.

7 Colchester

Location: Colchester (Essex) on the A12 from London.
Description: The largest and one of the oldest tower-keeps in England, partially demolished.
Opening hours: (Weekdays) 10am–5pm; (Sundays: April to September) 2.30pm–5pm.
History: Almost all that remains of the castle planted in the north-east quarter of the town by the Normans is the great tower-keep dating from the Conqueror's reign. Built on the foundations of a Roman temple, which may partly account for its vast size, it is even bigger than the Conqueror's White Tower at London which it closely resembles in plan. Both have in particular an apsidal projection at the south-east angle which housed the apse of the chapel serving the second and main residential floor within. Colchester, however, has lost its top levels by attempted demolition in and after 1683, and its remaining internal arrangements are unfortunately hidden by the municipal museum which occupies it. The present entrance at ground level is an early 12th-century insertion. The castle's active history ended dramatically and tragically with its heroic defence for Charles I (against Fairfax at the end of the 17th-century Civil War) by Sir Charles Lucas and Sir George Lisle who were shot upon their surrender.

8 Conisborough

Location: Conisborough (South Yorkshire) on the A630 between Sheffield and Doncaster.
Description: A mainly 12th-century castle dominated by a tower-keep of unusual design.
Opening hours: SH, SM.
History: The present castle was built *c.* 1180 by earl Hamelin 'Plantagenet', half-brother of Henry II (and who had married the Warenne heiress), on the site of the early castle founded here by the first William de Warenne, companion of the Conqueror and lord also of Lewes (Sussex), Reigate (Surrey) and Castle Acre (Norfolk). The curtain wall is interesting for its solid buttress towers, but the oustanding feature of the castle is its splendid keep of finest ashlar, a great cylindrical tower with six projecting buttresses, which closely resembles the tower-keep of another Warenne castle at Mortemer (Seine-Maritime) in Normandy.

9 Corfe

Location: Corfe Castle (Dorset) on the A351 between Wareham and Swanage.
Description: The most dramatic castle ruin in England, standing on an isolated hill along the spine of the Isle of Purbeck.
Opening hours: (March to October) 10am–dusk; (November to February) afternoons only.
History: This favoured royal castle was founded by the Conqueror and thereafter steadily developed in terms of walls and towers over the next two centuries. The inner bailey still has an 11th-century curtain wall and the western bailey the remains of an 11th-century hall. The rectangular tower-keep is attributed to Henry I, and King John built the beautifully elegant residence called 'La Gloriette' next to it. The towered curtain of the outer bailey dates mainly from the 13th century and its outer gate was completed by Edward I in the 1280s. The castle was viciously slighted by the Parliamentary forces after its prolonged resistance in the 17th-century Civil War.

10 Dover

Location: Dover (Kent).
Description: Powerful royal castle on 'the White Cliffs of Dover', called 'the key of England' in the 13th century, and regrettably 'modernized' in the 18th and early 19th centuries against the threat of French invasion.
Opening hours: SH, SM.
History: The first castle at Dover was planted within the existing Anglo-Saxon burgh (and former Iron Age fortress), in the vicinity of the Anglo-Saxon Church of St Mary-in-Castro and its Roman lighthouse, by William the Conqueror immediately after the Battle of Hastings. Little else is known until the great

Corfe

rebuilding and expansion begun by Henry II a century later and which in the 13th century took in the whole ancient site. Henry II built the towered outer curtain on the north-east from Avranches to Fitzwilliam, the whole towered curtain of the inner bailey and the great keep within it (and thus he fortified on the concentric plan in the 1180s). John continued the outer curtain as far round as Peverel, with a gateway at the northern apex. Then in 1216 the castle was besieged and nearly taken by undermining from the north. In the next reign, therefore, the weaknesses revealed were made good. The Fitzwilliam postern was built. John's northern gateway was blocked to form the present trinity of the Norfolk Towers. A new main gateway was built in the sophisticated shape of the present Constable's Gate. Finally the outer curtain was extended to the cliff's edge.

11 Dunstanburgh

Location: On the coast path 1 mile (1½ km) north of Craster, 7 miles (11 km) north-east of Alnwick, Northumberland.
Description: Large 14th-century castle built on 100-foot-high cliffs.
Opening hours: SH, SM.
History: When it was first built between 1313 and 1316, the castle was among the largest in England, occupying 11 acres. It was of great strategic importance in the Anglo-Scottish wars, guarding a harbour esential for local supplies if Berwick was in Scottish hands, as it frequently was after Bannockburn (1314).

In the tradition of Edward I at Harlech and Beaumaris, the gatehouse was the strong-point of the castle, being formed by two massive D-shaped towers. About 1380 John of Gaunt converted it into a veritable keep with much attention to comfort. He blocked the gateway and strengthened its defences by building a new wall within the vast bailey to form an inner ward round what had become his new donjon.

12 Framlingham

Location: Framlingham (Suffolk) on the B1120 north-east from Ipswich.
Description: Impressive late 12th-century towered walls topped by improbable Tudor chimneys.
Opening hours: SH, SM.
History: The first castle here of the Bigod lords of Framlingham, who became earls of Norfolk in 1141 (and were lords also of the Suffolk castles of Bungay and Walton), was demolished by Henry II after the rebellion of earl Hugh Bigod in 1173–4. It was refortified and rebuilt by the heir, earl Roger, c. 1190. What principally remains, between two baileys, is the inner enclosure whose splendid towered curtain still dominates the countryside. Within are vestiges of 12th-century (first castle) and early 13th-century halls and chambers, demolished in the 17th century, and an almshouse of that date. The Bigod earls were succeeded by the Mowbrays and the Howard dukes of Norfolk succeeded both (see tombs in the parish church) to proclaim Mary Tudor here as Queen in 1553 – and raise those chimneys.

Launceston

13 Kenilworth

Location: Kenilworth (Warwickshire) on the A46 south-west of Coventry.
Description: Massive castle first dating from the 12th century but with additional buildings up to Tudor times.
Opening hours: SH, SM.
History: Kenilworth by any standards was one of the most important castles in the realm and its lords themselves became kings of England when the House of Lancaster usurped the throne in 1399. Before this it had successfully withstood the greatest siege in English medieval history in 1266. The castle, moreover, had a longer active history than most, for the last period not only of lordly occupation but also of major works was the reign of Elizabeth I and the time of Robert Dudley, Earl of Leicester, her favourite. In the course of it all the fortress became a fortified palace and expanded from the original early 12th-century nucleus of Geoffrey de Clinton, Chamberlain of Henry I, represented today by the area of the keep and inner bailey, to the present extent of the great outer court – plus, of course, the huge expanse of its near-impregnable water defences (now drained away). Splendid, though ruined, buildings of all periods survive from the 12th to the 16th century, notably the 12th-century keep (grossly distorted by Leicester and slighted in the 17th century), John of Gaunt's 14th-century great hall and chambers, and Leicester's Building and Leicester's Gatehouse of the Elizabethan Indian summer.

14 Launceston

Location: Launceston (Cornwall) on the A30 west of Exeter.
Description: Powerful motte-and-bailey castle with later stonework dominating the historic gateway to Cornwall.

Opening hours: SH, SM.
History: Ever since Robert, Count of Mortain, the Conqueror's half-brother, planted it here soon after 1066, Launceston has been the most important castle of the earldom, later duchy, of Cornwall, controlling the main entrance to the country across the ford and ditch of Polston. A motte-and-bailey castle on a ridge, its most important feature now is the complex combination of mantlet wall, shell-keep and cylindrical tower-keep (12th- and 13th-century) forming its donjon on the original motte.

15 London, Tower of

Location: Tower Hill underground station (District and Circle Lines).
Description: Great royal castle of all dates from 1066 to the 16th century. Armouries and Crown Jewels.
Opening hours: Weekdays (March to October) 9.30am–5pm; (November to February) 9.30am–4pm. Sundays (March to October) 2pm–5pm.
History: The first castle of 1066 was an enclosure in the south-east angle of the Roman city wall, not extending further west than the present Bloody Tower (13th-century). Into this enclosure the Conqueror later inserted his great White Tower. An extension westward reached and included the Bell Tower under Richard I. In Henry III's time the present inner bailey was developed and largely built, involving an expansion northwards and also eastwards beyond the city wall. Edward I brought the Tower to its present maximum development as a great concentric castle with his new outer ward and outer curtain, and new moat, water-gate (St Thomas' Tower) and landward entrance via the Byward Tower, the Middle Tower and the vanished Lion Tower beyond. The notorious role of the Tower as a place of imprisonment and execution begins about the reign of Henry VIII who abandoned it as a residence.

16 Ludlow

Location: Ludlow (Shropshire).
Description: Splendid castle with work of all periods dominating a medieval town and the River Teme.
Opening hours: (May to September) 10.30am–7.30pm; (October to April: weekdays) 10.30am–4.30pm.
History: Founded by the Lacy lords from Lassy (Calvados) in Normandy and afterwards belonging to the Mortimers, Ludlow like Richmond in Yorkshire started as a walled enclosure in the 11th century, without motte or keep. Nearly all points of interest are concentrated in the inner ward. These include 11th-century mural towers and gate-tower which (again like Richmond) was converted into a tower-keep in the 12th century; the round nave of the 12th-century chapel, and the 14th-century great hall and chamber blocks of the Mortimer period. The fine 14th-century Mortimer's Tower, however, stands on the west wall of the great outer court. Much 16th- and 17th-century work marks the castle's later role as headquarters of the Council of the Marches.

17 Middleham

Location: Middleham (North Yorkshire), on the A6108 north-west from Ripon.
Description: Massive 12th-century rectangular keep with additions from the later Middle Ages.
Opening hours: SH.
History: Fifteen hundred feet south-west of the present building is the motte-and-bailey site of the first Middleham castle raised *c.* 1086. The pride of the present castle is the great tower-keep built by Robert fitz Ralph *c.* 1170 and marking the change of site. Wrapped close about this is a towered quadrangular enclosure of the 13th and 14th centuries. A further and subsidiary enclosure to the east has vanished. The great days of

Rochester

Middleham belong to the later Middle Ages under the Nevilles and ultimately Warwick 'the King-maker', whose daughter and heiress was married by Richard III.

18 Norham

Location: Norham (Northumberland). A698 and B6470 south-west from Berwick-upon-Tweed.
Description: Ruins of important border stronghold of the bishops of Durham.
Opening hours: SH.
History: Fortified against the Scots as late as the 16th century, Norham was founded by bishop Ranulf Flambard in 1121. In plan it has an inner enclosure and a larger kidney-shaped outer ward, all defended by towered walls of every period from the 12th to the 16th century (West Gate 15th-century). The main residential buildings stand in the inner ward, including the rectangular tower-keep built by bishop Hugh du Puiset (1153–95) and altered in the 15th century.

19 Nunney

Location: Nunney (Somerset) off the A361 3 miles (5 km) south-west of Frome.
Description: Late 14th-century castle set in beautiful surroundings.
Opening hours: SH.
History: Nunney was built by Sir John de la Mare, a veteran of the French wars, under licence granted by Edward III in 1373. An extensive enclosure to the north and west has gone, and what remains is what was always the principal part: the moated and machicolated donjon containing grand residential accommodation. This is very French in design (like the contemporary Bastille in Paris and Tarascon and Pierrefonds), being basically rectangular with a cylindrical tower at each corner. Damaged by guns in the Civil War siege of 1645, the north wall fell out in 1910.

20 Orford

Location: Orford (Suffolk). A12 and B1084 east from Ipswich.
Description: 12th-century polygonal keep on the coast.
Opening hours: SH, SM.
History: Orford was built by Henry II between 1166 and 1173 at a total recorded cost of £1,413 9s 2d. Its purpose was to control the port now vanished and to contain the Bigod castles of Framlingham and Walton. Only the keep survives and is unusual in design: a polygonal main tower (cylindrical within) with three rectangular buttress towers and a forebuilding covering the entrance. The interior comprises a basement and two residential floors each with hall, chamber and kitchen. There is a chapel in the forebuilding with separate accommodation for the chaplain.

21 Pevensey

Location: Pevensey (East Sussex) on the A27 between Eastbourne and Bexhill.
Description: 13th-century castle built on the

Middleham

foundations of a Norman castle and within the Roman fortress of Anderida.
Opening hours: SH, SM.
History: The Normans landed at Pevensey (the sea then washing the walls) in 1066 and raised a castle which became the centre of the rape, or military lordship, bestowed upon Robert, Count of Mortain. The early castle was simply an enclosure of bank, ditch and palisade cutting off one section of the Anglo-Saxon burgh (itself occupying the ancient Roman fort of Anderida). The chapel within (foundations only) antedates the castle, and the curiously shaped tower-keep was inserted in the 12th century. The present walls, towers and gate of the enclosure are 13th-century.

22 Portchester

Location: Porchester (Hampshire) on the A27 or M27 west of Portsmouth.
Description: Norman castle built within an earlier Roman fort.
Opening hours: SH, SM.
History: Portchester, like Pevensey, is an example of a Norman castle inserted into a pre-Conquest Anglo-Saxon burgh – that burgh, like Pevensey, occupying a surviving Roman fort. While the castle's ditch may be earlier, its oldest fabric is 12th-century, eg the tower-keep (though later heightened), the gatehouse (with 14th-century barbican) and curtain wall south and east. The elegant

ranges of hall and chambers on the south and west sides of the courtyard were built by Richard II in 1396–9 for his new French queen. In the opposite quarter of the Roman fortress to the castle is the church of an Augustinian priory founded in 1133.

23 Richmond

Location: Richmond (North Yorkshire) on the A6136 west from the A1.
Description: Imposing Norman castle dominating the town and the River Swale.
Opening hours: SH, SM.
History: Richmond Castle – the centre of the great Honor of Richmond bestowed by the Conqueror upon Alan the Red, Count of Penthièvre – was from the beginning, like Ludlow, a stone-built enclosure without motte or keep. In contrast to Ludlow, however, remarkably little has altered since. Here, too, the original 11th-century gateway was converted into a tower-keep in the 12th century (Henry II). However almost the entire curtain wall is 11th-century, including the important series of mural towers along the east side, and so is the very important (because such survivals are rare) Scolland's Hall in the south-east angle of the bailey.

24 Rochester

Location: Rochester (Kent) on the A2 from London.
Description: Powerful, early 12th-century castle standing with the cathedral above the River Medway whose crossing it controlled.
Opening hours: SH, SM.
History: The first Norman castle of the Conqueror's day was an enclosure within the Roman city walls on the lines of the present one. Gundulf, Bishop of Rochester built the walls of the existing castle for William Rufus. The splendid tower-keep was built *c.* 1127. In the most memorable of three sieges, King John in 1215 brought down the south-eastern section of this keep by undermining. The reparation of the damage is clearly visible in the cylindrical south-east angle of the great tower and in the cylindrical mural tower beyond it. Works by Edward III and Richard II in the 14th century are represented respectively by the two eastern rectangular mural towers and the north-west bastion.

25 Warkworth

Location: Warkworth (Northumberland) on the A1068 north of Amble.
Description: Magnificent ruin of the Percy family of the North.
Opening hours: SH, SM.
History: The castle evidently began as an early motte-and-bailey. It was developed thereafter into a veritable fortified palace, with walls, towers and buildings of every period from the 12th century to the end of the Middle Ages, a fitting monument to the Percy family (also of Alnwick) who held it from 1332. Crowning it all on the ancient motte is the extraordinary donjon of *c.* 1400 (though altered in the 16th century and partially restored in the 19th), in the form of a Greek cross surmounted by a lofty turret.

26 Warwick

Location: Warwick (Warwickshire).
Description: Magnificent castle rising sheer above the River Avon; seat of the earls of Warwick from the 11th century.
Opening hours: (March to October) 10am–5.30pm; (November to February) 10am–4.30pm. (Closed Christmas Day only.)
History: Warwick (like Alnwick, Arundel and Windsor) is one of the great castles of England in continuous occupation, but unlike them avoided the worst of 19th-century restoration and new building. Founded by William the Conqueror in 1068, it has been the seat of the earls of Warwick almost without interruption – Beaumont, Newburgh, Beauchamp and now Fulke Greville. At first a motte-and-bailey, fortified in stone at least from the 12th century, it owes its present architectural magnificence especially to the 14th-century Beauchamp earls. The most notable features of that period are the Water Gate south of the motte, the splendid range of residential buildings along the river-front and – especially for students of medieval military architecture – the east front towards the town. This has an elaborately defended gatehouse and barbican in the centre and, on either flank, a superb tower: the polygonal Guy's Tower to the north and the tri-lobed Caesar's Tower rising sheer from the river to the south.

Warkworth

27 Windsor

Location: Windsor (Berkshire).
Description: Magnificent royal castle, albeit much restored, and still going strong.
Opening hours: (January to 15 March) 10am–4pm; (16 March to 30 April) 10am–5pm; (May to August) 10am–7pm; (September to 25 October) 10am–5pm; (26 October to December) 10am–4pm. (Closed only on 16 June.)
History: Royal from the Conqueror's time to now, and England's premier castle, Windsor scarcely lends itself to brief description. There are two baileys, one on either side of the original motte, all crowned with the accumulated masonry of almost every reign. The shell-keep (Round Tower) is probably Henry II's, rebuilt by Edward III, and restored and heightened in the 19th century. Inevitably 19th-century work (by Wyatt and Wyatville) abounds, but the three great drum towers which dominate the High Street of the town are basically Henry III's, and the State Apartments in the upper bailey are of Edward III's time. Edward III, Edward 'of Windsor', indeed more than any other monarch made Windsor the fortified palace it has ever since remained – the medieval Versailles of his chivalrous age. It seems fitting that the last major addition to the castle should have been the splendid late 15th-century St George's Chapel, the spiritual home of Edward's Knights of the Garter, the senior chivalrous order of the realm.

Wales, Scotland & Ireland

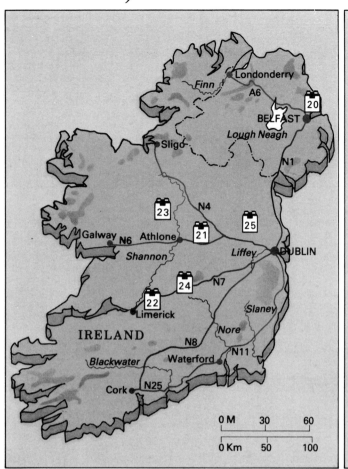

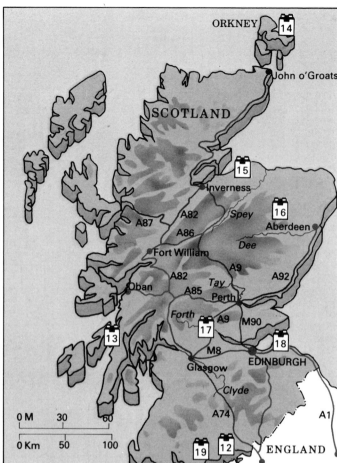

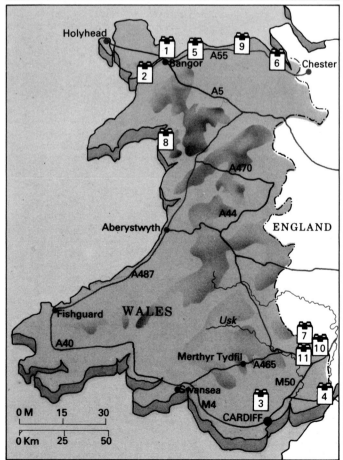

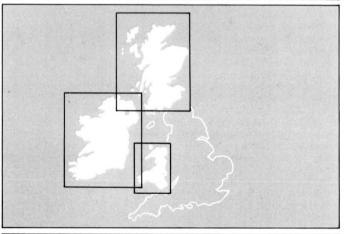

1	Beaumaris	17	Stirling
2	Caernarvon	18	Tantallon
3	Caerphilly	19	Threave
4	Chepstow	20	Carrickfergus
5	Conway	21	Castletown Geoghegan
6	Flint	22	Nenagh
7	Grosmont	23	Roscommon
8	Harlech	24	Roscrea
9	Rhuddlan	25	Trim
10	Skenfrith		
11	White Castle		
12	Caerlaverock		
13	Castle Sween		
14	Cobbie Row's Castle		
15	Duffus		
16	Kildrummy		

Wales

In the days of Edward the Confessor, Wales and the Welsh borders were a cause of concern, for two strong leaders – Gruffyd ap Rhydderch of Deheubarth and (after his death in 1055) Gruffyd ap Llewelyn of Gwynedd – began raiding the rich lands of Hereford and Gloucestershire. Harold Godwinson and his brother Tostig defeated and killed Gruffyd ap Llewelyn in 1063, which lessened the threat, but when William the Conqueror gained the English throne and began distributing lands on the Welsh borders he took no chances and deliberately favoured magnates whose qualities had already been proved on the borders of the Norman Duchy. William fitz Osbern was made Earl of Hereford in the south, Roger of Montgomery was entrusted with Shrewsbury, and Hugh, Vicomte of Avranches, was given Chester. In some cases (eg Chepstow) the castles these men built were of stone from the first, but the simplest and most effective means of penetrating the borders and furnishing a secure defensible base for offensive action to wrest the surrounding territory from the hands of the native inhabitants was the motte-and-bailey castle. To this day, the Welsh borders provide perhaps the best testimony to the enormous scope of the Norman castle-building programme, for as any Ordnance Survey map will reveal they are literally bristling with mottes and their remains.

Wales also takes credit for possessing some of the most sophisticated examples of the technique of castle-building in the whole of Europe and Latin Christendom. Taking advantage of the skills of the great Savoyard architect Master James of St George, Edward I spent some £80,000 in a programme of castle-building which resulted in such remarkable new royal castles as Beaumaris, Caernarvon, Conway, Flint and Rhuddlan. Not only were they masterpieces of design in their own right, but their carefully planned construction, hand in hand with a fortified township and their siting on tidal waters, reveals sound strategic planning. Edward's castles were vital to his success in the Welsh wars; they provided secure bases for settlement and further expansion backed up by safeguarded lines of supply and communication for his forces, since they could be reached by sea-going vessels and were not isolated inland.

The design features which characterize these castles are an enclosure without donjon or great tower as *pièce maîtresse* and ultimate stronghold, but with a much strengthened and improve gatehouse, usually twin towered, which often contains some of the best accommodation and takes on the former residential role of the keep. The mural tower on the curtain wall to provide flanking fire is an important element in the defensive planning and in several cases extra protection for the gatehouse is provided

Beaumaris

by the addition of a barbican or outwork.

The following is a standard reference for opening times:

SH:	Weekdays	Sundays
Mar–Apr	9.30am–5.30pm	2pm–5.30pm
May–Sept	9.30am–7pm	2pm–7pm
Oct	9.30am–5.30pm	2pm–5.30pm
Nov–Feb	9.30am–4pm	2pm–4pm

SM: Sundays from 9.30am, April to September.

Castles are closed on 1 January, 4 April, 24–26 December and some other bank holidays.

1 Beaumaris

Location: Beaumaris (Gwynedd) on the south-east coast of the Isle of Anglesey.
Description: Late 13th-century Edwardian concentric castle.
Opening hours: SH, SM.
History: Beaumaris, built by Master James of St George, was the last of Edward's Welsh castles to be undertaken but was never completed nor were the defences of the fortified township to the south-east. It was planned amid the Welsh rebellion and third Welsh war of 1294–5, but with the rebellion subdued as early as 1296 Edward's attention turned to Scotland and by 1300 construction ceased. Although work later resumed between 1306 and 1330, it proved unnecessary, for the castle's defences were never threatened, either by the Welsh princes or Owain Glyndwr, until 1646 when it was garrisoned for the king in the Civil War. However, the castle surrendered to Cromwell's commander Major-General Mytton after news arrived that Caernarvon had been successfully taken by siege and the Royalists defeated in a nearby battle.

2 Caernarvon

Location: Caernarvon (Gwynedd).
Description: A narrow-waisted enclosure castle conforming to the shape of the rock on which it stands with flanking towers and two gateways: the Queen's Gate at the east and

the King's Gate at the north front. Of the polygonal mural towers on the enceinte of the castle the Eagle Tower at the west end is the largest and has three turrets, each originally surmounted by a stone sculpted eagle. Adjacent to the Eagle Tower lies a dock to link the castle with the sea.
Opening hours: SH, SM.
History: Work began in June 1283 during the second Welsh war, and from the beginning Caernarvon was intended to be the finest of Edward's Welsh castles – the centre of royal government in the north and a deliberate exercise in propaganda and architectural symbolism. The siting of the castle upon the motte of Hugh, Earl of Chester, dating back to the first Norman penetration into Wales at the end of the 11th century, was intended to emphasize that Edward's campaigns were a reassertion of an established right, but a much more ambitious concept was embodied in the walls of Caernarvon. In France and England at the end of the 13th century, national monarchies were forming with imperial ideas derived from Roman Law. Philip IV's lawyers in France proclaimed that 'the king of France is emperor in his kingdom' and on the other side of the Channel, similar notions can be detected behind the building of Caernarvon. Caernarvon was formerly the Roman imperial city of Segontium and in 1283, the very year of the castle's foundation, the body of what was believed to be the Emperor Magnus Maximus (383–8), alleged father of the emperor Constantine, was discovered and on the king's orders was reburied in the church. It is no accident that the banded masonry and polygonal towers which distinguish Caernarvon from any of Edward's other Welsh castles directly recall the great walls of Theodosius II at Constantinople, and the imperial symbolism of the Eagle Tower is self apparent. Nor was it chance that brought Edward's queen, Eleanor, to Caernarvon to give birth to their son Edward, the future Edward II of England but also Edward of Caernarvon and the first English Prince of Wales; it was the culmination of a deliberate statement of an imperial ideal already interwoven in the fabric of one of the finest castles in Latin Christendom.

3 Caerphilly

Location: Caerphilly (Mid Glamorgan).
Description: A concentric castle of the late 13th century with extensive water defences.
Opening hours: SH, SM.
History: A baronial castle begun by Gilbert de Clare in 1271 (after the first attempt to the north-west was destroyed in 1268 by Llewelyn ap Gruffydd) it was not involved in Edward I's Welsh wars but later played a part in connection with the gruesome end of Edward II. Hugh le Despenser, a companion and favourite of Edward II, became Lord of Caerphilly by marrying into the Clare family and Edward sought refuge here from his wife, Isabella, and other enemies. Edward moved on elsewhere before he was finally captured, but Isabella persisted with the siege of the castle until it surrendered some months later. The king's wealth was given up to her and Despenser was beheaded. Apart from a brief struggle at the beginning of the 15th century when Owain Glyndwr captured and held it, the castle never featured again in Welsh military history.

4 Chepstow

Location: Chepstow (Gwent), 15 miles (24 km) north-east of Newport on the M4.
Description: One of the main features is the formidable Marten's Tower which is easily comparable with anything at Caerphilly or elsewhere. Built on a narrow spur of rock running eastward between the River Wye and a deep ravine, Chepstow Castle has several phases of construction. The rectangular keep (c. 1070) has the earliest datable tympanum in the British Isles.
Opening hours: SH, SM.
History: Chepstow, or 'Striguil', was begun by the great marcher lord William fitz Osbern c. 1070, but received the two new enclosures of the barbican and the Lower Bailey in the 13th century under the lordship first of Marshal (William) then of Bigod (Hugh), and Marten's Tower (c. 1270–1300) dates to Bigod's lordship as do the residential

Caernarvon

apartments in the Lower Bailey. It was also in the 13th century that the 11th-century keep was heightened and enlarged to improve its domestic accommodation, proving that despite contemporary trends to omit the keep and concentrate on the gatehouse as the ultimate strong-point, it remained, as before, in many castles the *pièce maîtresse* and final resort.

5 Conway

Location: Conway (Gwynedd), 13 miles (21 km) north-east of Bangor on the A55.
Description: Late 13th-century castle similar in overall plan to Caernarvon, with a series of mural drum-towers. The walled town is contemporary with the castle (as at Caernarvon) and it also stands upon tidal waters so that it might be supplied and, if necessary, relieved by sea.
Opening hours: SH, SM.
History: The castle was built with remarkable speed between 1283 and 1287. Edward I found himself stranded here in 1294 and cut off from the main army by an exceptionally full river. Later in 1399 Richard II visited the castle and there received Henry Percy, Earl of Northumberland, as Bolingbroke's ambassador and accepted from him a false

promise of safe conduct to meet Bolingbroke which resulted in ambush, imprisonment and the king's death within a year. During the Civil War, John Williams, Archbishop of York repaired the castle at his own expense (which had been described in 1608 as 'utterly decayed') but in spite of this it was taken without much difficulty in 1646 by the Cromwellian army under Major-General Mytton.

6 Flint

Location: Flint (Clwyd), 12 miles (19 km) north-west of Chester.
Description: Late 13th-century castle overlooking the estuary of the River Dee. Flint has an almost rectangular Inner Ward, with a detached cylindrical donjon at one of the corners.
Opening hours: SH.
History: Built 1277–86, Flint is by contrast with other Edwardian castles the most ruined in Wales, having been dismantled by the Parliamentarians after its final surrender in 1646.

7 Grosmont

Location: Grosmont (Gwent), 2½ miles (4 km) south of Pontrilas on the B4347. Pontrilas is 11 miles (18 km) north-east of Abergavenny on the A465.
Description: Grosmont, with White Castle and Skenfrith forming the Monmouthshire Trilateral, consists of an almost rectangular enclosure with deep ditches and a towered curtain. The main feature is the remains of a large first-floor hall.
Opening hours: Open at all times.
History: The castle dates from c. 1150, and the Pipe Rolls reveal that it was repaired in 1183–6. When it passed into the hands of Hubert de Burgh in 1201 (along with Skenfrith and White Castle) it appears that work was carried out on the curtain wall and gateway of the inner bailey.

8 Harlech

Location: Harlech (Gwynedd), 25 miles (40 km) south-east of Caernarvon on the A496.

Harlech

Description: Late 13th-century castle conforming to the concentric plan of fortification standing upon the estuary of the River Dwyryd with a dock to provide access by sea.

Opening hours: SH, SM.

History: Begun in spring or early summer of 1283 during the second Welsh war the castle was finished in 1290 and must rank as one of the superb achievements of Master James of St George who was himself appointed Constable of Harlech from 1290–93. In 1294 the Welsh rebels had to give up a futile attempt to besiege Harlech when a relieving force arrived from Conway and Caernarvon. However, in 1401 the castle was besieged by Owain Glyndwr who blocked the landward side, while his French allies patrolled the water below and with the sea route cut off the garrison had no choice but to surrender after holding out for as long as possible. During the Wars of the Roses, Harlech was strongly Lancastrian under the charge of Dafydd ap Ieuan, and his men were the 'Men of Harlech' who inspired the famous song. The castle endured a long and bitter siege before surrendering to the Yorkists under Lord Herbert, Earl of Pembroke, and Dafydd was the last of the Lancastrian commanders in England to surrender to the Yorkists, doing so on favourable terms in 1468. Finally, the castle withstood Parliament under the indomitable Major-General Mytton and was the last garrison to give in to the Cromwellians in 1647.

9 Rhuddlan

Location: Rhuddlan (Clwyd), 2½ miles (4 km) south of Rhyl on the A525.

Description: Late 13th-century castle with a diamond-shaped inner ward and concentric fortification.

Opening hours: SH, SM.

History: The second castle and borough at Rhuddlan (1277–82) replaced the earlier borough and motte-and-bailey to the south-east, built by Robert of Rhuddlan in the late 11th century. To link the castle with the sea the course of the River Clwyd had to be diverted into a deep-water channel between two and three miles long, specially dug for the purpose. As with other fine castles built by

Master James of St George, it fell before Major-General Mytton in the Civil War in 1646.

10 Skenfrith

Location: Skenfrith (Gwent), 12 miles (19 km) east of Abergavenny on the B4521.

Description: A cylindrical donjon built on an artificial mound with a quadrilateral ward with a drum tower at each corner.

Opening hours: Open at all reasonable times.

History: Though repaired in 1163 and 1183 onwards (according to the Pipe Rolls) most of the castle dates from after 1201 when it passed to Hubert de Burgh.

11 White Castle

Location: On a hill top 1½ miles (2½ km) north-west of Llantilio Crossenny (Gwent), 6 miles (10 km) east of Abergavenny on the B4233.

Description: The castle has an ovoid Inner Ward defended by a curtain wall with flanking towers, and to the north-west a fine twin-towered gatehouse. At the south-east end of the Inner Ward can be seen the square foundations of the 12th-century keep which was destroyed in the early 13th century so as not to obstruct the flanking fire of the towers then added to the curtain.

Opening hours: SH.

History: The Pipe Rolls confirm that work was carried out in 1161–2, and later between 1184 and 1186. In 1201 King John granted White Castle, Grosmont and Skenfrith to Hubert de Burgh, an officer in the king's service who gained fame in the war against Philip Augustus by his prolonged defence of Chinon. It was probably during Hubert de Burgh's time that most of the work on updating the castles was carried out; the destruction of the keep and the concentration upon the gatehouse as the ultimate stronghold illustrates a concept which was then well in advance of its time, and only brought to perfection with Edward I's castles at the end of the 13th century.

Conway

Scotland

Feudal institutions and, of course, castles came to Lowland Scotland in the 12th century under the influence of the Norman, French and other Continental adventurers and with the active assistance of the Conmore dynasty. As with Ireland, the castles which ideally suited the settlers for their ease of construction were of the motte-and-bailey variety. Stone castles do not seem to appear (at least in any number) until the beginning of the 13th century, when Lowland castles were being built of stone. But when Edward I turned his attention to Scotland after his Welsh wars, the standard of castle-building had caught up with contemporary developments in England and on the Continent as Caerlaverock and Kildrummy bear witness.

The first half of the 14th century in Scotland was occupied with the two devastating wars of Independence, and this was a time when more castles were dismantled than were constructed. Recovery came only at the end of the century, and the castles built during this period usually consisted of simple rectangular tower-houses, reverting in bare essentials to the principle of the old Norman keep. They provided the simplest and cheapest form of stronghold and residence for a landowner, whether small laird or great baron, and their design, which is simply a normal medieval hall-house with the apartments piled on top of one another for security instead of extending horizontally, can be seen as an important architectural development; perhaps this is the 'missing link' in the evolution from the medieval to the modern conception of house construction and layout?

12 Caerlaverock

Location: Caerlaverock (Dumfriesshire), 7 miles (11 km) south of Dumfries on the B725.

Description: A triangular castle with a fine twin-towered gatehouse at the apex of the triangle and a drum tower at each of the other two angles. A guesthouse range with an elegant Renaissance facade was added in the 1630s.

Opening hours: (April to September: weekdays) 9.30am–7pm, (Sundays) 2pm–7pm; (October to March: weekdays) 9.30am–4pm, (Sundays) 2pm–4pm.

History: An earlier rectangular castle (c. 1230) lies a few hundred yards away in the wood, but, as the poem makes clear, it was the magnificent shield-shaped castle built c. 1280 which Edward I besieged and captured in 1300 during his Scottish campaign. In 1313, when Sir Eustace Maxwell was in possession, he decided to declare for Robert Bruce rather than for Edward II and dismantled it in keeping with the Scottish policy to render useless any castle which might be of help to the English. The castle was later besieged, captured and dismantled by the Covenanters

Caerlaverock

in 1640 which meant that the splendour of the guesthouse range was extremely short lived. In spite of the dismantling and later reconstructions much of the original masonry remains and it provides a good example of the tendency in the Edwardian period to concentrate on the defensive strength of the gatehouse and enceinte rather than the keep.

13 Castle Sween

Location: On the south-east shore of Loch Sween, 11 miles (18 km) south-west of Lochgilphead (Strathclyde). Proceed via the A816 north of Lochgilphead for 2 miles (3 km) then the B841 west for 3 miles (5 km). At Bellanoch take the unclassified road south towards Achanamara and Kilmory. The castle is 7 miles (11 km) south-west of Achanamara.
Description: Considered to be the earliest stone castle in Scotland built after the Norman style (c. 1220) it consists of a rectangular keep with large pilaster and angle buttresses. Later additions include a great oblong tower-house with pointed loopholes, and a cylindrical tower.
Opening hours: Open at all times.
History: Built by a predecessor of Dugall McSwine, the castle was destroyed in 1647 by Sir Alexander MacDonald, one of Montrose's commanders.

14 Cobbie Row's Castle

Location: Isle of Wyre, Orkney Islands.
Description: Rectangular stone keep within an oval ditch-and-bank with the remains of a square building added on to the north corner of the east wall.
Opening hours: Open at all times.
History: Alleged to be the oldest datable Scottish castle of stone it was, of course, built on an island where timber for construction was unobtainable. It was not built by a Norman settler or a Scottish lord but by a Norse chief, Kolbein Hruga, c. 1145, and the modern name is merely a corrupted form. The Orkneyinga Saga mentions a *steinkastala* in Wyre at that date, and it is not altogether surprising to find a Norse castle of stone here;

the Norsemen had adopted feudalism by the 12th century and were quite capable of building stone castles as the excavations at King Sverre's, near Trondheim, have shown. Moreover, the Norsemen of these northern islands of Scotland (which still belonged to Norway until 1468) could command the services of the best masons of the Norman Romanesque, for Kirkwall Cathedral suggests a great affinity with Durham.

15 Duffus

Location: Duffus (Morayshire), 5 miles (8 km) north-west of Elgin on the B9021.
Description: A motte-and-bailey surrounded by an ovoid outer ditch. In the 14th century the bailey was enclosed with a curtain wall and a stone donjon was built on the motte which, however, subsided under its weight, splitting the donjon in two. Within the bailey are the remains of a hall which was reconstructed in the 15th century.
Opening hours: Open at all times.
History: The castle is said to have been built by Freskin the Fleming in 1151 and the lands were certainly in his hands by 1153. It is also the original seat of the Moravia or Murray family, now represented by the ducal houses of Atholl and Sutherland.

16 Kildrummy

Location: Kildrummy (Aberdeenshire), 30 miles (48 km) west of Aberdeen on the A944, then turning south on to the A97.
Description: A 13th-century enceinte castle to a design of St Gilbert consisting of a large semicircular walled enclosure with five cylindrical mural towers. It possesses an Edwardian gatehouse apparently built by Master James of St George.
Opening hours: (April to September: weekdays) 9.30am–7pm, (Sundays) 2pm–7pm; (October to March: weekdays) 9.30am–4pm, (Sundays) 2pm–4pm.
History: In 1305 Kildrummy, under the Earl of Mar, became involved in an attempt to put Robert Bruce on the Scottish throne. After Bruce's defeat at Methuen in the same year he sent his queen and her ladies to the castle while he fled to the Western Isles. The castle was besieged by Prince Edward (later Edward II) in 1306, but by that time the queen had escaped northward. It continued to feature in Scottish history from the Wars of Independence to the 1715 rising when it was dismantled.

17 Stirling

Location: Stirling (Stirlingshire).
Description: The early castle as it was even at the time of Bannockburn in 1314 has now disappeared and the earliest parts date from the 15th century. The main features of the castle are: the central turreted gatehouse with its flanking towers and curtain wall, the Great Hall, the Palace, the King's Old Buildings and the Chapel Royal, all dating from a period between the reigns of James III (acceded 1460) and James VI (acceded 1567).
Opening hours: (April, May and September: weekdays) 9.30am–6.15pm, (Sundays) 11am–

6pm; (June to August: weekdays) 9.30am–8pm, (Sundays) 11am–7pm; (October and March: weekdays) 9.30am–4pm, (Sundays) 1pm–4pm.
History: Stirling occupies the most powerful strategic position dominating the main ford of the River Forth, the link between the south and the north, the Highlands and Lowlands, and it has been very appropriately called 'the Key to Scotland'. Consequently the castle has changed hands more than any other and the Battle of Bannockburn took place to decide who should control it. Robert Bruce promptly dismantled the castle after his triumph in fear of the disastrous consequences should he lose control of it to the English. It is difficult to ascertain the date of the earlier castle at Stirling, but the castle chapel existed by 1115.

18 Tantallon

Location: On the coast 2½ miles (4 km) east of North Berwick (East Lothian), 20 miles (32 km) north-east of Edinburgh on the A198.
Description: The castle stands on a coastal promontory opposite the Bass Rock, and the principal feature is the huge curtain wall, with an imposing cylindrical tower at either end, which spans the promontory from cliff to cliff. In the middle of this curtain is the gatehouse and well appointed lord's residence. It has two great halls: the lower equipped as a mess for the garrison, and the upper a traditional festal hall for the lord.
Opening hours: (April to September: weekdays) 9.30am–7pm, (Sundays) 2pm–7pm; (October to March: weekdays) 9.30am–4pm, (Sundays) 2pm–4pm.
History: A Douglas stronghold in existence by 1374, Tantallon successfully withstood several sieges, but in 1651 it was dismantled by General Monck during the Cromwellian occupation.

19 Threave

Location: Kirkcudbrightshire, on an islet in the River Dee, 1¼ miles (2 km) west of Castle Douglas (accessible by ferry). Castle Douglas is 17 miles (27 km) south-west of Dumfries.
Description: The castle consists of a tower of four storeys enclosed by an outer barmkin wall with round towers pierced by gunloops. (This wall may date from 1455 when the castle endured its first long siege.)
Opening hours: (1 April to 30 September: weekdays) 9.30am–7pm, (Sundays) 2pm–7pm.
History: Threave was built by Archibald the Grim, 3rd Earl of Douglas c. 1360–70. In 1454, James Douglas, the 9th and last earl, openly accused James II of having murdered his brother, and rose against him with 40,000 men. In the course of this rebellion the king himself attended the siege of the Douglas stronghold (which was the last to hold out against him) and bombarded it with his formidable gun, Mons Meg, until it surrendered. (The barmkin wall may have been constructed following the damage inflincted by this siege. In 1640 the castle was dismantled after its capture by the Covenanters and it was finally used to house French prisoners in the Napoleonic Wars.)

Ireland

Giraldus Cambrensis, commenting on the nature of Irish fortification at the time of the first Norman invasion in 1169, states that the Irish had no castles, preferring to use such natural defences as forests and bogs. There are no references to the Irish standing siege in a castle; rather he emphasizes the need for a programme of castle-building, and when the Irish are besieged, it is in a walled town – and one walled by the Danes, as Giraldus makes clear.

Ancient defensive works existed: for example the *dun*, *lis* or *rath* (an earthen ring encircling the chieftain's hall) or, as in the case of the *rath* of Armagh described in the Annals of the Four Masters (1166), a very large enclosure containing streets, houses and churches, similar to the Old English *burgh*. There is no resemblence here to the private residence and stronghold of the Norman lord, though; Irish society put more faith in ties of blood, kinship and loyalty. A story survives of an Irish chieftain who rejected a castle offered to him by the Normans saying that he preferred a castle of bones to a castle of stones.

It might appear paradoxical that at a time when the technique of castle-building in stone was undergoing a remarkable development in the hands of Richard I's masons at Château-Gaillard, the simple motte-and-bailey with wooden donjon or *bretasche* was still being built in Ireland, but in the expediency of conquest and settlement its effectiveness and ease of construction were as indispensable to the Angevins in Ireland in the late 12th and the 13th centuries as to duke William in England in 1066.

20 Carrickfergus

Location: Carrickfergus (Co. Antrim), 8 miles (13 km) north-east of Belfast on the A2.
Description: One of the largest Irish castles standing on a rocky peninsula in Belfast Lough. It consists of a narrow enclosure covering the area of the peninsula and is defended by a twin-towered gateway at the landward end.
Opening hours: (1 April to 30 September: weekdays) 10am–1pm and 2pm–6pm, (Sundays) 2pm–6pm; (1 October to 31 March: weekdays) 10am–1pm and 2pm–4pm, (Sundays) 2pm–4pm.
History: Erected some time between 1180 and 1205 by John de Coucy, or by Hugh de Lacy, the younger, who succeeded him. King John stayed here on his visit to Ireland in 1210, and at the end of the 17th century William III first set foot on Irish soil on the quay under the castle's western wall before proceeding to the Battle of the Boyne.

21 Castletown Geoghegan

Location: Castletown Geoghegan (Co. Westmeath), 7 miles (11 km) north of

Trim

Kilbeggan on the T9, then the L108.
Description: Fine example of a motte-and-bailey, probably of 13th-century date, which remains the principal feature of the village.
Opening hours: Probably open at all times; permission to visit the site should be sought.
History: The name of the village derives from the MacEochagins, former county rulers.

22 Nenagh

Location: Nenagh (Co. Tipperary), 25 miles (40 km) north-east of Limerick on the N7.
Description: The castle consists of a cylindrical keep which is incorporated in the curtain wall at the northern apex of a small pentagonal ward.
Opening hours: Key available from Tourist Information Office, Kickham Street, Nenagh.
History: Nenagh is attributed to Theobald Walter, 1st Butler of Ormond (d. 1206).

23 Roscommon

Location: Roscommon, Co. Roscommon.
Description: Roscommon Castle consists of an almost rectangular ward defended by a fine twin-towered gatehouse. Comparison should be made with Ballintubber, on the L98 some ten miles north-west of Roscommon, built by the O'Connors *c.* 1300 which is almost identical in style.
Opening hours: Open at all times.
History: This royal castle was built, or perhaps restored (the records are confused), by Robert de Ufford, the Justiciary *c.* 1280, in place of earlier works begun by him in 1269 of which several appear to have been destroyed by his rivals, the O'Connors.

24 Roscrea

Location: Roscrea (Co. Tipperary), 25 miles

(40 km) south-west of Port Laoise on the N7.
Description: According to an inquisition of the 29th year of Henry III's reign a motte and *bretasche* was built here in King John's reign, but no motte now remains since it was completely swept away in Edward I's reign. The present castle, on a site a little distance away from the original motte, is an irregular polygon in plan, with no keep but a rectangular gatehouse-tower of 13th-century date.
Opening hours: Key available from the County Council offices in Damer House.
History: Roscrea is a good example of a castle updated in Edward I's reign, built 'from scratch' on a completely new site where the chief defensive feature was to be the gatehouse rather than the motte and *bretasche* of the earlier castle. The Irish Pipe Rolls of the eight years of Edward I's reign reveal that £700 was spent in the sixth and seventh years of Edward's reign on the new stone castle.

25 Trim

Location: Trim (Co. Meath), 27 miles (43 km) north-west of Dublin on the L3, off the N3.
Description: The donjon stands in a triangular ward defended by a curtain wall with mural towers.
Opening hours: Open at all times.
History: The 'Song of Dermot' relates the building of a castle at Trim by the first Hugh de Lacy in 1173 and of the burning of the *meysun*, or keep, in his absence and the levelling of the motte. The cylindrical gate-tower in the southern curtain was, for a time, the residence of the young Prince Hal, the future Henry V, when left here in 1399 by Richard II. The castle was virtually on the edge of the English Pale and played its part in all the uprisings and pacifications which would be too numerous to elaborate here.

Low Countries & Scandinavia

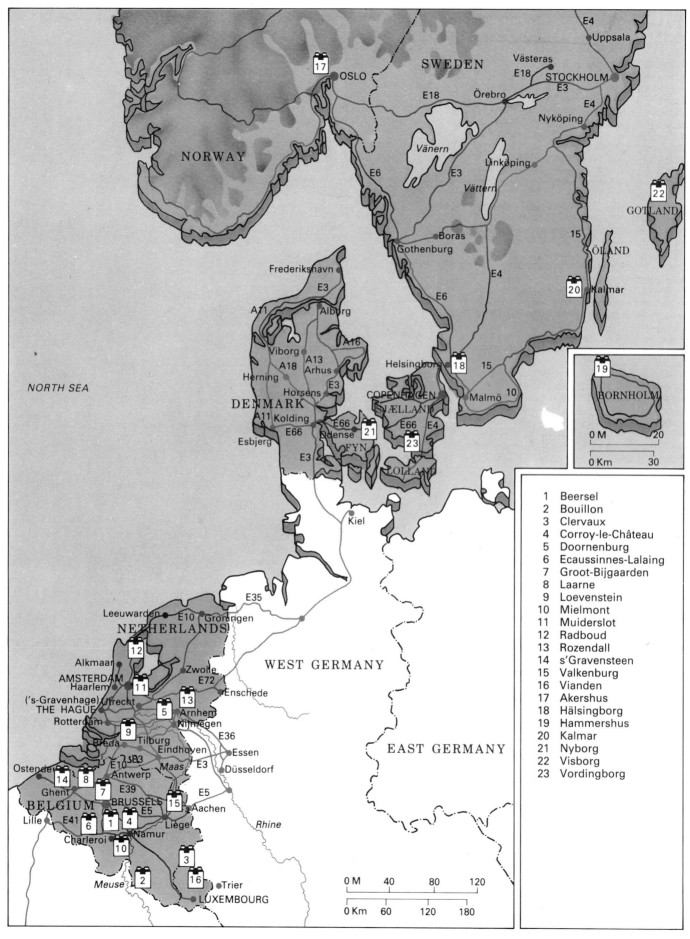

1 Beersel
2 Bouillon
3 Clervaux
4 Corroy-le-Château
5 Doornenburg
6 Ecaussinnes-Lalaing
7 Groot-Bijgaarden
8 Laarne
9 Loevenstein
10 Mielmont
11 Muiderslot
12 Radboud
13 Rozendall
14 s'Gravensteen
15 Valkenburg
16 Vianden
17 Akershus
18 Hälsingborg
19 Hammershus
20 Kalmar
21 Nyborg
22 Visborg
23 Vordingborg

Low Countries

Following the disintegration of the Carolingian Empire the Low Countries suffered both war and invasion. Founded by such men as Dirk I (Theodoric) of Holland and Godfrey I of Bouillon there gradually emerged strong, local, feudal dynasties that built castles within their domains. While the earliest Belgian castles date from the 11th century, most Dutch castles were constructed in the 13th century or later, after brick-making was developed enough to compensate for the lack of natural building materials.

1 Beersel

Location: Beersel (Brabant) off the A54 Brussels–Charleroi road, Belgium.
Description: 14th- and 15th-century moated castle with three towers presenting a protectively rounded exterior and a typically Flemish stepped style above the courtyard.
Opening hours: (1 March to mid November) 10am–12 noon and 2pm–6pm; (Open weekends and holidays in winter.)
History: Between 1300–10 a circular stone enclosure was erected. This suffered heavy damage in 1489 during the Revolt of The Towns when it was twice successfully besieged. The castle was greatly rebuilt in 1491 when it gained the towers and has been unoccupied since 1544 leaving the interior basically unaltered.

2 Bouillon

Location: Bouillon (Luxembourg province), on the N47 38 miles (61 km) south of Dinant and overlooking the River Semois, Belgium.
Description: Built on the living rock, this now mainly 14th- and 15th-century castle was 'modernized' in the 17th century by Vauban but retains the lower parts of two 13th-century, or earlier, halls.
Opening hours: (1 March to 30 November) 0am–4pm.
History: Originally built by the rulers of an independent duchy, the most famous of whom (Godfrey I of Bouillon) pledged it to the bishop of Liège in 1095 before going on crusade, this castle has been frequently besieged. Its possession has passed, with the duchy, through many hands before becoming part of Belgium in 1830.

3 Clervaux

Location: Clervaux, off the N7 37 miles (60 km) from Luxemburg city and overlooking the River Clerve, Grand Duchy of Luxemburg.
Description: Partially ruined 12th-century castle, with 17th-century alterations (at present being rebuilt). Contains an exhibition on the castles of the Duchy.
Opening hours: (Whitsun to 30 September, also during Easter and Christmas holidays) 10am–5pm; (in winter, on Sundays and holidays) 1pm–5pm.

History: This strategically placed castle was founded in the 1130s by Gerard of Clervaux and, remaining inhabited, it has been altered over the centuries. It was partly destroyed during the Battle of the Bulge in December 1944.

4 Corroy-le-Château

Location: Corroy (Namur), off the N4 Brussels–Namur road, Belgium.
Description: Well preserved, almost rectangular 13th-century castle, the exterior of which has altered very little. There are seven huge towers, one of which contains a 15th-century chapel while another two form part of the later gatehouse.
Opening hours: (May to 1 October) 10am–12 noon and 2pm–6pm.
History: Although erected during a time of stress between Brabant and Namur this frontier castle actually saw little action

Beersel

before the 16th century when, in 1542, Martin van Rossum took it, badly damaging the gatehouse. It was twice pillaged in the 1690s.

5 Doornenburg

Location: Doornenburg (Gelderland) off the A52 Arnheim–Nijmegen road, The Netherlands.
Description: 14th- and 15th-century brick castle of which the donjon (which stands apart in the surrounding moat) is a meticulous 20th-century reconstruction.
Opening hours: (Mid April to 31 October) generally after 2.30pm. (Closed most Mondays.) Appointments to view possible all year – tel. 08812-1456.
History: The site has been fortified since the 13th century with the present square bailey dating from the 14th century and exhibiting 17th-century alterations. Destroyed by German bombing in World War II, the 15th-century donjon took 20 years to rebuild.

6 Ecaussinnes-Lalaing

Location: Ecaussinnes-Lalaing (Hainaut) off the E10 Brussels–Mons road
Description: Mainly 15th-century castle. Noted for the two early 16th-century fireplaces in the great hall and a 14th-century Madonna attributed to Beauneveu.
Opening hours: (April to September) 10am–12 noon and 2pm–6pm. (Closed most Tuesdays and Fridays.)
History: A 12th-century frontier castle was erected here by the counts of Roeulx and it gained surrounding walls and towers during the course of the following two hundred years. When it passed into the hands of the counts of Lalaing it gradually lost its military importance and was drastically rebuilt in the 15th century.

7 Groot-Bijgaarden

Location: 4 miles (7 km) north-west of Brussels off the E5 road to Ghent, Belgium.
Description: Moated castle mainly consisting of 16th- and 17th-century rebuilding and additions, exhibiting a fine 14th-century donjon.
Opening hours: (From Easter weekend to the last Sunday of September, every Sunday and holiday) 2pm–7pm.
History: Some early fortifications existed here, with the first castle appearing in the early 12th century. The gatehouse originated in the 14th century, but was greatly altered, gaining twin towers, during the periodic building following the successful siege in 1548 when the owner was executed for heresy. Pillaged in the French Revolution it was restored in 1932.

s'Gravensteen

Muiderslot

8 Laarne

Location: Laarne (Oost-Vlaanderen), 6 miles (10 km) east of Ghent off the E3 road to Antwerp, Belgium.
Description: 13th- and 14th-century castle with early 17th-century alterations; some late 12th-century building is still visible.
Opening hours: 10am–12 noon and 2pm–6pm. (Closed most Mondays from September to June.)
History: By 1362 the counts of Flanders had acquired the right to garrison the castle and thus involved it in the troubles between the count and the people of Ghent, by whom it was besieged and occupied in 1382–5 and in 1449. After being occupied by mercenaries in 1453, it enjoyed a period of peace until it was sacked in 1583 during the religious wars.

9 Loevenstein

Location: Brakel (Gelderland) just off the E37 about 18 miles (29 km) north of Breda, The Netherlands.
Description: Recently restored 14th-century, moated, brick castle.
Opening hours: (1 March to mid October) 9am–5pm.
History: Dirk Loef van Horn built this castle in the 1350s as a base against the count of Holland, who gained its possession in 1386. It was later used as a state prison, from which Hugo de Groot (Grotius) escaped, in 1622, concealed in a chest of books. One tower was damaged in 1750 when a Dutch patriot blew himself up, having temporarily captured the castle from the occupying Spanish garrison.

10 Mielmont

Location: Near Temploux (Namur), on a rocky outcrop dominating the Orneau valley, off the N22 Namur–Mons road, Belgium.
Description: 12th-century castle, of interest for the mixture of building styles added over the centuries.
Opening hours: (Easter weekend to mid September, Sundays and holidays) 2pm–6pm.
History: Taken by the count of Hainaut in 1189, the castle was continually lived in and altered (especially during the Renaissance when it was partly rebuilt) causing the 12th-century donjon, towers and entrance-way to possess 17th-century roofs, windows and decoration. It was last restored in 1831.

11 Muiderslot

Location: Miden (Noord-Holland), 8 miles (13 km) east of Amsterdam on the E35 road, The Netherlands.
Description: Square, moated, 14th-century brick castle – one of the best preserved in the Netherlands.
Opening hours: (1 April to 30 September) 10am–5pm; (in winter) 10am–4pm. (Closed 25 December, 1 January, Friday mornings and holiday mornings.)
History: A fortified site since c. 1000. Much of the present castle was built in 1386 replacing the 13th-century work destroyed after Count Floris V's assassination here in 1296. Muiderslot was taken twice during the 16th century: by the Duke of Gelderland in 1508 and by the earl of Leicester in 1586.

12 Radboud

Location: Medemblik (Noord-Holland), off the N7 road 35 miles (56 km) north of Amsterdam on the shore of the Ijsselmeer, The Netherlands.
Description: The surviving quarter of a massive 13th-century, moated, brick castle.
Opening hours: (1 June to 31 August: Monday to Saturday) 10am–5pm; (Sundays) 2pm–5pm; (in winter: on Sundays and public holidays) 2pm–5pm. (Otherwise on application.)
History: On the reputed site of an 8th-century fort Count Floris V of Holland founded a large square castle in the 1280s to keep the West Frisians under control. Unfortunately much of the castle was demolished in the 17th and 18th centuries.

13 Rozendall

Location: Rozendall (Gelderland) off the A48 Arnhem–Zutphen road, The Netherlands.
Description: Moated brick castle, mostly rebuilt in the 17th and 18th centuries. Noted for the immense thickness – 13 feet – of the late 14th-century donjon walls.
Opening hours: (Mid June to mid September: Tuesday to Saturday) 10am–5pm; (Sundays) 1pm–5pm.
History: Originally built in the early 14th century by the dukes of Gelderland, the castle became a favourite ducal residence. In 1482 it was successfully besieged by the anti-Burgundian party and the damaged building was allowed to fall into disrepair until the early 16th century. It now houses the Museum of the International Castles Institute.

14 s'Gravensteen

Location: Ghent (Oost-Vlaanderen) which is situated at the confluence of the Lieve and the Lys rivers, Belgium.
Description: Built mainly in the 12th and 14th centuries and heavily restored between 1889–1908. The remains of an early 11th-century castle now form the cellars of the 12th-century square donjon that, with the counts' living quarters and several other buildings with vaulted basements, is protected by a wide moat and strong oval curtain wall possessing 24 two-storey projecting towers. The 12th-century gatehouse contains a room with blind arcading and an unusual cross-shaped window.
Opening hours: (April to September) 9am–6pm; (October to March) 9am–4pm. (Closed 25 December and 1 January.)
History: About 1000 a stone donjon was built on the site of an earlier timber fortification. This was besieged in 1128 by supporters of Thiery of Alsace. Philip of Alsace incorporated what survived in a much larger castle, built upon his return from crusade in the 1180s. It was twice successfully besieged in the early 14th century by the burghers of Ghent: in 1301 surrender was forced upon the aldermen of Ghent, sheltering within, by fire, and in 1338 the outer wall was breached. Repairs following these events account for much of the 14th-century work in the walls and gateway. The counts of Flanders only stayed here infrequently, using the living quarters where the Prince's Court of Justice sat from 1407–1708. From then on its use declined. It was sold in 1780 and used as a factory until 1887.

15 Valkenburg

Location: Valkenburg (Limburg), 7 miles (11 km) east of Maastricht, Belgium.
Description: This ruined, mainly 14th- and 15th-century castle displaying remains of a 14th-century *dwingel* (bent barbican) is the only hill castle in Holland.
Opening hours: (Easter to autumn school holidays) 9am–6pm.
History: Nothing survives of the late 11th-century castle of the counts of Valkenburg, destroyed during the successful siege by the count of Louvain in 1122, or of its immediate successor. Most of the 13th-century castle disappeared during rebuilding in 1329, which in turn was partly demolished in 1672 during the siege of Louis XIV.

16 Vianden

Location: Vianden, overlooking the Our valley, off the N7 road 25 miles (40 km) north of Luxemburg city, Grand Duchy of Luxemburg.
Description: This partially ruined 13th- and 14th-century castle is one of the largest in Europe. Of interest are the series of three entrance-gates; the 13th-century Knight's Hall, capable of accommodating 500 men, and the chapel displaying a hexagonal opening in the floor leading to an underground vault.
Opening hours: (1 April to 31 October) 9am–6pm.
History: 11th century in origin, the castle passed from the Counts of Vianden to the Orange Nassau family in 1417 and is now the property of the Grand Ducal family.

Vianden

Scandinavia

The feudalism of Western Europe barely affected Scandinavia and this fact is reflected in the small number of castles to be seen in the region. The few built were the work of kings and archbishops from the 12th and later centuries and resemble public fortresses in purpose. The nobles tended to live in defensible houses, generally of wood, and the great age of secular building in Scandinavia was the time of the Renaissance and the Reformation. The castles that had been raised were demolished or rebuilt in the new style heavily influenced by the development of artillery. Little remains that has not been drastically remodelled, often more than once, and the visitor must beware of the Scandinavian habit of referring to any fortress or palace as 'a castle'.

17 Akershus

Location: Oslo, Norway.
Description: Massive royal palace and fortress containing work of many dates with substantial medieval remains at the centre.
Opening hours: (2 May to 15 September: weekdays) 10am–4pm; (Sundays) 12.30pm–4pm and (Sundays in July) 11am–4pm; (15 April to 1 May and 16 September to 31 October: Sundays only) 12.30pm–4pm.
History: The castle was founded by Haakon V Magnusson (1299–1319) and although not completed until the end of the 14th century it was well enough advanced to withstand a siege in 1308. The site in the new capital of Oslo was originally a rocky promontory protected by sea and marsh but changes in the water level and the addition of further works and buildings have obscured these

Vordingborg

natural defences. Despite frequent modifications and continued use as a royal residence (the halls are still used for official functions) much of the fabric of Haakon's castle survives at the centre of the complex and the ground plan, too, is little changed.

18 Hälsingborg

Location: Hälsingborg, on the south-west coast of Sweden.
Description: Remains of a once-important fortress dominating the Ore Sund where tolls were once collected at the main entrance to the Baltic Sea.
Opening hours: (Summer) 9am–8pm.
History: Until 1658 the Danes possessed both sides of the strait that now divides Sweden from Denmark, and at the narrowest point they built a fortress on each shore. All that remains on the Swedish side is the Kärnan (keep) at Hälsingborg. Originally built in the 12th century this was rebuilt in brick in c. 1370 by Valdemar IV, and overmodernized in 1894. The walls are nearly 15 feet thick, and from the top of the 113-foot-high tower the corresponding fortress, the Kronborg, at Helsingør (the Elsinore of *Hamlet*) may be seen.

19 Hammershus

Location: 2 miles (3 km) south-west of Sandvig on island of Bornholm, Denmark.
Description: Massive remains of a 13th-century fortress much added to up to the 17th century. A ravine and barbican cover the approach to the two baileys, and the inner bailey (which has a 30-foot-high wall with flanking towers) is entered through Faestningsporten. The whole is dominated by the central Manteltaarnet.
Opening hours: Open at all times.
History: On Bornholm, a granite outcrop closer to Sweden and Germany than Denmark, the archbishop of Lund chose an inaccessible plateau 245 feet above sea level for the fortress erected in 1258 during his struggle with the king. Captured by forces from Lübeck in 1525, it was not abandoned until the 17th century when it was partially demolished. It was preserved in 1822. The four round fortified churches on the island are also of interest for although they are not castles they are nevertheless a contrast to Hammershus and provide an example of an alternative response to the threat of pirates.

20 Kalmar

Location: Kalmar, on the south-east coast of Sweden.
Description: A 13th-century castle later greatly modified and strengthened by Gustav Vasa with the addition of an outer rampart and massive artillery bastions.
Opening hours: (Mid-June to September; weekdays) 10am–4pm; (Sundays) 1pm–4pm; (rest of year: weekdays) 12 noon–2pm; (Sundays) 1pm–3pm.
History: This castle was built in the late 12th century (along with Stockholm and Borgholm) against the threat of heathen pirates, and rebuilt by Magnus Lådulus

Kalmar

(1275–90). His work was probably a roughly circular wall with four round towers and two gate houses and a keep but it was all much changed in the 16th century. Although it has seen more than twenty sieges and use as an armoury, granary, prison and museum, Kalmar, the 'Key to Sweden', still contains much of the 13th-century fabric, if in a Renaissance disguise.

21 Nyborg

Location: Nyborg, 18 miles (28 km) south-east of Odense, on the island of Fyn, Denmark.
Description: One wing of a royal palace built into an earlier castle and there are fragmentary remains of this 13th-century work. Little of the west wing is medieval but the foundations of the walls, the turret-shaped half towers and a gate-tower on the east side probably have medieval origins.
Opening hours: 9am–6pm.
History: This claims to be the oldest royal castle in Scandinavia and has the same origin as Vordingborg. It was the centre of royal government until 1416, when King Eric

moved to Copenhagen, and was the main meeting place of the parliament during the period 1282–1413. It remained a favoured royal residence, being used later as an armoury and granary before restoration. Three-quarters of the castle and palace were destroyed by the Swedes in the war of 1658–60.

22 Visborg

Location: Visby, on the island of Gotland, off the east coast of Sweden.
Description: Remains of a 15th-century castle set in a well preserved 13th-century town wall enclosing a town little changed since the Middle Ages.
Opening hours: Open at all times.
History: The Visborg, planned by the Teutonic Knights, was built by King Eric in 1411. The design was simple and secular (apparently not affected by the monastic discipline of the knights) and consisted of cutting off the south-west corner of the town wall. After being driven out by his subjects, Eric was able to hold out here for ten years. Only parts survived demolition in 1679 but a

wood mosaic view is in the town's Gotland Museum. The 2½-mile-long town wall is in better condition and it is possible to walk all the way round on top of it. There are 42 towers which range in height from 16 feet to 30 feet. Of interest is a simplified copy of the Severan gate in Cologne.

23 Vordingborg

Location: Vordingborg, at the southern extremity of the main island of Sjaelland (Zealand), Denmark.
Description: Ten acres of the ruins of a 14th-century royal castle. A curtain wall 765 yards long with brick flanking towers enclosed two wards and a small hill. Amid the ruins stands the Gaasetarnet (Goose Tower), which is well preserved and the best example of a mural tower in Denmark.
Opening hours: 8am–12 noon and 1pm–4pm. (Closed Mondays.)
History: Valdemar I the Great (1157–82) built the first castle to check the raids of Slavonic pirates. It was rebuilt by Valdemar IV (1340–75), the ruins of whose work are now to be seen.

France

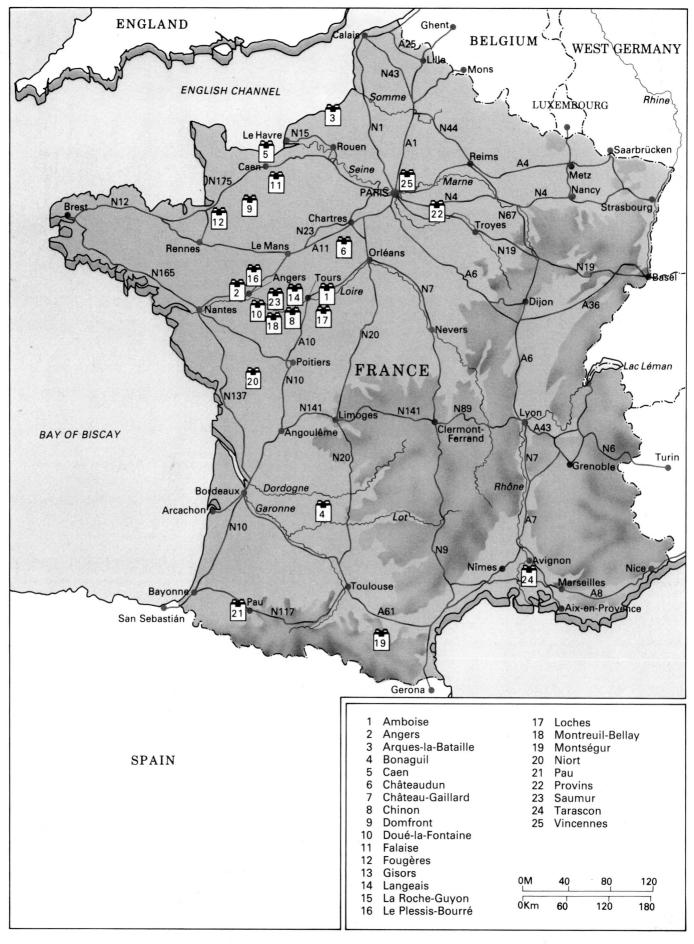

1	Amboise	17	Loches
2	Angers	18	Montreuil-Bellay
3	Arques-la-Bataille	19	Montségur
4	Bonaguil	20	Niort
5	Caen	21	Pau
6	Châteaudun	22	Provins
7	Château-Gaillard	23	Saumur
8	Chinon	24	Tarascon
9	Domfront	25	Vincennes
10	Doué-la-Fontaine		
11	Falaise		
12	Fougères		
13	Gisors		
14	Langeais		
15	La Roche-Guyon		
16	Le Plessis-Bourré		

France is the origin and home of the castle. In a country with such a wealth of remains, many favourites must of necessity be omitted. This selection tries to demonstrate the historical development of the castle from its beginnings in simple enclosures, mottes, and timber or stone towers. Doué-la-Fontaine is probably the oldest known keep, and many of the earliest castles seem to cluster on the borders of Anjou and Blois. The age of Philip Augustus, 1180–1226, saw the blossoming of the castle to a complex system of integrated defence, often with dominant keeps, subordinate enclosures, rounded towers and towers *en bec*. These ideas were worked out to perfection in the following century. The development of artillery inspired French architects to innovate, making loops for cannon and artillery platforms. The work of Bourré, for example at Le Plessis-Bourré, is notable. At the close of the medieval period there was greater emphasis on residential comfort such as one might note at Vincennes. This illustrates a development from the château-fort to the château, a move typified by the elegance of Amboise.

Amboise

1 Amboise

Location: Amboise (Indre-et-Loire) between Tours and Blois on the N152.
Description: Late 15th-century castle on a rocky plateau by the Loire.
Opening hours: (Summer) 9am–12 noon and 2pm–7pm; (Winter) 9am–12 noon and 2pm–dusk.
History: A fortress stood here in Frankish times but the present building is especially associated with Charles VIII, who was born here and completely rebuilt the castle before his death in 1498, also at Amboise. It is a Renaissance château, elegant in style and appearance. In 1560 the Hugenots tried to seize Francis II at Amboise. From a balcony the conspirators of Amboise were hanged. It became a prison and was later the residence of the Comte de Paris.

Angers

2 Angers

Location: Angers (Maine-et-Loire), on the N23, N160 and N162. On the east bank of the Maine, the castle is in the ancient capital of Anjou.
Description: 13th-century castle which dominates the riverside. Noted for the Apocalypse Tapestries made by Nicholas Bataille in the 14th century.
Opening hours: (15 June to 30 September) 9am–12 noon and 2pm–7pm; (1 October to 14 June) 9am–12 noon and 2pm–6pm.
History: A base for the counts of Anjou from the 9th century, a fragment of early wall remains. The present castle was built chiefly in the 13th century, its outer wall forming an irregular pentagon with 17 round towers.

3 Arques-la-Bataille

Location: Arques-la-Bataille (Seine-Maritime), 6 miles (10 km) south of Dieppe on the D154.
Description: Ruined 12th-century castle with a large rectangular keep, on an imposing site.
Opening hours: Open at all times.
History: William of Arques built the castle on its rocky promontory from 1038. Its main features now derive from the rebuilding by Henry I of England after 1123, including the keep with its flat buttresses, but the great northwest barbican is a 16th century addition. It was besieged by William the Conqueror in 1052–3, and was the last castle to yield to Geoffrey le Bel, Count of Anjou (1129–1151) when he conquered Normandy. It was taken by the French under Philip Augustus, and again in 1449. It was acquired by the state in 1868 and damaged in World War II.

4 Bonaguil

Location: Off the D673, 3 miles (5 km) northeast of Fumel (Lot-et-Garonne), 15 miles (25 km) west of Cahors.
Description: 13th-century castle on a rocky promontory between two valleys. It has strong rounded corner towers, a 13-foot-thick wall and its pentagonal keep forms a spur to the north. In the 15th century the defences were modified: new towers were built with loops for cannon to fire from a low level and an artillery terrace was added.
Opening hours: Every day from Easter to the end of September; also on Sundays and holidays from 1st October to Easter.
History: The early castle owed its strength to its position. The lordship passed from the de la Tour family to that of Roquefeuil, and the latter were responsible for changes that included the magnificent buttressed artillery terrace, the artillery towers and machicolation that may show Breton influence.

5 Caen

Location: Caen (Calvados), on the River Orne 9 miles (15 km) from the north coast.
Description: Massive remains covering a hill that dominates the town. Surrounded by 12th-century walls with the ruins of a large keep and a deep moat to the north. The famous Exchequer Hall dates from c1100.
Hours: Open at all times.
History: The castle was built by William the Conqueror soon after 1047. Henry I of England built a great keep, which was destroyed in 1793. Philip Augustus captured the castle but it twice returned to English control during the Hundred Years War, in 1346 and 1417, before its final loss in 1450.

6 Châteaudun

Location: Châteaudun (Eure-et-Loir) in the district of Dunois, 30 miles (50 km) north-west of Orléans on the D955.

Description: Dominated by the 148 ft (45 m) high cylindrical keep which dates from the time of Philip Augustus, the castle stands on a plateau overlooking the Loir. There are important 15th-century additions, including the Sainte-Chapelle and its statues.

Opening hours: (1 April to 30 September) 9am–12 noon and 2pm–6.30pm; (1 October to 31 March) 10am–12 noon and 2pm–5pm. (Closed on Tuesdays from 15 September to 1 June.)

History: Some believe the castle dates from Theobald 'le Tricheur', Count of Blois (966–978), but the castle seems to belong to the 12th century. The Bastard of Orléans transformed the castle in the 15th century, making it more comfortable, and building the Sainte-Chapelle. It was bought by the state in 1939 and restored.

7 Château-Gaillard

Location: Les Andelys (Eure), in the Norman Vexin, 22 miles (35 km) south-east of Rouen, off the N14.

Description: Magnificent ruined castle of outstanding architectural interest, dramatically sited overlooking the Seine. Its sophisticated keep *en bec* may be derived from the simpler version at La Roche-Guyon. The enclosure round the keep, with its rounded bastions almost touching, is especially notable. The outer walls protect the edges of the promontory, forming an angle at its point.

Opening hours: (Mid-March to mid-October) 10am–12 noon and 2pm–5.30pm. (Except Tuesdays and Wednesday mornings.)

History: Having lost Gisors by treaty to Philip Augustus, Richard the Lionheart built this castle to defend Normandy and the Seine. There is documentary evidence to show that it was built between 1196 and 1198. Built on a plateau and cut off by ditches, it is an

Château-Gaillard

Chinon

advanced work in triangular shape and has a massive keep. It represents a transitional stage towards the concentric castle and is an early example of integrated defence, with inner defences designed to command the outer walls. Philip Augustus captured it from John I of England after a siege and this was the most important advance in his conquest of Normandy. The castle was dismantled in 1603 on the orders of Henry IV.

8 Chinon

Location: Chinon (Indre-et-Loire), 25 miles (40 km) south-west of Tours on the D751.

Description: Spectacular stone mass of three castles in a row east to west along the plateau dominating the town and the valley of the Vienne, each fortress separated from its neighbour by a moat.

Opening hours: (Summer) 9am–12.30pm and 2pm–7pm; (Winter) 9am–12.30pm and 2pm–6pm.

History: The three separate castles are: the Château du Coudray, the Château du Milieu and Fort St-Georges. The two châteaux were begun in the 10th century by the counts of Blois, and in 1044 Chinon passed to Geoffrey Martel, Count of Anjou. The major work here was done by Henry II of England, who also built Fort St-Georges. Henry died at Chinon in 1189. The French kings added to the defences after acquiring Chinon in 1205. It was used as a prison for the Knights Templars. Under the Valois it became a more

comfortable residence with the addition of such works as the Tour de l'Horloge. A ruined wall of the Château du Milieu, with its fireplace, marks the spot where Joan of Arc first confronted the Dauphin in 1429.

9 Domfront

Location: Domfront (Orne) 30 miles (50 km) east of Avranches on the N176.
Description: Ruined 12th-century castle on the edge of a 200-foot height.
Opening hours: The 13th-century casements may be visited on request.
History: Probably begun by William de Bellême in 1011, Domfront was taken by William the Conqueror in 1052. The castle is particularly associated with Henry I of England, who developed it as a part of his defences of Normandy. It was one of the castles used by Geoffrey le Bel, Count of Anjou as a base for his conquest of Normandy; indeed, it was seen as the main Norman castle which supported the Empress Matilda. It was here that Henry II of England received the papal nuncio sent to reconcile him to Thomas Becket.

10 Doué-la-Fontaine

Location: Doué-la-Fontaine (Maine-et-Loire) 20 miles (30 km) south-east of Angers on the D748 and D761. Known as 'La Motte', it is at the edge of the village.
Description: A very important early tower-keep which recently has been discovered within a later motte.
Opening hours: Key can be obtained from the Mairie. Open 9am–12 noon, 2pm–6pm (Monday to Friday).
History: Excavations on this site between 1967 and 1970 showed its significance in the history of castles. It is the earliest known stone keep, probably built by Theobald, Count of Blois, in about 950. A stone hall dating to about 900 had been damaged by fire and then converted into the present stone keep. The ground-floor entrance was blocked and an upper storey and a forebuilding (both now gone) were added, and this became the prototype for early keeps. The castle was captured by Fulk Nerra, Count of Anjou, in about 1025.

11 Falaise

Location: Falaise (Calvados) 22 miles (35 km) south of Caen on the N158.
Description: Impressive ruin with a 12th-century keep and 13th-century walls. Its solid mass is perched imposingly on a rocky spur at the top of the steep cliffs which give the castle its name, overlooking the valley of the Ante.
Opening hours: 8am–12 noon and 2pm–7pm in summer.
History: The castle was a favourite residence of the early dukes of Normandy. Count Robert le Diable is said to have been in the castle when he spotted the tanner's daughter at the Fontaine d'Arlette. William the Conqueror, the outcome of their liaison, was born at Falaise and he formulated his plans for the invasion of England here. Henry I of England built the solid rectangular keep. Philip

Augustus, after his conquest of Normandy, built the Talbot Tower which is now named after the English hero who repaired it during the Hundred Years War. In World War II a shell went through its 13-foot-thick wall but otherwise the castle was not badly damaged. Restoration work was carried out in the 19th century.

Falaise

12 Fougères

Location: Fougères (Ille-et-Vilaine) 30 miles (50 km) north-east of Rennes on the N12.
Description: Extensive castle remains on a rock site, though it is overlooked by the town and the surrounding heights.
Opening hours: (15 April to 15 September) 9am–6pm; (15 September to 30 September) 9am–5pm; (October) 9am–4pm; (1 November to 24 December and from 28 February to 31 March) 10am–3pm; (1 April to 15 April) 9am–5pm.
History: The castle dates from the 11th century. It was taken and razed by Henry II of England in 1166 but reconstructed by the lords of Fougères later in the 12th century. It was altered in the 15th century to give a new walk-way with machicolation. In 1449 it fell to the English under the command of the Spaniard Surienne. The 12th-century keep was destroyed under Richelieu.

13 Gisors

Location: Gisors (Eure), which was the capital of the Norman Vexin. 19 miles (30 km) south-west of Beauvais on the D981.
Description: Ruined castle with an important early polygonal keep and early towers *en bec*.
Opening hours: 10am–12 noon, 2pm–6pm. (Except Tuesdays.)
History: The ruins of this important castle

are on the old frontier between Normandy and the lands of the Capetian kings of France. Chronicles and excavation agree an origin in the 11th century. The motte was built by William Rufus in 1096. It was later given an octagonal keep, early for its type, and an elliptical shell. After Philip Augustus took Gisors in 1193 he added the great cylindrical keep known as the 'Prisoners' Tower'.

14 Langeais

Location: Langeais (Indre-et-Loire), in Touraine, on a height dominating the valley of the Loire, between Tours and Sumur on the N152.
Description: Two castles on one site: an ancient stone keep in the park and an important 15th-century château.
Opening hours: (Summer, except on non-holiday Mondays) 9am–12 noon and 2pm–6.30pm; (Winter, except on Mondays) 9am–12 noon and 2pm–4.30pm. There is no access to the ancient keep.
History: Two walls of Fulk Nerra's very early keep are still standing. There is a 10th-century charter which refers to a siege 'before the castle of Langeais'. The castle played an important role in the struggles between Blois and Anjou. The 15th-century castle was the work of Jean Bourré, the minister of Louis XI from 1465, though only two wings were completed. It has an upper storey set back above the wall-walk, providing protection for this part of the defences. It was at Langeais in 1491 that Charles VIII married Anne of Brittany. Nearby is a house in which Rabelais lived.

15 La Roche-Guyon

Location: La Roche-Guyon (Val d'Oise), 6 miles (10 km) north-west of Mantes on the D193 near the N13.
Description: Late 12th-century castle with an especially notable keep *en bec*.
Opening hours: Private.
History: In about 1190 a castle was raised that pointed the way for Château-Gaillard. It was built on a chalky cliff overlooking the Seine, near its confluence with the Epte, and the isthmus was cut off with a ditch.

16 Le Plessis-Bourré

Location: Ecuillé (Maine-et-Loire), about 9 miles (15 km) north of Angers, on the D74.
Description: Excellent example of a late 14th-century castle, it became a model for later Renaissance châteaux. Built to accommodate artillery and with a very wide moat, it has a platform for artillery on the inner bank of the moat.
Opening hours: (Summer) 9am–12 noon and 2pm–7pm; (Winter, except for Tuesdays) 10am–12 noon and 2pm–4pm.
History: Acquired by Louis XI's minister, Jean Bourré, in 1462, his castle has a remarkable unity of style. It occupies a rectangular platform in an enormous moat. Machicolation has become unnecessary but there is a low terrace to carry artillery. The interior has a ceiling with early 16th-century decorations.

17 Loches

Location: Loches (Indre-et-Loire), in Touraine, on the Loire. 22 miles (35 km) south-east of Tours on the N143.
Description: Important example of an older castle in the Loire region, standing on a rocky plateau within solid walls. It has an important 12th-century keep containing traces of 11th-century work.
Opening hours: 9am–12 noon and 2pm–5pm. (Keep closed on Tuesdays in winter.)
History: Gregory of Tours refers to a fortress here in the early Middle Ages. It became a base for the Angevins against Blois, notably for Fulk Nerra, and the rectangular keep derives from this early period. Philip Augustus was responsible for the towers *en bec*. In the 15th century it became a prison, its most famous prisoner being Ludovico Sforza who is said to have painted frescoes here. The castle possesses the white marble tomb of Agnès Sorel, the mistress of Charles VII. The round keep incorporated in the 'Martelet' belongs to the 15th century.

18 Montreuil-Bellay

Location: Montreuil-Bellay (Maine-et-Loire). On the banks of the Thouet, 9 miles (15 km) south of Saumur on the N147 and the D761.
Description: Good example of a late medieval castle in French style.
Opening hours: (Easter to 1st November) 10am–12 noon and 2pm–6pm (except Tuesdays); (July to August) 3pm–7pm. Owner's permission required.

Vincennes

Tarascon

History: This is another of Fulk Nerra's castles dating from the late 10th/early 11th centuries, the Berlai family receiving it as a fief from him in the early 11th century. It sustained a three-year siege from 1148 to 1151, finally falling to Geoffrey le Bel, Count of Anjou. He transferred the fair from Saumur so that people visiting it could throw in rocks and fill the natural chasm which served as part of the defences. He broke through the defences in the end by hurling Greek fire at the gate – its first use in western Europe. Geoffrey demolished that castle but it was rebuilt in the last medieval centuries. The Petit Château was the dwelling for four chaplains, each with his own entrance door and stair turret.

19 Montségur

Location: 7 miles (12 km) south of Lavelanet (Ariège), 20 miles (30 km) east of Foix on the D117.
Description: Majestic ruin on the summit of a Pyrenean peak. The castle is pentagonal in plan and has a square donjon.
Opening hours: Open at all times.
History: The fame of this castle rests upon events in the 13th century. The site has become associated with the Cathar heretics, when Montségur, built in 1204, became their last refuge after defeat by Simon de Montfort. The castle was besieged in 1243 and the garrison under Ramón de Perella was forced to surrender after two months because of treachery. In 1244 over two hundred of the Albigensians who had refused to recant were burned alive in a great conflagration at the foot of the mountain. The castle was then dismantled.

20 Niort

Location: Niort (Deux-Sèvres), on the banks of the Sèvre Niortaise, between Poitiers and La Rochelle. The town is on the N11, N22, and N743.
Description: A most interesting double keep survives. There is a museum with local costumes.
Opening hours: Musée du donjon (All year) 9am–12 noon; (Summer) 2pm–6.30pm; (Winter) 2pm–5.30pm. (Closed Tuesdays all year.)
History: Founded by Henry II of England in the later 12th century. The twin keeps derive from this period. They were originally separated by a court, but were joined by a building in the 15th century. The machicolation on the southern keep is very early. The castle was finally taken by France in 1436. Although Niort favoured the Huguenots, the castle was severely damaged by the Protestants in 1588. The northern keep was reconstructed in the 18th century. Drawings from the 18th century show a bailey wall with 16 round towers. In 1815 Napoleon spent his last night on the mainland in a nearby house.

21 Pau

Location: Pau (Pyrénées-Atlantiques), in Béarn near the Spanish border on the N134 and N117.
Description: 12th-century fortress which was much altered in the later Middle Ages. It contains Renaissance tapestries and the restored apartments of Louis-Philippe and Napoleon III.
Opening hours: (16 April to 14 October) 10am–12 noon and 2pm–5.30pm; (15 October to 15 April) 2pm–5pm.
History: The castle was built in the 12th century to protect the ford through the *gave* (stream) at the foot of the promontory. Pau was held by the viscounts of Béarn, and it was Gaston Phoebus who most gave the castle its present appearance from about 1370. Henry IV was born here but never returned once he was king. At the time of the Revolution it became a barracks. Restoration was carried out in the 19th century.

Saumur

22 Provins

Location: Provins (Seine-et-Marne), at the confluence of the Voulzie and the Durteint, between Paris and Troyes on the N19.
Description: Large 12th-century keep with a surrounding wall from the 15th century. There is a good view of the splendid town walls from the west.
Opening hours: 10am–12.30pm; 2pm–4pm. (Until 6pm in the Summer.)
History: The keep is known as the 'Tower of Caesar', though it dates from Theobald II, Count of Champagne in the 12th century. It is an interesting structure with a rectangular plan that rises to an octagon. Philip IV (1285–1314) gained Provins for France but it was recaptured in the Hundred Years War. The English made alterations which involved the demolition of neighbouring houses, and the construction of the surrounding wall, the Pâté aux Anglais.

23 Saumur

Location: Saumur (Maine-et-Loire). On the convergence of the N147 and N152, between Nantes and Tours.
Description: Late medieval castle, transformed into a Renaissance palace. It houses a municipal museum containing tapestries and ceramics, and an equestrian museum with the skeleton of Flying Fox, the 1899 Derby winner.
Opening hours: (July to September) 9am–7.30pm and 8.30pm–11pm; (October to March) 10am–12 noon and 2pm–5pm (closed Tuesdays); (April to June) 9am–12 noon and 2pm–6pm; (Easter and Whitsun holidays) 9am–12 noon and 2pm–6pm and 8.30pm–11.30pm.
History: The castle possibly dates from the 10th century, but there have been several rebuildings, notably that in the 14th century by the duke of Berry. It then became a fairy-tale castle with fantastically decorated upper

parts, Gothic tracery, flying turrets and golden weathercocks. The gilding has gone, but it is illustrated under September in the *Très Riches Heures* of the duke of Berry. The building was abandoned in the 17th century, when the west wing collapsed. It became a prison, then a barracks, before being restored.

24 Tarascon

Location: Tarascon (Bouches-du-Rhône), on the river below Avignon on the N570.
Description: Magnificent late medieval

Loches

castle, rising sheer on rocks from the Rhône.
Opening hours: (April to September) Tours at 9, 10, 11am; 2, 3, 4, 5pm; (October to March) 10, 11am; 2, 3, 4pm. (Closed Tuesdays.)
History: Although it has an earlier history, the present castle derives from the late 14th and 15th centuries. It was begun in the late 14th century by Louis II of Anjou, Count of Provence. Additions were made by King René. The curtain wall was raised to the level of the towers to provide a continuous wall-walk, and the wall was machicolated. The interior was designed for comfortable residence. It passed to the king in 1481 and was later used as a prison until 1926. Restoration work has been carried out.

25 Vincennes

Location: Vincennes (Val-de-Marne), in the Ile-de-France, 1 mile (2 km) east of the Porte de Vincennes, Paris. It can be reached by the Métro – to Château de Vincennes.
Description: Outstanding royal palace, deriving from medieval military architecture. It has a keep with a massive, battered base, a large enclosing wall with nine other square towers.
Opening hours: 10am–12 noon and 2pm–5pm or 6pm.
History: Formerly a royal hunting lodge, Vincennes' life as a castle began in the 14th century with Philip VI. People who have died here include Louis X, Charles IV, Charles IX and Mazarin, as well as Henry V of England. It became a prison, with many famous captives including Diderot, Bonnie Prince Charlie and Mirabeau, who wrote his *Essai sur les lettres de cachet* here. In the castle in 1804 the Duke of Enghien was shot on the orders of Napoleon. In 1944 the Germans shot 30 men inside the ramparts before they moved out.

West Germany

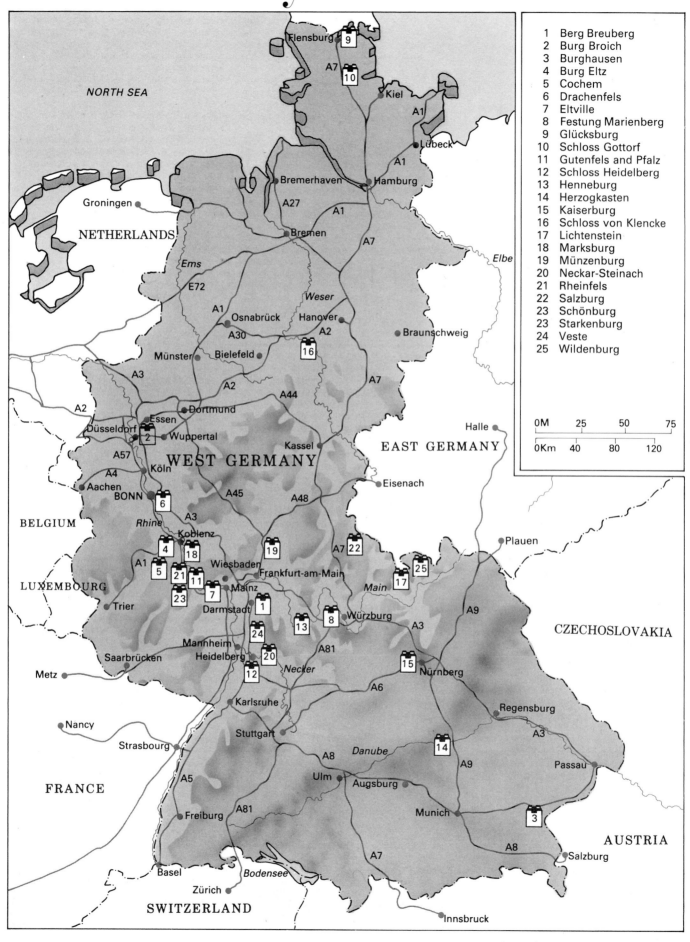

NORTH SEA

NETHERLANDS

BELGIUM

LUXEMBOURG

FRANCE

SWITZERLAND

WEST GERMANY

EAST GERMANY

CZECHOSLOVAKIA

AUSTRIA

Groningen

Flensburg
Kiel
Lübeck
Bremerhaven
Hamburg
Bremen
Osnabrück
Hanover
Braunschweig
Münster
Bielefeld
Dortmund
Essen
Düsseldorf
Wuppertal
Kassel
Köln
Aachen
BONN
Koblenz
Wiesbaden
Frankfurt-am-Main
Mainz
Trier
Darmstadt
Mannheim
Heidelberg
Saarbrücken
Metz
Nancy
Strasbourg
Karlsruhe
Stuttgart
Freiburg
Basel
Zürich
Ulm
Augsburg
Munich
Nürnberg
Regensburg
Passau
Salzburg
Innsbruck
Würzburg
Halle
Eisenach
Plauen

Ems
Weser
Elbe
Rhine
Main
Necker
Danube
Bodensee

A7 A1 A27 A30 A2 A3 A44 A57 A4 A45 A48 A5 A81 A6 A8 A9 E72

1	Berg Breuberg
2	Burg Broich
3	Burghausen
4	Burg Eltz
5	Cochem
6	Drachenfels
7	Eltville
8	Festung Marienberg
9	Glücksburg
10	Schloss Gottorf
11	Gutenfels and Pfalz
12	Schloss Heidelberg
13	Henneburg
14	Herzogkasten
15	Kaiserburg
16	Schloss von Klencke
17	Lichtenstein
18	Marksburg
19	Münzenburg
20	Neckar-Steinach
21	Rheinfels
22	Salzburg
23	Schönburg
23	Starkenburg
24	Veste
25	Wildenburg

0M	25	50	75
0Km	40	80	120

Early medieval defences in Germany were generally of earth and timber, motte and bailey type castles being quite common in low-lying areas. In mountainous country, where natural defences were good, they were more likely to consist of simple stone enclosures. From the 11th and 12th centuries, tall towers or *Bergfried* were an almost invariable feature of such castles, which proliferated with the feudalization of society. Initially free-standing, Bergfried tended to be moved closer to, or incorporated into, the curtain wall where it was most exposed to attack. At such points, the wall was often also made much thicker and higher, creating what is known as *Schildmauer* barring the approach to the castle. The Hohenstaufen emperors (1152–1250) engaged in systematic fortress-building to consolidate their rule. Their castles generally comprise a Bergfried and curtain wall with a palace, residential buildings and chapel (often above the gateway) adjacent to it, grouped around a courtyard, representing a re-arrangement of the elements of the relatively unfortified Carolingian palace to meet defensive requirements. The political fragmentation and weakening of the imperial power which followed the collapse of the Hohenstaufen dynasty created conditions favourable to castle building. Later medieval German castles exhibit a great deal of variety, partly because their ground plans are generally dictated by the terrain. Only in the late 15th and 16th centuries did regularly planned castles with angle towers become at all common. Another factor influencing their layout was the practice of partible inheritance, frequently causing them to be divided into several units belonging to different branches of a family (*Ganerbenburgen*). The construction of outer lines of defence with flanking towers, or their rebuilding in stone, has often created a sort of concentric plan with outer courtyards (*Zwinger*).

1 Burg Breuberg

Location: Neustadt im Odenwald (Hessen) on a hill above the town, 15 miles (25 km) east of Darmstadt on Bundesstrasse 426.
Description: The castle has a main courtyard with buildings ranged around it and a central Bergfried. To the west are two further enclosures.
Opening hours: (Daily) 9am–5pm.
History: In the 12th century, the castle belonged to the imperial abbey of Fulda. To this period belong the Bergfried and the gate to the main courtyard. The other buildings in this courtyard, which include a well-house, kitchen and chapel, date mainly from the 15th to 17th centuries. An outer line of defences comprising a curtain wall with round towers and ditches was added *c.* 1480–1515. The partially ruined palace separating the western and central enclosures was built in the late 16th and early 17th centuries.

2 Burg Broich

Location: Mulheim an der Ruhr (Nordrhein-Westfalen) at the edge of the town, on the opposite bank of the Ruhr.
Description: An approximately circular enclosure about 164 feet across resembling a shell keep, to which on the west side have been added the buildings of the post-medieval Hochschloss.
Opening hours: (Contact local tourist office) tel. 2 133 455267.
History: The castle was probably built to command an important bridgehead. Excavations 1965–68 revealed 9th-century structures comprising an enclosure similar in plan to the existing one, with buildings ranged around its interior. In the late 12th and early 13th centuries, the curtain wall was rebuilt much as it is today, and a round tower erected in the middle of the enclosure. This was razed in the 15th century when the fortifications were modernized. The half-timbered Hochschloss built above earlier stone buildings surrounding the gateway dates from the 17th century.

3 Burghausen

Location: Burghausen (Nieder Bavaria) above the town on a ridge between the river Salzach and the Wohrsee, about 63 miles (100 km) east of Munich and 31 miles (50 km) north of Salzburg, Austria. On Bundesstrasse 20.
Description: The castle extends for 1100 m along the ridge, and is divided by ditches into six enclosures.
Opening hours: (April to September) 9am–12 noon, 1pm–5pm; (October to March) 9am–12 noon, 1pm–4pm.
History: By the 12th century, there was a castle here belonging to the counts of Burghausen. In 1164, it passed to the dukes of Bavaria, and from the 13th to the 16th century, was one of their most important castles. Its present appearance is largely the result of major rebuilding by duke Georg der Reiche (1479–1503) who strengthened it against the Turks. To this period belong much of the outworks, notably the round Pulverthurm on the west side, and also the wall and round tower barring the entrance to the southern inner courtyard. However, parts of the fabric of the buildings in this courtyard are 13th century.

4 Burg Eltz

Location: Wierschem (Rheinland-Pfalz) on a crag above a bend in the river Eltz.
Description: A very impressive, approximately oval group of mainly post-medieval buildings ranged around a courtyard and surrounded by outworks. Restored in the 19th century, the interiors are supplied with medieval furnishings.
Opening hours: (April to October) 9am–5.30pm (Sundays and Holidays) 10am–5.30pm.
History: A castle is recorded from the 12th century. By 1268, the family of the counts of Eltz had split into several branches, which came to occupy the six *Hauser* that surround the courtyard. Most of these were rebuilt from the late 15th century, though the Haus Platt-Eltz at the west end of the courtyard still preserves something of its medieval appearance, and the chapel is 14th century.

Burg Eltz

5 Cochem

Location: Cochem (Rheinland-Pfalz) on a hill above the Moselle, about 25 miles (40 km) south-west of Koblenz, on Bundesstrasse 49.
Description: An attractive castle heavily restored in the neo-gothic style 1868–78.
Opening hours: (July to September) 9am–6pm; (Easter to October) 10am–5pm.
History: The original castle was probably built c. 1020. In the first half of the 14th century it was enlarged by archbishop Baldwin of Trier. It served as a toll station on the Moselle, a chain being used to bar the river. Of the medieval fabric the most notable survivals are the Bergfried, parts of the main gate, the Hexenturm, and a vaulted undercroft. The castle was sleighted by the French in 1689.

6 Drachenfels

Location: Konigswinter (Nordrhein-Westfalen) on a crag above the town, 6 miles (10 km) south of Bonn on the right bank of the Rhine, via Bundesstrasse 42.
Description: A picturesque ruin commanding excellent views.
Opening hours: No formal opening hours.
History: The castle was built by the archbishops of Cologne in the first half of the 12th century. In 1147 it was granted to the Cassius monastery at Boon which enfieffed it to the counts of Drachenfels. The ruinous Bergfried also dates from the 12th century. Of the 15th-century enlargement there survives a curtain wall with round towers on the east side. The castle has been abandoned since the 30 Years War. Quarrying activity in the 19th century destroyed much of the fortifications on the side facing the Rhine.

7 Eltville

Location: Eltville (Hessen) 9 miles (15 km) west of Mainz on the right bank of the Rhine.
Description: Most striking for its large residential tower about 39 feet square at the south-east corner of a quadrangular ditched enclosure. The tower has an octagonal turret with a spiral stair, and polygonal corner turrets at its summit. Inside is painted wall decoration of the 14th and 15th centuries. To the west of the tower are the remains of the palace. The kitchen on the west side of the courtyard, and the building to the east, are now much altered.
Opening hours: (Contact local tourist office) Tel. 6 123 4066.
History: Excavations have shown that the site was fortified from the early Middle Ages. Archbishop Baldwin of Trier began to build a castle above the remains of an earlier one 1330–32. The work was finished c. 1345 by the archbishops of Mainz whose residence the castle became until the second half of the 15th century. Destroyed by the Swedes in 1635, it was extensively restored in the 17th century.

8 Festung Marienberg

Location: Würzburg (Bavaria, Franconia) on a hill on the opposite bank of the Main to the town facing the Residenz, home of the prince-bishops in the 18th century.
Description: A large fortress of many periods now occupying the entire hilltop. Its nucleus is rectangular with buildings ranged round an inner courtyard.
Opening hours: Now the seat of the Mainfrankische Museum. (April to September) 9am–5pm; (October to March) 10am–4pm.
History: The hill was occupied in the Iron Age, and was the site of an ecclesiastical settlement from the 8th century, of which the round early romanesque Marienkirche in the courtyard is a survival. From c. 1250–1720, the prince-bishops lived here and built the castle to dominate the town. The round tower in the courtyard, and some parts of the fabric of the buildings on the east side of it, date from the 13th century. The curtain wall with round towers surrounding the inner nucleus is 15th century. The residential quarters were radically rebuilt by Julius Echter von Mespelbrunn (1573–1617). The bastions date from the 17th century.

9 Glücksburg

Location: Glücksburg (Schleswig-Holstein) in a park outside the town, which is about 8 miles (12 km) to the north-east of Flensburg.
Description: A square castle with octagonal angle towers typical of the late 15th and 16th centuries. Also a fine example of a Wasserburg, being situated on an island. Internally, it consists of three adjacent rectangular buildings with vaulted interiors,

Gutenfels and Pfalz

and furnishings and decoration of the 17th to 19th centuries.
Opening hours: (15 May to 15 October) 10am–4.30pm; (16 October to 14 May) 10am–11.45am, 2pm–4.45pm; (Sundays 11am–4.45pm. (Closed all Mondays.)
History: The castle was built 1582–87 by N. Karies for the duke of Holstein-Hadersleben near the site of a former Cistercian monastery.

10 Schloss Gottorf

Location: Schleswig (Schleswig-Holstein) on the east side of the town on what was formerly an island.
Description: A large rectangular building with a round tower at one corner and a central courtyard. Inside many rooms preserve decoration and furnishings of the 16th century.
Opening hours: (April to October) 9am–5pm; (November to March: weekdays) 10am–4pm; (Sundays and holidays) 9.30am–5pm. (Closed Mondays.)
History: The castle belonged to the dukes of Schleswig from 1268 and played an important role in the wars against Denmark. The late medieval castle was probably similar in plan to the present one, remains of it being incorporated into the existing fabric. From the 1490s and throughout the 16th and 17th centuries, it was rebuilt in a mixture of late gothic and early renaissance styles. The south facade dates from 1698–1703.

11 Gutenfels and Pfalz

Location: Kaub (Rheinland-Pfalz) about 22 miles (35 km) south of Koblenz on

Bundesstrasse 42. They comprise two separate contrasting castles, Gutenfels being on a spur above Kaub, and the Pfalz (Pfalzgrafenstein) on an island in the Rhine.

Description: Gutenfels consists of a residential block about 69 feet square, with wings either side of a rectangular courtyard, on the east side of which is attached a square Bergfried. It is surrounded by several outer curtain walls enclosing courtyards. The Pfalzgrafenstein is a small hexagonal enclosure with round turrets at the corners, within which there is a free-standing pentagonal tower.

Opening hours: The Pfalz is not open to the public; Gutenfels has no formal opening hours.

History: Gutenfels was probably built by the knights of Falkenstein in the first half of the 13th century. The nucleus of the castle, with the fine windows in the south wall, is substantially of that period, though restoration was carried out in the 19th century. The pentagonal tower of the Pfalzgrafenstein was built as a toll-station by King Ludwig of Bavaria in 1327. The hexagonal enclosure was added *c.* 1338–42. The southern end of it was reinforced by a bastion in 1607.

12 Schloss Heidelberg

Location: Heidelberg (Baden-Württemberg) on a spur above the south-east corner of the town, to the east of Europastrasse 4.

Description: A massive and imposing ruin, consisting of an approximately quadrilateral complex with round towers and a courtyard, round which are buildings of various periods, mainly of the 16th and early 17th century.

Opening hours: (April to October) 9am–12 noon, 1pm–5.30pm; (November to March) 9am–12 noon, 1pm–4pm, (Sundays) 9am–12 noon, 1pm–6pm.

History: Recorded from 1225, the castle was the seat of the counts palatine of the Rhine. Little of the medieval fabric survives, but the Ruprechtsbau at the south-west corner of the courtyard dates from the 15th century, as do the three round towers on the east side of the Schloss. The renaissance buildings in the courtyard were erected from 1508. The castle was destroyed by the French in 1689 and 1693. The Friedrichsbau (1601–07) was restored 1897–1900.

13 Henneburg

Location: Stadtprozelten (Bavaria, Franconia) on a hill to the west of the town, about 43 miles (70 km) south-east of Frankfurt am Main.

Description: An imposing ruin, approximately semi-circular in plan. The inner courtyard, with buildings ranged round it, is surrounded by an outer curtain wall, protected by ditches to the west and north.

Opening hours: (Contact local tourist office) tel. 9 392 7222.

History: At the end of the 12th century, the castle was the seat of the counts of Prozelten. To this period belongs the large square Bergfried in rusticated masonry. To the south of this are the remains of a 13th-century palace. The castle was much enlarged in the

Schloss Heidelberg

14th and 15th centuries, the range of buildings with the small square tower on the north side of the courtyard being constructed, together with the outer defensive wall with its round towers. Abandoned since the end of the 17th century, the castle was repaired on the instigation of Ludwig of Bavaria.

14 Herzogkasten

Location: Ingolstadt (Nieder Bavaria) about 50 miles (80 km) north of Munich, just west of Europastrasse 6. The Herzogkasten is near the present town centre. A second castle, the Neue Schloss, is at the south-east corner of the town walls on the Danube.

Description: The Herzogkasten is a large, three-storey brick building with stepped gables and a high saddle roof. The Neue Schloss comprises a rectangular enclosure, on the east side of which is the Hauptbau, a rectangular palace with a square and a pentagonal tower, and fine gothic vaulted rooms. To the north is a large warehouse with a round tower.

Opening hours: 9.30am–4pm. (Closed Mondays.)

History: The Herzogkasten is all that survives of the old castle dating from the 13th century. With the expansion of the town, the Neue Schloss was built on the present site

from the beginning of the 15th century. It has been restored since the damage of the last war.

15 Kaiserburg

Location: Nuremburg (Bavaria, Franconia) at north-east corner of town walls on a sandstone outcrop.

Description: The main part of the castle, the Kaiserburg, consists of two successive enclosures strung along the ridge, and surrounded by outer defenceworks. To the east lie the remains of the Burggraffenburg destroyed in 1420.

Opening hours: (April to September) 9am–5pm; (October to March) 10am–12 noon, 1pm–4pm.

History: The tower of the Burggrafenburg is the most notable survival of the original castle built by the emperor Henry III who founded Nuremburg *c.* 1040. This was added to by King Konrad III and the emperor Frederick I, the fine romanesque two-storey chapel and the round tower at the east end of the Kaiserburg dating from the 12th century. Most of the fabric of the palace and other buildings in the two courtyards date from 15th-century rebuilding. The huge Kaiserstallung next to the tower in the Burggrafenburg was built 1494–95. The outlying bastions were added in the 16th century.

155

16 Schloss von Klencke

Location: (Lower Saxony) on a low hill between Emmerthal and Hämelschenburg about 2 miles (3 km) to the west of Bundesstrasse 83.

Description: An outstanding example of North German renaissance architecture, the castle is a three-winged building surrounded by a moat. It is distinguished by very fine carved stonework and interior furnishings.

Opening hours: (April to 15 October) 10am–1pm; 2pm–5pm. (Closed Mondays.)

History: The castle recorded from the 14th century was demolished and rebuilt from the end of the 15th, the existing renaissance building dating from c. 1588–1610. To the north-east outside the moated enclosure are the 16th century Wirtschafthof and chapel belonging to the earlier castle.

17 Lichtenstein

Location: Lichtenstein (Bavaria, Franconia) to the north of Bamberg, near Pfarrweisach on Bundesstrasse 277.

Description: The northern part of the castle includes a square Bergfried, a round tower and a curtain wall in rusticated masonry dating from the 13th century, and also a romanesque chapel. The whole is in ruins. The southern part, comprising a Bergfried and adjacent living quarters with half-timbered frontages on a small courtyard, is well-preserved.

Opening hours: (April to October) 8.30am–12 noon, 1pm–5.45pm; (November to March: Saturday and Sunday only) 9am–12 noon, 1pm–5pm.

History: The castle is first recorded in 1232. Its irregular lay-out is the result of it having been a Ganerbenburg divided between three branches of the family of the lords of Lichtenstein. The northern Bergfried probably dates from the 14th century, and the buildings next to it were reconstructed in the 15th and 16th centuries.

Cochem

18 Marksburg

Location: Braubach (Rheinland-Pfalz) on a hill above the town, about 8 miles (12 km) south of Koblenz, on the right bank of the Rhine.

Description: The Marksburg is one of the best preserved of the Rhine castles. At the centre of it there are three ranges of buildings grouped round a triangular courtyard, in which there is a square Bergfried. This nucleus is surrounded by up to three lines of outer defences.

Opening hours: (16 March to 14 November) 8am–6pm; (Rest of year) 11am–4pm.

History: The castle is first recorded in 1231, and was probably built at the beginning of the 13th century by count Eberhard II von Eppstein. It later passed to the counts of Katzenelnbogen, and then in 1479 to the landgraves of Hesse. To the original castle belong the palace with romanesque windows and small blind arches on the north side of the courtyard, and the chapel-tower at its southern end. In the 14th century the first line of outer defences was added to the north, and another palace (with fine 16th-century interiors) was built on the east side of the courtyard. The curtain wall with round towers dates from the 15th century, whilst the bastions on the east side are 17th century.

19 Münzenburg

Location: Münzenburg (Hessen) on a basalt outcrop above the town, 25 miles (40 km) north of Frankfurt and 2½ miles (4 km) east of Europastrasse 4.

Description: An outstanding example of 12th-century architecture, the castle consists of an oval enclosure about 394 feet by 131 feet with a free-standing round tower at its east and west ends, and buildings ranged along its north and south walls. Round it is an outer curtain wall with round towers.

Opening hours: Apply to Herr Debus, 6309 Munzenburg 2, Burgweg 12, Münzenburg.

History: Of the castle built by Kuno von Münzenburg c. 1174, there survive those

parts of the enclosure wall in rusticated masonry; the southern palace (three-storey, first floors reached originally by external wooden stairs, fine romanesque windows); the adjacent chapel over the gateway, though these were altered c. 1500; and the east tower. In 1286 the Falkenstein family acquired a predominant share in the castle. They strengthened the defences and built the palace on the south side of the courtyard.

20 Neckar-Steinach

Location: Necker-Steinach (Hessen). There are actually four castles comprising the group, which can be reached on Bundesstrasse 37, about 9 miles (15 km) east of Heidelberg. The Hinter-, Mittel- and Vorderburg are behind the town on a ridge formed at the junction of the Steinach and Neckar. The Schadek is further to the west on the edge of the Neckar valley.

Description: Four small feudal castles in varying states of preservation.

Opening hours: (Contact local tourist office) Tel. 6 229 545.

History: The Hinterburg, an imposing ruin, was built by the lords of Steinach in the 12th century. To that period belong the Bergfried and irregularly-shaped enclosure, though the small palace next to the tower is probably 13th century. The two outer curtain walls are 14th and 15th century. The Mittelburg is a rectangular building much altered in the 16th and 19th centuries. The Vorderburg comprises a tower and adjacent palace, and an enclosure wall. it probably dates from the late 13th or early 14th century. The Schadek is a small enclosure with the ruins of internal buildings.

21 Rheinfels

Location: St Goar (Rheinland-Pfalz) about half a mile north of St Goar on a low spur above the Rhine, about 115 miles (35 km) south of Koblenz, Bundesstrasse 9.

Description: A large and impressive ruin, though only a fraction of its former size, it was originally the strongest fortress on the Rhine. Most of the surviving fabric is post-medieval.

Opening hours: No formal opening hours. Can be approached on foot.

History: The castle was originally built by count Diether von Katzenelnbogen in 1245. Of this there survives the approximately rectangular ground plan of the castle nucleus and the foundations of the Bergfried. Wilhelm II von Katzenelnbogen (1332–85) added a palace with round corner towers on the north side, and a massive screen wall with square towers at each end of it to the south. After 1479 it passed to the landgraves of Hesse-Kassel who rebuilt it as a residential palace and added the extensive outworks.

22 Salzburg

Location: Bad Neustadt an der Saale (Bavaria, Franconia) about 44 miles (70 km) north of Würzburg.

Description: A fine Ganerbenburg, or castle of the type divided up between several

Rheinfels

History: The hill was the original site of the early medieval settlement. The castle recorded from the 13th century was the seat of the counts of Henneberg and later of the dukes of Saxe-Coburg-Gotha until they transferred to Schloss Ehrenburg in the town. Of the early castle there survive only the foundations of the Bergfried and parts of the fabric of the buildings in the Hauptburg. The outer curtain wall with round towers is probably 15th century. The *Hohes Haus* or arsenal in the Vorburg was rebuilt in its present form in 1489. Much of the castle was reconstructed after a fire in 1500. Duke Johann Casimir (1586–1633) strengthened the outworks and built the bastions to either side of the entrance. Much restoration in the neo-gothic style was carried out in the 19th century.

families. The curtain wall is irregular in plan, following the gently sloping sides of the spur on which the castle is built. Inside there were six enclosures, those to the south and west being the best preserved. Especially notable is the so-called Munze palace of the mid-13th century, with stepped gables and early gothic windows. The approach from the east is barred by a ditch and a wall with four square towers, the gate-tower being of rusticated masonry and dated to *c*. 1200.

Opening hours: (Contact local tourist office) tel. 9 771 774.

History: The castle is first recorded in 1162. It was built by the bishops of Würzburg but soon passed under the control of the Voite family. Since the 16th century it has been allowed to fall into ruins.

23 Schönburg

Location: Oberwesel (Rheinland-Pfalz) on a hill above the town, about 29 miles (40 km) south of Koblenz on the left bank of the Rhine, off Bundesstrasse 9.

Description: Irregular in plan, the main approach from the south being barred by a rock-cut ditch and a high screen wall (Schildmauer) probably built in the 14th century. In the courtyard there is a small gothic chapel.

Opening hours: The ruins do not have regular opening hours but are accessible by a pathway from the town.

History: A eastle is first recorded in 1149. For much of the time from the 12th to 14th centuries, it belonged to the archbishops of Magdeburg. By the 14th century, it was a Ganerbenburg shared by the three branches of the family of the counts of Schonburg, and is divided accordingly into three parts, each with a Bergfried and palace. In 1689 the castle was sacked by the French.

24 Starkenburg

Location: Heppenheim (Hessen) on a hill above the town, about 19 miles (30 km) north of Heidelberg, on Bundesstrasse 3.

Description: The castle consists of an approximately rectangular enclosure surrounded by an outer curtain wall.

Opening hours: (Contact local tourist office) tel. 6 252 2515.

History: A castle was built here by the abbey of Lorsch *c*. 1065. In the 13th century it passed to the archbishops of Mainz who enfieffed it to a count who held it until the 30 Years War. The curtain walls of the inner and outer enclosures, with their round towers, date probably from the 13th century. The Bergfried must be of about the same period. It stood in the centre of the courtyard, but was demolished in 1924 and rebuilt in its present position. The north-west bastion was added in the 17th century.

25 Veste

Location: Coburg (Bavaria, Franconia) about 31 miles (50 km) north of Bamberg. The castle is on a hill to the east of the town, surrounded by a park.

Description: The castle is of several building periods. It is roughly oval in plan and divided into two courtyards, the Hauptburg to the east and the Vorburg to the west.

Opening Hours: (April to October) 9am–1pm, 2pm–5pm; (Rest of the year) 2pm–5pm. (Closed Mondays.)

26 Wildenburg

Location: Wildenburg (Bavaria, Franconia) in remote wooded countryside about 31 miles (50 km) north-east of Heidelberg, 4 miles (6 km) south of Amorbach.

Description: A well-preserved fortified complex of the late 12th and early 13th centuries. The enclosure wall is remarkably rectangular, interrupted only by a salient for the gateway, which has a chapel above it. At the western end, there is a large square Bergfried in rusticated masonry. Ranged along the east side, there is a palace and adjacent tower.

Opening hours: (Contact local tourist office) tel. 9 373 255.

History: The castle was begun by Rupert von Dürn soon after 1168, and continued by Konrad von Dürn in the 13th century who was responsible for the upper floor of the palace with its finely carved early gothic twin-light windows. The wall dividing the courtyard in two dates from the 15th century. The buildings were damaged by fire in 1525.

Veste

Austria & Switzerland

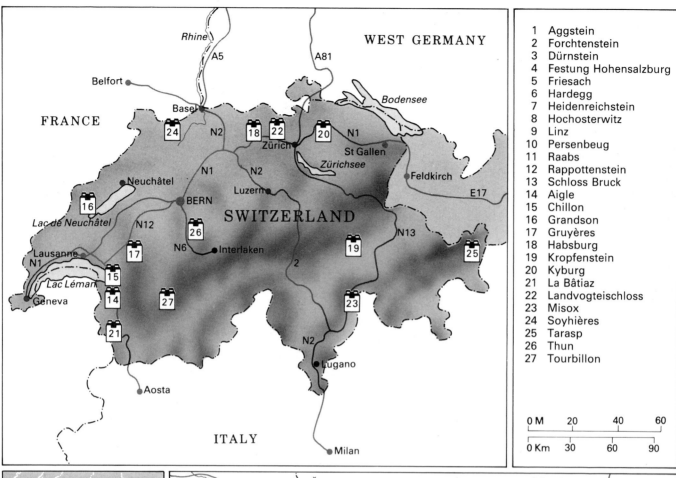

1	Aggstein
2	Forchtenstein
3	Dürnstein
4	Festung Hohensalzburg
5	Friesach
6	Hardegg
7	Heidenreichstein
8	Hochosterwitz
9	Linz
10	Persenbeug
11	Raabs
12	Rappottenstein
13	Schloss Bruck
14	Aigle
15	Chillon
16	Grandson
17	Gruyères
18	Habsburg
19	Kropfenstein
20	Kyburg
21	La Bâtiaz
22	Landvogteischloss
23	Misox
24	Soyhières
25	Tarasp
26	Thun
27	Tourbillon

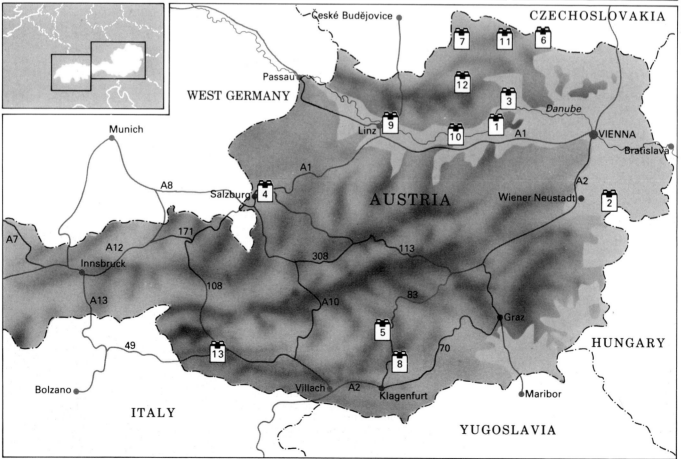

Austria

Austria and Switzerland are lands of castles, and these often combine with the mountains to give the splendid hilltop strongholds which are such a feature of both countries. The style of building in these castles is similar to that in Germany with the reinforcement of naturally strong or impregnable sites. The castles of Aggstein, Gruyeres and Hochosterwitz are particularly fine hilltop strongholds. Yet Austria and Switzerland also have excellent examples of lowland castles, often incorporating water defences, such as Heidenreichstein and Chillon, the latter dramatically imposing on its Lake Geneva setting. Some Swiss castles have affinities with Edward I's castles in north Wales because of his employment of the favoured mason, Master James of St. George. Most Swiss castles are closed on Mondays.

Durnstein

1 Aggstein

Location: Aggstein (Lower Austria), 8 miles (13 km) north-east of Melk.
Description: One of the most impressive of the many castles guarding the Danube frontier, Aggstein is perched on a narrow ridge about 1000 feet above the river. It comprises a long narrow courtyard with buildings ranged along its south side situated between two raised outcrops of rock, on which there are further buildings.
Opening hours: Ruined areas open daily. Restored parts (1 April to 15 October).
History: A castle was probably first built here in the early 12th century by Nizzo, son of Azzo von Hezzmannsweisen, founder of the powerful Kneuringer dynasty. It was captured by the dukes of Austria in 1231 and 1296, and thereafter it lay in ruins until 1429 when it was granted to Georg Scheck von Wald. In its present form, it is much as he rebuilt it, except for the middle courtyard buildings added in the 17th century.

2 Forchtenstein

Location: Forchtenau (Burgenland), 14 miles (23 km) south-east of Wiener Neustadt.
Description: The castle is situated on an outcrop of dolomite rock in the foothills of the Rosaliengebirge mountains. Mainly post-medieval, the approximately quadrangular nucleus is enclosed within outworks with bastions. The well, 466 feet (142 m) deep, with a treadmill, was excavated by Turkish prisoners, 1660–80.
Opening hours: Open daily.
History: The castle was originally built in about 1300 by the counts of Mattersdorf. To this period belongs the massive prow-shaped donjon on the west side of the central courtyard. In 1622 it passed to the Esterházy family who completely rebuilt the residential quarters and added the artillery defences. The castle played an important role in the defence of Austria against the Turks in the 16th and 17th centuries, and the museum has many relics of this period.

3 Dürnstein

Location: Dürnstein (Lower Austria), 4 miles (7 km) west of Krems.
Description: A mined castle on a cliff above the left bank of the Danube. It is of irregular ground plan, with an outer line of defences at the bottom of the cliff.
Opening hours: Open daily.
History: Like Aggstein, Dürnstein was probably built by the Kneuringer family early in the 12th century. The castle is famous as the place where Richard I of England was imprisoned and held to ransom by Duke Leopold V of Austria as he returned from the Third Crusade, and where he was discovered by the minstrel Blondel. It was largely destroyed by Duke Frederick II of Austria in the 13th century, but was rebuilt and became the main seat of the Kneuringer family. It continued to function as a castle as late as 1645 when it was captured by the Swedes.

4 Festung Hohensalzburg

Location: Above Salzburg. Reached by paths or funicular railway.
Description: The castle is an extensive complex of many different periods occupying the north end of the Mönschsberg ridge. It has some fine late-medieval interiors, notably the Golden Room (1501) with its gilded and painted carved wooden panelling, in which there is a superb glazed ceramic oven (1501). Museum.
Opening hours: (Summer) 9am–5.30pm; (Winter) 9.30am–4pm.
History: The castle was first built in 1077 during the Investiture Dispute by archbishop Gebhard. The oldest part of it is the central nucleus, the Altes Schloss, but even this was remodelled when, from the 15th century, the castle was strengthened and enlarged. To this period belong the round towers of the outer curtain walls. The residential quarters were modernized especially by archbishop Leonard von Keutschach (1495–1515), who was responsible for the decoration of the Golden Room. The outer bastions were added in the 16th and 17th centuries.

5 Friesach

Location: Friesach (Carinthia), on the hill of Petersberg above the town.
Description: Friesach is a fortified town with an almost unique combination of town walls within a moat and three castles. These are the Geiersberg which stands apart about ½ km to the north of the town; the Petersberg at the north-west corner of the town, which is the largest of the three; and the Virgilienberg, a small fortified priory on the south side of the town. In St Rupert's chapel in the Petersberg, there are beautiful 13th-century frescoes.
Opening hours: Open daily.
History: First recorded in 860, Friesach was important as a market and a strategic point on the Vienna–Venice road. It belonged to the archbishops of Salzburg, who built the three castles. The Geiersberg dates from about 1130. It preserves a romanesque Bergfried. Abandoned since 1750, it has been substantially restored from 1912. The Petersberg was built by archbishop Gebhard before 1077, enlarged by archbishop Konrad (1124–30), who erected the massive Bergfried, and further added to in the 16th century.

Festung Hohensalzburg

6 Hardegg

Location: Hardegg (Lower Austria),
8½ miles (14 km) north-west of Retz, on a
rocky ridge.
Description: A large castle situated on a
straggling ridge above a bridgehead on the
River Thaya. It has four massive towers, and
two residential buildings.
Opening hours: 9am–5pm.
History: A castle probably existed from the
early 12th century, but the existing layout
dates originally from c. 1200. It has been
partially restored since 1890.

7 Heidenreichstein

Location: Heidenreichstein (Lower Austria),
10 miles (17 km) north-east of Gmund.
Description: Whilst most Austrian castles
occupy hilltop sites, Heidenreichstein is a
Wasserburg and relies on wet-moats for its
defence. The castle has a square Bergfried
and three round angle-towers with conical
tiled roofs. It is reached by two former
drawbridges and a renaissance gateway.
Opening hours: (15 April to 15 October)
9am–12 noon and 2pm–5pm.
History: A castle existed here by the later
12th century, but the surviving buildings
date mainly from the 15th and 16th centuries.
The Bergfried, however, is 13th century.

8 Hochosterwitz

Location: Hochosterwitz (Carinthia),
5½ miles (9 km) east of St Veit an der Glan.
Description: A magnificent hilltop castle,
with a particularly strongly defended
approach, the road up to it passing through
fourteen gate-towers and over three ditches.
The nucleus of the castle is rectangular, with
three round angle-towers. Museum.
Opening hours: (May to October) 9am–6pm.
History: A castle is recorded as early as 960.
It later belonged to the archbishop of
Salzburg and the lords of Osterwitz. The
present structure was built between 1570 and
1586 by Georg Khevenhüller, governor of
Carinthia.

9 Linz

Location: Linz (Upper Austria), above the
south bank of the Danube.
Description: An elegant, roughly E-shaped
renaissance style building, with the remains
of medieval defences on its west side.
Provincial museum.
Opening hours: (Wednesdays) 10am–1pm
and 2pm–8pm; (Thursdays, Fridays,
Saturdays) 10am–1pm and 2pm–6pm;
(Sundays) 9am–12.30pm. (Closed Mondays
and Tuesdays).
History: A castle is recorded at Linz from
799. The curtain wall with round towers on
the west side was built by Emperor Frederick
III c. 1477–81. The castle was completely
reconstructed in its present form by Emperor
Rudolf II between 1599 and 1607. There was
once a south wing, but this, and part of the
east wing, were destroyed by a raging fire in
1800.

Aigle

10 Persenbeug

Location: Persenbeug (Lower Austria),
12½ miles (20 km) west of Melk.
Description: The castle stands on a cliff
above a bridgehead at a bend in the Danube.
The present building dates from the 17th
century, though a medieval belfry (with a
baroque cupola) survives.
Opening hours: Open daily.
History: A castle is recorded from the 10th
century, but it was completely reconstructed
1617–21. In 1800, it passed to the Habsburgs,
and it was the birthplace of the last Austrian
emperor, Karl I (1887–1922).

11 Raabs

Location: Raabs (Lower Austria), 31 miles
(50 km) north-east of Zwettl.
Description: Like Hardegg, Raabs was one of
a series of castles built to defend the River
Thaya. It stands on a narrow, rocky spur
above the town. The approach to it is defended
by a round and a pentagonal tower.
Opening hours: (Summer) 9am–12 noon and
1pm–5pm; (Winter: Mondays to Thursdays)
9am–12 noon and 1pm–4pm, (Fridays) 9am–
2.30pm.
History: In the 11th century there was an
important castle here belonging to the
margraves of Babenberg. It was extensively
rebuilt after 1358, when it passed to the
Puchheim family, and from the 16th century.

12 Rappottenstein

Location: Rappottenstein (Lower Austria),
6 miles (10 km) south-west of Zwettl.
Description: The castle occupies a
commanding position above the River Kamp.
The high walls of the compact, central
nucleus of the castle are surrounded by six
outer courtyards. Great skill has been shown
in the adaptation of the castle to the natural
defences of its site, especially in the creation
of the strongly defended approach to it.
Opening hours: (1 May to 15 September)
tours at 9am, 10am, 11am, 2pm, 3pm, 4pm
and 5pm; (16 September to 30 April)
Saturdays, Sundays and holidays only.
History: Like Aggstein and Durnstein,
Rappottenstein was a Kneuringer stronghold,
being first built by Rapoto von Kneuringer in
the second half of the 12th century. The five-
sided tower on the south side of the castle
nucleus has survived from this period. The
chapel of St Pancras dates from 1348. The
kitchen, the vaulted hall, and the
Archivzimmer on the north side of the inner
courtyard were built in the second half of the
15th century. In about 1548, the large outer
courtyard with the brew-house was added,
and the renaissance-style portico was erected
on the south side of the inner courtyard.

13 Schloss Bruck

Location: 1 km west of Lienz (Tyrol).
Description: A well-preserved 13th-century
castle situated on a rocky crag at the head of
the Isel valley. It consists of a large
rectangular Bergfried, to the east of which is
a courtyard with buildings ranged round it.
Museum.
Opening hours: 10am–5pm. (Closed
Mondays.)
History: The castle was built about 1270 by
the counts of Görz. The Knights' Hall
(Rittersaal) still retains its medieval
character whilst the vaulted chapel,
originally romanesque but rebuilt in the 15th
century, has frescoes of the 13th and 15th
centuries. In 1500 the Görz estates stretching
from the Tavern to Istria passed to the
Habsburgs. They modernized and
strengthened the castle, adding the outer line
of defence with bastions on the south side.

Switzerland

14 Aigle

Location: Aigle (Vaud), 29 miles (47 km) south-east of Lausanne.
Description: 15th-century castle. Wine museum.
Opening hours: (May to October: weekends only): 10am–5pm.
History: Magnificent in its Alpine setting, Aigle castle is fine testimony to the power of the city of Berne in the late 15th century. It was first built in the 11th century and extended 200 years later but the present structure dates largely from after its capture by the Bernese in 1475. The large donjon and its associated domestic buildings occupy one corner of a powerful curtain wall with three drum towers each topped by a conical tiled roof at the other three corners.

Grandson

15 Chillon

Location: South of Montreux on Lake Geneva (Vaud).
Description: Imposing castle possibly dating from the 10th century. Sited on an island in Lake Geneva.
Opening hours: Weekdays, basic hours (March to November) 10am–12 noon and 1.30pm–4pm; (Sundays: July and August only) 9am–6pm.
History: The earliest parts, the central Tower of Alinge and the Duke's Tower, probably date from the 10th and 11th centuries respectively. These earlier fortifications were developed in the middle of the 13th century by the architect Pierre Mainier into the imposing structure of today, for Peter II of Savoy.

Mainier reinforced a naturally strong position needing only to use mural towers, so common in Anglo-French castles, on the vulnerable landward side. The castle was later used as a prison, notably for François Bonnivard, a hero of the Swiss Reformation and immortalized in Byron's poem 'The Prisoner of Chillon'. The castle contains a fine series of 13th-century rooms and wall paintings.

16 Grandson

Location: Grandson (Vaud), on the Lake of Neuchâtel.
Description: Massive medieval castle. Historical and vintage car museum.
Opening hours: (15 March to 31 October) 9am–6pm; (1 November to 14 March: Sundays only) 9am–6pm.
History: The lords of Grandson first fortified the site in the early 11th century, but the present castle originates from the 13th century. It passed to the Châlons-Orange family in the early 1400s and they largely rebuilt it.

A historic date in Swiss history is 2 March 1476 when the Swiss Confederation defeated the Burgundian army led by Charles the Rash under the town walls. The castle then became the property of the towns of Berne and Fribourg.

The castle stands on the shore of Lake Neuchâtel. It has very high curtain walls with three circular and two semi-circular mural towers. Inside there is a fine renaissance hall and chapel, museum and impressive dungeons.

Chillon

Thun

17 Gruyères

Location: Gruyères (Fribourg), 3 miles (5 km) south-east of Bulle.
Description: A powerful hilltop castle dominating the adjacent fortified town. Museum.
Opening hours: (November to February) 9am–12 noon and 1pm–4.30pm. (March to May, and October) 9am–12 noon and 1pm–5.30pm. (June to September) 9am–6pm.
History: The castle belonged to the counts of Gruyères who dominated the Sarine valley for 400 years. The large round donjon at the south-east corner dates from the 13th century. For the most part, however, the castle is late medieval, having been rebuilt after a fire in 1480. In 1555 it was sold to Fribourg, which held it until the Bory family acquired and restored it in the 19th century. In 1938 it was returned to the canton.

18 Habsburg

Location: Near Brugg (Aargau), 27 miles (44 km) north-west of Zurich, on the summit of the Wülpelsberg.
Description: Large square Bergfried in rusticated masonry with adjoining palace and other buildings.
Opening hours: Open throughout the year during the hours of daylight.
History: This is the castle from which the Habsburg dynasty took their name, though they ceased to use it as a residence from about the 13th century. The Bergfried is generally attributed to the 11th century, though the castle is first documented in 1108. The palace and enclosure wall date from the 12th and 13th centuries, whilst the small square tower on the north side is 15th or 16th century. The interior of the palace was renewed in the 16th century. The castle passed on to the city of

Berne in 1529, and then in 1804 to the canton of Aargau.

19 Kropfenstein

Location: Near Waltensburg (Grisons), 27 miles (43 km) west of Chur below the Waltensburg-Brigels road.
Description: This is a cave stronghold, consisting of a main wall and two side walls enclosing the rock face on a narrow precipitous ledge to form a three-storey residential building.
Opening hours: Open at all times.
History: The castle has no recorded history, though a family bearing this name is known in the 14th century.

20 Kyburg

Location: Kyburg (Zurich), 3 miles (5 km) south of Winterthur.
Description: The castle comprises an irregularly shaped enclosure, within which there is a large courtyard. The chapel has some fine 15th-century frescoes and an interesting museum.
Opening hours: (March to October) 9am–12 noon and 1pm–5pm. (November to February) 9am–12 noon and 1pm–4pm. (Closed 25–31 December.)
History: First referred to in 1027. Ancestral residence of the counts of Kyburg. The square Bergfried and adjacent palace in the south-east corner of the courtyard, together with the chapel, date originally from about 1200. When the male line of the family became extinct in 1264, the castle passed to the Habsburgs, and then late in 1424 to Zurich, becoming like so many others a bailiff's residence. Rebuilding and alterations were carried out fairly continuously by these officials until the 18th century.

21 La Bâtiaz

Location: Above Martigny (Valais).
Description: Ruins of hilltop castle dominated by 13th-century circular donjon.
Opening hours: Open at all times.
History: The site was first fortified by the bishops of Sion. In 1259 it was successfully besieged by Peter II of Savoy who subsequently built the imposing circular donjon within the original fortifications. The bishops later regained the castle but it was destined to change hands several times before it was destroyed by George Supersaxo in 1518, since when it has been a ruin.

22 Landvogteischloss

Location: Baden (Aargau), 15 miles (24 km) north-west of Zurich, on the River Limmat.
Description: Landvogteischloss (Bailiff's Castle) is a tall building comprising a 12th-century tower to which later structures have been added. The town is also dominated by another castle, Stein, now in ruins.
Opening hours: (Tuesday to Sunday) 10am–12 noon and 2pm–5pm. Stein open at all times.
History: Both castles were Austrian strongholds in the 14th century. Despite Austrian defeats at Morgarten (1315) and Sempach (1386) they held out against the Swiss Confederation until 1415. Stein was burnt in that year, but the Bailiff's Castle became the residence of the provincial governor, being rebuilt 1487–90. The round tower with its renaissance portal dates from 1579–80, whilst the short wing to the north of it is 18th century. Stein was refortified in the 17th century but again destroyed in 1712.

La Bâtiaz

Tarasp

23 Misox

Location: Just outside Mesocco (Grisons).
Description: Ruins of massive border stronghold, crowning a rocky peak and guarding the San Bernardino Gap and the Val Mesolcina.
Opening hours: Open at all times.
History: The castle was built in the 11th and 12th centuries by the counts of Sax and consists of a strong donjon surrounded by a curtain wall with a fine chapel located in the inner ward. This chapel has a remarkable romanesque campanile with five storeys of arches. The outer defences at the foot of the castle incorporate another church, the Chapel of St Mary of the Castle. This also has a romanesque campanile, but in addition contains an interesting series of 15th-century frescoes, featuring among others St George slaying the dragon and St Bernardino of Siena, patron saint of the town. The castle was repeatedly besieged, being finally abandoned in the 18th century.

24 Soyhières

Location: Soyhières (Berne), 23½ miles (38 km) south-west of Basle.
Description: Ruins of early medieval hilltop castle, recently restored by the Société des Amis du Château de Soyhières.
Opening hours: (May to October: Sundays only) 2pm–6pm (weather permitting).
History: Probably built in the 11th century by the counts of Soyhières but by 1200 it had

fallen into the possession of the counts of Pfirt. It was finally destroyed in 1499 in the course of the Swabian War.

25 Tarasp

Location: Tarasp (Grisons), 2½ miles (4 km) south-west of Scuol.
Description: Magnificently positioned Alpine castle near the Austrian border. Best viewed from the summit of the Kreuzberg.
Opening hours: (For information Tel. 084/9 1229.)
History: The castle dates back to the 11th century when it was the seat of the lords of Tarasp. It passed through the hands of various Swiss and Austrian families before it came into the possession of duke Sigismund of Austria, remaining an Austrian and Catholic stronghold until 1803. The castle was fully restored at the beginning of this century. Still in private hands being the residence of the Grand-Duke of Hesse-Darmstadt.

26 Thun

Location: Thun (Berne), 17 miles (28 km) south-east of the city of Berne.
Description: Massive 12th-century donjon and later fortifications overlooking the town. Museum.
Opening hours: (June to September) 9am–6pm; (April, May and October) 10am–5pm.
History: The donjon was first built by the dukes of Zahringen at the end of the 12th century, later passing into the possession of

the powerful counts of Kyburg. It is massive both in size and strength with four towers at each corner of the rectangular structure. Inside is one of the largest baronial halls in Switzerland, now housing the museum. The rest of the castle is much later in date but it is the donjon which leaves the lasting impression.

27 Tourbillon

Location: Sion (Valais), positioned on one of the two steep rocks high above the town of Sion. The fortified church of Valere occupies the other.
Description: Ruined medieval castle with the remains of a donjon, several towers and the powerful curtain wall.
Opening hours: Tourbillon: Open at all times. Valere: (Summer) 8am–12 noon and 1.30pm–7pm. (Winter) 9am–12 noon and 1.30pm–5pm.
History: The castle of Tourbillon was built by the bishops of Sion who as lords of Valais faced a growing threat from the House of Savoy at the end of the 13th century. Tourbillon remained an episcopal residence until its destruction by fire in 1788. Throughout the Middle Ages it had a troubled history being frequently besieged and rebuilt. The fortified church at Valere is now partly a museum. The site has probably been occupied since Roman times, though the earliest parts of the church and fortress date from the 8th or 9th century. The present church is largely a very fine example of 12th- and 13th-century architecture.

Eastern Europe

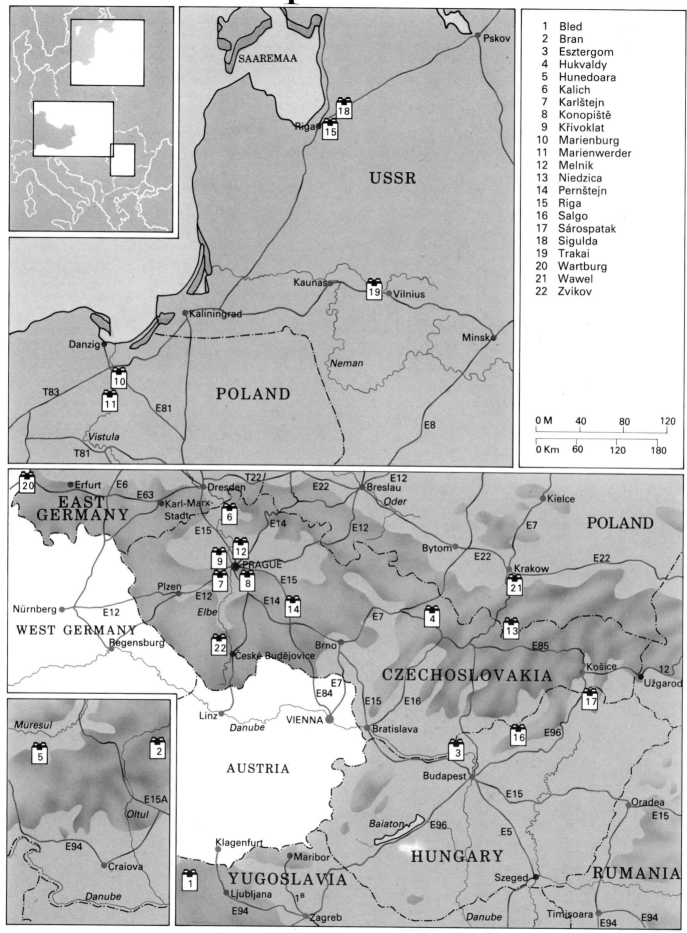

SAAREMAA

Pskov

USSR

Riga

18
15

Kaunas
19 Vilnius

Kaliningrad

Minsk

Danzig

Neman

10

T83

11

E81

POLAND

Vistula

T81

E8

1	Bled
2	Bran
3	Esztergom
4	Hukvaldy
5	Hunedoara
6	Kalich
7	Karlštejn
8	Konopiště
9	Křivoklat
10	Marienburg
11	Marienwerder
12	Melnik
13	Niedzica
14	Pernštejn
15	Riga
16	Salgo
17	Sárospatak
18	Sigulda
19	Trakai
20	Wartburg
21	Wawel
22	Zvikov

0 M   40   80   120

0 Km   60   120   180

20   Erfurt   E6   T22   Dresden   E22   E12   Breslau
Oder

EAST
GERMANY   E63   Karl-Marx-   Kielce
Stadt

E15   E14   E12   POLAND

6   Bytom   E22

E15   12   Krakow   E22

9   PRAGUE   21

7   8   E15

Plzen   E12

Nürnberg   E12   Elbe   14   E7   4   13

WEST GERMANY   E85   Košice   12

Regensburg   22   E7   Brno   CZECHOSLOVAKIA   Užgarod

České Budějovice   E15   E16   17

E7

E84   E15   E96

Linz   Danube   VIENNA   Bratislava   16

Muresul   3   Budapest   Oradea

5   2   AUSTRIA   E15   E15

E15A   Baiaton   E96   E5

Oltul   HUNGARY   RUMANIA

E94   Klagenfurt   Szeged

Craiova   Maribor

Danube   1   YUGOSLAVIA   Oradea

Ljubljana   1B   Timişoara   E94   E94

E94   Zagreb   Danube

The growing accessibility of countries behind the Iron Curtain has meant that some of the most impressive castles in Europe can be visited again. Over the centuries many wars have taken place in this part of Europe, usually instigated by external invaders, whether the Mongols from the east, the Turks from the south or the Germans from the west. The great number of fortifications in general and castles in particular in Eastern Europe reflect this historical insecurity. These wars, of course, did not cease with the end of the Middle Ages and the various governments can only be congratulated on their programmes of restoration – particularly in view of the appalling damage caused by World War II. The following examples represent a mere sample.

1 Bled

Location: Bled on the northern side of Lake Bled in Slovenia, 33 miles (53 km) north-west of Ljubljana, Yugoslavia.
Description: A hilltop castle first dating from the 11th century. Museum and restaurant.
Opening hours: (Summer) 9am–5pm; (Winter) 9am–3pm.
History: First mentioned in 1004, the castle controls the lake and the town of Bled. The latter is a particularly impressive fortified town founded at the time of Charlemagne. The castle stands on an imposing site on top of a bluff that rises vertically from the water's edge. Emperor Henry II presented the castle to the bishops of Bixen in the 12th century and they retained possession until the middle of the 19th century. The bishops carried out building works at fairly regular periods, much of which has survived today, notably the very fine Gothic chapel in the courtyard. Bled Castle was the favourite home of Regent Paul before World War II and later frequently visited by President Tito of Yugoslavia.

This is the only example drawn from Yugoslavia. It might not be a country full of castles but it is still one abounding with defensive fortifications, fully reflecting its historic role in resisting Turkish expansion. The Danube valley in particular contains the magnificent fortresses of Golubac, probably built in the 14th century and Smederevo, constructed between 1428 and 1430 by Djuradj Brankovic.

2 Bran

Location: Bran, in the Brasov region to the north-west of Bucharest, 15½ miles (25 km) south-west of the city of Brasov in the Transylvanian Alps, Romania.
Description: An imposing medieval castle usually associated with the legend of Dracula. Museum of medieval art.
Opening hours: (Summer) 9am–5pm; (Winter) 9am–3pm.
History: The most spectacular castle in Romania, Bran is positioned on a precipitous crag of rock commanding the entrance to the two valleys leading to the important medieval city of Sibiu. The first castle was a wooden structure dating from the early 13th century and the present building was constructed in 1377 by the men of Brasov to prevent attacks upon their city. Many features of the original Gothic castle can still be seen but it is as the vampire's Transylvanian castle in Bram Stoker's novel *Dracula* that Bran has achieved its recent notoriety. The legend originates from the middle of the 15th century when the castle was held by Vlad Tepes, the ruler of Wallachia. He is better known as Vlad the Impaler and in his struggles with the Turks and local opposition demonstrated an insatiable lust for cruelty and blood.

3 Esztergom

Location: Esztergom on the Danube 22 miles (35 km) north of Budapest, Hungary.
Description: The medieval seat of the Hungarian kings is dominated by the walls and bastions of the 18th-century fortress, but excavations have uncovered much of the original royal castle and its treasures which can now be seen in the castle museum.
Opening hours: Open at all times.
History: Its position on the River Danube has made Esztergom strategically important, a fact reflected in the continual reconstruction of the fortifications on Castle Hill until the middle of the 18th century. Initially it was a Roman fort but grew in the 9th and 10th centuries to become the capital of the country until the 14th century. It was at Esztergom that St Stephen (the patron saint of Hungary) was born and later in 1000 crowned the first king of Hungary. All traces of the principal

Bled

residence of the medieval Hungarian kings, destroyed by the Turks, seemed to have disappeared forever, until extensive excavations in the 1930s eventually uncovered remains of the original castle. Esztergom Castle was first built by Prince Geza, father of St Stephen, but its heyday was in the later 12th century and after when the Mongols were being successfully held back. The excavations of the 1930s revealed the predominant French influence in the work of the principal builder, Bela III (1173–96), which may be explained by the fact that his two wives were French princesses.

4 Hukvaldy

Location: 25 miles (40 km) south of Ostrava, in northern Moravia, Czechoslovakia.
Description: The ruins of an imposing 13th-century stronghold.
Opening hours: Open at all times.
History: Of all the Iron Curtain countries Czechoslovakia is the richest in terms of medieval castles, reflecting its strategic importance at the very heart of Europe. The vast majority have been rebuilt or remodelled since the Middle Ages. Thus it is a pleasant change to find a Czech castle in its original state, particularly one in the attractive surroundings of Hukvaldy where fallow deer graze in the game-preserve below the hill on which the castle is positioned. There is more than enough of the castle remaining to leave a lasting impression of the power and wealth of its occupants. The town itself is most remembered today as the birthplace of the famous Czech composer Leoš Janáček (1854–1928).

5 Hunedoara

Location: Hunedoara, 12½ miles (20 km) south of Deva, administrative capital of the region of Hunedoara, Romania.
Description: Much-restored 15th-century Transylvanian castle.
Opening hours: Open at all times.
History: The imposing site overlooking the medieval city of Hunedoara was first fortified in the 14th century but the present castle, though much restored, dates principally from the middle of the following century and the efforts of Janos Hunyadi, King of Hungary, in the face of the Turkish invasions. Hunyadi and his son Matthias Corvinus held out for some time. However, internal disunity instigated by George Dozsa helped the Turks under Soliman to defeat the Hungarian army at the battle of Mohacs (1526) in which King Louis II also perished. Hunedoara is the most impressive of the 15th-century castles built to hold out the Turks. The great hall is a particularly fine piece of architecture with its gallery of oriel windows, which suggest the influence of the Teutonic castles in Poland and Russia.

6 Kalich

Location: To the east of Litoměrice in the Labe valley, central Bohemia, Czechoslovakia.
Description: Ruins of the castle of Jan Žižka, military leader of the Hussites and builder of the fortifications at Tabor 54½ miles (88 km) south of Prague.
Opening hours: Open at all times.
History: Jan Žižka is one of the great patriots

Bran

of Czech history. A veteran of the Polish wars against the Teutonic Knights, he became deeply affected by Hussite doctrine and travelled to Tabor, the holy city founded by the Hussites in 1420. A military genius, Žižka turned the mountain-top town into a military stronghold by building a great double wall, roughly hexagonal in plan, around the town, with powerful towers at each projecting corner. The Hussites hated castles as symbols of oppression but they built Kalich for Žižka as it enabled him to change his name to Jan of Kalich (or Chalice) symbolizing the Hussite demand for communion in both kinds.

7 Karlštejn

Location: Karlštejn, 17½ miles (28 km) south-west of Prague, Czechoslovakia.
Description: A massive castle on an imposing hilltop and containing many Czech treasures.
Opening hours: (Summer) 9am–5pm; (Winter) 9am–3pm.
History: The castle was first begun in 1348 by Charles I of Hungary (1346–78) as a centre of his authority in Bohemia and as a depository for the crown jewels and his vast collection of relics. Earlier the Premysl dynasty had been replaced by the foreign house of Luxemburg. It was during the reign of Charles I, who also ruled as the Holy Roman Emperor Charles IV, that Bohemia experienced a Golden Age. Because of this, in height and internal splendour, Karlštejn rivals the contemporary Valois castles in France, but in terms of natural strength it bears more comparison with castles in Germany. The external appearance of the castle dates from the 19th century when it was completely restored. Fortunately the internal design has remained for the most

part in its original state. The castle consists of five independent towers with the final stronghold being the massive 121-foot-high keep which contains the Hall of the Empire and above it the Chapel of the Holy Rood where Charles kept his crown jewels and relics including the piece of the True Cross which gave the chapel its name. The military strength of the castle was clearly shown when it held out for Emperor Sigismund all through the Hussite Wars when every other imperial stronghold in the area was stormed.

Amongst other treasures, the castle contains a remarkable series of medieval wall paintings, particularly those by Theodric in the Chapel of the Holy Rood. This chapel is a magnificent tribute to Gothic art and architecture containing golden vaulting, a superb rood-screen and a triptych by Thomas of Modena above the altar.

8 Konopiště

Location: 2 miles (3 km) west of Benesov in central Bohemia, and 27½ miles (44 km) south-east of Prague, Czechoslovakia.
Description: A 14th-century castle extensively rebuilt in 1894. Museum (with a particularly fine collection of 16th- and 17th-century weapons).
Opening hours: Open at all times.
History: Konopiště was built in the early 14th century by the Stemberk family. The family arms of a golden star on an azure field are much in evidence at the castle. It was rebuilt several times, notably after it was bought by the Austrian Archduke Franz Ferdinand in the late 19th century. As a result of Franz Ferdinand's ownership, the castle has close ties with the outbreak of World War I. He met Kaiser Wilhelm II in the adjacent Choral Pavilion in 1914 to plan strategy for the war which erupted when the archduke was assassinated at Sarajevo later in the year. The castle is dominated by the round Gothic tower in which King Wenceslas IV was held prisoner by his rebellious nobility. The 82 rooms of the castle are packed with various collections while the corridors are decorated with hunting trophies. Bears are now kept in the moat rather than on the walls.

9 Křivoklat

Location: Křivoklat, in the midst of the deep woods near the town of Křivoklat in central Bohemia, 36 miles (58 km) to the west of Prague, Czechoslovakia.
Description: A picturesque medieval castle built on a hill and surrounded by dense woodland. Museum and library.
Opening hours: Open at all times.
History: The castle is built on top of a hill protected on three sides by the Rakovnicky valley. It is hardly surprising, considering that the site is in the heart of a wood, that the first castle was a timber structure and a favourite hunting residence of Czech rulers. The first stone castle was built during the reigns of Premysl Otakar II and Vaclav II at the end of the 13th century, but rebuilt during the period 1492–1522. It has a curious triangular plan but its buildings contain some of the finest Czech medieval

Karlštejn

architecture. The restored part of the castle houses the Furstenburg Library, and a hunting and local history museum.

10 Marienburg

Location: Malbork, 35 miles (56 km) south-east of Gdansk, Poland.
Description: The focal point of the 14th-century power of the Order of the Teutonic Knights in Eastern Europe. Museum.
Opening hours: (Summer) 9am–5pm; (Winter) 9am–2pm. (Closed Mondays.)
History: The great castles of the Teutonic Knights in Poland and north-west Russia formed the basis of the Order's power in the 14th century. The Teutonic Knights first came to the region in 1225 when the Polish duke, Conrad of Mazovia invited the Order and its Grand Master, Hermann of Salza to help with the conversion of a pagan Lithuanian tribe called the Pruzzi. The Order soon conquered the whole area and in 1309 made their headquarters at Marienburg, which subsequently became 'the queen of all the castles' of the Order in the East. Marienburg possesses the three main features of most Teutonic castles: first, the general rectangular layout, often built on low ground near a river; second, it was built of brick; and finally, it shows the dual characteristics of the Order, these being its religious nature and military power.

By 1280 the castle consisted of two main parts, the Hochschloss with the castle chapel, and the residential Mittelschloss. Between 1335 and 1341 a tower and a bridge over the River Nogat were added, the Mittelschloss was transformed internally and most important of all, a third element in the defences, the Unterschloss, was built.

The most splendid additions were those of the greatest Grand Master, Winrich von Kniprode who had the Rhenish architect Nikolaus Fellenstein design the magnificent Master's residence in the Mittelschloss. He also enlarged the chapel in the Hochschloss.

The great period of Teutonic castle-building lasted until their crushing defeat at the battle of Tannenberg (1410). Marienburg itself withstood a siege for two months in the same year until dysentery forced the Poles to give up. The castle eventually fell into Polish hands in 1457 and was greatly restored in later centuries. It was used by the Germans as a POW camp (Stalag XXB) during World War II, and was severely damaged in 1945, but has since undergone reconstruction.

11 Marienwerder

Location: Kwidzyn, 24 miles (39 km) south of Malbork, Poland.
Description: A magnificent castle of great height. Founded by the Teutonic Knights, it is attached to the 14th-century cathedral overlooking the River Liva. Museum.
Opening hours: Open at all times.
History: Like Marienburg, Marienwerder was constantly added to throughout the 14th century by the Grand Masters, to form a powerful defensive fortification on a steep bank overlooking the river. This probably replaced an earlier 13th-century wooden fortification as at Marienburg, built when the interests of rapid defence were paramount. Severely damaged in World War II it has now been excellently restored.

The most unusual feature at Marienwerder is the great *Danske* or sewage tower which is detached from the main body of the castle and accessible only by a gallery supported by five great arches. Provisions for waste disposal were not new in castles – they can be seen in Henry II's castles in England and at the Wartburg in East Germany – but not on this scale. It must be architecturally the most superb sewage-works in history, attributable no doubt to the horror of bodily functions felt by the celibate Order.

12 Melnik

Location: Melnik in central Bohemia, 18½ miles (30 km) north of Prague, Czechoslovakia.
Description: A rambling castle positioned on a strong site overlooking the confluence of the Elbe and Vltava rivers.
Opening hours: (Summer) 9am–5pm; (Winter) 9am–3pm.
History: A princely castle called Psov is recorded in the *Slavonic Chronicles* as existing on this site in the 10th century, and when the town acquired a charter in the 13th century a stone castle was already established. Both castle and town were then the property of the Czech queens.

Melnik castle was rebuilt in the 15th century, from which period the Prague Gate and the chapel have survived. Later modifications followed, the most striking being the renaissance work, in particular the double-tiered loggia. The town has been famous as the centre of the Czech wine industry since the early 14th century.

13 Niedzica

Location: Niedzica, 26 miles (42 km) east of Zakopane in the Beskid region, south of Krakow, Poland.
Description: The ruins of a rectangular hilltop Gothic castle built by the Teutonic Knights. Museum of local arts.
Opening hours: (Summer) 9am–5pm; (Winter) 9am–2pm.
History: The castle suffered extensive damage in World War II but has been carefully restored and is now under the management of the Polish Academy of Sciences. Despite being one of the smaller Polish castles of the Teutonic Knights, it is a fine example of their architecture, being built on a hill overlooking the Dunajec landing-stage in the Nowy Targ valley. It was built sometime before 1330 and greatly extended in the 17th century. The castle has a rectangular plan with high towers and walls decorated by elegant patterns in the brickwork.

Konopiště

14 Pernštejn

Location: Pernštejn, 13½ miles (22 km) north-west of Tišnov, Czechoslovakia.
Description: The most impressive castle in Moravia, the product of many centuries.
Opening hours: Open at all times.
History: Bohemia emerged from the Hussite Wars with a new independence from the Holy Roman Empire shown by the wholesale distribution of Church lands amongst the nobility, who proceeded to reconstruct the old castles on more comfortable lines. The greatest of these works was the rebuilding of Pernštejn after a fire in 1457 by William and John Pernstejn.

The castle, positioned on its inaccessible crag high above the River Svratka, was first built in the late 13th century, but the work of the Pernštejns turned it into an imposing medieval stronghold. It is built on several levels incorporating four gateways, five towers and two moats. The facade draws the visitor's immediate attention being of gleaming white marble (normally uncommon in Moravia). The bridge and entrance to the main residential tower are protected by a very strong polygonal tower surrounded at the top by a series of turrets, and the thick walls have a defensive parapet running through them. The late Gothic style is much in evidence with very fine cellular vaulting in the entrance hall.

15 Riga

Location: Riga in Latvia, USSR.
Description: A massive rectangular castle first built by the Teutonic Knights and thereafter the residence of the rulers of Riga. Now known as the Palace of the Young Pioneers. Various museums of Latvian arts. and crafts.
Opening hours: May be visited by contact with Intourist. (Closed Mondays.)
History: The castle was begun in 1330 by the Teutonic Knights as another phase in their expansion eastwards. Later it was controlled by the Livonian Knights (also known as the Knights of the Sword), a branch of the main Order who settled in the East after the Peace of Torun in 1466. It is an imposing rectangular structure with a powerful tower at each corner. There has been a great deal of later work carried out culminating in the extensive restoration necessary after World War II. Perhaps the most interesting part of the castle is the Pulvera or Gunpowder Tower. The name was first mentioned by chroniclers in 1330 but the present tower was built in 1650 on oak foundations.

16 Salgo

Location: Just outside Salgótarján in the region of Nograd, 74½ miles (120 km) north-east of Budapest, Hungary.
Description: A powerful baronial castle originally built in the 13th century against the threat from the Mongols.
Opening hours: Open at all times.
History: After the Mongol invasion of 1241, the kings of Hungary relaxed their strict control over the building of baronial strongholds. Therefore it seems fair to assume that Salgo, strongly positioned on a basalt rock 1875 feet high, was built in the second half of the 13th century with its powerful keep as the focal point of baronial authority.

It has had a varied history, being a Hussite stronghold until it was taken by Matthias Corvinus (also known as Matthias the Just, 1458–90). Later the castle became the residence of the Szapolyais family and István Werböczy, who was responsible for the codification of Hungarian law. Salgo suffered at the hands of the Turks and later, the Hapsburgs, and today the castle is in ruins. However, enough survives to show its strength in medieval times, notably a well-preserved pentagonal tower with very thick walls on the eastern side.

17 Sárospatak

Location: Sárospatak, 41 miles (66 km) north-east of Miskok, north-east Hungary.
Description: A 12th-century castle extensively restored and strengthened in the 16th and 17th centuries. Rakoczi family museum.
Opening hours: Open at all times.
History: Sárospatak was originally built in the 12th century and dominates the Bodrog valley. It was considerably strengthened to withstand Mongol invasions led by Batu Khan between 1241 and 1243 and is mostly associated with the powerful Rákóczi family whose wealth came from the Tokajhegyalja area famous for its wines. The most formative period in terms of what survives today was the 15th century when it was owned by Peter Perenyi. He had spent much time in Dalmatia and was greatly influenced by the Italian Renaissance. The very beautiful tile-roofed loggia in the central courtyard and the carved stone door lintels are all his work, though much of it is partially obscured by later re-strengthening. In the 18th century, the castle and town became a base for the movement against Habsburg rule. It was described as follows in 1847 when the nationalist movement was at its height: 'this is sacred soil. This town was the lion's den of Hungarian revolution. Here the lions of freedom dwelt.'

18 Sigulda

Location: Sigulda in Latvia, 33½ miles (54 km) north-east of Riga, USSR.
Description: After Riga, the first castle built in Russia by the Teutonic Knights.
Opening hours: May be visited by contact with Intourist.
History: The castle at Sigulda is one of several castles built by the Teutonic Knights in Latvia during the middle of the 14th century. Today the castle consists of two separate defences divided by a deep moat. However, this is not the original structure as the castle was rebuilt after undergoing a series of sieges by the Poles, Swedes and Russians during the course of the Livonian Wars in the 16th century. Nearby is another castle built by the Teutonic Knights – Turaida Castle – which has an impressive tower that gives extensive views over the surrounding countryside. Locals will be more than pleased to recount the sad story of the girl, Maja, known as the 'Turaida Rose', who died at a young age but whose love proved stronger than death.

19 Trakai

Location: Trakai in Lithuania, 17 miles (28 km) west of Vilnius, USSR.
Description: A powerful late medieval castle sited on an island in a picturesque lake. Museum.
Opening hours: May be visited by contact with Intourist.
History: The town of Trakai was originally known as 'the town on the water', being surrounded by a chain of lakes. Trakai castle was the home of Witold, Duke of Lithuania (1398–1430) during the time of the Polish-Lithuanian conflict with the Teutonic Knights and is situated on one of the numerous islands of Lake Galva. It is the only Lithuanian castle relying on this form of water defences. Though the site was no doubt fortified much earlier the present structure dates from the 14th and 15th centuries. It is an imposing castle with a powerful keep and curtain wall containing three large circular towers.

20 Wartburg

Location: Just south of Eisenach in the Erfurt region in the south-west of East Germany.
Description: A 12th-century baronial castle built on an impregnable site after the practice of contemporary imperial castles.
Opening hours: (Summer) 9am–5pm; (Winter) 9am–3pm. (Closed Mondays.)
History: The imposing site above the town of Eisenach was first fortified by Ludwig von der Schauenburg in the middle of the 11th

century. Like most early German castles it was constructed in wood, there being two timber towers in existence in 1080. The stimulus for the extensive castle-building in 12th-century Germany was the military and political activities of Frederick Barbarossa, who built an estimated 350 castles and residences. The Wartburg was one of the few baronial castles to be rebuilt by the Landgraves of Thuringia, a family firmly in the service of the Emperor and growing in power in order to offset that of the great territorial magnates.

The castle is built around an open courtyard within strong thick walls. However, it was in the site that the needs of defence were primarily placed, as residential comforts were given a higher priority than the military defences of the castle itself. Thus the adoption of Anglo-French flanking arrangements was delayed in penetrating central and eastern Europe. The castle has subsequently been extensively restored but the original design has survived.

21 Wawel

Location: Krakow, 28 miles (45 km) south-east of Auschwitz, southern Poland.
Description: Gothic castle and cathedral. Seat of the medieval kings of Poland. Museum. Cathedral containing tombs of many early Polish kings.
Opening hours: (Summer) 9am–5pm; (Winter) 9am–3pm.
History: An impressive hilltop castle overlooking the Vistula and formerly the seat of the secular and religious authorities in Poland during the Middle Ages. Originally a typical Slavonic hill fortress built in the 8th century, the stone castle existing today dates

from the 11th century when Krakow was the capital of Poland. It was further extended in the 14th century when the cathedral was also rebuilt (1320–64). In the 16th century the Polish kings moved their capital to Warsaw, but Krakow still remained an important religious and academic centre. During World War II, the castle was the home of Hans Frank the German Governor-General. Parts of the castle have undergone conservation, but basically it is intact from medieval times.

22 Zvikov

Location: Zvikov in southern Bohemia, 15 miles (24 km) north of Pisek, Czechoslovakia.
Description: A predominantly Gothic castle which has been called 'the Queen of Bohemian castles'.
Opening hours: (Summer) 9am–5pm; (Winter) 9am–3pm.
History: The castle is positioned on a spur dramatically overlooking the confluence of the Otava and Vltava rivers which the building of the Orlik Dam has turned into a large lake. In the 13th century Zvikov was the chief royal seat of the Premyslid rulers of Bohemia. The castle was started by Vaclav I and completed by Otakar II. The 30-foot-high wedge-shaped cylindrical watchtower and the squat Marcomanni Tower, named after the German tribe which may have once lived in the area, are all that remain from this period. The rest of the present castle is a magnificent example of early Gothic architecture. The residential building with its prismatic tower and arcaded courtyard is unique in Europe. The chapel is beautifully decorated with 15th-century wall paintings and was probably designed as a whole by a Frenchman.

Marienburg

Spain & Portugal

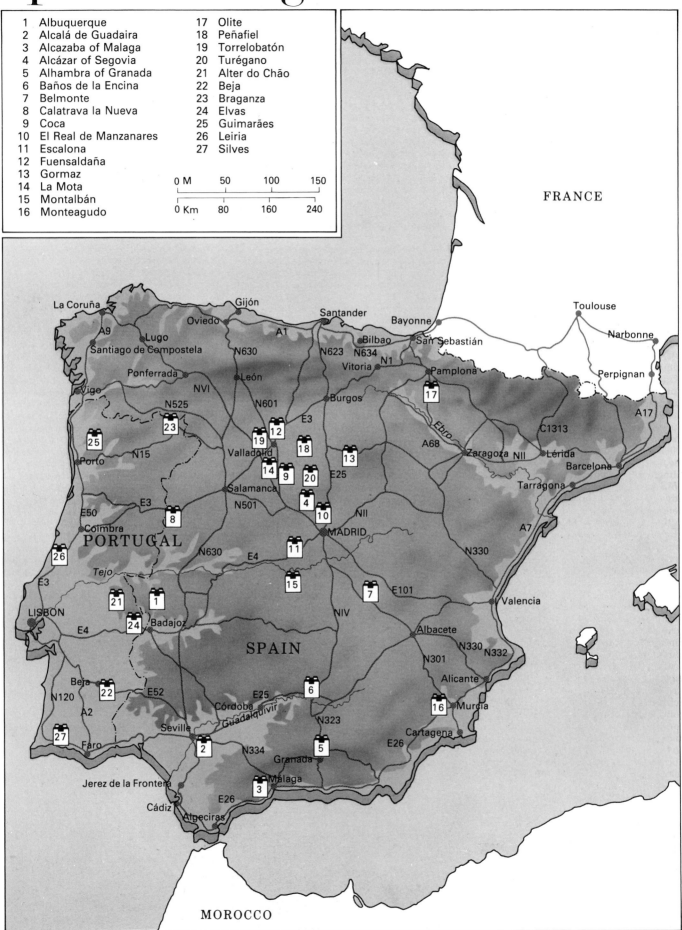

1 Albuquerque	17 Olite
2 Alcalá de Guadaira	18 Peñafiel
3 Alcazaba of Malaga	19 Torrelobatón
4 Alcázar of Segovia	20 Turégano
5 Alhambra of Granada	21 Alter do Chão
6 Baños de la Encina	22 Beja
7 Belmonte	23 Braganza
8 Calatrava la Nueva	24 Elvas
9 Coca	25 Guimarães
10 El Real de Manzanares	26 Leiria
11 Escalona	27 Silves
12 Fuensaldaña	
13 Gormaz	
14 La Mota	
15 Montalbán	
16 Monteagudo	

0 M   50   100   150

0 Km   80   160   240

FRANCE

La Coruña
Gijón
Toulouse
Oviedo
Santander
Bayonne
Narbonne
A9
Lugo
Santiago de Compostela
N630
A1
Bilbao
San Sebastián
Perpignan
Ponferrada
León
N623 N634
Vitoria N1
Pamplona
A17
Vigo
NVI
N601
Burgos
17
N525
E3
C1313
23
Ebro
25
N15
12
A68
Zaragoza
Lérida
Valladolid
19
18
A68
NII
Barcelona
Porto
14 **9** **13**
E25
Tarragona
Salamanca
20
N501
4
NII
A7
E50
E3
8
10
MADRID
Coímbra
PORTUGAL
N630
E4
11
N330
26
Tejo
15
E3
21 **1**
7
E101
Valencia
LISBON
E4
24 Badajoz
SPAIN
NIV
Albacete
N330 N332
N301
Beja
22
E52
Córdoba
E25
6
Alicante
N120
A2
Guadalquivir
N323
16 Murcia
27 Faro
Seville
2 N334
5
E26
Cartagena
Granada
Jerez de la Frontera
3 Málaga
Cádiz
E26
Algeciras

MOROCCO

Spain

Castles in Spain and Portugal owe their very distinctive evolution primarily to the Moorish occupation of the peninsula, from the invasion of 711 until the surrender of Granada to the Catholic Kings in 1492. The history of the Reconquest is, in essence, a confrontation of two civilizations.

The Moors introduced Western Europe to their own traditions of fortification and advanced Byzantine practice. In the peninsula their *alcazabas* (garrison forts) in the form of square or wedge-shaped tower enceintes, remained the basic model for castle design. The Christians added the *torre del homenaje* (tower-keep) of Galician-Basque derivation (also a symbol of victory) and from the 12th century showed a degree of preference for round tower construction. This was particularly evident with the advent of the knightly Orders who provided a synthesis of European-Syrian castle design with Moorish practice.

Christian Spain by the 11th century comprised kingdoms of differing spheres of interest and conflicting ambitions. Portugal only established real independence after the reconquest of Lisbon (1147). Occasional unity, with European support, produced the great Crusader vistories, the fall of Toledo (1085) and, after a Moorish revival under the fanatical Almorávides and Almohades, the battle of Las Navas de Tolosa (1212) which crippled Moorish power, but not cultural influence, in the peninsula. The great walls of Avila built in 1088–91 by Jewish, Moorish and Christian masons, epitomize the innovatory stimulus given to military architecture by the Reconquest.

The containment of the Moorish threat led to increasing involvement in Europe by the 14th century – a greater Anglo-French regularity overlaid the Moorish fortress tradition (which remained stronger in Portugal). The garrison role diminished with the belated advent of a feudal-palace function. It is in 15th-century Castile, with the internecine struggle between the nobility and the Crown, that the castle in the peninsula achieves its final form – a typically conservative but spectacular combination of Moorish technique and decoration with Christian design. By 1588 virtually all these castles had fallen into disrepair/disuse and last saw active service during the Peninsular War (1808–13). As a result we have concentrated predominantly on their architectural design.

1 Albuquerque

Location: Albuquerque (Badajoz) 25 miles (40 km) north of Badajoz on the C530.
Description: 14th-century castle spectacularly sited on a great pinnacle of rock commanding a wide range of country above the fortified town. A series of flanking walls

Alcazar of Segovia

cover the approach by a winding fortified passage. The walls with square towers on the north side extend down to enclose the town. Typical of Moorish-inspired Portuguese fortification, all the towers are square with pointed merlons. The Great Tower dominates the crest enceinte and there is an extra-mural tower, known as a *torre albarrana* with a monumental ogival bridge separated by a drawbridge from the barbican in the curtain.
Opening hours: Open at all times.
History: Albuquerque was built in 1354 by order of Alfonso Sanches, a son of King Dinis of Portugal and was often besieged during the border conflicts between Castile and Portugal in the 14th century. It held out successfully against Pedro the Cruel in 1354 but succumbed by treachery to Alvaro de Luna in the 15th century.

2 Alcalá de Guadaira

Location: Alcalá de Guadaira (Seville), 31½ miles (51 km) east of Seville on the N342.
Description: Extensive and impressive ridge-top fortress of very early Moorish origin with 13th- and 15th-century Christian alterations. An irregular triple enceinte of *tapiá* (a sun-cured mortar with pebble aggregate of great hardness) and stone with great lofty square towers encloses two large baileys. The tallest eastern tower is a notable Moorish innovation – a free-standing *torre albarrana* linked only by a high-set bridge to the main enceinte and commanding the latter and the bridge approach with its barbican and three gateways. The keep and the towers

Albuquerque

were altered by the Christians and are emblazoned with the Arms of Castile-León and the knightly Orders. There are subterranean corn magazines and cisterns.
Opening hours: Open at all times
History: Alcala was captured by King Ferdinand the Saint in 1246 and in the 15th century belonged to Don Rodrigo Ponce de León, Marquess of Cadiz.

3 Alcazaba of Malaga

Location: Malaga, on hill dominating the town and harbour, with the castle of Gibralfaro linked on the heights above.
Description: (Alcazaba of Malaga) A very early Moorish fortification comprising a square-tower enceinte and citadel dating from the 9th–11th centuries. (Gibralfaro) A double, partly triple, enceinte with square and hexagonal towers, the inner enceintes enclose a covered *chemin de ronde*. The Alcazaba and Gibralfaro are united to form a capital fortress by double zigzag curtain walls; although restored, they are a major feat of Moorish engineering.
Opening hours: (Alcazaba of Malaga) 9am–12 noon and 3pm–7pm. (Gibralfaro) Open at all times.
History: The Alcazaba is principally the work of Abdarrahman I (756–88) completed c. 1064 and with enlargements by Mohammed II of Granada. The Gibralfaro crowning the summit was a Phoenician-Greek site incorporating a *faros* (lighthouse), fortified by Abdarrahaman I and fully developed in the 11th century, and again in the 14th century by Yusuf I.

4 Alcázar of Segovia

Location: In the city centre of Segovia.
Description: A *gran buque* (great ship) castle commanding a spur between two rivers, the Alcázar dates from the Reconquest of Segovia in the 11th century.
Opening hours: 9am–12 noon and 3pm–6pm.
History: *Alcázar* is the Arab word for 'palace' and the royal castle of Segovia was adapted as such at the beginning of the 15th century. Its adaptation was due to Juan II, who separated the old keep from his magnificent *torre del homenaje*, decorated with Segovian plasterwork and a cluster of bartizans. The incredible richness of its *mudéjar* interiors shows the influence of the Alhambra. The original interiors were lost in the disastrous fire of 1862 but have been partially reinstated in the complete restoration.

5 Alhambra of Granada

Location: The Alhambra Hill east of the city centre beside the Alcazaba, Granada.
Description: Crowning a naturally fortified ridge is the magnificent Maghribian castle-palace, known as the Alhambra (Red Fort). The Alcazaba is the citadel holding the precipitous western end of the ridge.
Opening hours: 9am–12 noon and 3pm–7pm.
History: The Alhambra, begun in the 13th century, has an enceinte with towers incorporating parts of the palace, the strongest in military terms being the Justice Gate of 1348 with its vaulted passage turning through three right-angles. The famed interior decoration dates from 1334–1408. The Alcazaba is of 9th-century origin but was largely rebuilt in the 13th century by the Nazrite dynasty who ruled Granada after the decline of Almohade power. The adobe walls are reinforced by square and rectangular dominant towers with a massive wall to the east defending a depression, now the Plaza de los Aljibes. After a brief siege the Alhambra and Alcazaba were surrendered to the Catholic Kings on 2 January 1492, marking the end of the Reconquest and the 781-year presence of the Moors in the peninsula.

6 Baños de la Encina

Location: Baños de la Encina (Jaen), 7½ miles (12 km) north of Bailén, off the NIV by the Embalse del Rumblar.
Description: Fine Moorish *alcazaba* contouring the ridge commanding the village.
Opening hours: Open at all times.
History: The castle was built in 967–68 by the Caliph Hakam II to guard the line of the River Guadalqivir before Jaen. The single enceinte with 15 square towers and a fine ashlar double-horseshoe gateway is of typical Moorish build and shows how advanced the Moors were in fortification by comparison with Europe at this stage. Baños fell to the Christians just before Las Navas de Tolosa (1212) and they added the *torre del homenaje* symbol of victory and a further redoubt.

Coca

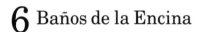

El Real de Manzanares

7 Belmonte

Location: South-west of Cuenca and 10 miles (16 km) north-east of the junction of the N301 with the N420.
Description: Belmonte has the most sophisticated regular geometric plan of the 15th-century castle-palaces. Built in *c.* 1456, the main enceinte is based on an equilateral triangle inscribed in a five-pointed star. The angles are bound by circular towers with prominent vaguely *mudéjar* crenellations and a massive *torre del homenaje* astride the entrance curtain defending the gateway. The low outer enceinte conforms in curved form to the plan of the main body and includes three round-towered gateways. The grand residential accommodation is provided by vaulted halls flanking the sides of the triangular patio, with *mudéjar* ceilings and carved fireplaces. Only the unique early 14th-century castle of Bellver, in Majorca, surpasses this plan in its circular perfection.
Opening hours: Open at all times.
History: The castle was built *c.* 1456 for Juan de Pacheco, Marquis of Villena, an eccentric and tyrannical noble. He was also the founder of the monastery of El Parral in Segovia (1447) built on a site on which he had fought three successful duels.

8 Calatrava la Nueva

Location: 5 miles (8 km) south-west of La Calzada de Calatrava (Ciudad Rodrigo), near the Puerto de Calatrava.
Description: Built by the Order of Calatrava as their new headquarters from 1216 onwards, this is a conventual castle, commanding a rocky height. It has a great, round towered fortified Romanesque church graced by a splendid rose west window; it is defended by a keep, double enceinte and flanking walls yet with Moorish-inspired battlements. The castle was almost certainly built by *mudéjar* masons.
Opening hours: Open at all times.
History: The Order takes its name from the older castle of Calatrava between Cordoba and Toledo (from 1216 onwards known as 'Calatrava la Vieja') which they had taken over from the Templars. However they failed to hold it against the Almohade counter-attack and only regained possession following the victory at Las Navas de Tolosa in 1212. The old castle was never restored and the Order moved their headquarters to Calatrava la Neuva in 1216. The Order of Calatrava, was in the vanguard of the Reconquest.

9 Coca

Location: Coca (Segovia), 30 miles (48 km) north-west of Segovia.
Description: Built in the mid 15th century for Alfonso de Fonseca, Archbishop of Seville (an incredibly rich and dissolute prelate) Coca is the *tour de force* of *mudéjar* brickwork. A very deep, brick-lined moat follows in curves the concentric rectangular plan of the castle, the outer curtain being broadly battered with provision for cannon. The square corner keep is approached only by a right-angle line from the bridge over the moat. But the military character is belied by the fantastic display of moulded brick crenellation and the clusters of bartizans around the octagonal angle-towers and keep. It had very rich stucco *mudéjar* interiors and was as much palace as castle.
Opening hours: (Interior only) 9am–12 noon and 3pm–7pm.
History: This castle-palace, in spite of its fortifications, was never in fact besieged and was the home of Alfonso de Fonseca, Archbishop of Seville until his death. From the early 16th century it belonged to the Dukes of Berwick and Alba.

10 El Real de Manzanares

Location: 20 miles (32 km) north of Madrid at the foot of the Guadarrama mountains.
Description: A 15th-century castle-palace, almost square in plan with a close-set, double, round-towered enceinte.
Opening hours: 9am–12 noon and 3pm–6pm.
History: El Real de Manzanares was built in 1475 for the first Duke of the Infantado adjacent to the remains of a Mendoza stronghold. A chapel was added to the east side incorporating parts of a 13th-/14th-century hermitage with its apse. In 1480 the second Duke of the Infantado added the exquisite *isabelino-mudéjar* gallery, the octagonal turret and the elaborate ball decoration and false machicolation – all made to the designs of Juan Güas, architect of the duke's Guadalajara palace and of San Juan de los Reyes, Toledo. Manzanares was the last of the castle-palaces, most successfully resolving the aesthetic duality of its function.

11 Escalona

Location: Approximately 6 miles (10 km) north of Maqueda (Avila) on the N403.
Description: One of the most extensive ruined castles in Spain with 1,476 feet of walls, built on the edge of a precipice. Of Moorish origin but with successive alterations in the 13th, 14th and 15th centuries, it consists of two baileys. The larger of these has a double enceinte on a trapezoidal plan whilst the smaller has a dry moat and is square with prominent *torres albarranas* commanding both walls. The construction of stone bonded by brick courses is principally *mudéjar* work (Moors remaining under Christian rule). The square enceinte was adapted as a palace in the 15th century and had very rich *mudéjar*-Gothic interiors around a patio.
Opening hours: Open at all times.
History: Conquered by Alfonso VI who ceded it to the Alvárez family, Escalona was received in 1281 as a fief by Don Manuel, brother of Alfonso X. Juana de Pimental defended the castle for her husband, Alvaro de Luna, in the famous siege of 1435. It was sacked by the French under Suchet in 1808.

12 Fuensaldaña

Location: 4 miles (7 km) off the N601, north of Valladolid.
Description: A fine 15th-century plains castle that was probably never completed. Fuensaldaña has a particularly well-proportioned three-storeyed *torre del homenaje* (with dungeons). Rectangular in plan it sits astride one of the short sides of its rectangular enceinte. The latter is provided with circular angle-towers and central small bartizans. The keep has full-height corner turrets with proper bartizans to the centre of the two longer sides. Both towers and bartizans have *mudéjar* merlons and machicolations.
Opening hours: 9am–12 noon and 3pm–7pm.

History: The castle was built *c.* 1450 for Alonso Pérez de Vivero, treasurer to Juan II, who was thrown to his death from a tower by the King's favourite, Alvaro de Luna, at Burgos in 1453.

13 Gormaz

Location: 10 miles (16 km) south-east of Burgo de Osma (Soria), off the N122.
Description: A huge Moorish frontier castle, one of the rare ones in the north built *c.* 965 (with some minor alterations in the 13th and 14th centuries) on the elongated summit of a crag near the River Ebro. The stone enceinte is nearly three-quarters of a mile in length with 33-foot-high walls girt with 21 towers and twin keeps (both on the curtain) all rectangular in plan, enclosing two irregular baileys. Gormaz compares with the best surviving *alcazabas* in Andalusia.
Opening hours: Open at all times.
History: Gormaz was used by the great Arab general Almanzor as a base for his summer raiding campaigns in the north. Reconquered by Ferdinand I in 1047, it was subsequently given to Rodrigo Díaz de Vivar 'El Cid Campeador' by Alfonso VI.

14 La Mota

Location: Medina del Campo (Valladolid), on the east side of this important market town.
Description: A great rectangular brick fortress of Moorish origin commanding a strategic crossroads. A series of restorations from the 12th century culminated in the major, mid-15th-century refurbishment which added to the earlier main enceinte the gigantic bartizaned *torre del homenaje* and

La Mota

the close-set, battered, outer curtain (pierced with gunloops) to face the increasing use of artillery. This curtain has built into it a remarkable, vaulted, two-tier *chemin de ronde* with stairs in the round towers. The brickwork is outstanding *mudéjar* craftsmanship rivalled only by Coca.
Opening hours: 9am–12 noon and 3pm–7pm.
History: Although La Mota is of *mudéjar* build, the architects, Fernando Carreño (1444) and Alonso Nieto (1479), were Christian. Having belonged to the Fonsecas, the castle was given as a wedding present to the Catholic Kings in 1475, and also served as a prison for Juana la Beltraneja and Cesare Borgia.

15 Montalbán

Location: 5½ miles (9 km) north of the C401, approximately 27 miles (44 km) south-west of Toledo.
Description: A Visigothic stronghold rebuilt by the Moors. Montalbán is situated on a rocky height overhanging the gorge of the Torcón. The castle has a vast irregular double stone enceinte with a massive gateway and two great wedge-shaped towers (pierced by arches) which project far out from the main enceinte with the low outer curtain following on plan. These towers are precursors of the *torres albarranas* and were developed to improve flanking cover. The brick crenellation with horseshoe loopholes is *mudéjar* work.
Opening hours: Open at all times.
History: Captured from the Moors after the fall of Toledo in 1085, Montalbán was held by the Templars in the 13th century. In the 15th century Juan II and his favourite Alvaro de Luna were besieged here by the King's cousin Enrique (later King Enrique IV).

Leiria

19 Torrelobatón

Location: 9 miles (15 km) north of Tordesillas (Valladolid), off the C611.
Description: A magnificent Castilian fortress of the mid 15th century rivalling in its military might the brick-built La Mota. Related in type to the nearby Fuensaldaña, Torrelobatón relied on its massive walls to resist cannon-fire. Three corners of the single sheer enceinte are held by lofty circular towers whilst the fourth is engulfed by the 150-foot-high *torre del homenaje* with eight bartizans which commands the entrance with its portcullis. A notable feature is that all the parapets, on false machicolations, are uncrenellated and smoothly curved inwards to impede the hold of grappling irons.
Opening hours: 9am–12noon and 3pm–7pm.
History: Torrelobatón was the seat of the Grand Admiral of Spain. It played an important role in the Comunero rebellion of 1521, being immune to the heavy cannon and falconets of Padilla's siege-train.

16 Monteagudo

Location: 3 miles (5 km) from Murcia on an isolated hill by the N340.
Description: A spectacularly sited Moorish fortress on a conical hill. Several lines of fortification wind up from the foot of the hill to the triple enceinte which rises in steps with close-set square towers. The whole is dominated by the impregnable main citadel (also square-towered), enclosing halls and provided with rock-cut underground cisterns.
Opening hours: Open at all times.
History: Dating from the early days of the Cordoban caliphate, Monteagudo was built as a key of the Murcian strategic system and once commanded the major stronghold of Los Castillejos at its foot.

17 Olite

Location: Olite (Navarre), 4 miles (7 km) from Tafalla on the N121 south of Pamplona. The castle incorporates the Parador Nacional del Príncipe de Viana.
Description: 15th-century castle-palace built on an immense rambling plan with wedge-shaped, polygonal and circular towers. Olite has a massive keep with belvederes, an octagonal tower rising in three machicolated stages and an *atalaya* (watch-tower) with a curious minaret-style turret. It is stylistically similar to French fortified architecture of the period (eg the Papal Palace, Avignon) and French masons certainly worked on the castle. The interiors had superb *mudéjar* decorations and in its heyday there were roof gardens, a menagerie and hot baths. A fine 15th-century church is incorporated and subterranean halls and passages abound. The architect was probably Semen Lezcano.
Opening hours: 9am–12 noon and 3pm–7pm.
History: Considerably restored, Olite was one of the earliest purpose-built castle-palaces constructed for Charles the Bold of Navarre *c*. 1403–1413. General Mina fired the castle in 1813.

18 Peñafiel

Location: Peñafiel (Valladolid), 24 miles (39 km) west of Aranda de Duero, above the town on the River Duero.
Description: 15th-century castle built on an ancient fortified site on a narrow ridge dominating the Duero valley. Peñafiel is the epitome of the *gran buque* type of castle – a great battleship 690 feet long by 74½ feet wide. The inner enceinte has 12 round towers to each flank, with one at the 'bow', another at the 'stern', two defending the gateway, and a 111-foot-high bartizaned rectangular keep as the 'bridge'. Machicolations crown the towers and the wall-walk is nearly continuous. A dry moat defends the keep, its only access being via a bridge.
Opening hours: Open at all times.
History: The present castle of Peñafiel dates from 1466, built by Don Pedro de Girón, Master of Calatrava. It owes its origin to the repopulation of the town by Count García Fernández of Castile in 1014. The former castle on the site was built by the Infante Don Juan Manuel in the early 14th century.

Peñafiel

20 Turégano

Location: Turégano (Segovia), 45 miles (72 km) south-west of Aranda de Duero on the C603.
Description: Commanding the town from a height, Turégano is a complex castle on account of its confused building history. Begun in the 10th century, its main body comprises the fine 12th- 13th-century Romanesque church of San Miguel. This has been strongly fortified as a keep with round towers. Large square towers were added in the 15th century, probably when it was a dependency of the bishops of Segovia. This work is in turn circumvallated with round towers with a machicolated pair flanking the only gateway. The outer square tower enceinte, however, appears to be earlier work.
Opening hours: Open at all times.
History: Turégano was founded by Fernán González of Castile in the 10th century. The feature of the round towers probably indicates that the castle was in Templar ownership in the 12th century as does the incorporation of the church. Loarre (Huesca), a chief Templar castle, also incorporates a church (as does Calatrava la Nueva).

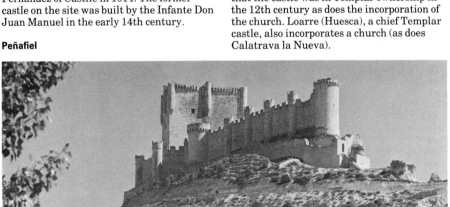

Portugal

21 Alter do Chão

Location: On the N245 south of Portalegre (Alentejo).

Description: An interesting 14th-century castle for its plan, Alter do Chão shows a greater, possibly French-influenced, regularity than is typical of Portuguese castles. It is virtually square with a single enceinte, two round, conical capped angle-towers, a lofty 144-foot-square keep in a third corner and a square gatehouse tower angled to the fourth. The crenellation of the parapet is swept up to the gatehouse.

Opening hours: Open at all times.

History: Alter do Chão was built in 1359, according to an inscription by order of King Pedro I (the date by our calendar would in fact have been 1321).

22 Beja

Location: Beja (Alentejo). The castle stands on the north side of the ancient town.

Description: The castle, on an irregular trapezoidal plan, is built on the site of a Roman fortification altered in turn by the Moors and with further additions in the 13th, 14th and 15th centuries.

Opening hours: 9am–12 noon and 3pm–7pm.

History: Beja was captured from the Moors during the reign of Alfonso III (1248–79), who rebuilt or restored the square tower enceinte commanding the hilltop overlooking the Alentejo plain. Surmounting these earlier fortifications is the fine keep built in 1310 in the reign of King Dinis. The corners of the parapet are pierced by carved loopholes and there are machicolated corner-galleries below the 15th-century top stage. The first floor has a star-ribbed vault with honeycomb corbelling, and *ajimez* (arched and twin-lobed) windows, denoting *mudéjar* craftsmanship.

23 Braganza

Location: Braganza (Tras-os-Montes), on the N15 in the far north district capital.

Description: The massive keep, rectangular in plan, is flanked by square watchtowers, and is unusual in Portuguese castles in that it is not detached. The keep is 108 feet tall and has corner bartizans, and, on the south and east sides, two gemiated Gothic *mudéjar* windows. These features are 14th- or 15th-century alterations. The enceinte, as with the keep, is built of massive local granite. The proximity of the León-Castile frontier probably influenced the more Spanish detailing of the *torre del homenaje*.

Opening hours: 9am–7pm. (Closed 12 noon to 3pm.)

History: Braganza was the birthplace of the dynasty of that name, being a duchy in 1444. The Braganzas ruled Portugal from 1640, and the ruined castle, with the adjoining walls of the old town, dates back to 1187 when Sancho I rebuilt an earlier fortification.

Guimarães

24 Elvas

Location: Elvas (Alentejo), on the N4 near Badajoz on the Spanish frontier.

Description: Elvas is the largest castle in Portugal, a major frontier fortress confronting Badajoz in Spain. It commands the steep ridge above the town and has a vast, polygonal, partly double enceinte extending 3,282 feet by 2,133 feet. Square towers predominate with a massive keep and a *torre del homenaje* built in 1488. Merlons are consistently of the Moorish pointed type, the castle originally being an important Moorish *alcazaba*. Cutting walls are used in the lists and there is a particularly strong gatehouse.

Opening hours: 9am–12 noon and 3pm–7pm.

History: Elvas was conquered from the Moors by Sancho II in 1226 and successive restorations took place under King Dinis in the 13th, João II in the late 15th (including the 1488 keep) and Manuel in the early 16th century.

25 Guimarães

Location: Guimarães (Minho), on the N101 south-east of Braga. The castle is on the north side of the town.

Description: Although considerably rebuilt in the 15th century and now restored, the castle, which stands on a rock outcrop, incorporates a much earlier 10th-century tower in its keep. The keep, in characteristic Portuguese fashion, remains isolated within the enceinte. Moorish crenellation predominates.

Opening hours: 9am–12 noon and 3pm–7pm.

History: The 10th-century tower, in the Galician-Basque tradition, was adapted as the keep of an enceinte castle by Henry of Burgundy following his creation as Count of Portucale by Alfonso VI of Castile in 1095. In the 15th century the castle was partially rebuilt on a regular trapezoidal plan with square angle-towers, two of which flanked the gateway. It was here that Henry of Burgundy's son Afonso Enriques, the first king of independent Portugal, was born, in 1110.

26 Leiria

Location: Leiria (Beira Litoral). The castle dominates the town from a rocky height.

Description: One of the finest castle-palaces in Portugal and spectacularly sited, Leiria has Roman origins with additions in the 12th, 14th and 15th centuries.

Opening hours: 9am–12 noon and 3pm–7pm.

History: Leiria was first fortified in 1135 by Afonso Enriques (prior to his election as the first king of Portugal in 1137) as a strategic southern frontier-post. After the reconquest of Lisbon and Santarém in 1147 its importance lapsed and the walls fell into disrepair. It revived, however, under King Dinis who built the dominating citadel in 1324 with the small, but elegant, twin-towered palace below and at an angle to it. The massive citadel is rectangular with close-set flanking towers on the irregular curtain taking advantage of the natural rocky defences of the outcrop. The palace underwent alteration in the late14th and early 15th centuries for João I; it retains an exquisite arcaded loggia commanding the view. Carved decoration and chimney-pieces also survive.

27 Silves

Location: Silves (Algarve) on the N124). The castle commands the ridge above the ancient town on the bank of the Arade.

Description: A red-sandstone garrison fortress built by the Moors in the 9th/10th centuries to control Xelb (Silves) the capital of the Moorish province of Alfaghar. The enceinte, with square towers, wall-walk and the prominent feature of the *torre albarrana*, contours the ridge. The bailey contains a fine Moorish cistern, 197 feet deep, and a whole complex of underground storerooms and passages with access only by a single entrance.

Opening hours: Open at all times.

History: Silves was captured from the Moors by Alfonso III who completed the reconquest of the Algarve in 1249. Silves was an important strategic fortress in the southern Algarve against the threat of Castilian ambitions in the province.

Italy

SWITZERLAND

AUSTRIA

HUNGARY

Innsbruck

Bolzano

Villach

Ljubljana

Lago di Como

Trento

Udine

A4

Lago di Garda

Aosta

Bergamo

Trieste

Rijeka

Brescia

A5

Milan

Verona

Padua

Venice

YUGOSLAVIA

A4

Adige

Turin

A1

Piacenza

Po

Ferrara

A21

A7

Modena

Genoa

Bologna

Ravenna

A12

Rimini

La Spezia

A1

Nice

Pisa

Florence

Ancona

A14

SS3

BASTIA

Tevere

A1

SS1

A12

Pescara

A1

L'Aquila

A24

ROME

ITALY

CORSICA

A2

Foggia

Bari

A16

A14

Brindisi

Naples

SS407

Potenza

Taranto

A3

Cosenza

A3

Messina

Palermo

Reggio di Calabria

A20

SS113

A18

A29

A19

A18

SS115

Catania

SICILY

Siracusa

1 Castello del
   Buonconsiglio
2 Castello Caetani
3 Castelvecchio
4 Castello dei Conti Guidi
5 Rocca Feltresca
6 Fenis
7 Castello dell'Imperatore
8 Lerici
9 Castello di Lombardia
10 Lucera
11 Rocca Maggiore
12 Rocca dei Malaspina
13 Rocca Malatestiana
14 Rocca di Montestaffoli
15 Castel del Morte
16 Narni
17 Castel Nuovo
18 Paternò
19 Castello di San Giorgio
20 Castel Sant'Angelo,
   The Savelli fortifications
   and Capodibove
21 Castello Sforzesco
22 Castel Sismondo
23 Castello Spagnolo
24 Castello Ursino
25 Caserta Vecchia
26 Castello Visconteo

0 M	40	80	120

0 Km	60	120	180

From about the 10th to the 13th century, throughout Italy, there was a change from open settlements to fortified ones known as *castra*. These are generally situated on a hilltop or spur, and their defences comprised a free-standing tower and curtain wall, which in later examples was made stronger by incorporating the tower into it and providing flanking towers. From about the late 12th century, that part of the *castrum* reserved to its lord or owners became more heavily fortified and began to resemble a true castle, a development marked in contemporary sources by the appearance of the words *cassaro* and *rocca*, both meaning castle, whereas *castello* generally refers to a fortified village. Some of the most important early Italian castles were those built by the emperor Frederick II (1220–50). The rectangular ground plan with corner towers so characteristic of many of these is modelled on Byzantine forts which he had seen during the Fifth Crusade (1228–29). This type of castle soon became the most common throughout Italy. Other types are those with a *mastio* (donjon) and an enceinte, those consisting of a large palace and tower, and those with a curtain wall heavily fortified with towers.

Because of the fragmentation of political power during the Middle Ages, Italy is rich in castles. The limited resources of their builders, however, meant that they are often relatively small and unimposing. Their strength generally lies in natural defences, in the difficulty of their approaches, and their outworks, which rarely survive. In the 14th century, scarped walls and machicolations in masonry became increasingly common. The 15th century saw the introduction of the gunloop, the widespread adoption of the round tower, and, by the end of it, the development of the first artillery fortifications.

1 Castello del Buonconsiglio

Location: Trento in Trentino-Alto Adige, to the north of Lake Garda on the River Adige.
Description: Series of buildings orientated north–south along the inside face of the pre-existing town wall. Much of the complex is residential in character and dates from the 15th century and later. There are some fine interiors with frescoes and wooden ceilings. The furnishings were brought here when the Museo Nazionale was set up in 1924.
Opening hours: (May to September) 9am–12 noon and 2pm–6pm; (October to April) 9am–12 noon and 2pm–4.30pm.
History: The Castel Vecchio built in the mid-13th century occupies the north end of the complex. It was a roughly rectangular enclosure with buildings grouped initially on two sides of the courtyard and it incorporated an earlier large round tower. From 1255 it belonged to the prince-bishops of Trento who enlarged and embellished it. The courtyard, loggia and ogee windows in the west wall are the work of Bishop Hinderbach (1465–86). Bernardo Cles (1514–39) built the Magno Palazzo to the south of the Castel Vecchio, the space between them being filled by the palace added by Bishop Francesco Alberti Poia from 1686. Used as a barracks in the 19th century, the castle was extensively restored after 1918.

2 Castello Caetani

Location: Sermoneta (Latina) in Lazio, about 7½ miles (12 km) north-east of Latina in the foothills of the Monti Lepini.
Description: The castle is separated from the town by a rock-cut ditch. Inside there is a courtyard surrounded by apartments of various dates built up against the back of the enclosure wall which is an irregular quadrilateral in plan.
Opening hours: 10am–11.30am and 3pm–6pm. (Closed Thursdays.)
History: The castle belonged to the Anibaldi family in the 13th century, who may have built the rectangular donjon on the south side of the courtyard. The hall to the east of it was probably added by the Caetani family who acquired the castle in 1297 and still own it. The castle was radically modernized in the 16th century by the Borgia family, who held it briefly, and by the Caetani.

3 Castelvecchio

Location: Verona in Veneto, to the south-east of Lake Garda, with access from the A4.
Description: The castle commands the approach to the Ponte Scaligero across the River Adige and is divided by the road leading to the bridge. The western part is approximately rectangular with square corner towers and housed the garrison; the smaller eastern part was the residence of the della Scala family.
Opening hours: Civico Museo d'Arte in the castle (Summer) 9am–12.30pm and 3pm–6pm; (Winter) 9am–12 noon and 2.30pm–5pm.
History: The castle was built by Cangrande II della Scala in 1354–7 to consolidate his control of the town. The tower guarding the bridge was finished in 1375. Extensive restoration has been carried out this century.

4 Castello dei Conti Guidi

Location: Poppi (Arezzo) in Tuscany, about 25 miles (40 km) north of Arezzo on the SS70.
Description: Comprises a fortified palace and tower. There is a small courtyard partly rebuilt in the 15th century. Many of the rooms preserve decoration and fittings of the same period.
Opening hours: Apply to caretaker (tel. 52012).
History: The existing castle was begun by Count Simone da Battifolle in 1274 and later rebuilt and enlarged by Count Guido di Simone from *c.* 1291.

Castello del Buonconsiglio

5 Rocca Feltresca

Location: San Leo (Forli) in Emilia-Romagna, about 6 miles (10 km) west of the republic of San Marino and off the SS258.
Description: The castle is defended by a sheer cliff on one side, and on the other by a long machicolated wall with a round tower at each end of it.
Opening hours: (Weekdays) 9am–12.30pm; (Sundays) 4pm–5.30pm. (Closed Mondays.)
History: San Leo was an important fortified site from the early Middle Ages. The round towers and the wall between them were built in the late 15th century for Federico da Montefeltro, possibly by Francesco di Giorgio Martini. Inside there survive some earlier buildings.

6 Fenis

Location: Fenis (Val d'Aosta) in Piedmont, about 8 miles (14 km) east of Aosta and just to the south of the A5.
Description: The residential part of the castle is an irregular polygon with a small courtyard with wooden balconies. There are two curtain walls: the outer one is partially collapsed but the inner has a fine gate-tower with a rectangular tower adjacent to it. Frescoes of the school of the 15th-century Piedmontese painter Giacomo Jaquerio are to be seen in the courtyard and the chapel. The castle preserves some fine internal fittings, such as coffered wooden ceilings, fireplaces

and ironwork, as well as furnishings brought here from elsewhere to constitute the Museo dell'Arredamento Valdostano.
Opening hours: (March to November) 9.30am–12 noon and 2pm–4.30pm; (December to February) 9.30am–11.30am and 2pm–4pm. (Closed Tuesdays.)
History: Of the castle recorded from the first half of the 13th century all that survives is the rectangular tower adjacent to the gate-tower. The existing building is thought to have been begun by Aimone di Challant in the middle of the 14th century. His son, Boniface I, was responsible for further building work in the 1390s and major additions and alterations were carried out in the 15th century. These included the outer curtain wall in its present form, the rectangular windows, the chapel and much of the interior. The castle was heavily restored in the 1930s.

7 Castello dell'Imperatore

Location: Prato (Florence) in Tuscany, 8 miles (13 km) north-west of Florence and off the A11.
Description: Rectangular with square corner towers, and intermediate towers which are both square and pentagonal.
Opening hours: Open during daylight hours.
History: This is the only well-preserved castle of Frederick II in Central Italy. It was probably substantially complete by 1241. The square towers half-way along the east and north walls are earlier structures which were incorporated into it.

Castel Nuovo

Lucera

8 Lerici

Location: Lerici (La Spezia) in Liguria, on the coast about 6 miles (10 km) southeast of La Spezia.
Description: Above the ditch stands a wall with a pentagonal tower in the middle of it. Behind there is an enclosure, and the buildings within it include a fine 13th-century chapel.
Opening hours: (May to September) 9.30am–12.30pm and 3.30pm–8.30pm; (October to April) 8.30am–12.30pm and 1.45pm–5.45pm.
History: The castle is of several building periods. The pentagonal tower may have been built by the town of Pisa which captured it in 1241. Inside this tower there is an earlier pentagonal one of uncertain date. The Genoese strengthened the castle when they recovered it in 1251 (inscription), possibly adding the walls with corner towers to either side of the pentagonal tower. The castle was radically modernized in 1555 (inscriptions).

9 Castello di Lombardia

Location: Enna, in the centre of Sicily. The Castello is on a spur on the east side of the town, the Torre de Federico is on a hill to the west of it.
Description: The Castello consists of three irregular shaped courtyards defended by square towers, many of which have now collapsed. The Torre is octagonal, with sides 26½ ft (9 m) long, and is surrounded by the remains of an octagonal wall.
Opening hours: From dawn to sunset (Castello only).
History: There were fortifications on the site of the Castello from Byzantine times but the existing structures are usually attributed to Frederick II, as is the Torre di Federico.

10 Lucera

Location: Lucera (Foggia) in Apulia, about 12 miles (19 km) west of Foggia.
Description: The castle is a large enclosure situated on a spur. One side of the ditch in front of it is revetted with a masonry glacis. Access was by steps in this glacis to the small gate set in a salient in the wall above. At each end of the ditch there is a round tower and between them there are seven pentagonal towers. The rest of the curtain wall is provided with square towers.
Opening hours: 8am–1pm. (Closed Mondays.)
History: Frederick II built a castle at Lucera but probably all that survives of it is the base of what was an enormous residential tower 165 feet (50 m) square with a tiny central courtyard. The existing fortifications were built by Charles I of Anjou in 1269–83.

11 Rocca Maggiore

Location: Assisi (Perugia) in Umbria, 15 miles (24 km) south-east of Perugia.
Description: Large well preserved castle on a ridge above the town. It consists of an enclosure with angle towers and within it a residential block comprising a palace with a large first-floor hall, a small courtyard and a *mastio* with a spiral stair.
Opening hours: Generally open during the hours of daylight.
History: The castle was built by the papal legate Cardinal Albornoz, possibly to the design of Ugolino da Montemarte. It is first recorded in 1365 but was probably unfinished on Albornoz's death in 1367. Further work was carried out by the mercenary captain Biordo Michelotti who seized control of Assisi in 1394. The details are not clear but he

Rocca Maggiore

probably completed the *mastio* and the enclosure wall. That the Rocca was slow to be built is indicated by a number of building joints and the fact that both the west and south walls of the enclosure have been raised in height. In the mid-15th century a 12-sided tower was built by Giacomo Piccinino west of the castle, linked to it by a wall with an enclosed gallery at the top. The entrance to the Rocca was reinforced by the construction of a round bastion beside it in 1538.

12 Rocca dei Malaspina

Location: Massa in Tuscany, about 31 miles (50 km) north-west of Pisa and just north of the A12.
Description: Large complex of buildings of several different periods. There is a handsome courtyard surrounded by porticoes, loggias and walls with painted plaster. Some of the rooms are decorated with Renaissance frescoes.
Opening hours: 9am–12.30pm and 2pm–5pm.
History: A castle is first recorded at Massa in 1164. The oldest part of the complex is that at the top of the hill, but even this seems to have been modified when, from the mid-15th century, the Malaspina family built a palace and the outer lines of defence.

13 Rocca Malatestiana

Location: Cesena (Forli) in Emilia-Romagna, 12 miles (19 km) south-east of Forli and just off the A14.
Description: Within the massive enclosure wall there stand a tower and a rectangular building with a polygonal tower at one corner. The castle was originally linked by a raised covered gallery to the polygonal tower of the Municipio in the piazza below.
Opening hours: The castle grounds are

generally open during the hours of daylight.
History: The two buildings inside the enclosure probably belong to the castle built *c.* 1380 by Galeotto Malatesta. Originally the rectangular block was not isolated but connected on its north side to structures which have now been demolished. The enclosure wall with its round and polygonal towers was for the most part built by Matteo Nuti for the papal governor, Lorenzo Zane, in the 1460s.

14 Rocca di Montestaffoli

Location: San Gimignano (Siena) in Tuscany, about 25 miles (40 km) north-west of Siena.
Description: Enclosure roughly pentagonal in plan with slightly rhomboid corner towers. It has a fine double gateway.
Opening hours: Generally open during the hours of daylight.
History: The *rocca* was built by the city of Florence from 1353 to hold down San Gimignano. It was partly demolished in 1558.

15 Castel del Monte

Location: About 10 miles (17 km) south of Andria (Bari) in Apulia, just off the SS170.
Description: The castle is a regular octagon in plan, with octagonal corner towers and an octagonal courtyard. Inside the rooms are trapezoid in plan, roofed with rib vaulting and decorated with polychrome masonry inlay.
Opening hours: 9am–2pm. (Closed Mondays.)
History: The building was begun by Frederick II *c.* 1240. It is one of the most idiosyncratic of the surviving examples of his architecture, representing a fusion of classical and gothic influences.

Castel Sant'Angelo

16 Narni

Location: Narni (Terni) in Umbria, about 7 miles (12 km) south-west of Terni.
Description: Rectangular castle with corner towers on a hill above the town. One of the towers is a *mastio* with a spiral stair at one side of it. Inside there is a small courtyard surrounded on two sides by rib-vaulted rooms.
Opening hours: Generally closed but can be seen on application to the Comune of Narni.
History: The castle was built in the mid-14th century on the orders of Cardinal Albornoz, the architect possibly being Ugolino da Montemarte. Its construction was probably a slow process, for two types of masonry occur in the south wall. The tops of the walls and towers with their machicolations are in rubble, and date from rebuilds carried out in the 15th century, notably during the pontificates of Eugenius IV (1431–47), Nicholas V (1447–55), Pius II (1458–64) and Paul II (1464–71), whose coats of arms, along with others, are to be seen inserted into the fabric. The surviving fragments of curtain wall round the castle are also mostly 15th century in date. In the 16th century and later the castle was strengthened through the addition of structures to its exterior, including a battery with nine gun-chambers on its east wall.

17 Castel Nuovo

Location: Naples in Campania.
Description: The castle is approximately trapezoid in plan with round towers.
Opening hours: Dawn to sunset.
History: Apart from the chapel to Santa Barbara virtually nothing remains of the castle built by Pierre de Chaule for Charles of Anjou from 1279–84, for it was completely transformed by Alfonso I of Aragon in 1442–

58. The work was carried out by both Spanish and Italian architects. Especially notable is the triumphal arch (1453–65) between two of the towers on the west wall.

18 Paternò

Location: Paternò (Catania) in Sicily, about 22 miles (35 km) west of Catania.
Description: Large rectangular tower measuring about 59 feet by 80 feet (18 m by 24 m). The small doorway is raised about 23 feet (7 m) above ground level and approached by a ramp overlooked by a small turret. At second-floor level there are two enormous double-arched windows in the long sides of the tower, creating a sort of loggia.
Opening hours: The castle is the property of the Comune and can be seen on application.
History: Although once thought to be Norman, the castle in fact dates from the 13th century, possibly from the time of Frederick II.

19 Castello di San Giorgio

Location: Mantua in Lombardy, south of Lake Garda and just west of the A22.
Description: Rectangular castle with square corner towers, those at the south-east and south-west having gate-towers adjacent to them. Drawbridges let down from these spanned the wet moat surrounding the castle.
Opening hours: (Summer) 9am–12.30pm and 2pm–6pm; (Winter) 9am–4pm; (Holidays) 9am–1pm. (Closed Mondays.)
History: Begun c. 1390–5 by the architect Bartolino da Novara for Francesco Gonzaga. From 1450 it was radically transformed as a residential palace by Ludovico II Gonzaga. Especially notable is the Sala degli Sposi with frescoes by Mantegna.

20 Castel Sant'Angelo, Savelli fortifications and Capodibove

Location: Castel Sant'Angelo is in Rome, on the River Tiber just to the east of the Vatican. The Savelli fortifications are on the Aventine next to Santa Sabina, and Capodibove is about 2 miles (3 km) outside the city on the Appia Antica.
Description: The nucleus of Castel Sant'Angelo is the tomb of Hadrian I. Since its use as a fortress meant frequent attacks, little of the original building survives. Sumptuously decorated apartments were added by the popes during the Renaissance. The Savelli fortifications consist of a wall with square towers enclosing the *castrum* where the Savelli family lived. At Capodibove a well preserved fortified palace adjoins the tomb of Cecilia Metella and to the south there are the remains of a large enclosure.
Opening hours: Castel Sant'Angelo: 9.30am–1pm (closed Mondays). The Savelli fortifications are laid out as a garden and are open during the hours of daylight. The palace at Capodibove can be visited on application to the custodian after 9.30am (closed Mondays).
History: Hadrian's tomb was used as a fortress from at least the sixth century AD. It was normally in the possession of the strongest power or family in the city, only being held consistently by the popes from the late 14th century. Nicholas V (1447–55) added round towers to the corners of the tomb and Alexander VI (1492–1503) strengthened them through the construction of polygonal towers. The outer bastions were built by Paul IV (1555–9) and Pius IV (1559–69). The Savelli fortifications date from the 13th century. The palace at Capodibove was built by the Caetani family c. 1300, though the enclosure might be earlier.

21 Castello Sforzesco

Location: Milan in Lombardy.
Description: The castle is 660 feet (198m) square with three internal courtyards. While the north side has square corner towers, the south side facing the town is designed to be more decorative and imposing, having stone-built round towers and a huge gate-tower in brick designed by Filarete and rebuilt in the nineteenth century.
Opening hours: 9am–7pm. (Closed Mondays.)
History: The castle built by Galeazzo II Visconti *c.* 1368 was destroyed by the short-lived Repubblica Ambrogiana in 1447. Francesco Sforza began to rebuild it in 1450, breaking one of the conditions on which the Milanese had agreed to make him duke. It was almost complete on his death in 1466 but work continued until the end of the century, Leonardo and Bramante being among the architects employed on it.

22 Castel Sismondo

Location: Rimini (Forli) in Emilia-Romagna, on the Adriatic coast just north of the A14.
Description: Outer defences have been demolished leaving the inner nucleus of the castle which comprises a rather irregular cluster of large square towers with battered bases.
Opening hours: Not open to the public (property of the Comune).
History: The castle was begun by Sigismondo Malatesta in 1437, possibly to his own design, though Brunelleschi may also have collaborated on the project.

23 Castello Spagnolo

Location: L'Aquila in Abruzzo, about 87 miles (140 km) north-east of Rome.
Description: One of the best preserved 16th-century fortresses in Italy. It is square with pentagonal angle bastions, and is surrounded by a wide moat. Inside there is an elegant courtyard.
Opening hours: Museo Nazionale d'Abruzzo in the castle: 9am–2pm. (Closed Mondays.)
History: The fortress was built by the Spanish from 1535–49 to consolidate their control of the town. The architects were the Spaniards known as Pirro Luigi Scriva from Valenza and Gion Girolamo Scriva.

24 Castello Ursino

Location: Catania, on the east coast of Sicily. Originally it stood on a slight spur jutting into the sea but its immediate topography was changed by the eruption of Mt. Etna in 1669.
Description: The castle is 165 ft square (50 m), with round corner towers and intermediate towers, of which only two survive. On each side of the courtyard there were originally five rib-vaulted bays with fine capitals. The first floor was identical but virtually nothing of it survives. The battered base of the castle and its outer defences were buried by the lava flows of 1669.

Opening hours: 8.30am–2pm.
History: The castle was begun by Riccardo da Lentini on the orders of Frederick II in 1239. It was radically altered in the 15th and 16th centuries, and used as a barracks in the 19th. The restoration of the 1930s has exposed what is left of the 13th-century fabric and conserved the more notable of the Renaissance alterations.

25 Caserta Vecchia

Location: Caserta in Campania, on the northern outskirts of the town.
Description: Castle with a roughly elliptical plan and buildings ranged round a courtyard. A large hall on the east side had windows with gothic tracery and vaults above its ground and first floors. Standing apart to the south there is a round tower about 66 feet (20 m) in diameter.
Opening hours: Open during daylight hours.
History: The round tower is attributed to Count Richard of Caserta, who married one of the daughters of Frederick II and died *c.* 1266. The main part of the castle is probably slightly later.

26 Castello Visconteo

Location: Pavia in Lombardy, about 18 miles (30 km) south of Milan.
Description: The castle is 470 feet square (142 m), with square corner towers and a spacious courtyard. It is a severe but elegant brick building, well provided with gothic windows with terracotta surrounds. Round it

Castello Sforzesco

is a moat over 66 feet wide (20 m) spanned by drawbridges.
Opening hours: Musei Civici in the castle (Summer) 10am–12 noon and 3pm–5pm; (Winter) 10am–12 noon and 2pm–4pm. (Closed on Mondays.)
History: The castle was built by Galeazzo II Visconte in 1360–65. It reflects the common tendency of the period for the residential role of castles to become as important as the military role, so that they became increasingly luxurious and comfortable.

Castello Visconteo

The Middle East

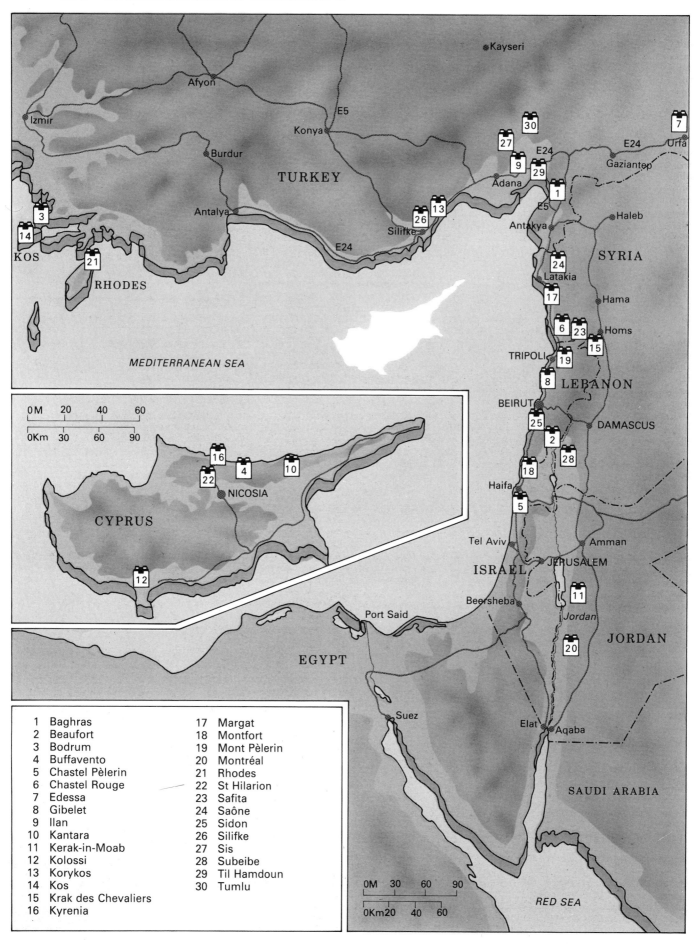

1	Baghras	17	Margat
2	Beaufort	18	Montfort
3	Bodrum	19	Mont Pèlerin
4	Buffavento	20	Montréal
5	Chastel Pèlerin	21	Rhodes
6	Chastel Rouge	22	St Hilarion
7	Edessa	23	Safita
8	Gibelet	24	Saône
9	Ilan	25	Sidon
10	Kantara	26	Silifke
11	Kerak-in-Moab	27	Sis
12	Kolossi	28	Subeibe
13	Korykos	29	Til Hamdoun
14	Kos	30	Tumlu
15	Krak des Chevaliers		
16	Kyrenia		

The castles of the Crusaders are the most solid memorial of their endeavours to take, and hold, the Holy Land. The mixture of the Latin, Byzantine, Armenian and Arabic civilizations and their architectural styles undoubtedly contributed to the development of castle design. Increasingly sophisticated defences grew up around the original simple donjon, the symbol of lordship.

Always in the forefront of these advances were the Military Orders, especially the Knights Hospitallers, who alone could afford the enormous expense of these works. Their magnificent creations at Krak des Chevaliers and Margat belong to the period of the kingdom of Jerusalem, while during their occupation of Rhodes they led in the construction of the new artillery bastions.

Bodrum

1 Baghras

Location: Baghras, 3 miles (5 km) north of the Iskenderun road, 12 miles (20 km) north of Antakya, Turkey.
Description: Partially ruined, with a fine early 13th-century hall and chapel.
Opening hours: Open at all times.
History: The refectory hall (with a wash-basin and beautiful large east window) and the lancet windows of the chapel, in the early Gothic style, are Templar work. On the south face the long gallery of loopholes is Armenian in inspiration. In case of siege an aqueduct supplied several cisterns and the cellars reportedly held 12,000 sacks of grain when Saladin captured the castle in 1188.

2 Beaufort

Location: Qalaat es-Shaqif, above Arnoun, 3 miles (5 km) south of Kefer Tibnit on the Saida–Marjayan road, Lebanon.
Description: Partially ruined early Crusader work, c. 1120, situated by a precipice.
Opening hours: Open at all times.
History: Beaufort, whose eastern face

Baghras

perches above a sheer drop, was made inaccessible by a rock-cut ditch and the construction of a curtain wall incorporating a massive square donjon. Only reduced by famine after Saladin's year-long siege in 1190, it was held by the Moslems until recovered by diplomacy in 1240. The Knights Templars bought Beaufort in 1260 but surrendered it to the Mamelukes, under heavy bombardment, in 1268.

3 Bodrum

Location: Bodrum, on the west coast of Turkey, opposite the island of Kos.
Description: Decorative 15th-century work behind an artillery bastion on a peninsular site.
Opening hours: 9am–6pm. (Closed Mondays.)
History: St Peter's (now Bodrum) was begun in 1415 on a site given to the Hospitallers in return for Smyrna (now Izmir). Completed by about 1450, it consists of a single curtain wall and the two tall square Towers of France and Italy, decorated with many carved escutcheons. The massive artillery outwork

was constructed between 1501 and 1522. The nearby mausoleum of Halicarnassus, one of the Seven Wonders of the World, was used by the Hospitallers as a quarry.

4 Buffavento

Location: 2 miles (3 km) north Güngör, 11 miles (17 km) south-east of Girne, Cyprus.
Description: 13th-century work of two wards on a broken mountain site.
Opening hours: 9am–5pm. (Closed Mondays.)
History: Buffavento was one of the mountain castles dismantled by the Venetians in the early 16th century in order to spare money for modernizing the island's defences against the Turks. Despite its strong position the castle's main role under the Lusignans was as part of a communications system, as it is in visual contact with Girne (Gk. Kyrenia), Lefkosa (Gk. Nicosia) and the castle of Kantara.

5 Chastel Pèlerin

Location: Atlit on the coast road 15 miles (25 km) south of Haifa, Israel.
Description: One tall tower and other ruins on a small promontory.
Opening hours: Open at all times.
History: In 1218 the Templars, aided by a band of pilgrims, built this simple but effective fortification in massive masonry. A rock-cut moat, an outer wall with three towers, and an inner wall with two tall towers (110 feet high), the five towers being spaced alternately, defied all Moslem attacks. The castle was only abandoned when the last Crusader ports fell in 1291. Quarrying in the 19th century for the rebuilding of Acre has left the present ruin.

6 Chastel Rouge

Location: Qalaat Yahmur, ½ mile (1 km) south of Beit Challouf, 9 miles (15 km) from Tortosa (now Tartus) on the N43 Safita road, Syria.
Description: Square donjon with a single curtain wall; in good repair.

Ilan

construction of a strong southern wall and a well defended gateway. Nevertheless the castle's main role was probably as a lookout post against the Genoese in Famagusta. It was dismantled by the Venetians in 1525.

11 Kerak-in-Moab

Location: El-Kerak on Route 49, 77 miles (124 km) south of Amman, Jordan.
Description: Rectangular towers defend a spur isolated by two rock-cut ditches.
Opening hours: Open at all times.
History: Built in 1142, in 'Oultre Jourdain', Kerak was positioned for raids on Moslem caravan and pilgrim routes. Reynald de Châtillon's ruthless exploitation of this potential led to determined sieges in 1183 and 1184, and to his death at Saladin's hands after the Battle of Hattin (1187). The castle fell after an eight-month siege in 1188 and, although regarded as vital to the defence of Jerusalem by Crusader negotiators in the 13th century, was never recovered.

12 Kolossi

Location: Kolossi, 6 miles (10 km) west of Limassol on the Paphos road, Greek Cyprus.
Description: Square, three-storeyed donjon decorated with coats-of-arms.
Opening hours: (Weekdays) 9.30am–4pm; (Sundays and holidays) 10am–4.30pm. (Closed Tuesdays.)
History: A Hospitaller work built c. 1460, Kolossi consists of a single massive square tower, with traces of a curtain wall. Designed like every donjon to be self-contained, there is a cistern in the basement, store-rooms at ground level and a kitchen on the first floor. The two barrel-vaulted rooms of the upper floor were the quarters of the Grand Commander of the Order.

13 Korykos

Location: 16 miles (26 km) east of Silifke on the E24 road on the south coast of Turkey.
Description: Land and sea castles built on a classical site and added to over the centuries.
Opening hours: Open at all times.

Opening hours: (Summer) 8am–1pm and 4pm–7pm; (Winter) 2pm–4pm. (Closed Tuesdays.)
History: Built c. 1112, Chastel Rouge is typical of the early, low, square towers found both within rectangular enclosures, as here and at Gibelet, or built into the curtain wall, as at Beaufort and Saône. Held by the Hospitallers in the late 12th century, the castle was lost to the Mamelukes in 1289.

7 Edessa

Location: Urfa, east Turkey.
Description: A large rectangular citadel, isolated by a rock-cut channel.
Opening hours: 9am–5pm. (Closed Mondays.)
History: Edessa was the first important stronghold to fall into Crusader hands in 1098 and the first significant gain of the Moslem counter-attack. Byzantine and Armenian work, on an old acropolis site, had produced a single curtain wall with evenly spaced towers. With their usual energy the Franks cut a 40-foot-deep ditch, faced with large polygonal bastions, against the town and constructed a square donjon.

8 Gibelet

Location: Jbail, on the coast of Lebanon.
Description: Large square donjon, tightly surrounded by a curtain wall, at the southern corner of the town walls.
Opening hours: (Summer) 9am–1pm and 2pm–5pm; (Winter) 9am–1pm & 2pm–4pm.
History: Built soon after the town's capture in 1103, the donjon (58 ft × 70 ft) is constructed of massive masonry *en bosse* in a style similar to another early work at Saône. Its solidity defied all Saladin's attempts to dismantle it when he captured it in 1188.

9 Ilan

Location: 4 miles (6 km) west of Ceyhan on the E5 road, Turkey.

Description: Three progressively higher wards occupy the summit of a long, sheer ridge.
Opening hours: Open at all times.
History: Ilan's history is obscure, although it may be the 'Govara' held by the Hospitallers in 1233 and it has a very similar donjon to their castle at Silifke. Each ward has a defended gateway. The uppermost, flanked by two tall horseshoe towers, is machicolated and requires two right-angled turns to enter. The carved figure between two lions rampant, above this gateway, may be the badge of the Armenian royal house.

10 Kantara

Location: Above Kantara, 24 miles (38 km) east of Girne, Turkish Cyprus.
Description: Irregular mountain site with a watchtower.
Opening hours: 9am–5pm. (Closed Mondays.)
History: Kantara's natural strength was improved in the late 14th century by the

Kyrenia

History: Originally fortified by the Byzantine admiral Eustathius in 1111, who constructed a single wall and a rock-cut moat, Korykos later fell into Armenian hands. King Leon II built the sea castle *c.* 1216 to protect the flourishing port. The imposing inner wall of the land castle belongs mainly to the mid 13th century, and *c.* 1360 King Peter I of Cyprus made further improvements. The different styles of building have left a diversity of tower shapes, and the use of classical masonry includes an entire Roman gate!

14 Kos

Location: Kos, on the island of Kos, Greece.
Description: Late 15th-century fortress rebuilt against artillery bombardment.
Opening hours: (Weekdays) 9.30am–4pm; (Sundays and holidays) 10am–4pm.
History: Between 1450 and 1478 the Knights of St John constructed a castle in support of St Peter's (now Bodrum) on the Turkish mainland opposite. An Ottoman siege in 1480, followed by an earthquake, led Grand Master Pierre d'Aubusson to begin an extensive reconstruction in 1495. The new work, built in the Italian style to withstand artillery, is typified by the broad cyclindrical Bastion del Carretto.

15 Krak des Chevaliers

Location: Qalaat al-Hosn, near Haret Toukman, 11 miles (18 km) north of Tall Kalakh, Syria.
Description: Large concentric fortification, restored in recent times.
Opening hours: (Summer) 9am–1pm and 4pm–7pm; (Winter) 2pm–4pm. (Closed Tuesdays.)
History: Krak des Chevaliers, originally a small 11th-century Arab fortress called 'the castle of the Kurds', was acquired by the Hospitallers in 1142. Severe earthquakes led to periods of rebuilding after 1157, 1170 and 1201. The small rectangular castle with square towers and masonry *en bosse*, typical of 12th-century work, was incorporated in a concentric work of great sophistication. First there is an outer curtain with evenly spaced towers and box machicolation, then an inner bailey whose tall projecting towers rise out of a sloping masonry talus. The interior halls and chapel, with their fine carvings, are reached only by a sharply-angled covered way. Unsuccessfully besieged on many occasions, this 'bone in the throat of the Moslems' as a Moslem chronicler described it, only fell in 1271, when there was no chance of relief.

16 Kyrenia

Location: Girne, on the north coast of Turkish Cyprus.
Description: Crusader work sited on a promontory, rebuilt as an artillery fort on the landward side.
Opening hours: 9am–5pm. (Closed Mondays.)
History: The town was easily captured by Richard the Lionheart's followers in 1191, and under Lusignan rule Kyrenia became a formidable fortress. It withstood a determined Genoese siege in 1374 and only fell to the Turks in 1570 through treachery. The three huge round bastions and 130-foot-thick wall on the west and south faces are the result of Venetian rebuilding after 1544.

17 Margat

Location: Qalaat Marqab, 2½ miles (4 km) above the town of Baniyas, on the coast of Syria.
Description: Fortified triangular area, with sides measuring 1,300 feet in length and a stong inner bailey, including a huge circular tower. In good repair.
Opening hours: (Summer) 8am–1pm and 4pm–7pm; (Winter) 2pm–4pm. (Closed Tuesdays.)
History: An Arab fortress in the 11th century, Margat came into Crusader hands in 1118. Unable to afford repairs after serious earthquakes, its lord sold the castle to the Hospitallers in 1186. The Order began an extensive rebuilding programme, constructing an inner bailey behind a wide ditch. This included vaulted halls, a fine chapel and a circular donjon. This two-storey tower, 100 feet in diameter, was central to the defensive system and when it was undermined during the Mameluke siege of 1285, the knights were forced to surrender.

18 Montfort

Location: 2½ miles (4 km) north-west of Mi'ilya, 10½ miles (17 km) east of Nahariyya, Israel.
Description: Long asymmetrical site, in ruinous condition, isolated by a rock-cut ditch.
Opening hours: Open at all times.
History: Handed over to the Teutonic Order by its lord in about 1229, Montfort was reconstructed by the knights of the Order as their headquarters. One of the latest Crusader works in the Holy Land, it defied attack by Sultan Baibars in 1266 but fell to him five years later.

Kantara

Safita

22 St Hilarion

Location: 3 miles (5 km) south of Girne on the Lefkosa road, Turkish Cyprus.
Description: Castle of three wards on a romantic and precipitous site.
Opening hours: 9am–5pm. (Closed Mondays.)
History: Set on a steep hillside, St Hilarion was first fortified by the Byzantines. Their thin wall to the large lower bailey was not improved by the Lusignan kings, who concentrated on more solid works higher up and on top of the mountain where they built, in the Gothic style, the apartments for their summer residence. Although reduced by the Venetians, the remains are impressive and from their great height command a fine view.

23 Safita

Location: Safita, 12 miles (20 km) south of Tartus (formerly Tortosa), Syria.
Description: Tall, two-storey donjon, with the remains of a curtain wall, situated on a round hill.
Opening hours: (Summer) 8am–1pm and 4pm–7pm; (Winter) 2pm–4pm. (Closed Tuesdays.)
History: The present magnificent donjon, 60 feet high, was probably built by the Templars in the early 13th century. It comprises a fine vaulted hall, lit by loopholes, above a chapel. An earlier work at Safita defied Saladin in 1188, but this castle fell easily to Baibars on his way to besiege Krak des Chevaliers in 1271.

24 Saône

Location: Qalaat Salah ad-Din, near Haffé village, on the N30 19 miles (30 km) from Lattaquié, Syria.
Description: Elongated triangular site between two gorges, with a 90-foot-deep rock-cut ditch at its base.
Opening hours: (Summer) 8am–1pm and 4pm–7pm; (Winter) 2pm–4pm. (Closed Tuesdays.)
History: Originally a 10th-century Byzantine fortress with a large citadel, Saône

Saône: the rock pillar by the entrance

19 Mont Pèlerin

Location: Tripoli, on the coast of Lebanon.
Description: Large rectangular castle with shallow square towers, much rebuilt.
Opening hours: (Summer) 9am–1pm and 2pm–5pm; (Winter) 9am–1pm and 2pm–4pm.
History: The great Crusader Raymond de St Gilles built the siege castle of Mont Pèlerin in 1103 to blockade the Moslem port which fell, after his death, in 1109. His donjon and a polygonal chapel were built over first during the Mameluke occupation after 1289, when the gatehouse was added, and then during extensive conversion for a Turkish garrison.

20 Montréal

Location: Shaubak on Route 49, 150 miles (243 km) south of Amman, Jordan.
Description: Early Crusader work, with much Moslem rebuilding, occupying the summit of a round hill.
Opening hours: Open at all times.
History: In 1115 King Baldwin I constructed a forerunner of the present castle in 'Oultre Jourdain', across Moslem communication routes. Montréal stood in a fertile area and was supplied with water by a subterranean spring, reached by a deep rock-cut stairway.

Inviolate until the destruction of the Latin field army at the Battle of Hattin in 1187, the garrison was eventually starved into submission.

21 Rhodes

Location: Rhodes, on the island of Rhodes, Greece.
Description: Fortified town with the Palace as an inner stronghold.
Opening hours: Perimeter walls (Monday and Saturdays) 3pm–5pm. Hospital and Palace (Weekdays) 9.30am–4pm; (Sundays and holidays) 10am–4.30pm. (Closed Tuesdays.)
History: The fortress of Rhodes, like its dependent castles of Bodrum and Ḳos, was designed to withstand artillery bombardment, by which the Turks eventually captured the place in 1522. Massively thick walls were constructed after the earthquake of 1481 and studded with towers like the Gate of Amboise (1512) and the Bastion del Carretto (1515). Within them stand the sumptuous Grand Master's Palace, the Inns for accommodation and the beautiful Hospital, now a museum. Lovingly restored in modern times, Rhodes stands at the end of the development of the castle and at the beginning of the new-style artillery forts.

was strengthened by the Franks in the 1100s. They cut an enormous ditch at the east end, leaving a rock needle to carry a bridge. A massive square donjon (with two vaulted floors carried on a central pillar) and small round towers were built above the ditch. Provision for a prolonged siege included two cisterns, one of an enormous size. Saône's understrength garrison fell quickly to Saladin's attack in 1188, however, and the castle was never recovered.

25 Sidon

Location: Saida, on the coast of Lebanon.
Description: Ruined land castle and a smaller sea castle.
Opening hours: (Summer) 9am–1pm and 2pm–5pm; (Winter) 9am–1pm and 2pm–4pm. (Sea castle only.)
History: Held by the Franks from 1110, Sidon was lost in 1187 and its fortifications were dismantled. The sea castle was begun in 1229 but the defences were reconstructed largely under the impetus of St Louis' great building campaign in the 1250s. Held by the Templars from 1260, it was abandoned with their other possessions in 1291.

26 Silifke

Location: Silifke, on the E5 road on the south coast of Turkey.
Description: Single circuit with many projecting towers.
Opening hours: Open at all times.
History: Known to be a Byzantine fortress in 1111, Silifke was held by the Hospitallers from 1210–25. In a similar style, though on a much smaller scale, to their castle of Krak des Chevaliers in Syria, projecting towers rise from a sloping talus above a dry moat. The fine hall, donjon and cisterns were probably built by the Hospitallers, but the gatehouse with its inscription of King Hethum I, dated 1236, is evidence of later Armenian work.

27 Sis

Location: Above Kozan, 25 miles (40 km) north of Adana, Turkey.

St Hilarion

Description: Long, straggling, asymmetrical fortress, probably from the 13th century, on a steep ridge.
Opening hours: Open at all times.
History: The site of the one-time royal Armenian city, now only the castle remains, sprawling half a mile in length. The Armenian style of placing walls only where the hillside is less than precipitous has a piecemeal look but it effectively defied Mameluke attacks in the 13th century. The two gateways of the lower eastern ward are heavily defended and a magnificent donjon overlooks a sheer drop to the south. Sis eventually fell through treachery, and with it the kingdom, in 1375.

28 Subeibe

Location: Qalaat Namrud, above the Baniyas–Majdal Shams road (reached by footpath) in the Israeli-administered area of Syria.
Description: Ruins, including the remains of a 12th-century donjon, occupying a 1300-foot-long ridge.
Opening hours: Open at all times.
History: Subeibe's strategic position as a base for attacks on Damascus, and overlooking routes to the coast, made it a much disputed and valuable possession. It was held only briefly by the Franks (1129–32 and 1139–64). Almaric, King of Jerusalem, died under the walls during a fruitless siege in 1174, when it was occupied by Moslem forces.

29 Til Hamdoun

Location: Toprakkale on the E5 road, 19 miles (30 km) east of Ceyhan, Turkey.
Description: Built of black asphalt, with many horseshore towers, and containing a large hall.
Opening hours: Open at all times.
History: Occupying an important strategic site overlooking routes to the east and south, Til Hamdoun was hotly disputed between the Armenians, Franks and Byzantines. The projecting towers of the upper ward, rising from a talus, as at Krak des Chevaliers, are probably Hospitaller works of the early 13th century. The two dozen, wide, brick-arched loopholes below them are, however, a distinctively Armenian provision for fire-power.

30 Tumlu

Location: Above Kermit, 12 miles (20 km) north-west of Ceyhan, Turkey.
Description: Small castle with massive towers perched on a rock above the river plain.
Opening hours: Open at all times.
History: Built in the late 12th century, the walls are well provided with loopholes, similar to nearby Toprakkale, in typical Armenian fashion. Tumlu fell to the Mameluke invaders in 1375.

Saône

Glossary

arrest – steel bracket on armour used as lance-stop
ashlar – cut or squared stone
aventail – mail face-defence
bailey – walled enclosure or courtyard
barbican – outwork, especially in front of a gate
barmkin – enclosure subsidiary to a pele (qv)
bartizan – projecting corner turret
batter – inclined face of wall (c/f 'talus')
beaked projection – see *en bec*
belvedere – a pavilion or raised turret
blind arcading – arcaded decoration on a wall face
bossed masonry – see *en bosse*
brattice-work – projection to allow the defence of the base of a building
castellan – one in charge of a castle
castellary – lordship attached to a castle
castle-guard – feudal knight-service in a castle
chemin de ronde – wall-walk
coat of plates – armour of iron plates riveted to inside of textile garment
corbel – load-bearing projection from a wall, eg for a rafter or vault
crenellation – battlements
curtain wall – enclosing wall of a castle
en bec – a tower *en bec* is one beaked or pointed towards the field
en bosse (en bossage) – cut stone with outer face left uncut or 'rustic'
enceinte – the fortified perimeter of a castle
gambeson – quilted garment worn under armour
glacis – smooth stone incline used as defence
great helm – iron helmet that completely encloses the head
habergeon – short hauberk (qv)
hauberk – iron mail shirt
hoarding – projecting timber on tower or wall-head
honor – lordship
hornwork – outwork
lists – tiltyard
machicolation – projecting stone gallery on tower or wall-head
march – a border district
mantlet wall – a subsidiary defensive wall closed about a tower or other building
merlon – the upright part of a battlemented parapet
meutrières – murder-holes
pele (or peel) – a tower-house, like a small keep, in or near the marches of Scotland
pilaster – a flat buttress of small projection
postern – a lesser, and privy gateway
ravelin – outwork
revetment – retaining wall or facing
rusticated masonry – see *en bosse*
seneschal – steward
spur – solid pointed projection at the base of a tower or wall
slight – to render indefensible
surcoat – textile coat worn over armour
talus – splayed-out base of tower or wall (c/f 'batter')
ward – see 'bailey'

Bibliography

Alberti, L. B. *Ten Books on Architecture* (1755, reprinted by Tiranti, London 1955)
Brinton, S. *Francesco di Giorgio Martini of Siena* (Besant, London 1934)
Colvin, H. M. (ed.) *The History of the King's Works* (HMSO, London 1963–70)
Davis, R. H. C. *History of Mediaeval Europe* (Longman, Harlow 1957)
Douglas, D. C. *William the Conqueror* (Eyre & Spottiswoode, London 1964)
Fowler, K. *The Age of Plantagenet and Valois* (Elek, London 1967)
Gabrieli, F. *Arab Historians of the Crusades* (Routledge and Kegan Paul, London 1969)
Gillingham, J. *Richard the Lionheart* (Weidenfeld and Nicholson, London 1978)
Hewitt, H. J. *The Black Prince's Expedition of 1355–7* (MUP, Manchester 1958)
Keen, M. H. *The Laws of War in the Late Middle Ages* (Routledge and Kegan Paul, London 1965)
Oman, Sir Charles *A History of the Art of War in the Middle Ages AD 378–1515* (1898, reprinted by Cornell University Press, Ithaca 1960)
Painter, S. *William Marshal – Knight-errant, Baron and Regent of England* (1933, reprinted by Johns Hopkins University Press, Baltimore 1968)
Powicke, Sir Frederick M. *The Loss of Normandy* (2nd edn. MUP, Manchester 1963)
Shipway, G. *The Paladin* (Peter Davies, London 1972)
Smail, R. C. *Crusading Warfare* (1956, reprinted by CUP, Cambridge 1972)
Southern, R. W. *The Making of the Middle Ages* (1953, reprinted by Hutchinson, London 1967)
Stenton, F. M. (ed.) *The Bayeux Tapestry* (2nd edn. Phaidon, London 1965)
The First Century of English Feudalism (OUP, Oxford 1932)
Verbruggen, J. F. *The Art of Warfare in Western Europe during the Middle Ages* (North Holland Publishing Company 1977)
Wood, M. E. *The English Medieval House* (Dent, London 1965)

Please note: For ease of reference the titles of the following works have been contracted in this book:
Longnon, J. and Cazelles, R. (ed.) *Très Riches Heures du Duc de Berry* (Thames and Hudson, London 1969)
– referred to as the *Très Riches Heures*

Monumenta Germaniae Historic ainde ab anno Christi quingentesimo usque ad annum millesimum et quingentesimum ... etc
– referred to as *MGH, Capitularies*

Further Reading

Anderson, W. F. D. *Castles of Europe* (Elek, London 1970)
Armitage, E. S. *Early Norman Castles* (1912, reprinted by Gregg International, Farnborough 1971)
Brown, R. A. *English Castles* (3rd edn. Batsford, London 1976)
Evans, J. (ed.) *The Flowering of the Middle Ages* (Thames and Hudson, London 1966)
Fedden, H. R. and Thomson, J. *Crusader Castles* (John Murray, London 1968)
Fenwick, H. *The Châeaux of France* (Hale, London 1968)
Hindley, G. *Castles of Europe* (Hamlyn, Feltham 1968)
Johnson, P. *The National Trust Book of British Castles* (The National Trust/Weidenfeld and Nicholson, London 1978)
Müller-Wiener, W. *Castles of the Crusaders* (Thames and Hudson, London 1958)
Ritter, R. *Châteaux Donjons* (Larousse, Paris 1953)
Toy, S. *The History of Fortification from 3000BC to AD1700* (Heinemann, London 1955)
Tuulse, A. *Castles of the Western World* (Thames and Hudson, London 1958)
Weissmuller, A. A. *Castles from the Heart of Spain* (Barrie and Rockliff, london 1967)

Also recommended are:
HMSO guides to individual castles in the care of the Department of the Environment in England, Wales and Scotland.

Index

The following index primarily records castles and personalities. Terminology connected with building, battle tactics and feudal life will be found in their respective chapters and the glossary. The page numbers of castles included in the gazetteer appear in **bold**; the page numbers of illustrated items appear in *italics*.

Acknowledgements

Material reproduced in this book was obtained from the sources listed below whose assistance is gratefully acknowledged. Pictures are listed by page number and additional numbers read in order clockwise around the page from top left.

Aerofilms Limited – 17/1, 24/1, 29/1, 44/1, 48/1, 53/1, 60/2, 89/3, 135/1, 136/2, 142/1, 157/2
Alinari – 121/1
David Andrews – 178/1, 179/1
Peter Baker Photography – 20/1, 90/3, 94/1, 136/1, 145/1
Barnaby's Picture Library – 169/1
Matthew Bennett – 40/1, 183/1, 183/2, 184/1
John Bethell Photography – Contents (top right), 20/3, 56/1, 86/4, 95/1
Bibliothèque Publique et Universitaire, Genève – 43/1
Bibliothèque Nationale, Paris – 15/3, 46/2, 77/2
Bodleian Library, Oxford – 68/2
British Architectural Library, RIBA – 171/2, 172/2
British Library – 29/2, 66/2, 66/3, 68/1, 69/2, 78/2, 87/1, 122/1, 123/2
British Tourist Authority – Contents spread (bottom right)
Professor R. Allen Brown – 15/2, 15/4, 18/1, 22/1, 45/1
J. Allan Cash Limited – 46/3, 86/3, 90/2, 98-99, 131/1, 143/1, 147/2, 160/1, 165/1, 166/1, 167/1, 168/1
Dean and Chapter of Canterbury – 12/4, 35/2
Chèze-Brown – Foreword, 19/1, 20/2, 28/1, 59/1,

85/1, 108/1, 130/2, 138/1
Christ Church, Oxford – 86/2
Cleveland Museum of Art – 102/1
Colour Library International Limited – 23/1, 153/1, 155/1
Commissioners of Public Works, Ireland – 139/1
Cooper-Bridgeman Library – 19/3, 66/1, 102/4, 122/2, 126-127
Corpus Christi College, Cambridge – 74/4
Country Life 100/1, 120/1
Courtauld Institute of Art/Corpus Christi College, Cambridge – 72/1, 73/1
Controller of HM Stationery Office, Crown Copyright – 10-11, 12/1, 17/2, 24/2, 45/2, 46/1, 49/1, 52/1, 52/2, 52/3, 52/5, 52/6, 86/1, 91/1, 92/1, 107/1, 124/3, 132/1, 132/2, 133/1,
C. M. Dixon – 88/1
Mary Evans Picture Library – 32/1, 32/3, 34/1, 35/1, 109/1
French Government Tourist Office – 25/1, 47/1, 105/1, 150/2
Sonia Halliday – 119/3, 123/4, 184/2
Dr. J. H. Harvey – 41/1
Alasdair Hawkyard – 118/2, 123/3, 124/1
Michael Holford Photographs – 14/1, 15/1, 19/2, 23/2, 26-27, 38/1, 49/2, 54/1, 58/1, 66/4, 82/1, 106/1, 148/2, 149/1, 151/2, 172/1
Hopcraft, Photography – 78/1
Italian State Tourist Office (ENIT) – 59/2, 115/1, 177/1, 178/2, 181/2
A. F. Kersting – 40/2, 57/1, 74/2, 82/3, 89/2, 90/1, 93/1, 93/2, 109/2, 112/1, 116/1, 116/2, 117/1, 159/1, 159/2, 171/1, 173/1, 185/1, 186/1, 186/2, 187/2
Mansell Collection – 32/4, 104/1

Middle East Photographic Archive – Half-title, 62-3, 113/1
National Gallery, London – 102/2, 119/2
National Monuments Record – 73/2, 74/3, 101/1, 130/1
National Trust – 129/1
Österreichische Nationalbibliothek – 118/1, 119/1
Picturepoint, London – Cover
Pierpont Morgan Library – 39/1, 82/2
Portuguese National Tourist Office – Contributors spread, 175/1
Dr Michael Prestwich – 60/3
Public Record Office, Crown Copyright – 12/3, 32/2, 37/1, 101/2
Peter Roberts – Title page, Contents spread (centre), 96/1, 124/2, 141/1, 147/1, 148/1, 156/1, 157/1
Jean Roubier – 12/2, 76/1
Royal Danish Ministry of Foreign Affairs – 144/1
Scottish Development Department, Crown Copyright – 42/1
Ronald Sheridan's Photo-Library – 119/4, 151/1, 180/1
Spectrum Colour Library – 16/1
Swiss National Tourist Office – 161/1, 162/1, 162/2
John Topham Picture Library – 60/1, 70/1, 89/1, 120/3, 163/1, 174/1, 174/2, 181/1, 187/1
Victoria and Albert Museum, Crown Copyright – 110/1, 116/3, 116/4, 116/5, 120/2, 123/1, 124/4
Weidenfeld and Nicolson Limited – 69/1, 74/1
ZEFA – 102/3, 111/1, 112/2, 137/1, 142/2, 150/1, 154/1, 161/2

Project Directors: Chris Milsome, Susan Ward. **Project Editor:** Mark Bryant. **Production Manager:** Chris Fayers. **Design and Visualization:** Mike Brown, Peter Burt, Steve Chilcott, Linda Francis, Andrew Sutterby, Keith Vollans. **Picture Research:** Tessa Pollitzer. **Editorial and Art Research:** Mike Doggart, David Hunter. **Sub-editing:** Colin Crewdson, Eric Smith. **Illustration:** Dan Escott, Chris Forsey, Chris Harrison, Kevin Maddison, Mike Saunders, Rob Shone, Rod Sutterby.